Wheels Across America

Volume 1

Tempo International
Publishing Co. LLC
8100 Wyoming Blvd.
Suite M4-234
Albuquerque, NM 87113

www.tempointernationalpublishing.com

Copyright © 2004 Tempo International Publishing Company

Published by: Tempo International Publishing Company
P.O. Box 28845, Santa Fe, NM 87592-8845 (505) 426–8633

All rights reserved. No part of this publication may be reproduced, stored in a retrieval system, or transmitted, in any form or by any means, electronic, mechanical, photocopying, recording, or otherwise, without the prior permission of Tempo Publishing Company.

ISBN # 0-9745106-0-2

Front Cover:

Hansen Wheel and Wagon Shop of Letcher, South Dakota built this authentic reproduction Concord Coach for Wells Fargo Company in 2002, closely following the design and construction details of the original Concord Western Mail Coach #599, originally manufactured by Abbot-Downing Company in 1897. *(Image Courtesy David Sietsema)*

Appearance of an advertisement in this publication does not constitute a recommendation, endorsement or warranties of goods and services offered. Neither the author nor the publisher makes any express or implied warranties or representations with respect to the correctness, physical condition, quality, importance, size or authenticity of items advertised.

Contents

Introduction iv

Acknowledgements v

The Craftsmen Listings 1

Vintage Ad's, Catalogs and Images 161

Carriage House: Presenting the Foremost Businesses in the Carriage Industry Today 217

Introduction

Numerous books have been written on carriages and wagons over the years.

Some have gone into great detail on a particular style, design, or use of vehicle. Others have offered extensive information on individual firms and factories. However, lacking from this important segment of our American history is an overall attempt to publish an industry and nationwide study focused entirely on the vehicle makers.

This ongoing series is dedicated to these artisans and craftsmen of horse-drawn vehicles.

Over 30,000 names of makers and those in the related early transportation construction trades are identified and listed in this multi-volume publication. Although this listing is extensive and the largest of its kind ever published, we are far from complete in our endeavor to chronicle this expansive field of craftsmen. From the early 1800's through 1920's there were literally tens of thousands of these carriage, buggy, and wagon makers. From coast to coast nearly every little town had a local blacksmith, wagon maker, general store and livery house. Here you could either buy, order or have built anything on wheels. In the larger cities the fine coach and carriage building factories thrived, employing hundreds of workmen manufacturing thousands of vehicles.

Unfortunately, today the majority of these vehicles are gone; worn out and discarded, along with any chance to identify the makers who applied their Carriage Art & Craftsmanship to send their *Wheels Across America*.

We now realize the importance of accurately documenting the names and history of these makers, which brings us to the concept of a multi-volume, sequential set of reference books to be released over the next several years. This will allow us the flexibility needed to list additional names, while updating and revising previous listings. It has always been our intent to enlist all resources available in the research and identification of these craftsmen, for no one individual can be considered an expert in such a diverse field of manufactured vehicles.

WE ENCOURAGE AND WELCOME ALL INFORMATIVE COMMENTS!

Anyone with additional material, resources, or other editorial comments are invited to contact the author, Daniel D. Hutchins, through the publisher—

Tempo International Publishing Co. LLC
8100 Wyoming Blvd.
Suite M4-234
Albuquerque, NM 87113

www.tempointernationalpublishing.com

Acknowledgements

The completion of this work would have been impossible without the generous assistance of many individuals and institutions around the country — and for the access to historical collections, the provision of historical images, trade literature, research material and their constructive critiques of manuscript. To all of these, the author is indebted.

I would also like to acknowledge the enormous contribution in spirt and encouragement given to me from my very supportive family. My beautiful wife Diana, son: Dustin Hutchins, daughter: Brandy Smith, brother: Edward Hutchins, sisters:, Linda McBurney and Karen Bast, and a very special Thank You! to my mother Polly Hutchins and father Douglas Hutchins for his incredible help and assistance sorting and organizing my research.

The smallest member of the "BIRDSELL" Wagon Family

I would also like to thank the following persons:
James and Peg Aplan, William Ayres, Karen Bast, Nathan Bender, Barbara A. Bertucio, Larry Bowman, Carolyn Brucken, Harold "Heavy" Burdick, E. Daniel Burkholder, Dan Bussey, Sharon Cooney, John Crockett, Fred Dahlinger, Jr., Eileen L. Davis, David B. Driscoll, Nancy Ehlers, Gail Esola, Kayo Fraser, Maxine Friedma, Sally Gambino, Mark Lee Gardner, Peter Georgi, Gretchen and Mike Graham, Robert D. Grant, James Gray, Susan Green, Russell Grills, Doug Hansen, John Hardy, Rozan Henning, Leona R. Heuer, Tammy Slade Honnell, Janet Houghton, Bob and Sharon Huxford, "Cap" Terrell Jacobs, Donna Rea Jones, Mark Knipping, Richard and Robert Kulp, Joe Leist, Dick Litschauer, Frank McMath, Greg M. Maddox, Lenard Magee, Mike Margerum, Andy Miller, Jeffrey T. Murray, George Oberst, Karen Del Principe, David B. Rietz, Dot Rugus, Fred W. Scott, Jr., Emily Seager, Brian Shovers, Jeff Shultz, Dave Sietsema, Samuel C. Slaymaker III, Marilyn Smiland, Jeffery Stein, Joanna Tobin, Ann VanCamp, Terry Wallace, Cathy Wegener, Joyce Welford, Don and Connie Werner, Betsy Whitmore, George Williams, Orley W. Yoder and Christa Zaros.

I am also indebted to the following organzations and companies:
Alaska Horse Journal; Abion Prairie Carriage Museum; Autry Western Heritage Museum; Berks County Heritage Center; Buffalo Bill Historic Center; Buggy Builders Bulletin; Bundoran Farm; California State Parks Dept.; Carriage Museum of America; Cheyenne Frontier Days Museum; Circus World Museum; FASNY Museum of Firefighting; Firesteel Photography; Gray-

Dort Motors, Wm. Gray & Sons Carriage Museum; Horse Drawn News; (The) Hubbard Museum of The American West; Janeway Carriage House; Long Island Museum of American Art, History and Carriages; Marsh-Billings-Rockefeller National Historic Park; Maymont Foundation; McCracken Research Library; Montana Historical Society; National Archives & Records Administration; National Cowboy & Western Heritage Museum; National Photo Archives; New York State Museum; New York State Parks Dept.–Lorenzo State Historic Site; Pueblo Historical Society, James Buchanan Foundation; Remington Carriage Museum; Santa Ynez Valley Historical Society, Museum & Carriage House; Smithsonian Institution; Staten Island Historical Society; State of Wyoming Library; Stratford Hall Plantation, Robert E. Lee Memorial; Werner Wagon Works; Wesley Jung Carriage Museum; Winmill Carriage Collection at Morven Park; (The) Westmoreland Davis Memorial Foundation; Wisconsin Historical Society.

Author: Daniel D. Hutchins and father Douglas A. Hutchins pictured here while doing research at the Wesley Jung Carriage Museum in Greenbush, Wisconsin, in June 2003.

The Craftsmen Listings

Abair
Frank Abair Jr., carriage maker; Red Cliff, Colorado, circa 1882–1890.

Abbith
Staver Abbith Carriage Co.; Chicago, Illinois, circa 1890–1910.

Abbott
E.C. Abbott, wagon maker; Johnstown Center, Wisconsin, circa 1885–1901.

Abbot-Downing
J. Stephens Abbot (1804–1871) and Lewis Downing (1792–1873) were early pioneers in the coach industry. This famous Concord, NH coach, wagon and motor-truck company, circa 1813–1928, gained world wide recognition for their "Concord Coach", used on stage and mail lines throughout the United States, Canada, South America, South Africa and Australia. Although mostly known for this coach, they actually manufactured over 40 different styles of wagons, buggies, coaches and commercial vehicles.

Starting in 1813, wheelwright Lewis Downing opened a small shop, building wagons, freight vehicles and two wheeled chaises. His business and reputation slowly grew, and by 1825 Downing employed a dozen workers and apprentices. In 1826 he was joined by an apprentice chaise builder named J. Stephens Abbot. Within the next two years, they would become full partners and known as Abbot and Downing, makers of the "Concord Coach". This was an extremely durable vehicle, with its oak frame, ash wheels and unique suspension of wide leather strips called thoroughbraces. These long leather strips ran lengthwise under the rounded coach body, giving it a swinging motion that was once described by Mark Twain as "an imposing cradle on wheels". Nearly 700 of these coaches were sold by the time the partnership dissolved in 1847.

Downing moved to another location in Concord, with his two sons, and formed Lewis Downing and Sons. Here, his business thrived and the new firm employed nearly 200 men by the 1860's, selling to retailers, wholesalers and U.S. government contracts. Meanwhile, Abbot continued on in the old shops, with his son, under the name J.S. and E.A. Abbot and Company. This new Abbot company also enjoyed much growth and success selling to retailers, wholesalers and U.S. government contracts.

In 1865, after more than half a century, Lewis Downing retired, and soon after his sons arranged a merger with his old partner, the Abbot company. The firm was incorporated in 1873 as Abbot-Downing Company, and soon was producing 2,000 coaches annually. Over the next 20 years, many more changes in the firms structure would take place.

In November of 1915, Rufus N. Elwell, then a major stock holder and plant operations manager, announced that the company would add motor trucks and motorized fire equipment to its line. The first of many Concord motor trucks rolled out the door, in 1916. Although they reorganized as the Abbot-Downing Truck and Body Co., the venture never really gained the same stature as their coaches, and after several more years of struggle, Abbot-Downing Company dissolved.

Wells Fargo & Company eventually purchased the Abbot-Downing name.

Abbott (see Staver & Abbott)

Abbots & Hill
Blacksmiths and wagon makers, 7th between I and J; Sacramento, CA, circa 1853–1865.

Abel
F.J. Abel, wagon maker; Fond du Lac, Wisconsin, circa 1879–1901.

Abels
W.P. Abels manufactured wagons, buggies and sleighs; Cicero, NY, circa 1850's.

Abercrombie
J.S. Abercrombie, blacksmith and wagon maker; American Falls, Idaho, circa 1905–1910.

Abercrombie
Thomas W. Abercrombie, blacksmith and wheelwright, 166 Camp; Dallas, Texas, circa 1890–1910.

Abercrombie
W.K. Abercrombie, blacksmith and wagon maker; Greenwood, Colorado, circa 1883–1890.

Ableiter
Melchior Ableiter, wagon maker; Boscobel, Wisconsin, circa 1885–1903.

Abresch
Charles Abresch manufactured wagons and carriages; Milwaukee, Wisconsin, circa 1879–1915.

Abts
Desire Abts, wagon maker; Champion, WI, circa 1885–1901.

Acker
Abram Acker devoted a large portion of his work to sleigh building; Sing-Sing, New York, circa 1870–1890.

Ackerman & Weber
Manufactured wagons and heavy horse-drawn trucks, 900 Lock; Syracuse, NY, circa 1899.

Ackerman (see Schneider & Ackerman)

Acme Harvester Co.
This Pekin, Illinois company started business about 1860, building farm implements, circa 1860–1910.

Acme Harvesting Machine Co.
Peoria, Illinois, circa 1890–1915.

Acorn Buggy Co.
Buggy manufacturer; Cincinnati, Ohio, circa 1880–1910.

Adam & Pretchett
Blacksmiths, wagon makers and machinists; Aspen, Colorado, circa 1883–1890.

Adams
T.A. Adams, blacksmith and wagon maker; Arapahoe Agency, Wyoming, circa 1902–1908.

Adams
William Adams & Son, blacksmiths and wagon makers; Idaho Falls, Idaho, circa 1905–1910.

Adams & Debose
Carriage painters and trimmers, 132 N. Ervay; Dallas, Texas, circa 1895–1905.

Adams & Grimmett
Blacksmiths and wagon makers; Meridian, Idaho, circa 1905–1910.

Adams (see Eicke & Adams)

Adams (see Henry & Adams)

Adkinson
P.D. Adkinson, blacksmith and wagon maker; Cottonwood, Idaho, circa 1905–1910.

Adriance, Platt & Co.
Adriance, Platt & Co., circa 1880–1912, manufactured a variety of farm implements, from the early 1880's, up to the time Moline Plow Co. bought them out in 1912; Poughkeepsie, NY.

Advance Buggy Co.
Buggy manufacturer; Cincinnati, Ohio, circa 1880–1910.

Aeschlemann
F. Aeschlemann, wagon maker: Pittsburgh and Allegheny, PA, circa 1854–1870.

Aetna Manufacturing Co.
Built their horse-drawn mower and reaper under the patents of Amos Rank; Salem, Ohio, circa 1860's–1870's.

Agnew
John Agnew, a noted hand fire engine builder, also manufactured three steam fire engines. The first in 1859 for the North Liberty Engine Co., and later another for Fairmont Engine Co.

Jacob L. Haupt succeeded Agnew in 1867 and would go on to build five more engines, using his own designs; Philadelphia, PA, circa 1859–1875.

Ahlbrand Carriage Co.
Seymour, Indiana, circa 1890–1910.

Ahrens
A manufacturer of fire engines from Cincinnati, OH. This company built over 700 steam fire-engines, making it one of the largest firms ever engaged in the construction of these vehicles.

Starting out in 1868, they purchased the established business of Lane & Bodley, who had purchased their business from the famous inventor, Moses Latta.

After a long and successful career, circa 1868–1891, Ahrens merged with Clapp & Jones of Hudson, NY; Silsby of Seneca Falls, NY; and Button of Waterford, NY, to form the American Fire Engine Company.

Aiken
H. James Aiken, carriage and wagon dealer and representative; Ashland, Wisconsin, circa 1890–1910.

Ainsworth (see Cloward & Ainsworth)

Albasing
Steve Albasing of Baraboo, Wisconsin lettered and gold leafed circus wagons for the Ringlings, circa 1920–1930's.

Albert
John Albert, wagon and truck manufacturer, 11 Canon; New York, NY, circa 1899.

Alberts
Mr. Alberts was a wagon maker; Mayville, Wisconsin, circa1865.

Alberthal
H.A. Alberthal, blacksmith and carriage maker; carriage painter and trimmer, 414–416 E. Overland; El Paso, Texas, circa 1900–1920.

Albion Manufacturing Co.
This Michigan company, circa 1880–1900, built farm implements, including a style called the Daisy Sulky Hay Rake. This hay rake was being advertised by Gale Manufacturing Co. of Albion, Michigan in 1889.

Alborn
H. Alborn, blacksmith and wheelwright, Franklin near Travis; Houston, Texas, circa 1887–1895.

Albrecht
Albert Albrecht, wagon maker; Mayville, Wisconsin, circa 1885.

Albrecht
Carl Albrecht Co, buggy manufacturer; Cincinnati, Ohio, circa 1880–1910.

Albright
A. Albright & Co., carriage makers; Easton, PA, circa 1880–1910.

Albright
August Albright, wagon and carriage maker; Rochester, Wisconsin, circa 1879–1919.

Albright
Edward Albright, wagon maker; Greenleaf, WI, circa 1885–1903.

Albuquerque Carriage Co.
Started at 301 N. 1st and moved to 111 W. Grand; Albuquerque, New Mexico, 1910–1923.

Aldrich
C.E. Aldrich, blacksmith and wagon maker; Kippen, Idaho, circa 1905–1910.

Alexander
William Alexander, carriage maker; Kirkland, NY, circa 1850's.

Alexander (see Brown, Sloan & Alexander)

Alexander (see McKay & Alexander)

Alf
Edward F. Alf Co., buggy manufacturer; Cincinnati, Ohio, circa 1880–1910.

Allen
Bonaparte Allen, entrepreneuer of Buford, Georgia, founded the Bona Allen saddlery & tannery in 1873. They made everything from saddles to boots, and their clientele list

included such noted celebrities as William Cody and Roy Rogers.

In 1900, in addition to the tannery, they operated a harness factory, a horse collar factory, the general store and Buford bank.

At one time the company employed nearly two thirds of the towns population. From the general store, you could purchase a complete outfit from head to toe, including an assortment of horse-drawn carriages, wagons and buggies, all a part of their vast inventory.

Bona Allen also enjoyed an extensive wholesale business, building the J.C. Higgins brand saddles and others, circa 1873– 1970.

In 1970, the Tandy Leather Co. bought out Bona Allen, and later sold at least the saddle making portion of the business to Foxwood of Olney, IL.

Allen
D.C. Allen, wagon maker; Okee, Wisconsin, circa 1879.

Allen
F.F. Allen, carriage maker; Applebachsville, PA, circa 1880–1910.

Allen
Frank H. Allen, wagon and carriage material, corner of Sac and Drumm; San Francisco, California, circa 1882–1890's.

Allen
Frederick Allen, wagon maker, Burnett Junction, WI, circa 1885–1919.

Allen
Lawrence Allen, blacksmith, horseshoer, wheelwright and wagon maker, 101 Junius, E., also Forney Ave, 3 E. Grand; Dallas, Texas, circa 1886–1910.

Allen
R. H. Allen & Co., carriage and wagon works; New York, N.Y, circa 1890–1910

Allen
R.L. Allen & Co. designed and developed the Empire Potato Harvester and other horse-drawn equipment; New York, NY, circa 1860's-1890's.

Allen
Robert Allen, blacksmith and wagon maker, J Street, between 14th and 15th; Sacramento, CA, circa 1853–1865.

Allen
Samuel Allen, carriage maker; Vernon, NY, circa 1850's.

Allen
Sidney D. Allen, blacksmith and wagon maker; Bedford, Wyoming, circa, 1900–1908.

Allen
S.L. Allen & Co. of Philadelphia, PA, built farm equipment, circa 1890–1910

Allen Buggy Co.
O.M. Allen Jr., carriages, buggies and wagons, D.H. Hughes, manager, 371 Elm; Dallas, Texas, circa 1891–1900.

Allen Supply Co.
(See Jucket & Freeman)

Allerton & Stevens
Around 1885, this company constructed a horse-drawn steam fire-engine. It was of the double horizontal style and the engraving was beautiful. It is unknown why the company went out of business; New Haven, CT, circa 1885.

Alliance Carriage Co.
Buggy manufacturer; Cincinnati, Ohio, circa 1880–1910.

Allis
A.D. Allis, wagon maker; Waupun, Wisconsin, circa 1865.

Allison
Frank J. Allison, blacksmith and wheelwright, 1907 Colita and 2100 Chicon; Austin, Texas, circa 1895–1905.

Allison & Kees
Carriage makers, 14 N. 15th; Denver, Colorado, circa 1883–1890.

Almers
E.H. Almers, buggy maker, 503 Chestnut Street; Mifflinburg, PA, circa 1862–1870.

Alstatter (see Long, Black & Alstatter Co.)

Alstatter (see Long & Alstatter)

Alvarez
F. Alvarez Sr., blacksmith and wheelwright—also carriage and wagon maker, 415 Perez (circa 1887–1895), moving later to 917 N. Laredo (circa 1895–1905); San Antonio, Texas.

His son, F. Alvarez Jr., joined his father as a blacksmith and wheelwright at the 917 N. Laredo location, circa 1901–1905.

Amarillo Carriage Works
Carriages, wagon makers and blacksmiths, 518–520 Tyler & 601 Harrison; Amarillo, Texas, circa 1903–1920.

Amell
Sameul Amell, blacksmith and wagon maker; Ranchester, Wyoming, circa 1901–1902.

American Buncher Manufacturing Co.
Built the American and the Improved Prairie Buncher; Indianapolis, IN., circa 1890–1910.

American Carriage Co.
Mr. Perrin P. Hunter, President of this buggy manufacturer; Cincinnati, Ohio, circa 1880–1910.

American Carriage Co.
Sleigh and carriage builders; Kalamazoo, Michigan, circa 1890–1920.

American Fire Engine Co.
This company was the result of the merger, in 1891, of the following fire engine companies: Clapp & Jones of New York; Silsby of Seneca Falls, NY; Button of Waterford, NY; and Ahrens of Cincinnati, Ohio.

The consolidation of these four firms brought together some of the foremost steam fire-engine builders in the world. They were officially incorporated on December 12, 1891. Their new machines included the "Columbian Engine" and the "New American", circa 1891–1910.

American LaFrance Fire Engine Company

In the early 1860's, Truckson LaFrance traveled from Pennsylvania to Elmira, New York looking for employment. He got a job at the Elmira Union Iron Works. It was while he was employed here that he first became interested in steam engines.

In the 1870's LaFrance obtained several patents on improvements he developed in the rotary steam engine. John Vischer, head of the Iron Works, became interested and was convinced by LaFrance to back him in the manufacture of a steam fire engine. They subsequently formed a business partership to manufacture fire apparatus.

Their success attracted the attention of Alexander S. Diven, a wealthy Elmira businessman, and his four sons, who bought the company in April of 1873. They renamed it LaFrance Manufacturing Company and appointed John Vischer as a Director and Truckson LaFrance as the company's Mechanical Engineer.

Within three months, the new company bought 10 acres of land and built a plant to manufacture steam engines and related equipment, including railroad locomotives.

By 1876 Truckson's brother, Asa LaFrance, joined the company as a traveling salesman.

In the hopes of promoting worldwide sales, the company built a steam fire engine and shipped it to France, in 1878, for the Paris Exposition. Unfortunately it did not comply with French law and they were not even allowed to demonstrate it. This was not only a huge disappointment, but, the expense nearly closed the plant.

Another Elmira businessman agreed to finance the manufacture of a fire engine if it was named after his wife. Sales depended upon entering and winning competitions. Thus the new "Jeanie Jewell" was off to Chicago for a three day competition, accompanied by Asa LaFrance and Thomas Hotchkiss. The LaFrance steamer, at the close of competition, was proclaimed "best in the industry".

In 1880, the company was once again reorganized; this time as LaFrance Steam Engine Company, to take advantage of the company's-reputation as the leading manufacturer of rotary, nest-tube boilers, invented and patented by Truckson LaFrance and used for fire engines.

Two years later, another major achievement took place when the firm arranged with Daniel D. Hayes to manufacture an extension ladder truck. This truck was considered a major technological advancement at the time. The LaFrance Steam Engine Company had clearly established itself as the leading manufacturer of fire engines.

The American Fire Engine Company was formed in 1891, by joining the Button Fire Engine Works, Silsby Manufacturing Company, Ahrens Manufacturing Company, and Clapp and Jones. LaFrance declined an offer to be included. However, in the late 1890's a group of New York investors desired to form a fire engine manufacturing monopoly and in 1900, the International Fire Engine Company was announced. This new organization included American Fire Engine Company, along with LaFrance Fire Engine Company, and Thos. Manning Jr. & Co., along with several other support equipment manufacturers.

This new company, with some reorganization, new officers, and J.H. Clarke as president, was named the American LaFrance Fire Engine Company and located its headquarters in New York, NY, until 1906 when they moved to Elmira.

The company continued its quest for inovation in design, quality of product and pride in furnishing the best equipment in the industry.

American Harrow Co.

Manufactured horse-drawn farm implements, including wagons and the New American manure spreader; Detroit, Michigan, circa 1890–1910.

American Oak Leather Co.

Buggy manufacturer; Cincinnati, Ohio, circa 1880–1910.

American Plow Co.

Farm implement and equipment manufacturer; Madison, Wisconsin, circa 1890–1910.

American Seeding Machine Co.

In 1903, a number of farm implement companies joined together and formed the American Seeding Machine Co. They also continued to build and sell the Black Hawk manure spreader, a line they acquired from D.M. Sechler Carriage Co.; Springfield, Ohio, circa 1903–1930.

American Shredder Co.

Built various farm equipment and a line of husker-shredders; Madison, Wisconsin, circa 1875–1910.

American Steel Gear Company

Manufactured steel buggy gear, axles and other carriage parts, at 381 and 383 Erie Street; Toledo, Ohio, circa 1870–1910.

American Wagon Co.

Buggy manufacturer; Cincinnati, Ohio, circa 1880–1910.

American Wheel Company

Manufactured vehicle wheels of every size and style; Chicago, IL, circa 1860–1900.

American Whip Co.

Westfield, Mass., circa 1890–1910.

Ames Buggy Co.

F.A. Ames, manufacturer of buggies; Owensboro, Kentucky, circa 1887–1926.

Ames Plow Co.
This Boston, MA company manufactured agricultural equipment and other farm implements—like Burt's Self-adjusting Horse Hay Rake, and the Perry Gold Medal mower, circa 1850's–1900.

By the mid-1860's Ames Plow Company had taken over the Nourse & Mason Company of Boston, MA.

Ames Plow Co.
Manufactured farm wagons and carts, 53 Beekman; New York, NY, circa 1899.

Ames-Dean
The Ames-Dean Carriage Co.; Jackson, Michigan, circa 1890–1910.

Ames (see Cliff & Ames)

Amesbury Carriage Factory
Amesbury, Mass., circa 1890–1910.

Ammon & Eilers Co.
Large jobbers of saddlery and carriage hardware. Later the name was changed to J.M. Eilers Co.; Cincinnati, Ohio, circa 1890–1910.

Amoskeag
Amoskeag Manufacturing Co. of Manchester, N.H. manufactured a variety of fire engines, pumpers and support vehicles, including a 9,240-pound steam pumper, named "T.J. Coolidge", after the chairman of the board of directors of the Amoskeag Manufacturing Co. (Coolidge was a great grandson of Thomas Jefferson).

This pumper was made of brass, copper and nickel-plated metal and was capable of pumping 900 gallons of water per minute.

Their first steam fire-engine was built in 1859. It was designed by N.S. Bean, and was named Amoskeag #1. This engine was in service for seventeen years. The firm constructed eleven more of this style engine. In 1861, they produced another sytle, available in three sizes, named the "Harp", because of its shape.

In 1866, they built their first double straight frame, in 1870, they added a crane-neck style, and in 1877, they offered what is known as the Single Short Frame. By now, over 700 vehicles had been sold, and in the spring of 1877, the firm changed management, and their company name to Manchester Locomotive Works; Manchester, NH, circa 1859–1900.

Anchor Buggy Co.
Buggy manufacturer, Cincinnati, Ohio, circa 1880–1910.

The largest buggy ever built was manufactured by the Anchor Buggy Co. of Cincinnati. Twice the size of an ordinary buggy with 80" and 88" wheels. It was used for advertising and shown at various state conventions.

Anderson
Alex Anderson, wagon maker; North Bend, WI, circa 1885–1898.

Anderson
A.M. Anderson, blacksmith and wheelwright, Lancaster Ave. between 9th and 10th and Oak Cliff, also 713 Elm; Dallas, Texas, circa 1891–1910.

Anderson
C. Anderson, wagon maker; Castle Rock, Wisconsin, circa 1879.

Anderson
H.J. Anderson, wagon maker; Manitowoc, Wisconsin, circa 1879.

Anderson
John Anderson, carriage and wagon dealer and representative; Augusta, WI, circa 1890–1910.

Anderson
Stephen Anderson, blacksmith and wheelwright, 2412 Postoffice; Galveston, Texas, circa 1890–1902.

Anderson
T. Anderson, wagon maker; Barre Mills, Wisconsin, circa 1879.

Anderson
Thomas Theador Anderson was born in Ohio, moved to Denver, circa 1870's. He then moved on to Cripple Creek, where he set up a carriage and wagon making business. Repairs and blacksmithing were also a large part of his business; Cripple Creek, CO., circa 1870–1900.

(*Author's note:* Thomas Theador Anderson is the great, great, grandfather of my son, Dustin Hutchins).

Anderson
T.T. Anderson, carriage maker, 3rd street, between I and J; Sacramento, CA, circa 1855–1875.

Anderson Bros.
Carriage and wagon dealers and representatives; Alban, Wisconsin, circa 1890–1910.

Anderson Buggy Co.
Buggy manufacturer; Anderson, Indiana, circa 1890–1910.

Anderson & Dallas
Blacksmiths and wagon makers; Coeur d'Alene, Idaho, circa 1905–1910.

Anderson & Harris Carriage Co.
Carriage makers; Cincinnati, OH, circa 1880–1910.

Anderson (see Bean & Anderson Mfg. Co.)

Anderson (see Heins & Anderson)

Anderson (see Pratt & Anderson)

Andrews
A.M. Andrews, wagon maker; Shawano, Wisconsin, circa 1879.

Andrews
Andrews & Son, carriage painters and trimmers, 313–1/2 E. 2nd; Ft. Worth, Texas, circa 1900–1910.

Andrews & Wyman
Wagon makers; Lafayette, Wisconsin, circa 1879.

Angelly
G.W. Angelly, blacksmith and wagon maker; American Falls, Idaho, circa 1905–1910.

Anger
Chris Anger, blacksmith and wagon maker, 163 15th; Denver, Colorado, circa 1878–1890.

Anger & Bitzer
Carriage and wagon makers, 163–15th, Denver, Colorado, circa 1880's–1900.

Ann Arbor Agricultural Co.
Manufactured a number of horse-drawn implements and other farm equipment, including their Columbia Hay press and a line of cutters and bailers, circa 1880's-1943.

The company continued to build agricultural equipment into the 1940's, before being sold to the Oliver Company.

Anson
Peter Anson, blacksmith and wagon maker; Mountain Home, Idaho, circa 1905–1910.

Ansted Axle & Spring Co.
Connersville, Indiana, circa 1890–1910.

Anthon
George Anthon, wagon maker, 507 West 54th; New York, NY, circa 1899.

Anthony (see Bean & Anthony)Appleton Manufacturing Co.
Built farm equipment, including heavy wagons, manure spreaders and a number of husker-shredders; Batavia, Illinois, circa 1872–1920.

Arceneaux (see Holmes & Arceneaux)

Archer
George W. Archer, light carriage and wagon maker, Jerone Ave. and 169th, New York, NY, circa 1899

Archer
Samuel Archer, wagon maker; Terre Haute, IN, circa 1858–1860's.

Arenburg (see Wanamaker & Arenburg)

Arfort
John Arfort, wagon maker, 623 Geary; San Francisco, California, circa 1880–1890.

Arkla Village
Over its many years of operation, this company took the opportunity to build every style of vehicle possible, from full size wagons to a line of pony carts—like their #454 style; Emmett, Arkansas, circa 1890–1976.

Arlington Iron Works
This firm manufactured several horse-drawn steam fire-engines; Waverly, IA, circa 1880–1890's.

Armleder Wagon Co.
Otto Armleder, proprietor, buggy manufacturer; Cincinnati, Ohio, circa 1880–1920. They issued their catalog #34 in 1910.

Armstrong
Mr. Albert Armstrong had previously operated Keystone Buggy Co. He then started this new firm, A. Armstrong Co., in Cincinnati, Ohio and operated it from 1904 to 1921. They manufactured vehicles mainly for the export trade.

They built rickshaws for China, cape carts for South Africa, victories for Cuba, South America and Mexico, and surreys, phaetons and vis-a-vis for Mexico, and South America.

Armstrong
C.W. Armstrong, wagon maker; Plainville, Wisconsin, circa 1865.

Armstrong Carriage & Buggy Co.
Carriage and buggy manufacturer; Cincinnati, Ohio, circa 1880–1910.

Armstrong
J.B. Armstrong Manufacturing Co. of Flint, Michigan built carriages and sleighs - also had a shop in Guelph, Ontario, Canada, circa 1890–1910.

Armstrong (see Fallon & Armstrong)
Arnett (see Foster & Arnett)
Arnett (see Vossbeck & Arnett)

Arnold
H.S. Arnold, carriage and wagon maker, dealer and representative; Argyle, Wisconsin, circa 1879–1910.

Arnold Buggy Works
Buggy makers; Grand Rapids, OH, circa 1880–1910.

Arp & Hammond Hardware Co.
Dealers in agricultural implements, carriages and other vehicles, 216 west 17th; Cheyenne, Wyoming, circa 1892–1910.

Arpe
C. Arpe, wagon maker; New Holstein, Wisconsin, circa 1879.

Artale (see Ciulla & Artale)
Arthur (see Burton & Arthur)
Ashbrook, Tucker & Co.
Buggy makers; Cincinnati, OH, circa 1880–1910.

Ashby
Soulert Ashby manufactured wagons and sleighs; Marcellus, NY, and at Camillus, NY, circa 1850's.

Ashby (see Hyde & Ashby)
Ashford (see Glenn & Ashford)
Ashley
Louis Ashley, wagon maker; Lyndon Station, Wisconsin, circa 1879–1885.

Aspinwall Manufacturing Co.
This Jackson, Michigan farm implement company would grow to offer the largest line of potato equipment in the world. As early as 1861, L.A. Aspinwall began his development of planters.

The business moved to Three Rivers, Michigan around 1880, but would eventually move back to Jackson, in 1891. By the 1920's, the firm went out of business.

Mr. Aspinwall was still active well into his 80's, working on new designs at McKenzie Manufacturing Company in LaCross, Wisconsin, circa 1861–1930.

Athearn
G.W. Athearn, wagon maker; Oshkosh, Wisconsin, circa 1879.

Atkinson
John F. Atkinson, wagon maker, 145 East Whitesboro; Rome, NY, circa 1899.

Atkinson
John Atkinson, blacksmith and wagon maker; Boise and Dayton, Idaho, circa 1905–1910.

Atkinson & Gray
Blacksmiths and wagon makers with special attention given to repairing farm machinery, Front St., near the Fresno Planing Mill; Fresno City, CA, circa 1882–1885.

Atkinson (see Bien & Atkinson)

Atlanta Buggy Co.
Buggy maker, Frank J. Lonig, President, (White Star A grade line of vehicles); Atlanta, GA; circa 1890–1914.

Atlas Carriage Co.
Buggy manufacturer; Cincinnati, Ohio, circa 1880–1910.

Audiss
J. Audiss, wagon maker; North Prairie, Wisconsin, circa 1879.

Auel
John Auel Co., buggy manufacturer; Cincinnati, Ohio, circa 1880–1910.

Aufderheide Buggy Co.
Buggy manufacturer; Cincinnati, Ohio, circa 1880–1910.

Augusten
J. Augusten, wagon maker; Cato, Wisconsin, circa 1879.

Augustin
Christian Augustin, wagon maker; St. Louis, Missouri, circa 1850–1870.

Ault & Wiborg Co.
Buggy manufacturers; Cincinnati, Ohio, circa 1880–1910.

Aultman
The Aultman Co. built the Star wagons; Canton, Ohio, circa 1900–1920.

Aultman-Miller & Co.
This well known company dates back to about 1856 and the invention of the Buckeye mower by Lewis Miller.

Over the years, they produced several catalogs in a variety of foreign languages to the benefit of immigrants and foreign customers.

The company became part of International Harvester around 1903; Akron, Ohio, circa 1856–1903.

Aultman, Miller & Co.
Carriages, wagons and buggies, A.G. Scherer, manager, 145 Main; Dallas, Texas, circa 1890–1910.

Aultman & Tayler Machinery Co.
Manufactured farm implements; Mansfield, Ohio, circa 1880–1910.

Austin (see Carver, Steele and Austin)

Austin (see Goulds, Austin & Caldwell Co.)

Austin Brothers
Blacksmiths and wagon makers, Cucharas St.; Colorado Springs, Colorado, circa 1877–1880's.

Austin & Tomlinson
These two men started in the wagon business around 1837. In the earlier years, the business was known as Davis, Austin & Co., changing their name in 1856 to Austin & Tomlinson. A later change made it Austin, Tomlinson & Webster, circa 1837–1900.

Their factory in Jackson, Michigan used prison labor—one of only two wagon factories known to employ convicts at that time, (as many as 120 did so, by 1872).

They also sold their farm, freight and lumber wagons at the Michigan Wagon Depot of St. Joseph, Missouri; and also with wagon dealer A. Woodworth, through his "Great Western Wagon Depot".

Auterman
William Auterman, wagon maker; Wateford, Wisconsin, circa 1885–1901.

Automatic Grip Neck Yoke Co.
Indianapolis, Indiana, circa 1890–1910.

Auto Vehicle Parts Co.
Buggy manufacturer; Cincinnati, Ohio, circa 1880–1910.

Auttenkamp Buggy Co.
Buggy manufacturer; Cincinnati, Ohio, circa 1880–1910.

Avery
G.V. Avery, wagon maker; Wonewoc, Wisconsin, circa 1879.

Avery Planter Co.
Robert Avery and his brother Cyrus M. Avery started to develop planters and other equipment in the 1860's in Galesburg, Illinois. They relocated to Peoria, Illinois in 1884. Their company continued to grow and by 1891 began to build threshers and steam engines. They continued to develop new lines—such as the Corn King and the Corn Queen in 1899—and the Perfection Planter in 1908, circa 1860–1912.

Avery & Sons
B.F. Avery & Sons was founded in 1825 by Benjamin Franklin Avery with only $400. This Louisville, Kentucky company, circa 1825–1951, would grow in worth to over 1.5 million dollars at the time of their incorporation, in 1877.

The Avery company built plows, planters and other farm implements, including the Avery Sure Drop Planter and the Avery Champion One-horse Mower.

They offered a series of catalogs, featuring their ever-growing line of plows and implements. Their continuing success and popularity forced a number of expansions, and the purchase of the Champion line harvest and hay equipment from the International Harvester Co.

After more than 125 years in business, the Avery Company merged with Mineapolis-Moline Co. in 1951.

Avery & Sons
B.F. Avery, carriages, wagons and buggies, Stanley Crabb, mgr., outlet for the main plant in Louisville, Kentucky, sw corner S. Market and Wood and se corner of Market and Pacific Ave., and 403–405 E. 6th; Dallas, Texas, circa 1897–1910.

Avery (see Pack & Avery)

Axelson
G.W.R. Axelson, blacksmith and wheelwright, 20th, between Avenue A and brick wharf; Galveston, Texas, circa 1901–1908.

Ayala (see Taylor & Ayala)

Ayers
A.W. Ayers, wagon maker; West Salem, Wisconsin, circa 1879.

Babcock
A. Babcock, wagon maker; Packwaukee, WI, circa 1879.

Babcock
W.H. Babcock Co., carriage and buggy builders; Watertown, NY, circa 1880–1910.

Babcock & Viele Carriage Co.
Manufactured buckboards, buggies, phaetons and wagons. Most of their vehicles were built with Vaughn gear, including the Vaughn pianobox top buggy; Evansville, Indiana, circa 1870's–1900.

Babler
H.L. Babler, wagon maker; Monticello, Wisconsin, circa 1885.

Bache
Frank Bache & Co., blacksmiths and wagon makers, 5th, between I and J; Sacramento, CA, circa 1853–1865.

Backensto
Benjamin M. Backensto, wagon maker; St. Louis, Missouri, circa 1850–1870.

Back Stay Welt Co.
Buggy valances, bindings, etc.; Union City, Indiana, circa 1890–1910.

Badie
William Badie, wagon maker; Chamberlin, Wisconsin, circa 1885.

Baer
Samuel Baer, wagon maker; Albany, WI, circa 1890–1910.

Baetz
A. Baetz, wagon maker (and Son after 1911); Two Rivers, Wisconsin, circa 1879–1919.

Baetz
H. Baetz, blacksmith and wheelwright, 202 Navarro; San Antonio, Texas, circa 1897–1898; and 519 Main Ave; San Antonio, Texas, circa 1901–1910.

Baetz
J. Baetz, blacksmith and wheelwright; carriage, buggy, phaeton and wagon manufacturer, corner of Navarro and Market; San Antonio, Texas, circa 1885–1900.

Bagwell & Gower
Bagwell & Gower Buggy Co., Gainesville, Georgia, circa 1890–1910.

Bailey & Co.
E.P. Bailey & Co., wagon makers; Knapp, Wisconsin, circa 1879.

Bailey & Co.
S.E. Bailey & Co. manufactured sleighs and buggies: Lancaster, PA. circa 1880–1900.

Bailey & Co.
S.R. Baily & Co., 1856–1910, was a renowned buggy manufacturer, located at 12 Chestnut St., Amesbury, Massachusetts.

Their buggies and wagons were distributed by The French Carriage Co. of Boston, (see listing on The French Carriage Co.).

Edwin W.M. Bailey of S.R. Bailey & Co., who was president of the Carriage Builders National Association, was elected to the Board of Directors of The French Carriage Co. in 1900.

By 1907, the S.R. Bailey & Co. was manufacturing and selling the Electric Victoria Phaeto automobile. The 1908 Bailey Electric Victoria Phaeton was exhibited at the Boston Auto Show. The batteries were supplied by Thomas Alva Edison.

Bain Wagon Company
Mr. Edward Bain purchased this wagon and carriage factory in Kenosha, Wisconsin from a Mr. Henry Mitchell, circa 1855–1915. Mitchell moved to Racine and started another wagon factory in 1855.

Baker
C.S. Baker, blacksmith and wagon maker; Buffalo, Wyoming, circa 1902–1908.

Baker
D.C. Baker, wagon maker; Marcellus, NY, circa 1899.

Baker
F. Baker, wagon maker; Marcellus, NY, circa 1899.

Baker
George B. Baker manufactured wagon and sleighs; Onondaga, NY, circa 1850's

Baker
J.G. Baker, blacksmith and wagon maker, 219 Taylor; Amarillo, Texas, circa 1910–1920.

Baker & Son
J. Baker & Sons, blacksmiths, horseshoers and wheelwrights, Camp between Lamar and Griffin; Dallas, Texas, circa 1886–1890.

Baker & Graham
Blacksmiths; Buffalo, Wyoming, circa 1905–1910.

Baker & Hamilton
Carriage and wagon dealers and agents, Sacramento, CA, circa 1875–1915.

Baker (see Burgess, Baker & Thomas)

Baker (see Philips, McCallum & Baker)

Baldwin Brothers
Blacksmith and wagon makers; Walsenburg, Colorado, 1878 and Trinidad, Colorado, circa 1879–1885.

Baldwin & Palmer
Blacksmith and wagon maker; Evans, Colorado, circa 1877–1880.

Baldwin & Sibley
Bought out E. Hy & Sons in 1899: Lemars, Iowa, circa 1899–1910.

Baldwin & Vossbeck
Carriages and wagons; Trinidad, Colorado, circa 1882–1890.

Baldwin (see Barker & Baldwin)

Baldwin (see Coles, Baldwin & Bentley)

Baldwin (see Cook & Baldwin)

Baldwin (see Darey & Baldwin)

Baldwin (see Davey & Baldwin)

Baldwin (see Howe & Baldwin)

Balgord
P. Balgord, wagon maker; New Lisbon, Wisconsin, circa 1879.

Ball
John Ball, blacksmith and wagon maker; Encampment, Wyoming, circa 1902–1908.

Ball
R.L. Ball, blacksmith, horseshoer and wagon maker, 897 Commerce; Dallas, Texas, circa 1910.

Ball Axle Works
Produced axles and parts for carriages and wagons; Lancaster, PA, circa 1890–1910.

Ball Bros. & Ferry
Blacksmiths and wagon makers; Encampment, Wyoming, circa 1900–1905.

Ball (see Witter & Ball)

Ballinger
C.C. Ballinger, proprietor, El Paso Stables, 106 S. Santa Fe; El Paso, Texas, circa 1898–1905.

Ballinger & Longwell
Carriage, wagon and buggy Dealers, 12–14 San Francisco; El Paso, Texas, circa 1900.

Balzer
John Balzer (John Jr. by 1901), carriage and wagon makers; Sheboygan, Wisconsin, circa 1879–1915.

B & B Buggy Co.
Marshall, MI, circa 1890–1910.

Baetz

Bandel (see Ferrel & Bandel)

Bandhauer
Robert Bandhauer, carriage and wagon maker, 382 Wazee and 185–187 15th; Denver, Colorado, circa 1879–1890.

Bandhauer & Fager
Blacksmith and wagon maker, 382 Wazee; Denver, Colorado, circa 1878–1880.

Banes
A.R. Banes, carriage maker; Feasterville, Bucks County, PA, circa 1880–1910.

Banks
Joseph Banks' firm was origanally known as Clapp & Banks, and later as Banks & Buckly.

Mr. Banks is credited with the construction of seven steam fire-engines, all of them used the patented pumps of M.R. Clapp, and look very similar to the Smith-style engines, (see James Smith); New York, NY, circa 1863–1870.

Banner Buggy Co.
Makers of The Perfect Banner Buggy; St. Louis, Missouri, circa 1880–1920.

Bantlin
J.J. Bantlin Co. manufactured buggies; Cincinnati, Ohio, circa 1880–1910.

Barber
C.A. Barber, blacksmith and wagon maker; Lusk, Wyoming, circa 1901–1910.

Barber
G. Barber, wagon maker; Eagle, Wisconsin, circa 1879.

Barber
J.M. Barber of North Adams, Massachusetts was a carriage and sleigh maker, circa 1870's-1890's.

Barber Mfg. Co.
Manufactured carriage and wagon springs; Anderson, Indiana, circa 1890–1910.

Barbian (see Miller & Barbian)

Barbian & Caire
Blacksmiths and wheelwrights, 114 Commerce; Dallas, Texas, circa 1900–1910.

Barbour Brothers
Terre Haute, Indiana, circa 1890–1910.

Barbour & Giambo
Blacksmiths and wagon makers; Boise, Idaho, circa 1905–1910.

Bare
Benjamin Bare, blacksmith and wagon maker; Trinidad, Colorado, circa 1882–1887.

Baright
Allen Baright, carriage maker; Lockport, NY, circa 1850.

Baright
S. Baright, carriage maker; Lockport, NY, circa 1835–1865.

Barker
Blacksmith and wagon maker, J.J. Barker, (mayor) of Newtown, situated on the Gunnison River at the mouth of the Uncompahgre river, in the center of the late Ute reservation, on the D. & G. RR, 21 miles West of Montrose and 51 miles East of Grand Junction.

County seat of Delta county. Population 200; Delta, Colorado, circa 1884–1890.

Barker & Baldwin
James P. Baker and Charles A. Baldwin of 51 Broadway; New Haven, CT manufactured quality carriage bodies for shipment throughout the country.

The firm offered a wide variety, including hearse bodies, rockaways, bretts, barouches, buggies, coaches, coupes and carriages, circa 1848–1900.

Barkley
The Frank B. Barkley Manufacturing Co. manufactured carriages and buggies; Cincinnati, OH, circa 1890–1910.

Barkow
Herman Barkow, wagon and carriage maker; Milwaukee, Wisconsin, circa 1885–1911.

Barlow
J.C. Barlow Corn Planter Co. of Quincy, Illinois started out with Vandiver Corn Planter Co., then went on his own around 1890, circa 1870–1900.

Barlows (see Smith & Barlows)

Barman
Frederick Barman, blacksmith and wagon maker, 9th, between J and K; Sacremento, CA, circa 1853–1865.

Barnack
C. Barnack, wagon maker; Concord, Wisconsin, circa 1879.

Barnard
Edward Barnard Co., carriage makers; Rome, NY, circa 1890's.

Barndt
J.G. Barndt, carriage maker; Line Lexington, PA, circa 1880–1910.

Barnes
Alfred Barnes, wagon maker, 15 Pearl; Lockport, NY, circa 1899.

Barnes (see Dunbar & Barnes)

Barnes Harness Co.
B.F. Barnes Harness Co., located at 124–126 Hobson Avenue; Sapula, OK, advertised as a manufacturer and dealer in harness, saddles and collars. They also offered a line of carriages, buggies and oil wagons, circa 1890–1920.

Barnesville Buggy Co.
Barnesville, Georgia, circa 1890–1910.

Barnett Carriage Co.
Manufacturer of buggies, surreys and road wagons; Cincinnati, Ohio, circa 1880–1910.

Barngrowver (see Clunningham & Barngrowver)

Barnhardt
Z. Barnhardt & Son, wagon makers; Arcadia, WI, circa 1879.

Barnick
E. Barnick, wagon maker; Richwood, Wisconsin, circa 1879.

Barnum & Davies
Wagon makers; Cassville, NY, circa 1899.

Barnwell & Fitler
Sales agent for Wilson, Childs & Company of Philadelphia, PA., circa mid-1800's.

Barr
J.H. Barr, blacksmith and horse-shoer, Commerce, 3 W River; Dallas, Texas, circa 1905–1910.

Barr
Olson Barr wagon maker; Brodhead, WI, circa 1885–1903.

Barrett
Joseph A. Barrett, blacksmith and wheelwright, 3219 Mechanic; Galveston, Texas, circa 1900–1905.

Barron
Moses Barron, wagon maker; Pepin, Wisconsin, circa 1865.

Barry
Charles Barry manufactured light and heavy carriages, 28 East 29th; New York, NY, circa 1899.

Barry
James Barry, wagon maker; Pepin, Wisconsin, circa 1865.

Barry
Thomas Barry, carriage and wagon dealer and representative; Arcadia, WI, circa 1890–1910.

Barta
John Barta, wagon maker; Casco, WI, circa 1885–1903.

Bartlet
Mr. Bartlet was a wagon maker; Albany, Wisconsin, circa 1865.

Bartlett
L.C. Bartlett & Sons, wagon makers; Brodhead, Wisconsin, circa 1879–1898.

Barz
A. Barz, wagon maker, 42 Vallejo; San Francisco, California, circa 1882–1890.

Bassett
E.C. Bassett manufactured sleighs and carriages; Sterling, Illinois, circa 1880–1900.

Bassford
E.C. Bassford, blacksmith and wagon maker; Sheridan, Wyoming, circa 1901–1902.

Bastian Bros.
Wagon makers; West Bend, Wisconsin, circa 1879.

Bastor
A. Bastor and Bro., wagon maker; Ahnapee, WI, circa 1879.

Batavia Carriage Wheel Co.
Successors to Batavia Wheel Co., they manufactured quality wheels and hubs including their special Sweet's Concealed band and the True Shell band; Batavia, NY, circa 1880's–1910.

Bateman
E.S. and F. Bateman of Spring Mills, New Jersey manufactured an extensive line of farm implements, including their Iron Age potato digger, (circa 1906), and other farm equipment. They later moved to Grenloch, NJ.

Bateman remained in business into the 1920's, before being bought out by A.B. Farquhar Co. of York, PA in 1930, circa 1880–1930.

Bates
Samuel Bates manufactured wagons and sleighs; Minlins, NY, circa 1850's.

Batey
B.F. Batey, blacksmith, 3201 Alameda Ave.; El Paso, Texas, circa 1905–1915.

Batzler
J.G. Batzler, carriage and wagon dealer and representative; Appleton, Wisconsin, circa 1890–1910.

Bauem
C. Bauem, wagon maker; Durand, Wisconsin, circa 1865.

Bauer
A. Bauer, carriage and wagon maker; Cedar City, Utah, circa 1884–1890.

Bauer
Charles J. Bauer, light carriage maker, 615 Hudson; New York, NY, circa 1899.

Bauer Bros. Mfg. Co.
Buggy manufacturer; Cincinnati, Ohio, circa 1880–1910.

Baum (see Jackson & Baum)

Bauman
R. Bauman, wagon maker; Shiocton, and Racine, Wisconsin, circa 1879–1898.

Baumgarten
A.G. Baumgarten, carriage and wagon dealer; Ableman, Wisconsin, circa 1890–1910.

Baumgasten
J. Baumgasten, blacksmith and wagon maker; Colorado Springs, Colorado, circa 1878–1890.

Baxter
John Baxter, blacksmith and wagon maker; Afton, Wyoming, circa 1900–1905.

Baxter
John Baxter, blacksmith and wagon maker; Emmett, Idaho, circa 1905–1910.

Baxter, Byrn & Ratterman
Buggy manufacturers; Cincinnati, Ohio, circa 1880–1910.

Bay City Buggy Works
Built sleighs and buggies; Bay City, Michigan, circa 1880's–1900.

Baylis
J. Baylis, wagon maker; Jennieton, Wisconsin, circa 1879.

Bazzlay & Gimon
Blacksmith and wagon maker, 765 Elm; Dallas, Texas, circa 1910.

Beach Carriage Mfg. Co.
This Ypsilanti, Michigan manufacturer built carriages, wagons and a variety of sleighs, circa 1870–1890.

Beacle
L. Beacle, wagon maker, 363 Ninth Avenue; New York, NY, circa 1899.

Beacom
W.H. Beacom; dealer of single seat top buggies, surreys, etc.; Sheldon, Iowa, circa 1890–1910.

Beaghen (see White & Beaghen)

Bean
P.S. Bean, wagon maker; Cataract, Wisconsin, circa 1879.

Bean & Anderson Mfg. Co.
Sleigh and carriage manufacturer; McGrawville, NY, circa 1880–1890.

Bean & Anthony
Wagon shop; Florissant, Colorado, 1882–1890.

Bean & Scott
Known to have built one horse-drawn steam fire engine in 1858; Lawrence, MA.

Bean (see Hoyal & Bean)

Bearer
J. Bearer, wagon maker; Young America, Wisconsin, circa 1879.

Beattie
James Beattie, wagon maker, 510 West 15th; New York, NY, circa 1899.

Beaty
Forrest M. Beaty, carriage, wagon, buggy and phaeton dealer, 417–419 Congress Ave.; Austin, Texas, circa 1898–1905.

Beaty (see Rosette & Beaty)

Beatty
C. & S. Beatty, carriage makers, 17th Ward; New York, NY, circa 1850.

Beaudoin
John Beaudoin, carriage and wagon maker, 3rd and Canby; Laramie, Wyoming, circa 1902–1910.

Beaumont Carriage & Implement
Carriage and wagon makers and repairers, 252–260 Fannin; Beaumont, Texas, circa 1906–1911.

Beck
John Beck, wagon maker; South Germantown, Wisconsin, circa 1879–1903.

Beck
M.P. Beck, blacksmith and wagon maker, 205 W 4th; Amarillo, Texas, circa 1915–1920.

Becker
L. Becker, blacksmith and wheelwright, 306 North, (circa 1897–1898), and corner of Austin and Lamar, (circa 1900–1910); San Antonio, Texas.

Becker
R.A. Becker Co., buggy manufacturer; Cincinnati, Ohio, circa 1880–1910.

Becker Co.
John Becker, wagons, buggies and implements; Belen, New Mexico, circa 1900–1915.

Bedell
J.W. Bedell, carriage and wagon dealer and representative; Appleton, Wisconsin, circa 1890–1910.

Beebe
F.C. Beebe, wagon maker; Navarino, NY, circa 1899.

Beebe & Boardman
Wagon makers; Boardman, Wisconsin, circa 1865.

Beecher
Charles Beecher, wagon maker; Racine, Wisconsin, circa 1865–1903.

Beedle & Kelly Co.
Built corn planters and other farm equipment; Troy, Ohio, circa 1895–1905.

Beeman
H. Beeman, wagon maker; Rock Falls, Wisconsin, circa 1879.

Beeman
H.D. Beeman, blacksmith and wheelwright, 834 Elm and 877 Commerce; Dallas, Texas, circa 1891–1905.

Beeman
J.W. Beeman, wagon maker; Trempealeau, WI, circa 1879.

Beeman Bros.
Blacksmiths and wheelwrights, 302 Exposition Ave.; Dallas, Texas, circa 1900–1910.

Beeman & Cashin Mercantile Co.
Dealers in agricultural implements; Evanston, Wyoming, circa 1900–1908.

Beeman & Stogsdill
Blacksmiths and wagon makers, 304 Exposition Ave.; Dallas, Texas, circa 1910.

Beers
D.G. Beers & Co. manufactured tops and trimmings for the wagon and carriage industries; Newton, CT, circa 1890–1910.

Beers
John Beers, blacksmith and wagon maker; Fort Collins, Colorado, circa 1884–1890's.

Beery
Jesse Beery Co. manufactured carriages; Pleasant Hill, OH, circa 1890–1910.

Beggs
James Beggs was born in 1898. His father, Samuel M., and uncle, James W., owned the Beggs Wagon Co. Young James was around wagons, and particularly circus wagons, his entire life.

When he was in his 20's, he joined a rail circus, called Eschman, and traveled throughout the midwest to "gain firsthand knowledge and to satisfy his curiosity."

He had never planned to be a permanent member of circus life. Once his sense of adventure was accomplished, he returned to the family business of wagon making.

His father and uncle were originally from St. Joseph, Missouri, but had moved the business to a small town in Iowa, (circa 1875–1900), where they made freight wagons and other farm wagons. Almost by accident, the company got into making wagons for the F.J. Taylor Circus, a small outfit that spent winters in the town. They made a few wagons for them and learned a little bit about the circus life.

After a few years the brothers moved the company, first to Carrolton, Missouri, and then in 1904, to Kansas City where they built a wagon factory. They continued to build mostly farm and business wagons. However, in the winter season when circuses were resting up and preparing new acts for the next season, they would be ordering new equipment.

The Beggs Wagon Co., almost by accident, became one of only a half dozen companies making wagons for the more than 100 circuses touring in the early 1900's throughout the country.

These circuses would commission Beggs Wagon Co. to make carnival wagons, baggage wagons, ticket wagons, band wagons, racing chariots, cages and calliopes.

Some would come in with an idea, but need help with the details.

James W. would start suggesting decorative touches like scrolls, while sketching each idea until he had drawn something the customer liked.

Though he had never taken a lesson, the senior Beggs was a natural artist.

They even made some wagons for the Tony Lowenda Circus, based in Buenos Aires, Argentina. A picture of the band wagon they made for the Lowenda Circus became a permanent part of the letterhead for the Beggs Circus Wagons.

About 1918 the demand for wagons decreased dramatically and the company abanded the wagon business and began building and selling their own line of automobiles. They sold the "Beggs Six" until the depression, when they went out of business.

Beggs' father and uncle both died shortly thereafter and Beggs tried his hand as an automobile dealer, later switching to insurance.

He never lost his love of circuses. He was a member of the Circus Historical Society, based in Baraboo, Wisconsin. A circus museum there houses many of the circus wagons still in existence.

Beggs felt that more than half of all the circus wagons still around are in the museum in Baraboo. The rest have all fallen apart or rotted away.

Beggs Bros.
Manufactured a variety of farm wagons, including many with fancy designs and engravings.

This company may have had a connection to Beggs-Goodson Wagon Company of Hannibal, Missouri. They both offered similar designs; Carrollton, Missouri, circa 1880–1910.

Beggs-Goodson Wagon Co.
This Hannibal, Missouri company advertised themselves as "wholesale wagon manufacturers".

They may also have had some connection to Beggs Bros. of Carrollton, MO, circa 1880–1910.

Beggs & Rowland
Built wagons, drays, carts, heavy trucks and timber wheels at 220–222 North Front Street; Philadelphia, PA., circa 1850–1870's.

Behlen
Charles Behlen Sons' Co., carriage builders; Cincinnati, Ohio, circa 1890–1910.

Behlen Carriage Co.
Buggy manufacturer; Cincinnati, Ohio, circa 1880–1910.

Behnisch
C. and G. Behnisch, wagon and carriage makers; Milwaukee, Wisconsin, circa 1879.

Behnman
G. Behnman, wagon maker; West Bloomfield, WI, circa 1879.

Behr (see Meller & Behr)

Behrend
Nicholas Behrend, wagon and carriage maker; Madison, Wisconsin, circa 1873–1885.

Behrens
F.D. Behrens Co., makers of metal buckle shields, ornamental accessories for fancy harness trimmings and carriage door handles; Cincinnati, Ohio, circa 1890–1910.

Behrens-Malone Vehicle Co.
Carriages, wagons and buggies; Dallas Club building, Dallas, Texas, circa 1900–1910.

Belanger
A. Belanger, Ltd. was established in 1867 at Montmagny, Quebec, Canada. They built plows, cultivators and other farm implements, circa 1867–1920.

Belcher
F.L. Belcher, blacksmith and wagon maker; Guernsey, Wyoming, circa 1900–1905.

Belcher & Taylor Agricultural Tool Co.
This well-known maker of farm implements also built the Eclipse Two-Row Two-Horse Corn Planter; Chicopee Falls, MA., circa 1890–1920.

Beldsmeyer
H.W. Beldsmeyer & Co. manufactured commercial horse-drawn equipment related to road construction; St. Louis, Missouri, circa 1880–1900.

Belknap Wagon & Sleigh Co.
Manufactured wagons, sleighs and carriages; Grand Rapids, Michigan, circa 1880–1900.

Bell
J.M. or J.W. Bell, wheelwright and wagon maker; Manitou Springs; Colorado, 1877–1890.

Belle City Manufacturing Co.
Built a variety of farm implements; Racine, Wisconsin, circa 1890–1910.

Bellefontaine Carriage Body Co.
Manufactured all styles of first class bodies; including the Jagger jump seat surrey; Bellefontaine, Ohio, circa 1870's–1910.

Bellis
Samual B. Bellis, wagon maker; St. Louis, MO, circa 1850–1870.

Bench
Albert Bench, wagon maker, Arcadia, Wisconsin, circa 1865.

Bender
C. Bender, wagon maker; Baraboo, Wisconsin, circa 1879.

Benedict & Co.
G.M. Benedict & Co., blacksmiths and wagon makers; Fairplay, Colorado, circa 1882–1890.

Benedict & Schumann
Wagon makers; Sheboygan Falls, Wisconsin, circa 1879.

Benjamin
G.W. Benjamin, wagon maker, 22 White Plains Ave.; New York, NY, circa 1899.

Bennett
Thomas H. Bennett, blacksmith, carriage and wagon maker, 224 S Oregon; El Paso, Texas, circa 1904–1914.

Bennett
Wilder Bennett, wagon maker; Marcellus, NY, circa 1850's.

Bennett (see Heath & Bennett)

Bennison
Samuel Bennison, blacksmith and wheelwright, 1701 Mechanic; Galveston, Texas, circa 1890–1900.

Benson
H.L. Benson, blacksmith, wheelwright, carriage painter and trimmer, 362 Commerce, and 431 Jackson; Dallas, Texas, circa 1900–1910.

Benson & Monschke
Blacksmiths, horseshoers, carriage and wagon manufacturers, also carriage painters and trimmers, 363–365 Commerce; Dallas, Texas, circa 1900–1915.

Bentel & Margedent Co.
This firm manufactured every necessary piece of carriage wood working machinery; including wheel polishers, wheel planers, rim planers and wheel press machines; Hamilton, OH, circa 1860–1900.

Bentley
J.L. Bentley, blacksmith and wagon maker; Big Horn, Wyoming, circa 1900–1905.

Bentley (see Coles, Baldwain & Bentley)

Berg
P.C. Berg, wagon maker; Oconomowoc, Wisconsin, circa 1879–1885.

Berg
Peter Berg, carriage and wagon dealer and representative; Ashford, Wisconsin, circa 1890–1910.

Bergmann
R.J. Bergmann & Co., blacksmith and wheelwright, 2606 Mechanic; Galveston, Texas, circa 1886–1894.

Bergschicker
A. Bergschicker & Co. of 226 Main Street; Memphis, TN, were dealers in phaetons, buggies, surreys and spring wagons.
They also manufactured and repaired saddles and harnesses, circa 1890–1920.

Bering (see Chambers, Bering, Quinlan Co.)

Bernard
H.M. Bernard, blacksmith and wagon maker, corner L and 6th; Sacramento, CA, circa 1853–1865.

Bernard (see Musser & Bernard)

Bernauer
R. Bernauer, carriage painters and trimmers, 119 W. Overland; El Paso, Texas, circa 1898–1905.

Bernhard
B. Bernhard, wagon maker; Appleton, Wisconsin, circa 1879.

Berry
Clark Berry manufactured wagons and sleighs; Lysander, NY, circa 1850's.

Berry
Jesse Berry Co., wagon maker; Pleasant Hill, Ohio, circa 1900.

Berry
John Berry, carriage painter, 837 Folsom; San Francisco, California, circa 1888–1894.

Berry
Hebron & Fletcher Berry, buggy makers, (William Berry's sons), 303 Walnut Street (rear); Mifflinburg, PA, circa 1902–1918.

Berry
William Berry, blacksmith and buggy maker, 303 Walnut Street (rear); Mifflinburg, PA, circa 1860's-1902.

Berry Spring Sleigh Co.
Established 1889, this firm manufactured a variety of sleighs and a few other vehicles; Concord, NH, circa 1889–1900's.

Best
G. Best, wagon maker; Millhome, Wisconsin, circa 1879.

Beters
Henry Beters, wagon maker, worked in the shop of Joseph Murphy (see Joseph Murphy); St. Louis, Missouri, circa 1850–1870.

Bettis
O.J. Bettis, wagon maker, 1434 Jackson; San Francisco, California, circa 1882–1890.

Betts Spring Co.
Carriage and wagon materials, 218 Fremont; San Francisco, California, circa 1888–1894.

Betz
F. Betz, carriage and wagon maker; LaCrosse, WI, circa 1865.

Betze
L. Betze, wagon maker; Fountain City, Wisconsin, circa 1865.

Biddle & Smart
Manufacturers of the famous 400 Buckboard; Amesbury, Mass., circa 1890–1910.

Biehle Wagon & Auto Body Works
Built carriages and wagons, including a number of commercial vehicles; Reading, PA, circa 1900–1920.

Bien & Atkinson
Carriage and wagon makers; Casa Grande, Arizona, circa 1884–1890.

Biesemeier
E.E. Biesemeier, blacksmith and wagon maker; Kimberly, Idaho, circa 1905–1910

Bigden
Alfred Bigden, blacksmith and wheelwright, 217 W. Woodard; Denison, Texas, circa 1887–1890's.

Biggs
G.J. or G.I. Biggs, wagon maker; Jackson County, Missouri, circa 1850–1860.

Biggs
J.H. Biggs & Co., blacksmith and wagon maker; Pueblo, Colorado, circa 1883–1900.

Big Horn Transportation Co.
Carriage and wagon makers; Buffalo, WY, circa 1902–1908.

Billing
Robert Billing, carriage maker; Syracuse, NY, circa 1850's

Billings
Fletcher Billings was a blacksmith and wagon maker; Rippleton, NY, circa 1830–1860.

He also built some farm equipment with his son Charles, who later moved to Madison, Wisconsin and became a partner in a plow manufacturing business; named Firmin, Billings and Noe.

Billings
J.E. Billings, wagon maker and painter; Idaho Springs, Colorado, 1877 and Greeley, Colorado, circa 1878–1883.

Billings (see Firmin, Billings and Noe)

Billington
Edgar Billington, wagon maker; Arena, Wisconsin, circa 1885–1919.

Bimel Buggy Co.
Sidney, Ohio, circa 1890–1910.

Bingham
R.M. Bingham & Co. was a well known sleigh maker from Rome, New York. They turned out a variety of styles, including a Berlin Victoria Sleigh, designed by their draftsman Paul Steinbeck.

They also offered Canadian style sleighs, vis-à-vis, portlands and other cutters.

Bingham specialized in pony wagons and carts. They also built carriages and other vehicles, like their No. 152 Brighton wagon and No. 232 Bingham buckboard, both shown in their 1890 catalog; Rome, NY, circa 1880–1910.

Birch
Jas. H. Birch, carriage, coach and sleigh manufacturer, located in Burlington, NJ and Philadelphia, PA. (This may have been the main location.) In the 1880's, they manufactured thousands of coaches annually, including some stage and other road styles, circa 1862–1910.

Bird
G.M. Bird & Co. was known to have built one horse-drawn steam fire-engine in 1858; Boston, MA.

Bird
T.E. Bird, carriage and wagon maker; Madison, Wisconsin, circa 1873.

Bird (see Osgood, Morrill, Bird & Schofield)

Birdsall, Waite & Perry Mfg. Co.
This firm built a number of styles of vehicles, including wagons, carriages and as many as 18,000 sleighs

in the 1887–1888 season alone; Whitneys Point, NY, circa 1870's-1900's.

Birdsell
John C. Birdsell; West Henrietta, NY, received his first huller patent in 1855. He moved to South Bend, Indiana in 1863 where he continued to build the Birdsell wagon and perfect the Birdsell Huller.

They advertised as the largest "Steel Skein" wagon works in the world, circa 1855–1915.

Birmingham
W.R. Birmingham, manufacturer of carriages, wagons and buggies, 112–114 S. Wall; Paris, Texas, circa 1891–1900.

Birsner & Bockmann
Carriage and wagon makers; La Crosse, Wisconsin, circa 1879.

Bishop
P.T. Bishop and Bro., wagon makers; Winneconne, Wisconsin, circa 1879.

Bishop
Thomas Bishop, wagon maker; Medina, Wisconsin, circa 1865.

Bitzer
Conrad Bitzer, carriage and wagon maker; Denver, Colorado, circa 1884–1890.

Bitzer (see Anger & Bitzer)

Black
George W. and S.H. Black, dealers in agricultural implements; Basin, Wyoming, cira 1902–1908

Black
H.M. Black & Co., carriage makers, stages and express wagons of every description made to order. General jobbing done with neatness and dispatch. Importers of all kinds of spring and thoroughbrace, 590–592 Mission Street; San Francisco, California, circa 1888–1894.

Black
Moritz Black, blacksmith and wagon maker, 158 Orange; Dallas, Texas, circa 1900–1910.

Black (see Long, Black & Alstatter Co.)

Black (see Mason & Black)

Blackburn
Scott Blackburn, blacksmith and wagon maker; Idaho Falls, Idaho, circa 1905–1910.

Blacklock
J. Blacklock, wagon maker; Alloa, Wisconsin, circa 1879.

Blackwell
J.F. Blackwell of 128 S. Poydras; Dallas, Texas, was a blacksmith, wheelwright and wagon maker, circa 1890's–1910.

Blahnik
W. Blahnik, carriage and wagon dealer and representative, Algoma, Wisconsin, circa 1890–1910.

Blair
Samuel Blair, buggy maker, 345 Walnut Street (rear); Mifflinburg, PA, circa 1850's-1886.

Blake Manufacturing Co.
George F. Blake built steam fire-engines, though most were not used for that purpose. His market was in West India and South America. Here, they were used primarily on plantations and public grounds for irrigation, drainage and fire service; Boston, MA, circa 1855–1900.

Blanik
C. Blanik, carriage and wagon dealer and representative; Antigo, Wisconsin, circa 1890–1910.

Blankenship & Woodcock
Wagons, farm machinery and harness; Portales, New Mexico, circa 1900–1910.

Blaser
C.F. Blaser, carriage painters and trimmers, 103 Lake Ave.; Dallas, Texas, circa 1897–1905.

Blaser
E.M. Blaser, blacksmith, carriage painter and trimmer, 122 Montgomery, 711Ft Worth Ave., Commerce 1W Lancaster Ave.; and So. Commerce and 2 W Trinity river; Dallas, Texas, circa 1901–1910.

Blees Carriage Co.
Macon, Georgia, circa 1890–1910.

Bleiler
James Bleiler, carriage maker; Doylestown, PA, circa 1880–1910.

Blenkle
Markus Blenkle, blacksmith and wagon maker; Blackfoot, Idaho, circa 1905–1910.

Blessing
John Blessing, blacksmith and wagon maker; Casper, Wyoming, circa 1902–1910.

Blessing (see Svendsen & Blessing)

Blewett
William Blewett, blacksmith and wagon maker, 17th and Larimer; Denver, Colorado, circa 1878–1890.

Blickfeldt
H. Blickfeldt, blacksmith and wagon maker; Rawlins, Wyoming, circa 1902–1910.

Blind
William H. Blind, carriage and wagon maker; New Columbia, PA, circa 1850–1860.

Bliss & Sweetser
Wagons and agricultural implements, 355–361 Wazee; Denver, Colorado, circa 1882–1890.

Blomquist (see Eklund & Blomquist)

Blondin (see Delker & Blondin)

Bloom
James R. Bloom, blacksmith; Marion, Iowa, circa 1855–1863.

Bloom
J.S. Bloom started building farm equipment in Nashua, Iowa. By 1903, they added the Bloom Spreader to their expanding line of implements.

Bloom eventually moved to Independence, Iowa, circa 1890–1920.

Blount Carriage Co.
East Point, Georgia, circa 1890–1910. A Mr. Peter J. Zimpelmann joined this company after many years with American Carriage Co. of Cincinnati, Ohio.

Blount Plow Works
This Evansville, Indiana manufacturer built farm equipment, circa 1900–1930.

Blunck
J.C. Blunck, blacksmith and wheelwright, 630 East Commerce; San Antonio, Texas, circa 1900–1910.

Blydenburgh
Charles Blydenburgh was a carriage manufacturer. He patented 23 items between 1880 and 1890, including a vehicle body, carriage poles, springs, and gears. His most successful designs were the Suffolk and Montauk wagons.

Blydenburgh also ran a cranberry farm; Riverhead, NY., circa 1870–1910.

Boam
Thomas Boam, blacksmith and wagon maker; Downey, Idaho, circa 1905–1910.

Boardman (see Beebe & Boardman)

Bobo (see Scrimshire & Bobo)

Bockmann (see Birsner & Bockmann)

Bode
Henry Bode manufactured plows in the mid 1880's. His son, Albert, continued the business as the Bode Wagon Co. in Cincinnati, Ohio.

They made custom-built truck bodies, specializing in heavy-duty ice wagons. Albert designed and built circus wagons for several circuses—Hagenbeck-Wallace, Ringling Bros. and the 101 Ranch Wild West Show.

When a circus came to Cincinnati they would have their equipment repaired by Bode Wagon Co., who hired skilled Spanish and Portuguese wood carvers to design animals on cage wagons.

Boehle
Herman Boehle, blacksmith and wheelwright, 157 Marilla, 218 College Ave. and 1218 McKinney Ave.; Dallas, Texas, circa 1891–1905.

Boehm
Anton Boehm, carriage and wagon maker; Appleton, Wisconsin, circa 1890–1910.

Boehm
G. Boehm, wagon maker; Helenville, Wisconsin, circa 1879.

Boehmer
M. Boehmer, carriage and wagon maker; Madison, Wisconsin, circa 1873.

Boellert
Matt Boellert, blacksmith and wagon maker; Black Hawk, Colorado, circa 1890.

Boellert & Fick
Blacksmiths and wagon makers; Black Hawk, CO, circa 1883–1890's.

Boellert (see Leitzman & Boellert)

Boering
C. Boering, blacksmith and wheelwright. 109 W. 30th; Austin, Texas, circa 1906–1912.

Boerner
E.R. Boerner, blacksmith and wheelwright, 719 Elm; Dallas, Texas, circa 1898–1905.

Bogart
Elbert Bogart was a farmer, blacksmith and wagon maker. He operated his shop on the family farm; Hempstead, NY, circa 1880–1897.

Bohn
Nic Bohn, blacksmith and wheelwright; carriage and wagon manufacturers, 214—17th; Galveston, Texas, circa 1886–1902.

Bohon Carriage Co.
George Bohon of Harrodsburg, Kentucky, circa 1878–1930, established a business selling buggies, carts, harness and farm machinery. His sons Davis T. and Hanly, grew up in the business with their father.

In 1914, George sold his company and helped his two sons establish the D.T. Bohon Co. They started a business selling buggies, carts, harness, etc. as a mail order service. The sons operated this company for the next 15 years.

Bohrnsteilt
George Bohrnsteilt, carriage and wagon maker, also manufactured carriage lights; Arcadia, Wisconsin, circa 1890–1910.

Boles & Hughes
Blacksmiths and wheelwrights, 165 Camp; Dallas, Texas, circa 1898–1905.

Bolles & Prochazka
Wagon makers; Watertown, Wisconsin, circa 1879.

Bolser (see Neal & Bolser)

Bomar
R.F. Bomar, blacksmith and wheelwright; Sherman, Texas, circa 1893–1900.

Bommer
Adam Bommer, carriage and wagon maker, 612 Soulard; St. Louis, Missouri, circa 1884–1890.

Bonnell
W.T. Bonnell, wagon makers; North Freedom, Wisconsin, circa 1879.

Bonell Bros.
Wagon makers; Eau Claire, Wisconsin, circa 1879.

Bonte (see Lame & Bonte)

Bonts
Isaac N. Bonts, blacksmith and wheelwright, 509 E. 7th; Austin, Texas, circa 1898–1905.

Boob
William W. Boob supplied single elliptic spring gear and other parts to the carriage and wagon makers in the Centre Hall, PA. area, in the late 1890's. In 1900, Boob moved to Cincinnati, Ohio where he would offer a wide variety of wagon and carriage gears in his shop, and through his catalogs. He also built

wagons, carriages, road carts, and sleighs, circa 1880–1920.

Books & Neil
Blacksmiths, carriage and wagon makers, sw corner Eddy and 18th; Cheyenne, WY, circa 1895–1896.

Bookwalter
Bookwalter Wheel Co., buggy wheel manufacturing; Miamisburg, Ohio, circa 1890–1910.

Border & Simmons
Blacksmiths, carriage and wagon makers; Boulder, Colorado, circa 1882–1890.

Borgman
H. Borgman, wagon maker; Kewaunee, Wisconsin, circa 1879.

Borgman
J.M. Borgman, wagon maker, Kewaunee, Wisconsin, circa 1879.

Borland
F.L. Borland, carriage painters and trimmers, 204 W. 6th; Amarillo, Texas, circa 1900–1915.

Bose
N.E. Bose, blacksmith and wheelwright, 165—167 Camp; Dallas, Texas, circa 1900–1901.

Bose (see Hughes & Bose)

Bosisto
R. Bosisto, wagon maker; Edgerton, Wisconsin, circa 1865.

Boston Carriage Works
Carriages and wagons; Denver, Colorado, circa 1882–1890's.

Bothmer
William Bothmer, blacksmith and wheelwright, 118 E. 8th; Austin, Texas, circa 1898–1905.

Botsch
P.J. Botsch, carriage and wagon makers; Milwaukee, WI, circa 1879.

Bourne
Z.H. Bourne, blacksmith and wheelwright, Holmes and McDonald; Dallas, Texas, circa 1900.

Bouser
S. Joh Bouser, specialized in trim work on carriages and wagons; Appleton, WI, circa 1890–1910.

Bovee
Samuel Ball Bovee manufactured wagon hubs and wheel parts at Cogan Station, located several miles north of Williamsport, PA., circa 1900–1910.

Bowden
J.A. Bowden, carriage and wagon maker; Almond, Wisconsin, circa 1890–1910.

Bowden
J.W. Bowden, 1st and Ford St.; Gold Hill, Colorado, circa 1877–1890.

Bowden & Miller
Wagon makers; Alma Ceter, Wisconsin, circa 1879.

Bowdoin (see Fitzpatrick & Bowdoin)

Bowe
W.H. Bowe Co., buggy manufacturer; Cincinnati, Ohio, circa 1880–1910.

Bowen
Lee Bowen, blacksmith and wagon maker; Montpelier, Idaho, circa 1905–1910.

Bowles
Samuel Bowles, blacksmith, horseshoer and wheelwright, 1327 Main corner of Preston; Dallas, Texas, circa 1886–1900.

Bower Roller Bearing Co.
Dayton, Ohio, circa 1890–1910.

Bower & Davis
Carriage makers; Salida, Colorado, circa 1882–1890.

Bowerman
William T. Bowerman, wagon maker, 10th, between J and K; Sacramento, CA, circa 1853–1865.

Bowers
J.W. Bowers, blacksmith and wagon maker; Rosita, Colorado, circa 1882–1888.

Bowman
E.P. Bowman & Co., dealers in agricultural implements; Meeteetse, Wyoming, circa 1902–1908.

Bowman
E.W. Bowman, wagon maker, K street, between 9th and 10th; Sacramento, CA, circa 1855–1875.

Bowman
O. Bowman, wagon maker; New London, Wisconsin, circa 1879.

Bowman (see Jackson & Bowman)
Box Elder Wagon and Hdwe. Co. Carriage and wagon makers; Box Elder, Utah, circa 1884–1890.

Boyd (see Whittet & Boyd)

Boyer
Enos Boyer, carriage maker; Tylesport, PA, circa 1880–1910.

Boyer
H. Boyer, wagon maker; Waupun, Wisconsin, circa 1865.

Boyer
Boyer Wheel Co., buggy wheel manufacturer; Aurora, Indiana, circa 1890–1910.

Boyle
S. Boyle, carriage maker; Saguache, CO, circa 1882–1890.

Bozarth (see Stephens & Bozarth)

Braasch
H. Braasch, carriage and wagon maker; Milwaukee, WI, circa 1879.

Brach & Kubera
Wagon makers, 336 East 4th; New York, NY, circa 1899.

Bradford & McDonald
Makers of wagons and ice wagons, 165 Christopher; New York, NY, circa 1899.

Bradley
David Bradley Manufacturing Co. started out in the retail seed and implement business in the 1860's. The company eventually became involved in the production of farm implements and equipment, includ-

ing their X Rays Sulky Plow and XX Rays Gang Plow and their Tu Ro riding cultivator; Bradley and Chicago, IL, circa 1860's–1910.

Sears, Roebuck & Co. marketed a number of the Bradley implements, and eventually bought out the company.

Bradley
J.W. Bradley, buggy manufacturer; Cincinnati, Ohio, circa 1880–1910.

Bradley
Robert B. Bradley & Co. manufactured farm implements, 93 State Street; New Haven, CT, circa 1850's–1880's.

Bradley
S.H. Bradley Co. carriage and wagon maker, developed a good reputation state-wide for their spring wagons. Bradley also had success early-on building stages and Concord coaches for mountain travel; Marysville, CA, circa 1850's–1880's.

Bradley
W.F. Bradley, blacksmith and wheelwright, 210 E. 5th; Austin, Texas, circa 1900–1915.

Bradley & Sons
Blacksmiths and wagon makers; Lusk, Wyoming, circa 1905–1910.

Bradley (see Lawrence, Bradley & Pardee)
Bradley Shaft Coupler Co. Syracuse, New York, circa 1890–1910.

Bradt
W. Bradt, wagon maker; Wyalusing, Wisconsin, circa 1879.

Brady
J. Brady & Co., blacksmiths and wagon makers; Douglas, Wyoming, circa 1902–1908.

Brady, Langdon & Briggs
Wagon makers; Seneca, Wisconsin, circa 1879.

Brady (see Cline & Brady)

Braekke
M.O. Braekke, wagon makers; Boscobel, Wisconsin, circa 1879

Braeuer (see Gunther & Braeuer)

Bragg
S.A. Bragg, wagon maker; Cambridge, Wisconsin, circa 1865.

Brandenstein
H. Brandenstein & Co., dealers in carriages, top phaetons, top and open buggies, jump seat wagons, top and open rockaways, single seat business wagons, two seat country wagons; and every description of harness, saddlery, whips, blankets, robes, etc., corner New Montgomery and Mission Streets; San Francisco, California, circa 1882–1900.

Brandt
F. Brandt, wagon maker; Sandusky, Wisconsin, circa 1879.

Brandt
H. Brandt, wagon maker; Iron Ridge, Wisconsin, circa 1879.

Brannan
F.A. Brannan, blacksmith and wagon maker; Mohler, Idaho, circa 1905–1910.

Brant
A. Charles Brant, blacksmith and wheelwright, 3108 Washington; Houston, Texas, circa 1900–1910.

Brantford Carriage Co.
Carriage manufacturer; Brantford, Ontario, Canada, circa 1890–1910.

Brantingham (see Emerson-Brantingham Co.)

Bratton
Peter Bratton and Son, blacksmiths and wheelwrights, 306 W 3rd; Austin, Texas, circa 1887–1894.

Bratton
Willis M. Bratton, blacksmith and wheelwright, 310 Lavaca; 1105 E. 4th; Austin, Texas, circa 1897–1910.

Breal (see Fessmer & Breal)

Brebme
Ernst Brebme, wagon maker; Fort Howard, Wisconsin, circa 1865.

Brecht
H. Brecht, wagon maker; Cedar Grove, Wisconsin, circa 1879.

Brede
Henry W. Brede, wagon maker, 343 East 63rd; New York, NY, circa 1899.

Breed (see Crane & Breed)

Breen
R. Breen, wagon maker; Sacramento, CA, circa 1850–1860.

Breese
Charles Breese, blacksmith and wagon maker; Pinedale, Wyoming. He also operated a shop in Cora, Wyoming, circa 1905–1910.

Brehme
A. Brehme, wagon maker; Fort Atkinson, Wisconsin, circa 1879.

Brein
Richard Brein, wagon maker, at McGuire's, 6th, between J and K; Sacramento, CA, circa 1853–1865.

Breisseur
Rodger Breisseur, blacksmith and wagon maker; Challis, Idaho, circa 1905–1910.

Breit
Peter Breit, a New York, NY master wood carver, worked on circus wagons built by Sebastian Wagon Works, circa 1860–1890.

Breiten
Henry Breiten, blacksmith and wheelwright, 103 Texas; El Paso, Texas, circa 1895–1905.

Breitung
Albert A. Breitung, wagon maker; Appleton, Wisconsin, circa 1890–1910.

Brennan
M.F. Brennan, blacksmith and wagon maker, 410 west 17th; Cheyenne, Wyoming, circa 1892–1905.

Brennan
Thias Brennan, blacksmith and wagon maker, 1722 Thomes; Cheyenne, Wyoming, circa 1903–1910.

Brennan & Worlaumont
Carriage and wagon makers; Cheyenne, WY, circa 1884–1890.

Brensicke
August Brensicke, wagon maker; Hustisford, WI, circa 1879–1919.

Bresemann
J.J. Bresemann, wagon maker; Neenah, Wisconsin, circa 1879.

Bresemeister
J. Bresemeister, wagon maker; Hustisford, Wisconsin, circa 1879.

Brewer
T.P. Brewer, farm implements and blacksmith; Aztec, New Mexico, circa 1910–1920.

Brewster
James Brewster was born in Preston, Connecticut in 1788, the second of eight children. His father died at a young age, leaving his mother, with limited resourses, to raise the children. James remained in school untill the age of fifteen.

In 1804, he apprenticed with coach maker Colonel Charles Chapman of Northampton, Massachusetts. Brewster then worked briefly as a journeyman in Pittsfield, Massachusetts, and then in Stratford, Connecticut. On a trip to New York, seeking work, he chanced to meet John Cook, and gained employment with this New Haven coach maker.

Brewster married in 1810 and, having spent a mere 16 months as a journeyman, opened a shop of his own before years' end. The war of 1812 slowed most coach makers from making anything luxurious, as the public just wasn't buying. Mr. Brewster studied the market, and the need for improved wagons. Soon after the war, in 1816, his advertisements were offering elegant and fancy wagons for one or two horses and soon the Brewster wagons were all the rage.

Brewster bought only the best of ash plank, white oak spokes and basswood panels. He was a stickler for quality in both materials and workmanship—and his reputation, and that of his shop, flourished.

James Brewster continued to relocate—always to bigger factories—before finally constructing his own factory in 1832.

Two of Brewster's sons, the oldest—James B., and youngest—Henry, upon reaching the age of 21, would join him in the carriage trade.

While the Brewster name is one of the most recognized in the history of carriage making, it is also one of the most confusing. The Brewster name was associated with several companies, partnerships, titles and locations. There was James Brewster, J.B. Brewster, Brewster & Sons, and more. Some of these were at different locations and different cities.

There was also Brewster, Lawrence, & Co.; Brewster & Collis, Coach Makers—and later such combinations as Collis & Lawrence in New Haven; Lawrence & Collis in New York; Lawrence & Bradley; Lawrence, Bradley & Pardee, etc. All of these firms, in later years, refered to Brewster in reverent terms in many of their advertisements.

In 1827 Brewster expanded his business again, by buying the Broad Street shops from Abram Quick of New York. Records, at times, were incomplete, and even misleading and contradictory. Brewster had partnerships with Lawrence and also with Collis. By 1833, Lawrence and Collis seemed to assume management of the carriage companies, when Brewster became closely associated with the New-Haven and Hartford Railroad. He resigned as President of the Railroad in 1837. The next year he returned to the carriage building trade, with son James B. Brewster as his partner.

Young Henry Brewster, in 1838, eschewed a formal education at Yale University and apprenticed to a hardware merchant in New York. By 1845, at age 21, Henry joined his father and brother in James Brewster & Sons. Ten years later Henry was starting to drift away from the family firm. Records are not clear on just why he left, but there seemed to have been some rancor or bitterness between the two firms. He had joined with James Lawrence in the partnership of Brewster & Lawrence—John W. Britton became a third partner and the firm became Brewster & Co. It wasn't long, or unusual—for the name to change again—this time to Messrs. Brewster & Co. of Broome Street. They remained in competition with the original James Brewster firm.

During this time of the 1820's and 30s, these two companies expanded their businesses to many locations in the southern states. Sales to Martin VanBuren and Andrew Jackson were well publicized, to enhance the company name in the U.S.

In the 1860's, James Brewster joined with Henry Hooker and two other coach maker-financiers to buy out G. & D. Cook & Co., which subsequently became Henry Hooker & Co. by 1868.

James Brewster lived long enough to see his grandson, William, born in June of 1866. James died at New Haven of typhoid fever, November 11, 1866.

James B. Brewster continued management of the original firm and as it continued to grow and excel, it was said to be "the standard of merit wherever wheels turn." However well J.B. Brewster continued on with this excellent firm, it was said "the man who made the name famous was the father of the present Brewster."

J.B. Brewster & Co. prospered during the 1870's when they were assigned the rights to Ward's influential side-bar carriage patent, which was combined with Caffrey's cross spring and Benezet's shackle coupling to produce a frame for light road wagons. These patent features remained in control of the company through the 1890's.

James B. Brewster, genial, approachable, and much loved by his employees, died in New York on March 9, 1902.

After the company's demise in 1895, it was revived at least twice, by the three partners who tried to market a lesser product to a wider middle-class cliental, and at the same time, trying to live on the Brewster reputation and long established good name. Henry Brewster, president of Brewster & Co., challenged them in court, and won.

This was the end of the J.B. Brewster Co. as it had been so admired for its beauty and quality in its workmanship and service. In no way, did it diminish the accomplishments of its rival, the Brewster & Co.

Henry, as president of Brewster & Co., headed an ambitious internationally recognized firm on superior manufactures, design, finishes and a penchent for image exclusiveness. In 1868 Brewster & Co. moved into a five story repository on Fifth Avenue that was resplendent in beauty. Materials of whitewood, varnished walnut and ceiling panels, in addition to special lighting, gave a wonderous effect, and enhanced the reputation of where this company wanted to go.

In 1858 the firm developed the Guard Wheel Machine, allowing one operator, in a span of seven hours, to assemble twelve wheels. A few years later, the firm developed a new form of wood filler that entered the pores and sealed the wood, forming a firmer base for painting and varnishing. At the 1878 Paris Exposition, a French observer stated "for skilled workmanship and brilliant finish" the Brewster vehicles were unequalled.

In 1870, Brewster & Co. developed a profit-sharing plan whereby at the end of the year, the employees could divide 10% of the yearly profits. In later years the company matched employee contributions to a benefit fund; provided free medical services and developed a second profit-sharing plan for twenty-year veterans of the shop.

Brewster & Co., of Broome Street added sleighs to their diverse and ever-enlarging product line. This was enhanced with the purchase of C.P. Kimball's name and services in 1875. They supplied the largest carriage display at the Centennial Exhibition in Philadelphia, with seven carriages, three sleighs and one sulky. Reviewers were favorably impressed, not only with the stylish equipment and lustrous finishes, but with the attention given to minor details and passenger comfort.

Perhaps the biggest event in the Brewster & Co.'s long and illustrious history was the 1878 Paris Exposition Universelle. Most of the prominent carriage builders in the world, 72 in all, competed for honors. Medals were awarded to Brewster craftsmen, to the firm for best display, and to Henry Brewster personally. These honors were significant in the acceptance of Brewster carriages on the European market and at home. The firm prospered on the business that followed these distinctions.

By the 1880's Brewster & Co. was considered internationally, by some, to be "the most complete carriage shop anywhere." A few of the finest carriage shops throughout Europe sent their sons to study here.

In keeping with their design to cater to a wealthy clientele, the sale to conspicuous politicians and businessmen, was good for future sales. Four U.S. presidents—Grant, Hayes, Garfield and Arthur—had Brewster carriages. John D. Rockefeller and his brother William purchased, in an eleven year period, over 40 vehicles. Between 1858 and 1886 production increased by 240 percent.

Henry Brewster died September 20, 1887, following two years of bad health. By July of 1888 young William Brewster was brought in as a third partner and preserved the Brewster & Co. lineage.

William Brewster, grandson of the founding James Brewster, served as a partner from 1888 until 1903, when he was elected president. He had a fetish for beautiful finishes, and no carriage left the shop without his personal inspection.

By the 1890's he identified with the more affluent clients. The Brewsters joined several exclusive clubs, supported charities and did some traveling to Europe.

One of the refinements of William Brewster was driving. He maintained stables in New York City and in Connecticut.

In the early 1900's, with the advent of the automobile, Brewster & Co. began to confront the change. They dabbled first in auto bodies and later in the manufacture of automobiles. This was not a great success.

William Brewster resigned in 1927. He spent the next 22 years of his life traveling the world and serving as a director for many firms. He died in 1949.

The largest group of Brewster carriages, available for viewing by the public, is in the collection of The Museums at Stony Brook, Stony Brook, New York.

Brickhouse

B.D. Brickhouse, blacksmith and wheelwright, E. 4th near San Marcos; Austin, Texas, circa 1887–1900.

Bridgeport Coach Lace Company

The firm designed and manufactured fine lace and trimming materials for coaches and carriages.

They advertised themselves as the original manufacturer of patent tufts and that they were the largest U.S. importers of Wulfing dyed yarns; Bridgeport, CT, circa 1870–1910.

Bridges

James Bridges, blacksmith and wheelwright,133 S. Jefferson, Dallas, Texas, circa 1898–1908.

Bridges

S.A. Bridges, wagon maker; Ft. Atkinson, Wisconsin, circa 1879.

Bridges
William Bridges, carriage maker; Scofield, Colorado, circa 1882–1890.

Bridgewater Carriage Co.
Established in 1873, manufacturers of spring wagons, buggies and carriages, corner of Grove and Water streets; Bridgewater, Virginia, circa 1873–1900.

Briese
A. Briese, wagon maker; Columbus, Wisconsin, circa 1879.

Briggs
D.G. Briggs, blacksmith shop; carriage and wagon maker; Buena Vista, Colorado, circa 1882–1890.

Briggs & Son
George W. Briggs, blacksmith, wheelwright and wagon maker, 145–147 S. Akard; also 231 S Harwood; Dallas, Texas, circa 1901–1910.

Briggs & Enoch Manufacturing Co.
Built the Rockford Corn Planter; Rockford, Illinois, circa 1895–1910.

Briggs (see Brady, Langdon & Briggs)

Brigham, McRay & Co.
This carriage and sleigh maker from Ayer Junction, Massachussets built a commercial line of business and store sleighs, circa 1870–1900.

Bright (see Van Pelt & Bright)

Brighton Buggy Co.
Mr. McCurdy, buggy manufacturer; Cincinnati, Ohio, circa 1880–1910.

Brill
A.W. Brill, manufacturer of buggies, road and spring wagons, 204 E. 6th Street; Austin, Texas, circa 1905–1915.

Brinegar
T.E. Brinegar, carriage and wagon manufacturer and dealer; Hailey, Idaho, circa 1908.

Brinker & Keefe
Wagon makers; Stevens Point, Wisconsin, circa 1879.

Britz
Georte Britz, wagon and carriage maker; Racine, WI, circa 1879–1885.

Brock
Charles Brock manufactured wagons and sleighs; Pompey, NY, circa 1850's.

Brock
J.M. Brock, blacksmith and wheelwright, Washington, between 3rd and 4th; Houston, Texas, circa 1882–1890's.

Brockway
W.N. Brockway made carriages, wagons and commercial vehicles. He also produced a large number of sleighs, building over 14,00 in the 1887–1888 seasons; Homer, NY., circa 1880–1910.

Brodbeck
John J. Brodbeck, wagon maker, 191 Lewis; New York, NY, circa 1899.

Broell
William Broell, blacksmith and wagon maker; Lusk, Wyoming, circa 1901–1902.

Brogden
William Brogden, carriage painter, 107 Jones; San Francisco, California, circa 1888–1894.

Bromlard
John Bromlard, blacksmith and wagon maker, Mission near 13th; San Francisco, California, circa 1882–1885.

Bromwell
Samuel Bromwell, blacksmith, horseshoer and wheelwright, sw corner of Elm and Crowdus; Dallas, Texas, circa 1886–1890's.

Bronder
J. Bronder, wagon maker; Wyoming, Wisconsin, circa 1879.

Bronson
Ira A. Bronson manufactured light carriages, 1 to 7 Park Avenue; Lockport, NY, circa 1899.

Brooke
Thomas Brooke, wagon maker; Hingham, Wisconsin, circa 1865.

Brooks
Amos Brooks, blacksmith and wagon maker; Boise, Idaho, circa 1905–1910.

Brooks
Clarence Brooks & Co. offered a full line of coach and carriage varnishes from their store, located at the corner of West and 12th Streets; New York, NY, circa 1870–1900.

Brooks
G.W. Brooks Sr., blacksmith and wheelwright, 415–417 Elm and 590 Main; Dallas, Texas, circa 1891–1901.

Brooks
G.W. Brooks Jr., blacksmith, horseshoer and wheelwright (rubber tires a specialty); also carriage and wagon maker; carriage painter and trimmer, 590 Main; Dallas, Texas, circa 1898-1910.

Brooks
Thomas V. Brooks, a master wood carver from New York, NY, worked on circus wagons and other horse-drawn vehicles.

Brooks also had his own shop in Chicago, Illinois, circa 1860–1900.

Brosius
Brosius Brothers, blacksmiths and wheelwrights, 212 Clarksville; Paris, Texas, circa 1891–1900.

Broussard
A.P. Broussard, blacksmith, wheelwright, carriage manufacturer and repairer, 458 Orleans; Beaumont, Texas, circa 1906–1910.

Brow (see McClary & Brow)

Brower
Benjamin Brower, blacksmith and wagon maker, 915 2nd; Laramie, WY, circa 1902–1910.

Brower
Law Brower, carriage maker, 19th Ward; New York, NY, circa 1850.

Brower & Stumpf
Blacksmiths and wheelwrights; carriage and wagon makers, 512 Colorado; Austin, Texas, circa 1887–1899.

Brown
A. Brown & Sons, blacksmiths and wheelwrights, carriage and wagon makers, 659 Main; Beaumont, Texas, circa 1910–1915.

Brown
Albert H. Brown, carriage maker; Cumbria, NY, circa 1850.

Brown
Ben Brown, blacksmith and wagon maker, 519 south 2nd; Laramie, WY, circa 1901–1902.

Brown
B.F. Brown was a carriage and coach maker from Dorchester, MA, circa 1815–1830.

Brown
E. Brown, wagon maker; Glendale Wisconsin, circa 1879.

Brown
F.A. Brown, blacksmith and wagon maker; Afton, Wyoming, circa 1900–1905.

Brown
George W. Brown & Co. built mostly corn planters, beginning with his first of many patents in the 1850's. Brown built the Excelsior and Admiral Dewey and many other styles; Galesburg, Illinois, circa 1850–1910.

Brown
Gus Brown, blacksmith; Cumberland, Wyoming, circa 1905–1910.

Brown
Henry F. Brown, blacksmith and wagon maker; Meeteese, Wyoming, circa 1901–1902.

Brown
J.W. Brown, carriage and wagon maker; Milwaukee, Wisconsin, circa 1879.

Brown
L.W. Brown, blacksmith and wagon maker; Clearwater, Idaho, circa 1905–1910.

Brown
N.R. Brown, wagon maker; Milton Junction, WI, circa 1879–1903.

Brown
O.P. Brown, wagon maker and blacksmith; Alamosa, Colorado, circa 1883–1890.

Brown
Philip I. Brown, carriage and buggy builder was born in 1838 in Rahway, New Jersey. Brown started out in the shops of Lawrence, Bradley & Co., and spent six more years at J.B. Brewster before opening his first shop back in his home town of Rahway, NJ, in 1866. When the shop burned down in 1872, Brown moved to Staten Island and two years later, he opened a shop on Richmond Terrace, West New Brighton.
   The P.I. Brown Carriage Company, circa 1866–1920, manufactured carriages, wagons, carts, contractor dumping wagons and other commercial vehicles. They also ran a successful carriage rental business and livery stable. The livery business eventually became the Richmond Storage Warehouse and Van Company, and the carriage works branched off into automobile sales.

Brown
S.M. Brown Co.; Dayton, Ohio, circa 1890–1910.

Brown
S.N. Brown & Co. of Dayton, Ohio, manufactured carriage and wagon wheels, circa 1870's–1900.

Brown
T.H. Brown & Co., carriage and wagon makers; Milwaukee, Wisconsin, circa 1879–1901.

Brown
W.H. Brown, blacksmith and wheelwright, se corner Ft. Worth Ave. and Rush Road; W. Dallas, Texas, circa 1898–1905.

Brown
William F. Brown, buggy maker and owner of the Brown Carriage Works; Mifflinburg, PA. Located at 526 Market Street, 1880–1895, and North Fifth and Mill Streets, circa 1895–1920.

Brown
W.O. Brown, carriages, wagons and buggies, 126–128 Elm; and sw corner Main and Broadway; Dallas, Texas, circa 1910.

Brown Carriage Co.
Manufactured wholesale carriage and wagon parts, including Brown's patented Double Tire; New London, CT, circa 1880's–1910.

Brown Carriage Co.
Buggy manufacturer; Cincinnati, Ohio, circa 1880–1910.

Brown Lamp Co.
Surrey Lamp manufacturer; Columbus, Ohio, circa 1890–1910.

Brownlee (see Crane & Brownlee)

Brown Manufacturing Co.
This Zanesville, Ohio firm built the Brown wagon, and farm equipment of all types, circa 1880–1930. They pioneered in building cultivators as early as 1880.
   They eventually merged into Brown-Manly Plow Company of Malta, Ohio.

Brown, Sloan & Alexander
Carriages and wagons, 414 Dolorosa; Houston, Texas, circa 1900–1905.

Brumm
August Brumm, blacksmith; carriage and wagon maker; Nevadaville, Colorado, circa 1881–1890.

Brundage (see Isham, Brundage & Co.)

Bryan (see Carlson & Bryan)

Bryan Plow Co.
Manufactured farm implements; Bryan, Ohio, circa 1890–1920.

Bryant
J.L. Bryant of Hillsdale, MI was a sleigh builder, circa 1870–1890.

Bryant
Tobe S. Bryant, blacksmith and wheelwright, 1193 Poquita; Austin, Texas, circa 1910–1915.

Bryant & Co.
Wagon makers, 291 Morris Ave.; New York, NY, circa 1899.

Bryden & Scott
Carriage and wagon makers, Denver, Colorado, circa 1884–1890.

Bryden (see Magill & Bryden)

Bucannon
J. Bucannon, wagon maker; Lodi, Wisconsin, circa 1879.

Bucher & Gibbs Plow Co.
Established in 1864, Bucher & Gibbs would grow to offer a full line of implements and equipment. By the 1880's they featured their Imperial Prairie Plow and the Imperial Gang Plow.

Bucher & Gibbs Plow Co. came under control of the F.E. Myers Co. for an unknown period of time. However they continued well past the horse-drawn equipment era, and are listed in advertisements and trade publications well into the 1960's; Canton, Ohio, circa 1864–1960's.

Buchholz (see Hodge & Buchholz)

Buchner
A. Buchner, wagon maker; Fond cu Lac, Wisconsin, circa 1879.

Buckeye Buggy Co.
Buggy maker, Columbus, OH, circa 1870–1900.

Buckeye Wagon Works
Wagon maker—farm and commercial vehicles; Dayton, Ohio, circa 1900–1915.

Buckley Brothers
Carriage makers; Tin Cup, Colorado, circa 1882–1890.

Budde
Henry Budde, wagon maker; Schleisingerville, Wisconsin, circa 1879–1919.

Budlong
C.M. Budlong, carriage and wagon dealer and representative; Allen's Grove, Wisconsin, circa 1890–1910.

Buell
Nelsen Buell manufactured wagons and sleighs; Van Duren, NY, circa 1850's.

Buerkens Manufacturing Co.
Built farm wagons of all types; Pella, Iowa., circa 1890–1910.

Buffalo Carriage Co.
Manufacturer of carriages and sleighs, including their Buffalo Speeding Cutter; Buffalo, N.Y., circa 1880–1910.

Buffalo Hardware Co.
Dealers in agricultural implements, carriages and wagons; Buffalo, Wyoming, circa 1902–1910.

Buffalo-Pitts Co.
The Pitts brothers were building threshers as early as the 1830's and continued into the early 1900's; Buffalo, New York, circa 1830's–1910.

Buford
B.D. Buford & Co., an early Rock Island, Illinois farm implement manufacturer, circa 1855–1937, may have started out as Tate & Buford.

They built a variety of farm equipment, including the Browne gang plow and Browne sulky plow. Around 1880, B.D. Buford became part of the Rock Island Plow Co. (See Rock Island Plow Co).

Buford
S.R. Buford & Co. of Virginia City, Montana, agents for the Mitchell & Lewis Co. of Racine, Wisconsin, circa 1880–1910.

Bugen
J. Bugen, wagon maker; Cascade, Wisconsin, circa 1865.

Bulian
Charles Bulian, blacksmith and wheelwright, 818 W. 11th; Austin, Texas, circa 1906–1912.

Bulian (see Smith & Bulian)

Bull & Grant
Farm Implement Co., fine carriages, buggies and wagons; also farm implements, road grading machinery, steam well-boring outfits, engines, etc. There ad stated, "Any tubular axle broken or bent, no matter what the load or circumstance, will be replaced with a new one free of charge", 233 North Los Angeles Street; Los Angeles, California, circa 1888–1900.

Bulles
I.P. Bulles, wagon maker; Milton Junction, Wisconsin, circa 1879.

Bumbrey
S. Bumbrey, blacksmith and wheelwright; also carriage and wagon manufacturer, E. Commerce, bottom of Lasalle and Sycamore; San Antonio, Texas, circa 1887–1895.

Bunge
H.F. Bunge, maker of light carriages, 118 West 52nd; New York, NY, circa 1899.

Bunz & Nicholas
Manufactured wagons and sleighs; Clay, NY, circa 1850's.

Buob Carriage Co.
Buggy manufacturer; Cincinnati, Ohio, circa 1880–1910.

Buob Wheel Co.
Cincinnati, Ohio, circa 1880–1910.

Buob & Scheu
Buggy manufacturer, Cincinnati, Ohio, circa 1880–1910.

Burbrige
J.B. Burbrige, blacksmith and wagon maker; Gifford, Idaho, circa 1905–1910.

Burch Plow Works Co.
Manufactured farm implements, from plows to pulverizers; Crestline, Ohio, circa 1910–1930.

Burdick
M.S. Burdick, wagon maker; Milton, Wisconsin, circa 1879.

Burger & Heilig
Blacksmiths' supplies, 129 Military Plaza; San Antonio, Texas, circa 1897–1905.

Burgess, Baker & Thomas
J.C. Burgess, J.G. Baker and W.L. Thomas, blacksmiths, carriage and wagon makers, 302 Tyler; Amarillo, Texas, circa 1910–1920.

Burg Wagon Co.
This firm was established in 1851 in Burlington, Iowa. They built quality wagons, buggies and a large number of sleighs, circa 1851–1900.

Burgum
John Burgum of Concord, NH was a coach painter. He was born in Birmingham, England in 1826. He moved to Boston, MA in 1850, then on to Concord, NH that same year.

Burgum served as chief artisan in charge of ornamental painting for the Abbot-Downing Company.

His work also included painting and ornamental design on steampumpers for Amoskeag Company of Manchester, NH. He also produced numerous sketchbooks and easel paintings. John Burgan worked for Abbot-Downing Company until his death in 1907; Concord, NH, circa 1826–1907.

Burgy
T. Burgy, wagon maker; Ogdensburg, Wisconsin, circa 1879.

Burkart & Mackey Mfg. Co.
Wagon makers; West De Pere, Wisconsin, circa 1879.

Burke
George Burke, blacksmith and wagon maker; Mountain Home, Idaho, circa 1905–1910.

Burkhard
F. Burkhard Saddlery and Implement Co.; Trinidad, Colorado, circa 1900–1922.

Burkholder's Buggy Shop
Everette Burkholder, buggy shop; Dayton, Virginia, since 1967. Daniel and Joseph Burkholder worked in the shop with their father.

Their two-story building contains almost 10,000 sq. ft. of area. In addition to their buggy work, they do repair and limited restoration work, and provide supplies, such as horseshoes, tools and nails, to farriers in the area.

Burman
J.G. Burman, carriage and wagon dealer; Amery, Wisconsin, circa 1890–1910.

Burns
Thomas Burns, wagon maker, Mottville, NY, circa 1899.

Burns
Wallace N. Burns, blacksmith; Marion, Iowa, circa 1882.

Burns & Sell
Wagon makers; Janesville, Wisconsin, circa 1879.

Burns (see Dawson & Burns)

Burr
A. Burr, wagon maker; North Bend, Wisconsin, circa 1879.

Burr
J. Burr, wagon maker; North Bend, WI, circa 1879.

Burr
L.S. Burr and Co., carriage and wagon maker, also built commercial delivery vehicles; Memphis, TN, circa 1850–1870.

Burr & Co.
Makers of light and heavy carriages, 1709 Broadway; New York, NY, circa 1890–1910.

Burroughs
E. Burroughs of Burroughs, Winters & Co., corner K and 7th; Sacramento, CA, circa 1853–1865.

Burroughs
L. Burroughs, wagon maker; Lone Rock, Wisconsin, circa 1879.

Burrows
Mr. Burrows was President of the Standard Wagon Co., Cincinnati, Ohio, circa 1890–1910.

Burrows, Winters & Co.
Blacksmiths and carriage makers, corner K and 7th; Sacramento, CA, 1853–1865.

Burrows (see McDaniel & Burrows)

Burt
J.M. Burt, blacksmith and wheelwright, Guadalupe, bottom of 3rd, 4th; Austin, Texas, circa 1900–1901.

Burt
William Burt, wagon maker, Newfane, NY, circa 1899.

Burt Bros.
Carriage and wagon makers; Madison, Wisconsin, circa 1865.

Burton & Arthur
Blacksmith and wagon maker; Elkhorn, Colorado, circa 1880–1890.

Burton Implement Co.
Wagon and carriage dealers; Ogden, Utah, circa 1905–1910.

Burwell
George Burwell manufactured carriage name plates, carriage lamps and carriage mountings; 713 So. Broad St., Philadelphia, PA, circa 1880–1900.

Burwell & Butler
Wagon makers; Platteville, Wisconsin, circa 1865.

Busbee
L.D. Busbee, blacksmith and wagon maker, 327 Cedar Springs Ave.; Dallas, Texas, circa 1910.

Busbee & Busby
Blacksmiths and horseshoers, 327 Cedar Springs Ave., Dallas, Texas, circa 1908.

Busby (see Busbee & Busby)

Busch
H. Busch, wagon maker; New Cassel, Wisconsin, circa 1879.

Bushnell
Charles W. Bushnell, wagon maker; Omro, WI, circa 1865–1898.

Bushnell
Henry and William Bushnell, carriage factory; Harrisonburg, Virginia, circa 1890–1910.

Bushnell (see Warder, Bushnell & Glessner Co.)

Buss
J.J. Buss, wagon maker; Delavan, Wisconsin, circa 1865.

Buss
W. Buss, wagon maker; Richmond, Wisconsin, circa 1865.

Bussey (see Law & Bussey)

Butler
Alexander Butler, wagon maker; Platteville, WI, circa 1879–1915.

Butler
C.W. Butler, wagon maker; Clark Mills, Wisconsin, circa 1879.

Butler (see Burwell & Butler)

Butler (see Haible & Butler)

Butt
A.W. Butt Implement Co. built the Daisy Corn Harvester and claimed it was capable of cutting 10 acres a day; Springfield, Ohio, circa 1885–1905.

Button
Mr. L. Button headed one of the oldest and well received companies by firemen everywhere. This manufacturer ranks among the foremost of pioneers in the construction of fire engines; Waterford, NY, circa 1834–1895.

Their first hand-engine was built in 1834, and their first steam fire engine, in 1862. Many more would follow before they merged, circa 1891, with three other companies: Silsby of Seneca Falls, NY; Ahrens of Cincinnati, OH; and Clapp & Jones of Huidson, NY. They became known as the American Fire Engine Company.

Buxton & McWilliams
Blacksmiths and wagon makers; Casper, Wyoming, circa 1900–1905.

Bybee & Cole
Blacksmiths and wagon makers; Grace, Idaho, circa 1905–1910.

Byrn (see Baxter, Byrn & Ratterman)

Byrne
Frank Byrne, dealer in agricultural implements; Piedmont, Wyoming, circa 1900–1905.

Cabe
L. Cabe, carriage maker, 19th Ward; New York, NY, circa 1850.

Cable
David Cable manufactured wagons and sleighs; Pompay, NY, circa 1850's.

Cadena
Juan Cadena, blacksmith and wheelwright, 917 N. Laredo; San Antonio, Texas, circa 1897–1908.

Caffrey
Charles S. Caffrey Co., carriage and sulky maker; Camden, NJ, circa 1890-1919.

Cahoon
H.R. Cahoon, blacksmith and wagon maker; Almo, Idaho, circa 1905–1910.

Caire (see Barbian & Caire)

Caffall Carriage Co.
Carriage, buggy, and wagon dealer, 814–848 Pearl; Beaumont, Texas, circa 1910–1911.

Caldwell
J. Caldwell, blacksmith and wheelwright; carriage, wagon and buggy dealer, 110–118 W. Overland, corner of Santa Fe; El Paso, Texas, circa 1898–1905.

Caldwell
Oliver S. Caldwell, blacksmith, wheelwright and horseshoer; 1103 Railroad Ave.; Corpus Christi, Texas, circa 1913–1918.

Caldwell (see Goulds, Austin & Caldwell Co.)
Caledonia Bean Harvester Works Manufacturer of bean harvesters, mostly on the east coast; Caledonia, New York, circa 1866–1900.

Calhoun
Patrick H. Calhoun, blacksmith, carriage and wagon maker; Cazenovia, NY, circa 1879–1909.

Calkins
Milo Calkins, wagon maker; Lowell, Wisconsin, circa 1879–1903.

Calkins
See Electric Wheel Co.

Call
A.V. Call, dealer in agricultural implements; Afton, Wyoming, circa 1900–1910.

Callai
Peter Callai, wagon and carriage factory; Holly, Colorado, circa 1884–1890.

Callanan
Edward Callanan & Son, makers of light carriages, 57 West 44th; New York, NY, circa 1899.

Calmes
Frank Calmes, wagon maker; Appleton, WI, circa 1890–1910.

Calvert
P. Calvert, carriage and wagon maker; Sheridan, Wyoming, circa 1902–1908.

Cameron
William Cameron, blacksmith and wheelwright, corner Dallas and Lancaster Ave.; W. Dallas, Texas, circa 1900.

Cameron & Chisholm
Carriage and wagon makers; Evanston, WY, circa 1900–1910.

Cameron (see Maschek and Cameron)

Campbell
A.R. Campbell, carriage maker; Walsenburg, CO, circa 1882–1890.

Campbell
E. Campbell, wagon maker; Blanchardville, Wisconsin, circa 1879.

Campbell
John Campbell, carriage maker; Teller, Colorado, circa 1882–1890.

Campbell
Neil Campbell, blacksmith and wagon maker; Bellevue, Idaho, circa 1905–1910.

Campbell
W.A. Campbell, wagon maker; Rochester, Wisconsin, circa 1879.

Campbell & Hommel
Wagon makers, Neilsville, Wisconsin, circa 1879.

Campbell & Rickards
Under the direction of a Mr. H. Johnson, from the Philadelphia Fire Dept. repairs division, this firm constructed five steam fire-engines, using the patterns and designs of John L. Knowlton; Philadelphia, PA, circa 1885.

Campbell & Smith
Blacksmiths and wagon makers; Buffalo, Wyoming, circa 1900–1905.

Campbell & Whittier
This company constructed their fire-engines from the designs of J.M. Stone from Manchester, NH. They built the "Tremont Engine No. 13" and the "Dearborn Engine No. 14"; Roxbury, MA, circa 1860–1865.

Campbell (see Perkins & Campbell Co.)

Campos
Don Campos, wagon maker; Ojo Caliente; New Mexico, circa 1900–1910.

Campos
Vincente Campos, blacksmith and wheelwright, E. 5th, 1 mile east of Comal; Austin, Texas, circa 1910–1915.

Canada
Taylor Canada; Oxford, N.C., circa 1890–1910.

Canada Carriage Co.
Carriage manufacturer, moved from Gananoque, Ontario to Brockville, Ontario, Canada, circa 1890–1910.

Cann & Wilson
Wagon makers 245–247 27th; Denver, Colorado, circa 1881–1890.

Capital Buggy Co.
Henderson, North Carolina, circa 1890–1910.

Capital City Carriage Co.
Buggy makers; Columbus, OH, circa 1880–1910.

Capital City Carriage Co.
Manufactured a wide range of wagons, carriages, surreys, buggies and many other horse-drawn vehicles; Des Moines, Iowa, circa 1890–1920.

Carey
Mrs. A.H. Carey, retail sales and repair of wagon and agricultural implements; Raton, New Mexico, circa 1900–1910.

Carlisle
Charles Carlisle built farm implements, including Carlisle's Patent Improved Horse Rake in the 1840's; Quechee Village, Vermont, circa 1840's-1860.

Carlow
J.Carlow, blacksmith and wagon makers; Alpine, Colorado, circa 1878–1890.

Carlson & Bryan
Blacksmiths and wagon makers; Montpelier, Idaho, circa 1905–1910.

Carmean (see Rhoades-Carmean Buggy Co.)

Carmichael Buggy Co.
Jackson, GA, circa 1890–1910.

Carnegie Plow & Manufacturing Co.
Built farm implements, including land rollers and pulverizers; Carnege, PA, circa 1890–1910.

Carney
J.J. Carney Manufacturing Co.; Kittery, Maine, circa 1890–1910.

Carolus (see Mayer & Carolus)

Carpenter
A.B. Carpenter, carriage and wagon maker; Beloit, Wisconsin, circa 1879.

Carpenter
A.H. Carpenter, blacksmith and wagon maker; Deary, Idaho, circa 1905–1910.

Carpenter
D.L. Carpenter Co., buggy manufacturer; Cincinnati, Ohio, circa 1880–1910.

Carpenter
S.A. Carpenter; Potage, Wisconsin, circa 1865.

Carr
E. Carr, carriage maker; Broadaxe, Montgomery county, PA, circa 1880–1910.

Carr (see Phelps, Carr & Co.)

Carr & Koch
Blacksmith, carriage and wagon maker, Larimer and 11th Denver, Colorado, circa 1878–1880's.

Carreon
Jose Carreon, blacksmith, and wagon makers, 501 S Stanton; El Paso, Texas, circa 1905–1914.

Carriage Sun Shade Co.
Carriage manufacturer; Troy, OH, circa 1880–1910.

Carrier
Carlos Carrier, blacksmith and wagon maker; Bernalillo, New Mexico, circa 1905–1910.

Carrington
Albert Carrington, blacksmith and wheelwright, 520 E. 6th; Austin,Texas, 1887–1888; 1106 E 11th; and 602 Red River; Austin, Texas, circa 1889–1918.

Carroll
C.E. Carroll, blacksmith and wagon maker; Mountain View and Burntfork, WY, circa 1900–1908.

Carroll
John Carroll, blacksmith and wagon maker; Opal, Wyoming, circa 1901–1902.

Carruthers & Pias
Blacksmiths and wheelwrights, 1606 E. 6th; Austin, Texas, circa 1893–1900.

Carson
Hugh M. Carson, blacksmith and wheelwright, 309 W. 16th; 1106 E. 6th; Austin, Texas, circa 1900–1913.

Carter
J.D. Carter, blacksmith and wheelwright, 1203 E. 6th; Austin, Texas, circa 1906–1910.

Carter
W.C. Carter, blacksmith and wagon maker; Ilo, Idaho, circa 1905–1910.

Carter, Chapman & Co.
This Ludington, Michigan firm was best known for their sleighs, including the Twentieth Century Pleasure Bob, circa 1890–1910.

Caruth (see Cooter & Caruth)

Carver & Steele Manufacturing Co.
Built farm implements at their Illinois location and may also have been known as Carver, Steele and Austin, in Grinnell, Iowa; Harvey, Illinois, circa 1870–1910.

Carvill Manufacturing Co.
Manufacturer of fine carriages of every description, two locations, No. 7—9 Powell St., opposite the Baldwin, and 180 Jessie St. and 184 Stevenson St.; San Francisco, California, circa 1882–1890.

Cary
The Cary-Ogden Co. manufacturers of carriage and coach colors. They advertised their Derby Red as "Deep Beautiful Shade—Most Durable Made"; Chicago, Illinois, circa 1870–1910.

Cashin (see Beeman & Cashin Mercantile Co.)

Case
George Case, wagon maker; Johnson Creek, WI, circa 1885–1903.

Case
J.J. Case & Co., wagon makers; Racine, Wisconsin, circa 1865.

Case Plow Works
J.I. Case Plow Works of Racine, Wisconsin manufactured a wide variety of farm implements for years before selling out, in 1928, to Massey-Harris Company of Ontario, Canada, circa 1880–1928.

Case (see Roberts & Case)

Case (see Roberts, Case & Spring)

Casey
James Casey, blacksmith, horseshoer and wheelwright, 28 Live Oak and 126 N., 130 Crodus, 116 Patterson Ave. and 174 N. Akard; Dallas, Texas, circa 1886–1908.

Casey
James D. Casey, wagon maker; Watertown, WI, circa 1879–1901.

Casey & Miller
Blacksmiths and wagon makers; Silverton, Colorado, circa 1884–1890.

Casler
E.S. Casler, wagon maker; Rutland, Wisconsin, circa 1879.

Casson
E.C. Casson, wagon maker; Oconto, Wisconsin, circa 1879.

Castree-Mallery Co.
Sold bobsleds, sleighs and various farm implements; Flint, Michigan, circa 1880–1900.

Catherman
Oliver Perry Catherman, buggy maker, 133 Market Street (rear); Mifflinburg, PA, circa 1880's-1914.

Cayuga Chief Manufacturing Co.
This firm built horse-drawn reapers, rakes and mowers, along with a few other implements, before being bought out by D.M. Osborne, in 1874; Auburn, NY, circa 1860's–1874.

Cazell
G.F. Cazell Jr., blacksmith and wheelwright, 104 Navarro; San Antonio, Texas, circa 1897–1900.

Cedar Rapids Implement Works
Manufactured a variety of farm equipment, including the Up-2-Date manure spreader; Cedar Rapids, Iowa, circa 1890–1920.

Cella
The Cella Company, makers of carriage leather handles, leather tips wiffle trees, carriage shaft tongues, and street car straps for hangers for trolley riders; Dayton, Kentucky, circa 1890–1910.

Celina Mfg. Co.
Celina, Ohio, circa 1890–1910.

Cenly (see Creegar & Cenly)

Central Ohio Buggy Co.
This Ohio buggy company burned down in 1900, City unknown at this time, circa 1870's-1900.

Central Shoeing Shop
Blacksmiths and wheelwrights, 366 Commerce; Dallas, Texas, circa 1901–1906.

Century Wagon Co.
Blacksmiths and wheelwrights, carriage and wagon makers, 399 Forsyth; Beaumont, Texas, circa 1905–1915.

Chabb
Mathias Chabb, wagon maker; Highland, WI, circa 1885–1919.

Chaffin & Duncan
M. Chaffin and J. Duncan, livery and feed stable, distributor of spring wagons and buggies. They were agents for the celebrated Rushford wagons; East Las Vegas, New Mexico, circa 1895–1905.

Challenge Corn Planter Co.
Established in 1872, and claimed to have sold over 30,000 Challenge corn planters by the late 1880's; Grand Haven, MI, circa 1872–1895.

Challenge Mill Co.
Farm equipment and implement manufacturer; Batavia, IL, circa 1880–1920.

Chamberlin
J. Chamberlin, wagon maker; Randolph Centre, WI, circa 1869.

Chambers, Bering, Quinlan Co.
Built farm equipment, mostly corn planters. This company was acquired by International Harvester around 1910; Decatur, Illinois, circa 1885–1910.

Chambey
Jason Chambey, blacksmith and wagon maker; Erie, Colorado, circa 1879–1890.

Chamluss
Lee Chamluss, blacksmith and wheelwright, corner Ft.Worth Ave.

and Cedar Hill Rd.; W. Dallas, Texas, circa 1891–1900.

Champagne
M. Champagne, wagon maker; Appleton, Wisconsin, circa 1879.

Champaigne
A. Champaigne, blacksmith and wagon maker; Beulah, Wyoming, circa 1902–1910.

Champion Wagon Co.
Circa 1890–1910.

Chandlee
E.B. Chandlee, blacksmith and wagon maker; Idaho Falls, Idaho, circa 1905–1910.

Chandler Carriage Wks.
Blacksmiths and horseshoers; carriage and wagon makers, 116 Bryan; Dallas, Texas, circa 1908–1915.

Chandler
Herbert C. Chandler, blacksmith, horseshoer and wheelwright, 1509 Elm; Dallas, Texas, circa 1886–1890's.

Chandler
Moses Chandler, blacksmith and wagon maker; Monument, Colorado, circa 1884–1890's.

Chandler & Wolfram
Blacksmiths, wheelwrights, carriage painters and trimmers, 407–411 Elm, 116–118 Live Oak; Dallas, Texas, circa 1891–1910.

Chapmen
G.J. & J.L. Chapman of Philadelphia, PA, built seven steam fire-engines in their short career. Two of them were built for the engine companies of the volunteer fire department of Philadelphia, circa 1860–1865.

Chapman
R.E. Chapman, carriages, buggies, phaetons and wagons, 18 Main Plaza; San Antonio, Texas, circa 1887–1900.

Chapman
W.S. Chapman, circa 1840's–1890, manufactured carriage and wagon parts, including "Chapman's Elastic Anti-rattling Carriage Shaft Fastener", patented August 8th of 1854; Cincinnati, OH.

Chapman (see Carter, Chapman & Co.)

Charles
G.W. Charles, wagon maker and blacksmith; Morrison, Colorado, circa 1880–1890.

Charlton
James Charlton, blacksmith and wheelwright; manufacturer of carriages, wagons, buggies and phaetons, 106–108 Milam; Houston, Texas, circa 1900–1910.

Charlton, Lynch & Co.
Blacksmiths and wheelwrights; carriage and wagon manufacturer, 8–10 Travis; Houston, Texas, circa 1887–1900.

Chartrand
P. Chartrand, carriage and wagon maker; Green Bay, WI, circa 1879.

Chase Plow Co.
Manufactured farm implements; Lincoln, Nebraska, circa 1900–1930.

Chase (see Katzner, Russell & Chase)

Chase (see Pratt & Chase)

Chatin
A. Chatin, blacksmith and wagon maker; Walsenburg, Colorado, circa 1882–1890.

Chattanooga Plow Works
This small company, circa 1890's–1919, offered a few styles of walking plows and horse-drawn implements, mostly marketed in southern states.

They were bought out by International Harvester, in 1919; Chattanooga, Tennessee.

Chaudron
Jule Chaudron, carriages, wagons and buggies, 193 Elm; Dallas, Texas, circa 1898–1905.

Cheever
O. Cheever, wagon maker; Raymondville, Wisconsin, circa 1879.

Cherek
Joseph Cherek, wagon maker; Bevent, Wisconsin, circa 1885–1903.

Cherokee Manufacturing Co.
Built horse-drawn commercial and construction vehicles including the 20th Century cement mixer; Cherokee, Iowa, circa 1900–1920.

Chester & Porter
Carriage makers; Cumbria, NY, circa 1850's.

Chestnut
H.E. Chestnut, carriages, wagons and buggies, 403 Polk; Amarillo, Texas, circa 1910–1920.

Cheyenne Carriage Co.
Manufacturer of carriages, phaetons, brewster buggies, concord wagons, village carts, frazier road carts; also blacksmithing and repairing, nw corner 18th and O'Neil, (N. Robertson, general manager; G.A. Coffman, supt.); Cheyenne, Wyoming, circa 1872–1896.
They advertised as "The oldest carriage works in the west".

Cheyenne Hardware Co.
Dealers in hardware, agricultural implements and farm machinery—their ads boasted "largest stock west of the Missouri river"; Cheyenne, Wyoming, circa 1884–1900.

Child
A.J. Child primarily acted as general western agent of Mishawaka Wagon Co. of Mishawaka, Indiana, 209 Market Street; St. Louis, Missouri, circa 1880–1920.

Childs
Charles H. Childs, wagon and carriage maker; Utica, NY, circa 1890's.

Child
J.M. Child & Co. manufactured farm and freight wagons, as well as a line of heavy wheeled trucks, 12–18 Fayette Street; Utica, New York, circa 1870–1910.

Childs
J.M. Childs & Co., carriage makers; Flemington, NJ, circa 1880–1910.

Childs (see Wilson, Childs & Co.)

Chisholm (see Cameron & Chisholm)

Chockelt
John A. Chockelt built sleighs and a few other vehicles; South Bend, Indiana, circa 1880's–1900.

Chollar
J.J. Chollar, wagon maker; Hancock, Wisconsin, circa 1879.

Christenson
Charles Christenson, wagon maker; Mount Morris, Wisconsin, circa 1879–1901.

Christian
J.C. Christian, buggy maker; Mifflinburg, PA, circa 1881–1890.

Christian
W.T. Christian, blacksmith and wheelwright, sw corner of Lamar and Church; Paris, Texas, circa 1891–1900.

Christianson
C. Christianson, blacksmith and wagon maker; Grant, Wyoming, circa 1900–1910.

Christie
The A.E. & J.H. Christie firm was one of the foremost sleigh builders of their time. They had a fine reputation for many original designs and patterns representing both American and foreign styles.

One example of their unique work is the Berlin Jumper sleigh shown in an August 1883 issue of *The Hub*, (a major trade publication of the day); Nyack, New York, circa 1870–1900.

Christine
D.W. Christine, buggy maker; Mifflinburg, PA, circa 1881–1885.

Christnacht
J.O. Christnacht, wagon maker; Addison, Wisconsin, circa 1879.

Christofferson
M. Christofferson, wagon maker; Menasha, Wisconsin, circa 1879.

Christoffersen
M. Christoffersen and Son, wagon makers; Neenah, Wisconsin, circa 1885–1911.

Church
E.A. Church, wagon maker; Prospect Hill, Wisconsin, circa 1865.

Cilly
D.C. Cilly & Co., wagon makers; Independence, WI, circa 1879.

Cincinnati Carriage Goods Co.
Cincinnati, Ohio, circa 1880–1910.

Cincinnati Carriage & Buggy Co.
Buggy manufacturer; Cincinnati, Ohio, circa 1880–1910.

Cincinnati Panel Co.
Cincinnati, Ohio, circa 1880–1910.

Cincinnati Varnish Co.
Cincinnati, Ohio, circa 1880–1910.

Cincinnati & Hammond Springs Co.
Cincinnati, Ohio, circa 1880–1910.

City Blacksmith Shop
Blacksmiths; also manufacturer of carriages, wagons and buggies, 1416 San Antonio; El Paso, Texas, circa 1911–1914.

City Carriage Works
Carriage, buggy and sleigh builders; Fort Wayne, Indiana, circa 1880–1900.

Ciulla & Artale
Blacksmiths and wheelwrights, 1318 San Felipe; Houston, Texas, circa 1900–1910.

Clapp
E.D. Clapp Manufacturing Co., buggy manufacturing; Cincinnati, Ohio, circa 1880–1910.

Clapp
E.D. Clapp Wagon Co.; Auburn, N.Y. Built a variety of farm wagons, from the light weight $50 Little Giant with a 1500# rated capacity, to the Auburn with a 5,000# rated capacity.

Clapp & Jones
This well known Hudson, New York company, circa 1862–1891, constructed their steam fire-engines using the designs of co-owner M.R. Clapp. Starting out in 1862, they offered five sizes of these machines; the smallest weighing about 3,200 lbs.

Later, to keep pace with changing times and the competition, they began to build a crane-neck sytle, and offered it in six different sizes. The largest of this style weighed 8,500. lbs. In all, Clapp & Jones manufactured over 600 machines before consolidating , circa 1891, with the following builders: Silsby of Seneca Falls, NY; Button of Waterford, NY; and Ahrens of Cincinnati, OH, to form American Fire Engine Co.

Clark
Alfred J. Clark, wagon maker, 242 East 122nd; New York, NY, circa 1899.

Clark
B.E. Clarke, blacksmith and wheelwright; Sherman, Texas, circa 1893–1900.

Clark
C. Clark's Sons manufactured horse-drawn trucks, 723 Washington; New York, NY, circa 1899.

Clark
James D. Clark, blacksmith and wheelwright, Brunner, circa 1900–1910.

Clark
James L. Clark (Carriage Co. by 1915) wagon and carriage makers; Oshkosh, WI, circa 1885–1915.

Clark
J. Clark, wagon maker; Attica, Wisconsin, circa 1879.

Clark
J. Max Clark, blacksmith, agricultural implement and wagonmaker; Greeley, Colorado, circa 1880–1890.

Clark
J.W. Clark, wagon maker; Spring Valley, Wisconsin, circa 1879.

Clark
M.A. Clark, wagon maker; Hammond, Wisconsin, circa 1879.

Clark
R.L. Clark, blacksmith and wagon maker; Collins, Idaho, circa 1905–1910.

Clark
S.P. Clark, wagon maker; Winneconne, Wisconsin, circa 1879.

Clark
Willard Clark, carriage maker; Porter, NY, circa 1850's.

Clark
William Clark, blacksmith and wagon maker; Meadows, Idaho, circa 1905–1910.

Clark
William Clark, blacksmith; Burlington, Wyoming, circa 1905–1910.

Clark
W.F. Clark, wagon maker; Orfordville, Wisconsin, circa 1879.

Clark & Co.
Manufactured sleighs and carriages; Lansing, Michigan, circa 1880's–1910.

Clark Carriage
Advertised their Clark line of vehicles, and offered for sale to other manufacturers, their Clark patented long spring cushion seats; Oshkosh, Wisconsin, circa 1880's–1910.

Clark Carriage Co.
Coach maker, established in 1831; Ravenna, Ohio.

Clark Carriage Co.
Buggy manufacturer; Cincinnati, Ohio, circa 1880–1910.

Clark & Gidcumb
Blacksmiths and wheelwrights, 181 N. Lamar; Dallas, Texas, circa 1890–1910.

Clarke
Ervine Clarke, blacksmith, wagon and carriage maker, 517 west 16th; Cheyenne, WY, circa 1895–1910.

Clarke
P.S. Clarke, blacksmith and wagon maker; Meeteetse, Wyoming, circa 1902–1908.

Clarkson
J.T. Clarkson, vehicle manufacturer; Amesbury, Mass., circa 1890–1910.

Clausing
Gustav Clausing, wagon maker; Grafton, WI, circa 1885–1915.

Clauter
John Clauter, wagon maker, 234 East 113th Street; New York, NY, circa 1899.

Clayton
A.B. Clayton, blacksmith and wagon maker; Denver, Idaho, circa 1905–1910.

Clegg
J.H. Clegg, blacksmith and wheelwright, 1220 W. 25th, Rosen Heights; Ft. Worth, Texas, circa 1900–1910.

Clelland
L.J. Clelland, blacksmith and wagon maker; Trinidad, Colorado, circa 1877 and 1879, also Walsenburg, Colorado, circa 1878–1880's.

Clemens & Garing
Wagon makers, 422 East 62nd; New York, NY, circa 1899.

Clement
Ferin Clement, blacksmith and wheelwright, 1003 Red River; Austin, Texas, circa 1887–1901.

Clements
Nathan Clements, blacksmith and wheelwright, 1003 Red River; Austin, Texas, circa 1900–1910.

Clemons
H.H. Clemons & Co., carriage and wagon makers; Oshkosh, Wisconsin, circa 1879.

Clemtson
Joseph Clemtson, wagon maker; Hazel Green, Wisconsin, circa 1865.

Cleveland
J.W. Cleveland, wagon maker; Union Grove, WI, circa 1879–1901

Click & Miller
Joseph Click and Peter S. Miller, proprietors of The Bridgewater Carriage Co., established in 1873, manufacturers of spring wagons, buggies and carriages, corner of Grove and Water Streets; Bridgewater, Virginia, circa 1873–1900.

Cliff
S. Cliff, carriage and wagon maker; Arkansaw, Wisconsin, circa 1890–1910.

Cliff & Ames
Wagon makers; Arkansaw, Wisconsin, circa 1879.

Clifton
Joseph Clifton, wagon maker; Mount Vernon, Wisconsin, circa 1865.

Clifton Farm
T.D. Elliott, proprietor, Holstein cattle, carriages, wagons and buggies, Maple Ave., N of Oak Lawn, Dallas, Texas, circa 1900.

Clifton & Hayford
Wagon makers; Patch Grove, Wisconsin, circa 1865.

Cline & Brady
Blacksmiths, horseshoers, and wheelwrights, 117 Camp; Dallas, Texas, circa 1886–1900.

Clinedinst
J.W. Clinedinst Co., carriage factory of great reknown known all over the eastern U.S. Manufacturers of carriages, barouches, rockaways, phaetons, buggies, spring wagons, etc.; New Market, Virginia, circa 1865–1910.

It is noted that Clinedinst, at one time, employed 19 blacksmiths, plus many woodworkers, painters and trimmers. A finished carriage, circa 1875, was said to sell for anywhere from $125 to $1,000; and at times production under way might top 50 vehicles.

Clinton
J.G. Clinton, carriage maker; Saguache, CO, circa 1882–1890.

Clipper Mower & Reaper Co,.
Manufactured farm implements and equipment, including their one-horse clipper mower; Yonkers, NY, circa 1860's–1870's.

Clipper Plow Co.
Built the Defiance Sulky Corn Cutter, and other equipment; Defiance, Ohio, circa 1890–1910.

Closson
Charles Closson Livery, also blacksmith and wagon repair; Santa Fe, New Mexico, circa 1906–1918.

Cloward & Ainsworth
Blacksmiths and wagon makers; Iona, Idaho, circa 1905–1910.

Coan & Ten Brocke
Built circus wagons and other vehicles; Chicago, Illinois, circa 1890–1910.

Coates
Leander Coates, carriage and wagon maker; Alloa, Wisconsin, circa 1890–1910.

Cobb
H. Cobb, wagon maker; Clinton, Wisconsin, circa 1879.

Cobett & Co.
May have constructed one or more horse-drawn fire-engines; New York, NY, circa 1875.

Cochran (see Holt & Cochran)
Cochran (see Overshiner & Cochran)

Cock
William C. Cock manufactured wagons, buggies and sleighs; Cicero, NY, circa 1850's.

Cockshutt Plow Co., Ltd.
This company had a long run of building farm plows and implements, from the 1870's until merging (in the 1960's) with others to form White Farm Equipment Co; Brantford, Ontario, Canada, circa 1870–1960.

Cody Trading Co.
Dealer in agricultural implements; Cody, WY, circa 1905–1910.

Coe
Jonas L. Coe, wagon maker, Park Avenue and N. 131st; New York, NY, circa 1899.

Coe
Samuel H. Coe, wagon maker, 1932 Park Avenue; New York, NY, circa 1899.

Coekell
W.J. Coekell, carriage painter, 604 west 18th; Cheyenne, Wyoming, circa 1900–1905.

Coffeyville Implement & Manufacturing Co.
Building farm equipment and implements for the midwest farmer; Coffeyville, KS, circa 1890–1910.

Cofiele
Charles Cofiele, carriage maker; New Hartford, NY, circa 1850's.

Coghill
Thomas Coghill, carriage maker; Cincinatti, Ohio, circa 1860–1880.

Coin
Thomas B. Coin, blacksmith, horseshoer and wheelwright, 227 Camp; Dallas, Texas, 1886–1890.

Cole
Frederick C. Cole, blacksmith; carriage and wagon makers; carriage painter and trimmer, 407 East Overland Street; also, 600 Texas; El Paso, Texas, circa 1905–1911.

Cole
John M. Cole, wheelwright; South Pueblo, CO, circa 1880–1890.

Cole
W.P. Cole & Co., Louisville, Kentucky, circa 1890–1910.

Cole Brothers
The well known firm of Cole Brothers manufactured their first steam fire-engine in 1867, using the designs of George A Saunders and George Baker, two former William Jeffers employees.

Over the next several years they would offer three classes of steam fire-engines. The "Rough and Ready" No. 2, built for the City of Pawtucket, was a third class, or the smallest. It weighed 4,600 lbs. 1883 was their last year in business; Pawtucket, RI, circa 1867–1883

Cole (see Bybee & Cole)

Coleman
Nicholas Coleman, manufactured wagons, drays and carts; Philadelphia, PA., circa 1844–1860.

Coleman Carriage & Wagon Co.
Manufactured carriages, wagons, surreys and seven styles of pony carts; Ilion, NY, circa 1880–1910.

Coleman & Underwood
Blacksmiths and wheelwrights, 208 Rusk; Ft. Worth, Texas, circa 1900–1910.

Coleman (see Langly & Coleman)

Coleman (see Simons, Coleman & Co.)
Coleman, Eskridge & Rowley Blacksmiths and wagon makers; Rico, Colorado, county seat of Dolores county in 1881, 40 miles from Durango; Pop. 1,000, circa 1881–1890.

Coles, Baldwin & Bentley
Carriage and wagon makers; may have started out as Coles & Bentley; Port Jefferson, NY, circa 1890–1910.

Colfax
The Colfax Co., (Schuyler Colfax, president) manufacturer of pony carts, wagons and carriages; South Bend, IN, circa 1890–1910.

Collins Plow Co.
Built agricultural equipment; Quincy, Illinois, circa 1890's-1940.

Collins & Sons
B.A. Collins & Sons; Akron, Ohio, circa 1900.

Collins & Johnson
Blacksmiths and wagon makers; Mohler, Idaho, circa 1905–1910.

Collins & Jones
Wagon makers; Winchester, Wisconsin, circa 1879.

Collins (see Zumhof & Collins)

Collmann
Henry Collmann, blacksmith and wheelwright; and carriage and wagon manufacturer, 39 Acequia; San Antonio, Texas, circa 1887–1900.

Colman
O.P. Colman, wagon and carriage maker; Milwaukee, Wisconsin, circa 1885–1898.

Colonial Buggy Co.
Circleville, Ohio, circa 1890–1910.

Colorado Carriage Works (See listing—also known as Melburn & Co.)

Colsher (see Everham & Colsher)

Colson
R.L. Colson, blacksmith and wagon maker; Ashton, Idaho, circa 1905–1910.

Columbia Carriage Co.
Cincinnati, Ohio, carriage manufacturer, circa 1890–1910.

Columbia Wagon & Body Co.
Columbia Wagon & Body Co.; Columbia, PA. offered four sizes of the Columbia Wagon with a load capacity ranging from 2,500 to 7,000 pounds, circa 1890–1915.

Columbus Bolt Works
Columbus, Ohio, circa 1890–1910.

Columbus Buggy Co.
Buggy maker; Columbus, OH, circa 1890–1910.

Columbus Carriage & Harness Co.
Carriage manufacturer; Columbus, OH, circa 1890–1910.

Columbus Vehicle Co.
The Columbus Buggy Co. was founded by C.D. Firestone, Geo. M. Peters and O.G. Peters; Cincinnati, Ohio.

In 1888 they advertised the factory as the largest in the world. They were operating branches in Kansas City, Chicago, Detroit and San Francisco, circa 1875–1913.

Combs
Charles E. Combs, carriage maker; Cazenovia, NY, circa 1845–1870.

Combs
Joseph Combs, carriage maker; Boenville, NY, circa 1850's.

Combs
Thomas Combs, wagon maker; North Andover, WI, circa 1885.

Commercial Wheel Co.
Manufactured wheels for every style of vehicle; Indianapolis, Indiana, circa 1870's–1910.

Commins
P.W. Commins, wagon maker, Mission near 29th; San Francisco, California, circa 1882–1888.

Comstock
Randall Comstock & Co., carriage and wagon dealer; Albany, Wisconsin, circa 1890–1910.

Concord Carriage Builders
Manufacturer of carriages and wagons, circa 1870–1910, including commercial vehicles like the Omnibus named Grace Darling, built in 1880. This vehicle was built for the Huntress family of South Berwick, Maine, owners of a livery business. Concord Carriage Builders occupied the New Hampshire prison works—1876 to 1891.

The interior panels of this Omnibus were painted by John Burgum, an easel painter and the chief ornamenter for the famous Abbot-Downing Company of Co cord, NH.

Condon
Charles E. Condon, blacksmith and buggy maker; Mifflinburg, PA, circa 1876–1886.

Condon
J. Harry Condon, buggy maker, opened his blacksmith shop on Chestnut Street after moving to Mifflinburg from Long Island in 1865. Here he specialized in buggy gears and ironing vehicles. By 1868, Condon moved to 526 Market Street, a much larger shop, for carriage and buggy building; Mifflinburg, PA, circa 1865–1879.

Condon Carriage Co.
Carriage, buggy, phaeton and wagon manufacturing, nw corner ofSt. Mary and Travis; San Antonio, Texas, circa 1887–1900.

Conner
George Conner was a carriage and wagon maker. Conner operated the 10th ward carriage shop in the same building as blacksmith George W. Setley, at west fourth and Bieber street; Williamsport, PA., circa 1890–1915.

Conner
J.E. Conner, wagon maker; West Superior, Wisconsin, circa 1885.

Conner Brothers
Built horse-drawn vehicles, including the famous Ada Road Cart; Ada, Ohio., circa 1880's-1900.

Connersville Buggy Co.
Connersville, Indiana, circa 1890–1910.

Conningham
Rochester, New York, circa 1890–1910.

Connolly
Patrick Connolly, carriages, wagons and buggies, 224 N. Lamar; Dallas, Texas, circa 1900–1915.

Connor
Daniel Connor; wagon maker, Central City, CO, circa 1884–1890.

Connor
R. Connor Company, carriage and wagon dealer and representative; Auburndale, Wisconsin, circa 1890–1910.

Conover Buggy Co.
Conover, N.C., circa 1890–1910.

Conrad
Peter Conrad, wagon maker; St. Louis, Missouri, circa 1850–1870.

Consolidated Implement Co.
Dealers in agricultural implements; Afton, WY, circa 1900–1905.

Consolidated Wagon & Machine Co.
Carriage and wagon manufacturer and dealer; Grace, Malad, Preston and Montpelier, Idaho.

They were also dealers in agricultural implements in Afton, Wyoming, circa 1890–1915.

Consumers Carriage & Manufacturing
Started building carriages in 1874. The company offered a 30-day free trial to farmers, on its $28.50 buggy, in an 1895 advertisement; Chicago, Illinois, circa 1874–1910.

Continental Carriage Co.
Buggy manufacturer; Cincinnati, Ohio, circa 1880–1910.

Cook
Charles Cook, carriage maker; Lewisburg, PA., circa 1830's–1850.

Cook
G. & D. Cook & Co., New Haven, Connecticut manufacturer of fine carriages, circa 1850's to 1868, sold primarily to the southern market. When the Civil War broke out, the G. & D. Cook & Co. was owed over $120,000 by dealers in the seceeding southern states. This led to the demise of G. & D. Cook & Co.

The firm was reorganized a couple of times, before 1868, when it eventually became Henry Hooker & Co. (see listing on Henry Hooker & Co).

Cook
Hannibal H. Cook, (and son, 1910) blacksmith and wheelwright, 507 Trinity and 608 Colorado; Austin, Texas, circa 1900–1920.

Cook
John Cook was an early carriage maker from New Haven, MA, circa 1790–1810, credited with the construction of a two wheeled chair—or chaise, in 1794.

Cook
John Cook established a wagon factory and grew it into one of the largest in the St. Louis, MO area. By 1853, he added a large blacksmith shop to his factory in order to place the entire process needed to complete a wagon, under one roof and under his immediate supervision.

Cook offered a wide variety of vehicles including the manufacture of wagons for the Army during the Civil war.

Cook
T. Cook and Bros.; Chester, PA, wagon and carriage maker also known for a specialty type of gypsy wagon decorated with gold and silver leaf, bright colors and other ornate or gaudy decorations, circa 1890–1910.

Cook
Thomas Cook, blacksmith, carriage and wagon maker; Douglas, Wyoming, circa 1902–1910.

Cook
W.G. Cook, wagon and carriage maker; Appleton, Wisconsin, circa 1865.

Cook & Co.
Blacksmiths and wagon makers; Marysville, Idaho, circa 1905–1910.

Cook Carriage Co.
Buggy manufacturer; Cincinnati, Ohio, circa 1880–1910.

Cook Wagon Co.
Carriage and wagon manufacturers; Marion, OH, circa 1890–1910.

Cook & Baldwin
Louis H. Cook and W. Baldwin, blacksmiths and wagon makers, 340 Larimer; Denver, Colorado, circa 1880–1890.

Cook & George
Blacksmiths and wagon makers; Douglas, Wyoming, circa 1900–1905.

Cook, Brinkley Co.
Produced a number of fine wagons, carts and light vehicles from their shop on Broadway; New York, NY, circa 1890–1910.

Cooley
M.L. Cooley, distributor and carriage repository, Bridge St., and he also operated Cooley Stables and Carriage Repository at their 713–715 Douglas Avenue location; Las Vegas, NM, circa 1890–1910.

Cooley
Oren Cooley manufactured wagons and sleighs; Pompey, NY, circa 1850's.

Coolidge Carriage Co.
Carriage, wagon and sleigh maker; Woodville, MA, circa 1880's–1910.

Coolidge (see Weatherford & Coolidge)

Cooper
A.A. Cooper Wagon & Buggy Co., Dubuque, Iowa, circa 1850–1920, manufactured a variety of wagons and carriages, including their Flex-Tight wagon. They also built a large number of sleighs.

Cooper wagons were available through many other dealers.

Cooper
C.G. Cooper & Co. manufactured farm equipment and implements in association with Mt. Vernon Iron Works; Mt.Vernon, OH, circa 1880–1900.

Cooper
C.H. Cooper, blacksmith and wheelwright, 400 Bonham, corner of Mill; Paris, Texas, circa 1891–1900.

Cooper
Edward Cooper, blacksmith and wagon maker; Bellevue, Idaho, circa 1905–1910.

Cooper
J.A. Cooper, wagon maker; De Soto, Wisconsin, circa 1879.

Cooper
Samuel Cooper, carriage painters and trimmers, 201 W 5th; Austin, Texas, circa 1887–1900.

Cooper
W. L. Cooper, blacksmith; Marion, Iowa, circa 1866–1879.

Cooper
Mr. Cooper was a carriage maker; Lockport, NY, circa 1850's.

Cooper Tire Co.
Cincinnati, Ohio, circa 1880–1910.

Cooter & Caruth
Blacksmiths and wheelwrights, 503 Main; Dallas, Texas, circa 1900.

Copeland
E.R. Copeland, wagon maker; Monroe, Wisconsin, circa 1879.

Coppenhauer
George Coppenhauer, blacksmith and wagon maker; Como, Colorado, circa 1883–1890.

Coquillard Wagon Works
Established in 1865, they built all types of wagons and carts, including some heavy log wagons and drays. These were called the Henderson and Coquillard wagons; Henderson, Kentucky, circa 1865–1920.

Corbett Buggy Co.
Henderson, North Carolina, circa 1890–1910.

Corbett & McAuliff
Manufactured light and heavy carriages, 140 East 41st; New York, NY, circa 1899.

Corcoran
Thomas Corcoran & Sons, buggy manufacturers; Cincinnati, Ohio, circa 1880–1910.

Corcoran (see Morrison & Corcoran)

Cornelius
A.A. Cornelius of Babylon, NY owned and operated a successful carriage manufacturing business with the help of a few key employees like carriagesmith Andrew J. Weeks. The woodshop was run by John Hilton, trimming by John Place and painting was done by Frank Holdridge, circa 1880–1900.

Cornelius (see Sammis & Cornelius)

Corning Company
Carriage and cart makers; Corning, NY, circa 1880–1910.

Corrigall & Wyland
Wagon and carriage makers; Oshkosh, Wisconsin, circa 1879.

Corry Machine Co.
Built farm implements and equipment like their Climax mower; Corry, PA., circa 1860's–1870's.

Cortland Cart & Carriage Co.
New York, circa 1890–1910.

Cortland Implement Co.
This Cortland, NY company built farm equipment, including wagons and spreaders. They also used agents like J.I. Case Plow Works to expand their market throughout the midwest.

Cortland Top & Rail Co., Ltd.
Manufacturers of carriage tops, shifting rails, carriage trimmings and hardware; Cortland, NY, circa 1880–1900.

Cortland Wagon Co.
Carriage and wagon manufacturer; at one point they were building and shipping over 100 vehicles a day. Cortland also made a number of sulkies and sleighs, including an unusual Sulky Sleigh, first published in the June 1893 Carriage Monthly, a major trade publication of the day.

The construction of this style sleigh was exceedingly light, the arched braces and seat were similar to sulkies of the time period. This sulky-sleigh was built for fast driving; Cortland, NY, circa 1885–1910.

Cory
Watts G. Cory of Amsterdam, NY, built one 5,000 lb. horse-drawn steam fire-engine shortly before his death, around 1873. This engine was used for many years in the central part of New York state, circa 1873.

Cosgriff
Cosgriff Bros. Co., dealers in agricultural implements; Opal, Wyoming, circa 1900–1908.

Cosmon
William H. Cosmon, blacksmith, horseshoer and wheelwright, 1013 Elm and 18 Live Oak; Dallas, Texas, circa 1886–1900.

Cosman (see Sheets & Cosman)

Cossett
L.G. Cossett, blacksmith and wagon maker; Kellogg, Idaho, circa 1905–1910.

Costello
D.D. Costello manufactured light and heavy carriages; North Manlius, NY, circa 1899.

Costigen
T. Costigen, wagon maker, 404 Jackson; San Francisco, California, circa 1882–1890.

Cottman & Son
W.F. Cottman, blacksmiths and wheelwrights, 526 Main, Dallas, Texas, circa 1895–1905.

Coultress & Hettler
Blacksmiths and wheelwrights, 1114 S. Alamo; San Antonio, Texas, circa 1900–1910.

Courtland Forging Co.
Courtland, New York, circa 1890–1910.

Courtland Wagon Co.
Courtland, New York, circa 1890–1910.

Cowles
C. Cowles & Co., general agents and sole manufacturer of Kimball's Improved Carriage Top Prop. They also offered a large variety of carriage and coach lamps; carriage hardware, mountings, trimmings and fringes, 27 & 29 Orange Street; New Haven, CT, circa 1850–1910.

Cowles (see Hanna, Cowles & Co.)

Cowley
J. Cowley, wagon maker; Esdaile, Wisconsin, circa 1879.

Cox
Edward Cox, blacksmith and wagon maker; Kooskia, Idaho, circa 1905–1910.

Cox & Eager
Blacksmiths and wagon makers; Saratoga, WY, circa 1901–1902.

Cox & Roberts
(See Roberts, Thorp & Co.)

Crabb Bros.
Wagon makers; Union Grove, Wisconsin, circa 1879.

Crabtree
P. Crabtree, blacksmith and wheelwright, 118 McKinney Ave.; Dallas, Texas, circa 1897–1905.

Craig & Henderson
Blacksmiths and wheelwrights, 902 N. Flores; San Antonio, Texas, circa 1897–1905.

Craigue
H. Craigue, carriage painter; Manitou Springs, Colorado, circa 1877–1890.

Cramer
J. Cramer, wagon maker; Boscobel, Wisconsin, circa 1879.

Crampton & Company
Blacksmith and wagon makers; Canon City, Colorado, circa 1877–1890.

Crandal, Stone & Co.
Manufactured a full line of carriage hardware and trimmings; Binghamton, NY, circa 1870–1900.

Crane
Crane and Breed Manufacturing Co.; Cincinnati, Ohio. Famed hearse builder, circa 1890–1910.

Crane & Brownlee
Carriage and wagon dealers; Adams, Wisconsin, circa 1890–1910.

Crane & McMahon
Manufactured wagon and carriage wheels, including the Nut brand, the Acorn brand and the Star brand. They also built rims, spokes, hubs, shafts, bows, poles and wiffletrees, 38 Park Place; New York, NY, circa 1870–1910.

Cranson
John Cranson, blacksmith and wagon maker, operated a small shop on Farnham street; Cazenovia, NY, circa 1870's–1910.

Cratzer
Charles Cratzer, buggy maker; Mifflinburg, PA, circa 1881.

Craus
J. Craus, wagon maker; Maple Grove, Wisconsin, circa 1879.

Craven
G.W. Craven, blacksmith and wheelwright; carriage and wagon makers, 106 Congress Ave., 410 Colorado, and 207 E. 5th; Austin, Texas, circa 1887–1905.

Crawford
E.D. Crawford, blacksmith and wagon maker, Longmont, Colorado, circa 1884–1890.

Crawford
G.W. and H.D. Crawford manufactured carriages, 1623 Broadway; New York, NY, circa 1899.

Crawford
N.A. Crawford, dealer in agricultural implements; Guernsey, Wyoming, circa 1902–1908.

Crawford Carriage Works
J.A. Crawford, blacksmiths and wheelwrights, 108–110 Main, Dallas, Texas, circa 1900–1910.

Crawford (see Post & Crawford)

Cray Brothers
Cray Brothers; bobsled and wagon maker—also offered for sale materials and tools for making carriages and wagons, 57–59 Water St.; Cleveland, Ohio, circa 1890–1920.

Creed
W.T. Creed, blacksmith and wheelwright, Ft. Worth Ave., and corner of Dallas Ave. and Cedar Hill; W. Dallas, Texas, circa 1891–1899.

Creegar & Cenly
Blacksmiths; Big Horn, Wyoming, circa 1905–1910.

Creighton
J. Creighton, wagon makers; Lyons, Wisconsin, circa 1879.

Cretors
The Chicago, Illinois firm of C. Cretors & Company was famous for their design and manufacture of wheeled popcorn-making machines.
   Although not in the true wagon and carriage building business, they built a great popcorn wagon, circa 1890–1920.

Criswick
J. Criswick, wagon maker; Racine, Wisconsin, circa 1865.

Crocker
Benjamin Crocker, of Cronkite, Crocker & Co., 7th between J and K; Sacramento, CA, circa 1853–1865.

Cromeans
John B. Cromeans, blacksmith and wheelwrights, 1310 E. 6th; Austin, Texas, circa 1910–1920.

Cronce (see Slater & Cronce)

Crone Carriage Co.
Celina, Ohio, circa 1890–1910.

Cronk
B.B. Cronk, wagon maker; West Salem, Wisconsin, circa 1879.

Cronkite
Jose Cronkite, of Cronkite, Crocker & Co., 7th between J and K; Sacramento, CA, circa 1853–1865.

Cronkite, Crocker & Co.
Blacksmiths and wagon makers, 7th, between J & K; Sacramento, CA, circa 1853–1865.

Crosby
Manson H. Crosby, a native of Maine, was a blacksmith by trade, and a wagon and carriage maker. He became a resident of Marion,

Iowa in 1856. Two years later, he built a wagon factory on the ne corner of seventh avenue and thirteenth street.

Crosby was commissioned 2nd lieutenant in the 20th Iowa Infantry in 1862, and later became captain.

Upon his retirement from the army, he secured the contract to complete the trackage of Marion's first railroad.

Cross
Arthur Tyler Cross learned the trade of carriage trimmer while working in the shop of his father, Asahel Cross. Arthur was also a talented artist, opening his own shop, offering carriage, sign and fancy painting, as well as carriage trimming.

Cross worked for a brief time in the shops of Combs & Shute, before going back into business for himself, doing trimming, painting and carriage and sleigh repair work; Cazenovia, NY, circa 1860–1885.

Cross
Asahel Cross, carriage trimmer; Cazenovia, NY, circa 1840–1865.

Cross
William Cross, carriage and wagon dealer and representative; Arkansaw, Wisconsin, circa 1890–1910.

Crossitt
D. Crossitt, wagon maker; Kenosha, Wisconsin, circa 1865.

Crotty
Mike Crotty Carriage Co., buggy manufacturer; Cincinnati, Ohio, circa 1880–1910.

Crow & Crow
B.D. Crow and A.J. Crow, blacksmiths, horseshoers, carriage and wagon makers, 219 Taylor; Amarillo, Texas, circa 1919.

Crown Point Manufacturing Co.
Built a combination husker-shredder and other farm equipment; Crown Point, IN, circa 1890–1905.

Cruz
D.G. Cruz, blacksmith and wheelwright, 801–825 S. Laredo; San Antonio, Texas, circa 1897–1902.

Cruz
Juan Cruz, blacksmith and wheelwright, 620 Utah; El Paso, Texas, circa 1898–1905.

Culbertson
H.M. Culbertson, wagon maker; Eau Claire, Wisconsin, circa 1879.

Cummings
C.J. Cummings of Tully, NY, circa 1880–1920, manufactured horse-drawn farm implements and equipment, including his special potato diggers—later known as the Cummings-Ostego potato diggers, built by Babcock Mfg. Co. of Leonardsville, NY.

Cummings
W. Cummings, wagon maker; Avalanche, Wisconsin, circa 1879.

Cunningham
James Cunningham & Son Co.; Rochester, N.Y. Builders of fine carriages, but mostly known for their wide variety of hearses and ambulances, circa 1890–1910.

Cunningham
R.D. Cunningham, blacksmith and wheelwright; carriage and wagon manufacturer, 504 Trinity; Austin, Texas, circa 1887–1894.

Cunningham
Z.H. Cunningham & Son, wagon maker, 2313 Mission; San Francisco, California, circa 1882–1890.

Cunningham & Barngrowver
This company specialized in the construction of fruit dryers and packers' vehicles and supplies—offering a full line of horse-drawn orchard trucks, wagons and cultivators, 338–340 West Santa Clara street; San Jose, CA, circa 1880–1920.

Cunningham (see Kerr, Cunningham & Co.)

Cunningham (see Watson & Cunningham)

Curley
John Curley established his carriage business in 1867. He built a variety of vehicles—including carts, carriages, cabriolets, phaetons and vis-à-vis; Brooklyn, NY., circa 1867–1880's.

Curnow
Edward Curnow, wagon maker; Mineral Point, Wisconsin, circa 1885–1919.

Currin (see Morris & Currin)

Cutaway Harrow Co.
Manufactured farm implements; Higganum, CT, circa 1890–1930.

Cutts
A.W. Cutts, carriage and wagon maker, may have been one of the first to build a wagon in this city in 1852.

Cutts joined Suber in 1854, to form Suber & Cutts; Marysville, CA, circa 1852–1880's.

Daab (see Kappe & Daab)

Dael & Hopkins
Manufactured carriages and sleighs; Manlius, NY, circa 1850's.

Dagnal & Stokey
J.D. Dagnal, blacksmiths and wheelwrights, 692 Ross Ave.; Dallas, Texas, circa 1900–1910.

Dagnon & Flannery
Wagon makers; Seneca, Wisconsin, circa 1879.

Dahl (see Jones & Dahl)

Dahlberg
Oscar Dahlberg, carriage and wagon maker; Staten Island, NY, circa 1870–1900.

Dahlstrom
Nephi Dahlstrom, blacksmith and wagon maker; Idaho Falls, Idaho, circa 1905–1910.

Daigger
B. Daigger, wagon maker, West Las Vegas, New Mexico, circa 1882–1900.

Dain Manufacturing Co.
This company, circa 1881–1911, built the Dain Steel Corn Cutter, the Dain

Power Lift Hay Rake and the Dain Center-Draft Mower They also perfected a side delivery rake that became very popular and was marketed widely through the John Deere organization.

This company was established by Joseph Dain in 1881 in Kansas City, Missouri. They moved to Carrollton, Missouri in 1899, then Otumwa, Iowa in 1900.

They eventually became part of Deere & Company in 1911.

Dale
Dennis Dale, wagon maker; Jackson County, MO, circa 1850–1860.

Dallas Buggy & Wagon Co.
Carriages, wagons and buggies, 198–200 Pacific Ave.; Dallas, Texas, circa 1908.

Dallas City Carriage Co.
Dallas City, Illinois, circa 1890–1910.

Dallas Transfer Co.
Carriage lines, 316 Commerce; Dallas, Texas, circa 1910.

Dallas Transfer & Cab Co.
Carriage lines, 107 S. Akard; Dallas, Texas, circa 1905–1915.

Dallas (see Anderson & Dallas)

Daly
Edward Daly, blacksmith and wagon maker, 2311 Pine; San Francisco, California, circa 1882–1887.

Dalzell Axle Co.
South Egremont, Mass., circa 1890–1910.

Damm (see Moldenhauer & Damm)

Damme (see Weber & Damme Wagon Co.)

Dancy
T. Dancy, wagon makers; Oak Hill, Wisconsin, circa 1879.

Danels & Sides
Blacksmiths and horseshoers, 182 Leonard; Dallas, Texas, circa 1905–1912.

Daniel
Mr. Daniel was a carriage maker; Utica, NY, circa 1850's.

Daniels (see Pinneo & Daniels Wheel Co.)

Danley
A. Danley, blacksmith and wagon maker; Cloudcroft, New Mexico, circa 1900–1910.

Danley
Minos C. Danley, blacksmith and wheelwright; carriage painters and trimmers; carriage and wagon manufacturer, 505–507 Colorado; Austin, Texas, circa 1910–1918.

Dann Brothers Mfg.
This firm offered a full line of carriage wood work, 137 State Street; New Haven, CT, circa 1850–1900.

Darey & Baldwin
Carriage makers; Shaneobiles, NY, circa 1850's.

Darling
John Lincklaen Darling, wagon and carriage maker, worked as a wagon maker in his shop on Albany street, before selling it to a blacksmith named Eber Peet.

Darling then went into business as J.L. Darling's Carriage Shop, with two local blacksmiths, brothers Frank and Nathan Soult. Bennett Vollmer, from Syracuse, New York also leased and worked as a blacksmith and wagon maker in one of the Darling wagon shop buildings; Cazenovia, NY, circa 1845–1890.

Darr (see Irby & Darr)

Dash & Carriage Goods Co.
Buggy manufacturers; Cincinnati, Ohio, circa 1880–1910.

Dassler
William Dassler, wagon maker, 627 West 47th; New York, NY, circa 1899.

Dater
J.Y. Dater & Co., carriage, wagon and buggy builder; Ramsay, New Jersey, circa 1850's–1870.

Dau
Mrs. Hermina Dau, carriage and wagon dealer and representative; Appleton, WI, circa 1890–1910.

Daumeyer (see Klein & Daumeyer)

Davenport Wagon Co.
Davenport, Iowa, circa 1890–1910.

Davey & Baldwin
Carriage makers; Skancateles, NY, circa 1850's.

David
W.M. David, blacksmith and wagon maker, Aransas St.; Alice, Texas, circa 1910–1915.

Davies (see Barnum & Davies)

Davis
Alfred Davis, wagon maker, 1523 N. Salina; Syracuse, NY, circa 1899.

Davis
B.M. Davis, blacksmith and wagon maker; Bellevue, Idaho, circa 1905–1910.

Davis
C.W. Davis, blacksmith and wheelwright, E. 5th east of city; Austin, Texas, circa 1893–1901.

Davis
David R. Davis operated a repair shop, working on wagons and farm implements; Cazenovia, NY, circa 1870–1905.

Davis
D.R. Davis, wagon maker; Bangor, WI, circa 1879.

Davis
E. Davis, wagon maker; Watertown, Wisconsin, circa 1879.

Davis
E.J. Davis, blacksmith and wheelwright, 1053 S. Central Ave.; Dallas, Texas, circa 1897–1908.

Davis
G.W. Davis, wagon maker; Towerville, Wisconsin, circa 1879.

Davis
Hiram W. Davis & Co., successors to Davis, Gould & Co., carriage makers; Cincinnati, Ohio, circa 1880–1910.

Davis
Joseph W. Davis, carriage trimmers and painters, 209 Milam; Houston, Texas, circa 1900–1910.

Davis
J.W. Davis, carriage trimmer, 10 Travis; Houston, Texas, circa 1882–1890.

Davis
L.A. Davis & Brother's wagon building company advertised their combination spring platform as the best carrying, easiest riding and most duirable wagon in use; Port Crane, New York, circa 1870's–1910.

Davis
L.W. Davis, blacksmith and wheelwright, State lunatic asylum; Austin, Texas, circa 1905–1913.

Davis
M.C. Davis & Brother, blacksmith amd horseshoer; wagon and carriage ironing; Fairbury, Nebraska, circa 1882–1888.

Davis
N.A. Davis, wagon maker; Cato, Wisconsin, circa 1879.

Davis
N.F. Davis, wagon maker; Mazomanie, Wisconsin, circa 1879.

Davis
O.C. Davis, wagon maker; Wautoma, WI, circa 1885–1901.

Davis
W.C. Davis & Co., carriage trimmers; Tucson, AZ, circa 1884–1890.

Davis
W.T. Davis, wagon maker; Palmyra; Wisconsin, circa 1898–1903.

Davis Carriage Co.
Buggy manufacturer; Cincinnati, Ohio, circa 1880–1910.

Davis Carriage Co.
Richmond, IN, circa 1890–1910.

Davis & Dixon
Carriage makers; Utica, NY, circa 1850's.

Davis & Gramse
Wagon makers; Dakota, Wisconsin, circa 1879.

Davis & Smith
Wagon and carriage makers; Madison, Wisconsin, circa 1879.

Davis (see Bower & Davis)
Davis (see Parren & Davis)
Davison (see Roehm & Davison)

Dawson
Andrew J. Dawson was a wagon maker from Oskaloosa, Kansas. Not much is known of him outside of his attempt to build a windwagon. The vehicle he constructed was lighter and much smaller than the one built by William Thomas of Westport, Missouri.

Dawson's wagon made a successful trip all the way to Denver, Colorado, circa 1860.

Dawson
Dawson & Burns, blacksmiths; Marion, Iowa, circa 1866–1879.

Day
J.S. Day, carriage maker; Trinidad, Colorado, circa 1882–1890.

Day & Son
Manufactured light carriages, l07 Seventh Ave.; New York, NY, circa 1899.

Day Carriage Works
William S. Day, blacksmith, wheelwright, carriage painter and trimmer, 128 S. Poydras and 108-110 Main; Dallas, Texas, circa 1898–1908.

Day & Waechter
Blacksmiths, 707 Red River; Austin, Texas, circa 1915–1920.

Dayton Plow Co.
Offered their Perfected Perfection Plow; Dayton, Ohio, circa 1880–1900.

Deal
Jacob J. Deal, carriage and sleigh builder, established in 1857, was the maker of the Quick Deal Wagons; Jonesville, Michigan, circa 1857–1910.

Dean
W.Y. Dean, wagon and carriage material, 53 Beale, San Francisco, California, circa 1882–1890.

Dean (see Ames-Dean Carriage Co.)

Deane
Elkanah and William Deane came to New York from Dublin, Ireland, in 1764. They established their carriage shop that same year.

They advertised landaus, two-wheeled chairs, phaetons, carriages and sleighs; New York, NY., circa 1764–1790.

Deatz
V. Deatz, wagon maker; St. Cloud, Wisconsin, circa 1879.

DeBorde
Abel B. DeBorde, blacksmiths and horseshoers, Fort Worth Ave, Harrison Ave; Dallas, Texas, circa 1905–1910.

Debose (see Adams & Debose)

Decatur Buggy Co.
Carriage makers, circa 1890–1910, moved to Middletown, Ohio from Indiana.

Decker
E.E. Decker, blacksmith and wagon maker; Gooding, Idaho, circa 1905–1910.

Decker
J.C. Decker built straps, shafts and poles in his shop several miles south of Williamsport; Montgomery, PA, circa 1900–1910.

Dederich
Peter L. Dederich, wagon maker; Bear Valley, WI, circa 1879–1911.

Deere
John Deere Wagon Co. and John Deere Plow Co. in Moline, Illinois,

played a major role in the horse-drawn vehicle era in America.

John Deere Plows, Wagons and Carriages of Moline, IL. See the complete history of this company, including their connection to the White Elephant Buggy Factory, Mansur & Tebbetrs Implement Company, Fort Smith Wagon Co., Moline Wagon Co., Cavenport Wagon Co., Deere & Weber Co. and Reliance Buggy Co. in volume 2 of Wheels Across America.

Deere & Mansur Co.
Established by Deere in 1877 to manufacture corn planters, was later merged into Deere & Co.; Moline, Illinois, circa 1877–1910.

Deering Harvester Co.
Established by William Deering in the early 1870's. This company would grow to employ over 6,000 workers by 1898.

A harvester manufacturer, they built the Horizontal Corn Binder, (1899). They also offered several styles of mowers from the Ideal One-horse to the Ideal Giant mowers of the 1880's.

They published their catalogs in several languages much to the benefit of immigrant farmers.

In 1902 Deering Company became part of International Harvester Co.; Chicago, IL, circa 1870–1902.

Defiance Hub, Wheel & Spokes
Defiance, OH, circa 1890–1910.

Degen Bros.
Wagon makers; Stevens Point, Wisconsin, circa 1879.

DeGlover
Watts DeGlover Company supplied carriage, coach and wagon makers with a variety of colors and varnishes; Chicago, Illinois, circa 1860–1900.

DeGolier
H.D. DeGolier, carriage and wagon dealer and representative; Amery, Wisconsin, circa 1890–1910.

Deibler & Smith
Wagon makers; Berlin, Wisconsin, circa 1879.

Deinzer
L. Deinzer & Son of 113 to 117 Water Street, Hamilton, Ohio manufactured a variety of carriage and wagon parts, including rims, shafts, poles, bows and more, circa 1880–1900.

DeKalb Implement Works
Built a variety of farm implements, including their Rustler design; DeKalb, Illinois, circa 1890–1910.

Delaney (see Jones & Delaney)

Delker
Frank H. Delker, Delker Bros. Buggy Co.; Henderson, Kentucky, circa 1901–1927.

Delker
George Delker, buggy manufacturer; Henderson, Kentucky, circa 1863–1891.

Delker
John Delker Co., buggy manufacturer; Henderson, Kentucky, circa 1890–1910.

Delker & Blondin
Manufactured carriage and buggy parts. They offered, for sale, their July 8, 1873 patented body design, fully ironed with royalty rights, for $23.00. Additionally, they offered a side-bar phaeton, d-boy, 30" wide at the bottom, patented November 9, 1880, fully ironed with royalty rights for $47.00; Henderson, KY, circa 1860's-1890.

Dell
John B. Dell, wagon maker; Sheboygan, Wisconsin, circa 1879–1898.

Demarest
A.T. Demarest & Company, 13th street, New York, NY, and New Haven, CT, circa 1860's–1915, was a successful New York carriage, wagon and sleigh maker. In 1873, they purchased what was left of the Lawrence, Bradley and Pardee company from sole remaining owner, Bradley, (see Lawrence, Bradley and Pardee listing).

Demars (see Hebert & Demars)

Demerritt & Newell
Wagon makers; Muskego, Wisconsin, circa 1865.

Deming Carriage Works
F.C. Peterson (proprietor), corner of Gold Ave. and Hemlock St.; Deming, New Mexico, circa 1910–1923.

Demming
W.S. Demming, blacksmith and wagon maker; Clark Fork, Idaho, circa 1905–1910.

Dempster Mill & Manufacturing Co.
Built farm implements; Beatrice, Nebraska, circa 1890–1910.

Dennis & VanAlstyne
Wagon makers; Glenbeulah, Wisconsin, circa 1865.

Dennisson
John N. Dennisson was known to many as "Pop". Mr. Dennisson, like others, started out designing and building hand-pump fire-engines; Newark, NJ, circa 1845–1875.

He moved on to design and build the steamers, not only for his own company, but he also lent his designs to other builders, like the firm of R.J. Gould.

Denniston
G.W. Denniston, wagon maker; Foster, Wisconsin, circa 1879.

Denver Carriage Works
379 and 381 Arapahoe; Denver, Colorado, circa 1882–1890.

Departee
W.J. Departee, blacksmith and wagon maker; Culdesac, Idaho, circa 1905–1910.

Depp
George Depp, blacksmith and wagon maker; Longmont, Colorado, circa 1877–1880's.

Deppel
John Deppel, blacksmith and wagon maker, Railroad Ave. near 6th; San Francisco, California, circa 1882–1890.

Derby
D. Derby, wagon maker; Plover, Wisconsin, circa 1879.

Dersham
Alexander Dersham, buggy maker; Mifflinburg, PA, circa 1881.

Desmond & Pool
Wagon makers; Monroe, Wisconsin, circa 1879.

DeSoto Agricultural Manufacturing Co.
Built a variety of farm equipment including the Carrey Perfect Corn Shredder; DeSoto, Missouri, circa 1890–1910.

Dessecker
Gustav Dessecker, manufacturer of heavy carriages and hearses, 154 Elizabeth; New York, NY, circa 1899.

Detton
Clarence Detton, blacksmith and wagon maker; Hatch, Idaho, circa 1905–1910.

Detzler Color Co.
Detroit, MI, circa 1890–1910.

Deuchler
Phillip Deuchler, carriage, buggy and sleigh maker; Lyons, NY, circa 1880–1910.

Deuscher
H.P. Deuscher Co., established 1878, built corn planters and other farm implements; Hamilton, Ohio, circa 1878–1910.

Devoe
F.W. Devoe & Co., established 1852, manufactured fine colors, oils, and varnishes for coach and carriage painters; also brushes, striping and artists materials; New York, NY. Devoe paint is still available today.

DeVoe & Hilton
Carriage and wagon dealers and representatives; Argyle, Wisconsin, circa 1890–1910.

Devoe (see Raynolds, Devoe & Pratt) DeVoursney
Offered fine cut-glass coach lamps for sale; 46 Green, New York, NY., circa 1860–1890.

Dhonau
F. Dhonau & Sons manufactured buggies; Cincinnati, Ohio, circa 1880–1910.

Diamond Body & Seat
Kansas City, Missouri, circa 1890–1910.

Diamond Rubber
Akron, Ohio, circa 1890–1910.

Dicke
Charles Dicke, wagon maker, 407 East 75th; New York, NY, circa 1899.

Dickenson & Rentfrow
Blacksmiths; buggy and wagon makers; Capitan, New Mexico, circa 1900–1910.

Dickey
W.K. Dickey, wagon maker; Nielsville, Wisconsin, circa 1865.

Diefenderfer & Dinwiddie
Dealers in agricultural implements; Sheridan, Wyoming, circa 1902–1908.

Dieterle
Fred Dieterle, blacksmith and wagon maker; Gilbert, Idaho, circa 1905–1910.

Dietsch
J.F. Dietsch, blacksmith and wheelwright, 621 Navarro; San Antonio,Texas, 1897–98; and 326 St. Mary; San Antonio, Texas, circa 1901–1905.

Dill
William J. Dill, carriage painter and trimmers, 505 Neches; Austin, Texas, circa 1905–1915.

Dillon
Edward Dillon, blacksmith and wheelwright; and carriage and buggy manufacturer, nw corner Travis and Ave. D; San Antonio, Texas, circa 1887–1900.

Dillon
T.F. Dillon, blacksmith and wagon maker, 184 15th; Denver, Colorado, circa 1880–1890.

Dillon (see Varian & Dillon)
Dilts
S.M. Dilts, carriage and wagon maker; Colorado Springs, Colorado, circa 1882–1890.

Dilts (see Hogan & Dilts)
Dimock
F.H. Dimock, wagon maker; Avoca, Wisconsin, circa 1879.

Dinwiddie (see Diefenderfer & Dinwiddie)
Dippel
J. Dippel, carriage and wagon maker, corner Railroad and 6 Ave.; San Francisco, CA, circa 1888–1894.

Dishmaker
F.J. Dishmaker, wagon maker; Carleton, Wisconsin, circa 1885.

Dixon
The J. Dixon Carriage and Sleigh Works of Toronto, Canada, circa 1880's–1900, manufactured carriages, carts and sleighs, including their original Dog Cart Sleigh as seen in the May 1892 Hub, a major trade publication of the day.

Dixon (see Davis & Dixon)
Doak (see Swalm & Doak)
Dobson
F.P. Dobson, buggies, wagons, ect.; Evans, CO, circa 1882–1883.

Dockett (see Happy & Dockett)
Dockstader
G. Dockstader, wagon maker; Greenbush, Wisconsin, circa 1879.

Dodd
George Dodd, and later George Dodd's Sons, carriage makers, 5th and Race streets; Philadelphia, PA, circa 1880–1910.

Dodd
Samuel Dodd, blacksmith and wagon maker, 6th, between J and K; Sacramento, CA, circa 1853–1865.

Dodds
J. Dodds manufactured farm implements including the 1875 introduction of the Hollingsworth rake, featuring a very early all-steel design; Dayton, Ohio, circa 1870's–1880.

Dodge
John Dodge, wagon maker; Tomah, Wisconsin, circa 1865.

Dodge
Stephen Dodge, an early carriage, wagon and sleigh maker; Cazenovia, NY, circa 1810–1840.

Dodge & Manville
Wagon makers; Ripon, Wisconsin, circa 1865.

Dodson
S.T. Dodson, wagon maker, 10th street between J and K; Sacramento, CA, circa 1855–1875.

Doebert & Stehwein
Carriage and wagon makers; Milwaukee, Wisconsin, circa 1879.

Doerle
Victor Doerle, blacksmith, horseshoer and wheelwright, Broadway between Main and Commerce; Dallas, Texas, circa 1886–1896.

Doersch
G.M. Doersch, carriage and wagon dealer and representative; Antigo, Wisconsin, circa 1890–1910.

Doherty
M. Doherty, wagon maker; Sturgeon Bay, Wisconsin, circa 1879.

Dohr
J. Dohr, wagon maker; Pheasant Branch, Wisconsin, circa 1879.

Dohs
Charles Dohs, blacksmith and wagon maker, 972 Harrison; San Francisco, CA, circa 1882–1890.

Doll (see Robertson & Doll)

Dom Carriage Co.
Philip Dom manufactured buggies; Cincinnati, Ohio, circa 1880–1910.

Donahu
John & Thomas Donahu, coach and wagon makers; Pittsburgh and Allegheny, PA, circa 1840–1870.

Donahue
John Donahue, carriage and wagon makers, Albuquerque, New Mexico, circa 1884–1890.

Donald
J.M. Donald, blacksmith and wheelwright; also carriage, buggy and phaeton manufacturer, 208 Rusk; Ft. Worth, Texas, circa 1900–1915.

Donald
Jefferson M. Donald, blacksmith and wheelwright, 1/4 mile ne of stockyards; N. Ft. Worth, Texas, circa 1905–1910.

Doney & Pearson
Wagon makers; Excelsior, Wisconsin, circa 1879.

Donnelly
R. Donnelly, blacksmith and wheelwright, 610–622 Elm, also 128 Patterson Ave., 507 and 830 Main; Dallas, Texas, circa 1891–1905.

Donovan
M.M. Donovan, carriage painter, 200 Bartlett; San Francisco, California, circa 1888–1894.

Doolittle
P. Doolittle, wagon maker; Dayton, Wisconsin, circa 1865.

Dorman
S. Dorman, blacksmith and wagon maker; Georgetown, Colorado, circa 1880–1890.

Dort
Durant Dort Carriage Company, (formerly the Flint Road Cart Co.), was established 1886. The name was changed in 1896 when they incorporated as Durant Dort Carriage Co. They had a capacity of 35,000 vehicles annually in their peak production years.

The Road Cart had a unique feature known as the cold-water patent—a spring connecting the shaft to the seat for easier riding. Durant Dort, of Flint, Michigan, makers of the Famous Blue Ribbon Line, continued making carriages until approximately 1917.

Doty
C.R. Doty, wagon maker; Stevens Point, Wisconsin, circa 1879.

Doubek
Wenzel Doubek, wagon maker; Greenstreet, WI, circa 1885–1903.

Doucet (see Palmer & Doucet)

Doucette
M.A. Doucette Carriage Co.; Cincinnati, Ohio, circa 1890–1910.

Dougherty
D. Dougherty, wagon maker; Eldorado Mills, Wisconsin, circa 1879.

Dougherty
The firm of Robert Dougherty & Brother of St. Louis, Missouri (circa 1850–1890), designed and manufactured the Dougherty wagon, an ambulance so popular it was used by the U.S. Army from the early 1870's through 1900. Dougherty built a number of other vehicles—including wagons, buggies and carriages.

In 1850, he was a partner in the carriage business of Osborne & Dougherty. By 1852 he had joined with another carriage maker, Alexander Finley. Dougherty established his own business by 1856 and changed the name of the firm to Robert Dougherty & Brother in 1866.

Doughty Bros.
Wagon makers; Durand, Wisconsin, circa 1865.

Douglas
D. Douglas, blacksmith and wheelwright, 159 N. Market; Dallas, Texas, circa 1897–1905.

Dow
Alphonso Dow, blacksmith and wagon maker; Fairplay, Colorado, circa 1878–1885.

Dowagiac Manufacturing Co.
Built farm implements; Dowagiac, MI, circa 1880–1920.

Dowe
A.H. Dowe, wagon maker; Sextonville, Wisconsin, circa 1879.

Downer
F. Downer, wagon and carriage maker; Milwaukee, WI, circa 1865.

Downie & Ladd
Wagon makers; Sharon, Wisconsin, circa 1879.

Downing
J. Downing, wagon and carriage maker; Milwaukee, WI, circa 1879.

Downing & Hamilton
Dealers for the "Old Reliable" Schuttler wagons—they also offered a line of farm implements, including plows, reapers, cultivators and mowers; Clinton, IN, circa 1870–1910.

Downing (see Abbott-Downing)

Downing (see Abbott-Downing Co.)

Downs
William T. Downs of Huntington, NY manufactured carriages and wagons. They also offered repairs and jobbing for customers throughout Suffolk County, New York., circa 1870–1890.

Dow, Sheman & Co.
Blacksmith and wagon maker; Denver Street; Fairplay, Colorado, circa 1877–1885.

Doyle
E. Doyle, carriage and wagon maker; Milwaukee, WI, circa 1879.

Doyle
H.H. Doyle, blacksmith and wagon maker; Doyleville, Colorado, circa 1880–1890.

Doyle (see Flynn & Doyle)

Drake
Phillips Drake, manufactured wagons and sleighs; Van Buren, NY, circa 1850's.

Drake
William W. Drake, wagon maker; Columbus, Wisconsin, circa 1865.

Dralle
George Dralle, wagon maker; Saguache, Colorado, circa 1880–1890.

Dresser
Benjamin Dresser, wagon maker; Jackson County, MO, circa 1850–1860.

Drew & Hall
Wagon makers; Omro, Wisconsin, circa 1879.

Drew & Hicks
Wagon makers; Omro, Wisconsin, circa 1865.

Driscoll (see Schmidlin & Driscoll)

Dromgold (see Hench & Dromgold)

Drumheller (see Myers and Drumheller)

Drummond
Robert Drummond & Son built a number of extention top surreys, cabriolets, phaetons, piano-box buggies and speeding wagons; 12 Carriage Avenue, Amesbury, MA, circa 1880–1910.

Drury (see Hinckley & Drury)

Druse
J. Druse, wagon maker; Muskego, Wisconsin, circa 1879.

Dubois Mfg. Co.
Manufactured Dubois patented cushioned tires for all style of vehicles; Philadelphia, PA, circa 1880–1910.

Duenkel
C. Duenkel, wagon maker; Sheboygan, Wisconsin, circa 1879.

Duenkel
E. Duenkel, wagon maker; Sheboygan, Wisconsin, circa 1879.

Duescher
William Duescher, wagon maker; Wrightstown, WI, circa 1879–1903.

Duff
Michael Duff was a carriage and wagon maker who worked for a number of local shops before opening his own on Post Avenue. Duff also made carts and child size vehicles; (Port Richmond) Staten Island, NY, circa 1880–1910.

Duff
W. Duff, wagon maker; Hillsboro, Wisconsin, circa 1879.

Dugan
Hugh Dugan, wagon yards, 415 W. Weatherford; Ft. Worth, Texas, circa 1896–1906.

Duhamel
H. Duhamel; Brooklyn, N.Y., hearse and carriage builder, circa 1890–1910.

Duke
G.B. Duke & Son, blacksmiths and wheelwrights, 1919 W. Commerce; San Antonio, Texas, circa 1900–1910.

Dukes (see Middleton & Dukes)

DuMenil
A. DuMenil, blacksmith and wheelwright, 818 E. Commerce; San Antonio, Texas, circa 1897–1902.

DuMenil & Sons
August DuMenil & Sons, blacksmiths and wheelwrights; carriage manufacture and repair, Southern Carriage Works, 761 Liberty Ave.; Beaumont, Texas, circa 1900–1910.

Dummann
Henry Dummann, wagon and carriage makers; Milwaukee, Wisconsin, circa 1911–1919.

Dunbar & Barnes
Edward L. Dunbar and Wallace Barnes manufactured carriage and wagon springs; Bristol, CT, circa 1850–1890.

Duncan & Tuttle
Blacksmiths and wagon makers; Cambridge, Idaho, circa 1905–1910.

Duncan (see Chaffin & Duncan)

Dunham Co.
J.W. Dunham & Son built farm implements, including various kinds of landrollers and their Dunham Culti-Packer; Berea, Ohio, circa 1890–1920's.

Dunlap
Dunlap Vehicle Co.; Pontiac, Michigan, circa 1890–1910.

Dunlap
William Dunlap of the Phoenix Coach Works, carriage maker; Philadelphia, PA, circa 1880–1910.

Dunn (see Sanford & Dunn)

Dunne
James Dunne, wagon maker, 145 Valencia; San Francisco, California, circa 1882–1888.

Dunning
Lewis Dunning, wagon maker, 9th, between J and K; Sacramento, CA, circa 1853–1865.

Dunning
Thomas Dunning, carriage maker, 19th Ward; New York, NY, circa 1850.

Duran
Rosalio Duran, blacksmith, 1004 Fauntleroy; Austin, Texas, circa 1910–1920.

Durham
Durham Buggy Co.; Durham, North Carolina, circa 1890–1910.

Durr, Martin & Co.
Dealer for Columbus Buggy Co.; Marion, Ohio, circa 1895–1913.

Durre
F. Durre, wagon maker; Thiensville, Wisconsin, circa 1879.

Dusenbury
D.J. Dusenbury, carriage manufacturer at 102 Laurens; New York, NY., circa 1850's–1870's.

Dutton
J.Q.A. Dutton, blacksmith; Marion, Iowa, circa 1866–1879.

Dykins
James Dykins, wagon maker; Baraboo, WI, circa 1879–1901.

Eads
Alvah Eads, blacksmith and wheelwright, 304 W. Weatherford; Ft. Worth, Texas, circa 1896–1906.

Eager (see Cox & Eager)

Eagle Carriage Co.
Buggy manufacturer of Cincinnati, Ohio, circa 1880–1910.

Eagle Manufacturing
Carriages, wagons and buggies, P.E. Stromberg, state manager, 123 N. Broadway; Dallas, Texas, circa 1898–1908.

Eagle Manufacturing Co.
Built the Eagle Kaffir Corn Header. This special device was mounted on the side of a wagon; Kansas City, MO, circa 1900–1910.

Eagle Steam Fire-Engine Co. #1
In 1859, under the direction of George Wilson, this firm constructed a horse-drawn fire engine designed by James Nelson. This vehicle was hung on platform springs and weighed over 6,000 lbs. when fully loaded; Pittsburgh, PA, circa 1859–1860's.

This engine was in service on the streets of Pittsburgh until it was swept away and destroyed in a flood on May 31, 1889.

Eagle Wheel & Bending Works
This firm, owned by Philip Lebzelter, was established in 1856. They built and distributed all styles of wheels, shafts, rims, spokes, bows, poles and reaches. They also offered a variety of sleigh runners to makers throughout the country; Lancaster, PA, circa 1856–1910.

Eagle (see Sullivan and Eagle)

Ealies
H. Ealies, wagon maker; Hayton, Wisconsin, circa 1879.

Eames
Jacob Eames, blacksmith and wagon maker; Meridian, Idaho, circa 1905–1910.

Earl
James D. Earl manufactured wagons, and also advertised the Dearborn carriages for sale; St. Louis, Missouri, circa 1820–1830's.

Earl
J.I. Earl, carriage and wagon maker; Bunkerville, Nevada, circa 1884–1890's.

Easton & White
Wagon makers; Marysville, CA, circa 1853.

East Williston Cart Company
Owned by Lyman W. Valentine who patented the Hempstead cart. This vehicle was originally produced by Robert H. Nostrand; East Williston, NY, circa 1890's–1910.

Easy Wagon Gear Co.
Manufactured the Easy wagon gear used by wagon makers in the U.S. and Canada; 210 Jefferson Ave., Detroit, MI, circa 1880–1910.

Eaton
Cyrus Eaton, carriage and buggy maker, who moved from Massachusetts to Mifflinburg, PA, where he would specialize in iron work—mostly gears for vehicles. Eaton later worked with silver plating and vehicle trimming; Mifflinburg, PA., circa 1850–1860's.

Eaton & Gilbert
Orasmus Eaton and Uri Gilbert were early carriage and coach makers from Troy, New York. They started their business in the 1820's. By the 1850's, they boasted they had made more than 5,000 coaches for use in North America, and that they were the first to install a railing around the top of coaches to carry baggage, circa 1820–1860.

Eaton & Price
Although this company was engaged in other lines of work, they also constructed about twelve steam fire-engines over a three or four year period, beginning in 1875. The engines were all the same size (6,000 lbs.) and of a plain finish, allowing them to be sold at the remarkably low price of $1,800 each; Chicago, IL, circa 1875–1878.

Ebbert (see Hickman-Ebbert Co.)

Eberhard Mfg. Co.
Buggy manufacturer; Cincinnati, Ohio, circa 1880–1910.

Eberhard Manufacturing Co.
Carriage makers; Cleveland, OH, circa 1890–1910.

Eberhart
A. Eberhart & Co. of Mishawaka, Indiana, circa 1850–1867, manufactured farm and freight wagons.
They entered into a brief partnership with M.T. Graham (see M.T. Graham & Co).

Eberly & Orris Co.
Wagon wheels; Mechanicsburg, PA, circa 1890–1910.

Ebert
W. Ebert, blacksmith and wagon maker; Georgetown, CO, circa 1890.

Ebert
William H. Ebert, blacksmith and wheelwright; manufacturer of carriages, wagons, buggies and phaetons, 702 Willow; Houston, Texas, circa 1900–1910.

Eccles
Richard Eccles Co., manufactured couplings and carriage and sleigh hardware; Auburn, New York, circa 1880–1900.

Eckels
J. Edkels, wagon maker; Meehan, Wisconsin, circa 1879.

Eckenbach
Charles Eckenbach, wagon maker; Waterford, WI, circa 1865.

Eckenroth Brothers
Blacksmiths and wheelwrights; also manufacturer of carriages, buggies, phaetons and wagons, 212–214 Market; San Antonio, Texas, circa 1887–1900.

Eckert
George Eckert, blacksmith and wheelwright, se corner Ave. O and 42nd; Galveston, Texas, circa 1886–1887.

Eckhardt
Charles Eckhardt, carriage maker; Hilltown, Bucks County; Philadelphia, PA, circa 1880–1910.

Eckstein
C.G. Eckstein, wagon and blacksmith shop; Buena Vista, Colorado, circa 1880–1890.

Economist Plow Co.
This South Bend, Indiana firm produced farm implements, circa 1880–1900, including an early version of the Solid Comfort Sulky Plow. This plow was also being built by the Syracuse Chilled Plow Company in the early 1900's.

Economy Vehicle Co.
Buggy manufacturer; Cincinnati, Ohio, circa 1880–1910.

Eddington
E.E. Eddington, wagon maker; Janesville, Wisconsin, circa 1879.

Edelbrock
J.A. Edelbrock & Son, carriage painters and trimmers; also carriage, wagon, buggy and phaeton dealers, 1213–1215 Houston; Ft. Worth, Texas, circa 1900–1910.

Edgarton
Cicero Edgarton, sleigh and wagon maker; Pompey, NY, circa 1850's.

Edmond & Quinsler
Carriage and sleigh makers; Boston, Massachussets, circa 1880–1900.

Edmond (see Ettenger & Edmond)

Edmonds
J.W. Edmonds, wagon maker; Burlington, WI, circa 1865–1879.

Edwards & Williams
Wagon makers; Arena, Wisconsin, circa 1879.

Edwin
N. Edwin, maker of carriages, wagons and sleighs; Manlius, NY, circa 1850's.

Eeles
Harry Eeles, blacksmith, horseshoer and wheelwright, 1208 Elm, and 515 Main; Dallas, Texas, circa 1886–1905.

Eeles & Brothers
Blacksmiths and wagon makers, County seat of Conejos county (in 1883) 279 miles southwest of Denver, population 800; Conejos, Colorado, circa 1883–1890.

Eells & Co.
Rufus S. Eells, carriage maker; Sacramento, CA, circa 1853–1865.

Eells (see Haworth, Eells & Co.)

Egelhoff
John and J. Egelhoff, carriage and wagon makers, circa 1865–1879.

Eggert
Fred Eggert was a master woodcarver. He created carvings on the Ringling circus wagons and other horse-drawn vehicles while employed by the Milwaukee Ornamental Woodcarving Company, circa 1910–1930.

Ehing
John B. Ehing, carriage and wagon maker; Alma, Wisconsin, circa 1890–1910.

Ehlers
Herman H. Ehlers, wagon maker, Park Avenue, East 160th; New York, NY, circa 1899.

Ehlert
C. Ehlert, wagon maker; Marcy, Wisconsin, circa 1879.

Ehling
John B. Ehling, wagon maker; Alma, Wisconsin, circa 1879–1898.

Ehrenberg
Thomas Ehrenberg, carriage painters and trimmers, 326 S. El Paso; El Paso, TX, circa 1898–1908.

Ehrhardt
C. Ehrhardt, wagon maker; Centreville, Wisconsin, circa 1879.

Ehser
Henry A. Ehser, wagon maker, 537 West 40th; New York, NY, circa 1899.

Eibel
Gustavus Eibel, carriage and wagon maker, Albuquerque, New Mexico, circa 1884–1890's.

Eicke & Adams
Wagon makers, 476 Eleventh Avenue; New York, NY, circa 1899.

Eickelberg
H. Eickelberg, wagon maker; Horns Corners, WI, circa 1879.

Eilenberger (see Smith & Eilenberger)

Eilers
J.M. Eilers & Co., buggy manufacturer; Cincinnati, Ohio, circa 1880–1910.

Einspahr
C.F. Einspahr, blacksmith and wagon maker, 403–3rd; Laramie, Wyoming, circa 1902–1910.

Eitelman
Eitelman Bros., blacksmiths and wheelwrights, 713 Rusk; Ft. Worth, Texas, circa 1896–1906.

Eilers (see Ammon & Eilers Co.)

Eklund
A.P. Eklund, blacksmith and wheelwright, corner 5th and Pearl and 300 W. 14th; Austin, Texas, circa 1906–1913.

Eklund
C.P. Eklund, blacksmith and wheelwright; carriage and wagon maker, corner Lavaca and W. 14th; Austin, Texas, circa 1906–1918.

Eklund & Blomquist
Blacksmiths and wheelwrights, corner Lavaca and W. 14th; Austin, Texas, circa 1903–1909.

Eklund & Martin
Blacksmiths and wheelwrights, se corner W. 13th and Lavaca; and nw corner W. 14th and Lavaca; Austin, Texas, circa 1889–1901.

Elber
George Elber, carriage and wagon maker; Candelaria, Nevada, circa 1884–1890.

Eldred
E.D. Eldred, wagon maker; Minnesota Junction, WI, circa 1879.

Eldred
J.W. Eldred, blacksmith and wagon maker; Banner, Wyoming, circa 1902–1910.

Eldridge
M.F. Eldridge manufactured for wholesale to carriage and buggy builders, the Eldridge Automatic buggy top; Toledo, OH, circa 1880–1910.

Electric Wheel Co.
Their #38 catalog offered steel wheels for every style of vehicle—they also built Calkins farm wagons, Walton farm wagons, and freight and logging wagons; Quincy, Illinois, circa 1880–1920.

Elizabeth City Buggy Co.
John Quincy Adams Wood, was president of this plant which annually produced about 450 buggies, surreys, traps, buck boards, carts, etc. in peak years; Elizabeth City, N.C., circa 1890–1910.

Elizabeth Wagon Works
Wholesale wagon manufacturer, 392 Hudson; New York, NY, circa 1899.

Elkhart Carriage & Harness
Elkhart, IN, circa 1873–1920.

Ellenwood
Dura Ellenwood, carriage maker; Kirkland, NY, circa 1850's.

Elliott
B.C. Elliott, wagon maker; Ironton, Wisconsin, circa 1879.

Elliott
E. Elliott, blacksmith, 1722 Eddy street; Cheyenne, Wyoming, circa 1892–1893.

Elliott
W. Elliott & Co., blacksmith, carriage and wagon maker, 1812 Eddy Street; Cheyenne, Wyoming. Preceeded the Sever Severson Co., circa 1895–1908.

Elliott & Hynds
Blacksmiths, carriage and wagon makers, ne corner 18th and O'Neil; Cheyenne, WY, circa 1884–1896.

Ellis
Henry W. Ellis manufactured team and express wagons, carts and timber wheels. They also made hickory buggy spokes, shafts, bows, felloes and more, junction of Dyer, Orange & Clifford streets; Providence, Rhode Island, circa 1870's–1910.

Ellis
William Ellis & Sons, vehicle manufacturer; Amesbury, Mass., circa 1890–1910.

Ellis & Kenner
Blacksmiths and wheelwrights, 1015 Main; Houston, Texas, circa 1900–1907.

Ellison
Charles Ellison, carriage maker, patented the Mineola cart in 1885; Long Island, NY.

Ellwein
William Ellwein, wagon maker, 616 West 58th; New York, NY, circa 1899.

Elmer
William Elmer, wagon maker; Fair Water Village, WI, circa 1865.

El Paso Buggy Works
Hillard & Perry (proprietors), blacksmiths; carriage, wagon and buggy makers, 901 Texas, corner of Chihuahua; El Paso, Texas, circa 1910–1923.

El Paso Carriage & Auto Painting Co.
Carriage painters and trimmers, 301–303 S. Oregon; El Paso, Texas, circa 1905–1915.

El Paso Saddlery Co.
Carriage, wagon and buggy dealers, 402 El Paso; El Paso, Texas, circa 1898–1908.

El Paso Vehicle Works
Charles LeBaron, Mgr., blacksmith, carriage makers; carriage painters and trimmers; carriage, wagon and buggy dealers, 416 E. Overland, 600 Texas Street; also 700–706 Texas Street; El Paso, Texas, circa 1904–1918.

Emerson
C.J. Emerson, carriage and wagon maker; LaCrosse, Wisconsin, circa 1865.

Emerson
John W. Emerson, carriage maker; Porter, NY, circa 1850's.

Emerson Mfg. Co.
Carriages, wagons and buggies, J.M. Wendelken, manager, 193–193-1/2 Elm, also se corner N. Austin, Pacific Ave.; Dallas, Texas, circa 1897–1908.

Emerson-Brantingham Plow Co.
Carriage, wagons and buggies, se corner N Austin and Pacific Ave.; Dallas, Texas, circa 1910.

Emerson-Brantingham Co.
This Rockford, Illinois firm was established in 1852 as Emerson Manufacturing Co., building corn planters and other tillage implements in the mid-1800's. They also built the New Standard mower, as well as other mowing machines. They changed their name to Emerson-Brantingham Company in 1909. They also offered a line of wagons and buggies after the purchase of Newton Wagon Co. of Batavia, Illinois around 1911. Theybought out American Drill Works at Marion, Indiana in 1913, and the D. M. Osborne & Co. in 1919. They were later acquired by J.I. Case, in 1928.

Emerson & Fisher
Buggy manufacturer; Cincinnati, Ohio, circa 1880–1910.

Emery
Michael Emery was a carriage maker; Amesbury, MA., circa 1800–1820's.

Emigsville Wagon Co.
Built wagons, sleighs and bobsleds; York County, PA, circa 1880's–1910.

Empire Bending Works
Supplied bent woodwork, shafts, bows and rims to the carriage makers; Lancaster, PA., circa 1890–1910.

Empire Buggy Co.
Buggy manufacturer; Cincinnati, Ohio, circa 1880–1910.

Empire Buggy Co.
Jackson, Georgia, circa 1890–1910.

Empire Gear & Top Co.
Manufactured tops, gears and trimmings for the wagon and carriage industries; Buffalo, New York, circa 1890–1910.

Empire Manufacturing Co.
Wagon maker; Quincy, Illinois. They also offered farm implements, including the Empire Steel Frame disc harrow, at their Rock Falls, Illinois location, circa 1890–1920.

Engelhardt
V. Engelhardt, wagon maker; Schleisingerville, WI, circa 1879.

Engelke Harness Co.
Cincinnati, Ohio, circa 1880–1910.

Engelman
August Engelman, blacksmith and wagon maker; also built ore carts for gold mines; Hillsboro, New Mexico, 1906, Hillsboro County Seat of Sierra County (Est. 1877). To date (1906) the local mines have produced over $9,000,000 in Gold. Population 1,000, Altitude 5,400.

Enger Buggy Co.
George Enger, buggy manufacturer; Cincinnati, Ohio, circa 1870–1910.

England
Frank England, wagon maker; Patch Grove, WI, circa 1879–1903.

England
P. England, wagon maker; Cambridge, Wisconsin, circa 1879.

Engle
H.T. Engle, blacksmith and wagon maker, 420 Wazee; Denver, Colorado, circa 1880–1890's.

English & Kingsley
Manufactured wagons and sleighs; Comillus, NY, circa 1850's.

English & Mersick
Manufacturers of carriage and coach lamps, curtain fasteners and Landau hinges. They also imported English canopies; New Haven, CT, circa 1870's–1910.

Enoch (see Briggs & Enoch Manufacturing Co.)
Enright (see Lonsdale & Enright)
Enterprise Brass & Plating Co. Cincinnati, Ohio, circa 1880–1910.

Enterprise
Enterprise Carriage and Wagon Works; Morrisville, PA., manufactured everything from carriages to farm and hay wagons, circa 1880–1900.

Enterprise Carriage Co.
Blacksmiths and wheelwrights; carriage, buggy and wagon manufacturing, 1013 Houston; Ft. Worth, Texas circa 1896–1908.

Enterprise Carriage Mfg. Co.
In the late 1890's, Charles H. Albrecht, Cincinnati manufacturer of parts for buggies, shipping all over the U.S., was desirous of starting a buggy company in Miamisburg, Ohio.

William J. Kauffman, son of the founder of the Kauffman Buggy Co., was selected to join the company. It's new building was built on Pearl street, just east of the New York Central Railroad. William Kauffman was elected president of the new firm—called Enterprise Carriage Manufacturing Co.

About 1916, the demand for buggies decreased. There was some talk at that time of converting the business into the manufacture of autos—but the Enterprise investors were uninterested in the new venture.

Eplett
John Eplett, wagon maker; Edgerton, Wisconsin, circa 1865.

Erdman (see Sievers & Erdman)

Erickson
Frederick Erickson, blacksmith and wagon maker; Lund, Idaho, circa 1905–1910.

Erickson
Henry Erickson, blacksmith and wagon maker; Fort Bridger, Wyoming, circa 1902–1910.

Erickson
K. Erickson & Bro., wagon makers; Stoughton, WI, circa 1879.

Ericsson
John Ericsson—Although it is believed by some that Capt. John Ericsson built steam fire-engines, he did not. Ericsson did however, receive a gold medal in an 1840 contest from the Mechanics' Institute in New York city for the best design. Capt. John Ericsson, who was born in Sweden in 1803 and died in New York city on March 8, 1889, is probably best remembered for designing the iron war ship Monitor.

Ernisse
P. and M. Ernisse, wagon makers; Oostburg, Wisconsin, circa 1879.

Ernst
Dan Ernst, blacksmith and wagon maker; Georgetown, Colorado, circa 1880–1890.

Ervin
John Ervin, blacksmith and wheelwright, 2803 Nueces; Austin, Texas, circa 1910–1915.

Esch
John Esch (and Son-1885), wagon and carriage makers; Milwaukee, Wisconsin circa 1879–1898.

Eskridge (see Coleman, Eskridge & Rowley)

Espenschied
Louis and Henry Espenschied of 148 Broadway, St. Louis, Missouri were German natives who started out as blacksmiths in 1843. They soon expanded to wagon making and by the 1850's, their freight wagons were popular on all western trails.

The Union Army purchased large numbers of wheels and wagons from the Espenschied factory during the Civil war.

Louis died around 1887, but the Espenschied name continued to appear on St. Louis made wagons as late as the 1930's.

Espinosa
Esteban Espinosa, carriage painter and trimmer, 105 E. 2nd; El Paso, Texas, circa 1900–1912.

Esser
J. Esser, wagon maker; Springfield, Wisconsin, circa 1879.

Esser
P. Esser, wagon maker; Waunakee, Wisconsin, circa 1879.

Estes & Son
Blacksmiths and wagon makers; Boise, Idaho, circa 1905–1910.

Etnyre
E.D. Etnyre & Co. manufactured wagons of all types, including many commercial vehicles; Oregon, Illinois, circa 1890–1920.

Etscheid
Frederick Etscheid (and son by 1911), wagon makers; Reeseville, Wisconsin, circa 1879–1919.

Ettenger & Edmond
Using the designs of Alexander McCausland of Philadelphia, PA, this Richmond, VA firm produced five steam fire-engines, circa 1859–1877.

The first engine was built for Winans, Harrison & Winans of St. Petersburg, Russia. Three more were built for the city of Richmond, VA.

One of these engines was designed by H.P. Edmond. Their last steamer was built in 1877 for another Russian customer.

Eureka Carriage Co.
This firm advertised The Worlds Fair road wagon. They manufactured mostly road carts, road wagons, spring wagons, phaeton carts and delivery wagons; Rock Falls, Illinois, circa 1870–1910.

Eureka Carriage Co.
Buggy manufacturer; Cincinnati, Ohio, circa 1880–1910.

Eureka Carriage Shop
H.M. Bernard built carriages, wagons, and sulkies. They also did carriage painting, trimming, etc., corner of sixth and L streets; Sacramento, CA, circa 1855–1875.

Eureka Wagon Co.
Maker of wagons; Americus, Missouri, circa 1870–1900.

Evans
A.A. Evans, blacksmith and wagon maker; Boise, Idaho, circa 1905–1910.

Evans
A.C. Evans Manufacturing Co. built farm implements and the Buckeye Grain Drills. Evans joined with other companies in 1903 to establish The American Seeding Machine Co.; Springfield, IL, circa 1865–1929.

Evans
George Evans, wagon maker; Stoughton, WI, circa 1879–1903.

Evans
G.O. Evans, carriages, wagons and buggies; nw corner Elm and Houston; Dallas, Texas, circa 1906–1912.

Evans
H.J. Evans, blacksmith and wagon maker; Malad, Idaho, circa 1905–1910.

Evans Manufacturing Co.
Built wagons, sleds and sleighs; Hammond, NY, circa 1890–1910.

Evans & Ventress
Blacksmiths and wagon makers; Black Hawk, CO, circa 1883–1890.

Everett & Krepser
Blacksmiths and wheelwrights, 16th, between Ave. A and brick wharf; Galveston, Texas, circa 1900–1908.

Everett & McConough
Blacksmiths and wheelwrights, 17 N. 18th, Galveston, Texas, circa 1893–1900.

Everham & Colsher
Wagon makers; Philadelphia, PA, circa 1840's–1860.

Everidge
George W. Everidge, blacksmith and wheelwright, 102 N. Rusk; Ft. Worth, Texas, circa 1905–1906.

Exall
Henry Exall, proprietor, carriages, wagons and buggies, Lomo Alto farm office, 310 Ross Ave.; Dallas, Texas, circa 1900.

Excelsior Supply Co.
Cincinnati, Ohio, circa 1880–1910.

Faber (see Siefert & Faber)

Fager
Joseph Fager & Co., blacksmith and wagon maker, 163–164–15th; Denver, Colorado, circa 1877–1888.

Fager (see Bandhauer & Fager)

Fairbairn
D. Fairbairn, wagon maker in Rollinsville, Colorado, a mining settlement on South Boulder Creek in Gilpin County, 52 miles northwest of Denver, circa 1882–1889.

Falk
W. Falk, wagon maker; Burlington, Wisconsin, circa 1879.

Fallon & Armstrong
Buggy manufacturer; Cincinnati, Ohio, circa 1880–1910.

Falls City Buggy Co.
Louisville, Kentucky, circa 1890–1910.

Fancher
Alanson Fancher manufactured wagons and sleighs; Lysander, NY, circa 1850's.

Fancher
C.H. Fancher, wagon maker; Menasha, Wisconsin, circa 1879.

Farber
N. Farber, carriage and wagon makers; Columbus, Nevada, circa 1884–1890.

Farhardt
F. Pierce Farhardt, buggy maker, 361 Walnut Street; Mifflinburg, PA, circa 1882–1890.

Farkle
J.H. Farkle, blacksmith, wagon and carriage maker; Monument, Colorado, circa 1878–1879; and 15th and Wewatta; Denver, Colorado, circa 1880–1885.

Farley (see Herndon & Farley)

Farmer
E.H. Farmer, wagon maker, 315 J street; Sacramento, CA, circa 1855–1875.

Farmers Friend Manufacturing Co.
Built farm equipment; Dayton, Ohio, circa 1870–1905.

Farmers Handy Wagon Co.
This firm was known for the construction of many heavy farm wagons and horse-drawn trucks; Saginaw, Michigan, circa 1890–1915.

Farmers Manufacturing Co.
Built farm implements; Sebring, Ohio, circa 1890–1910.

Farquhar
A.B. Farquhar Co. Ltd. of York, PA, circa 1850's–1952, manufactured farm implements, including their Non-Wrap manure spreader (in the 1930's), and other implements for almost 100 years.

In 1952 they were acquired by the Oliver Corporation.

Farrar
G.W. Farrar & Sons, carriage and wagon makers; Peterboro, N.H., circa 1890–1910.

Farrell
William Farrell, carriage and wagon maker; Madison, WI, circa 1873–1879.

Farrell & McAfee
Blacksmiths and wheelwrights; Sherman, Texas, circa 1890–1900.

Farren
J.W. Farren, blacksmith and wagon maker, 121 Beale; San Francisco, California, circa 1882–1894.

Farrer
O.F. Farrer, wagon maker; Whitewater, WI, circa 1879.

Farrington & Tucker
Carriage makers; Sagauche, Colorado, circa 1882.

Farthing, Petree & Co.
George E. Farthing, blacksmiths and wagon makers, 8th, between J and K; Sacramento, CA, circa 1853–1865

Farver
R. Farver, wagon maker; Cazenovia, WI, circa 1879–1885.

Fashion Carriage Factory
Every description of carriages, wagons, buggies, etc. made to order—of the best material and workmanship. Repairs of all kinds executed with neatness and dispatch.

Albert Folsom, proprietor, 217 Ellis Street, between Mason and Taylor; San Francisco, California, circa 1880–1900.

Fassett & Kelly
Wagons and farm implements; carriage painters and trimmers; carriage, wagon and buggy dealers, 208 S. El Paso; El Paso, Texas, circa 1896–1906.

Favorite Carriage Co.
Buggy manufacturer; Cincinnati, Ohio, circa 1880–1910.

Fay
J.A. Fay & Company of Cincinnati, Ohio (W.H. Doane, President), built

carriage and wagon-making machinery; circa 1880–1900.

Fay Bros.
Carriage and wagon dealers; Amery, Wisconsin, circa 1890–1910.

Fecht
F.J. Fecht, wagon maker; Highland, WI, circa 1879.

Fedder
Jacob Fedder, coach and wagon maker; Pittsburgh and Allegheny, PA., circa 1840–1870.

Feese
Charles & R.F. Feese, buggy makers; Mifflinburg, PA, circa 1881.

Fehlauer
Louis Fehlauer, blacksmith and wheelwright; carriage painters and trimmers, 2322 Postoffice; Galveston, Texas, circa 1900–1908.

Feigelson
Alexander Feigelson, blacksmith and wheelwright; carriage and wagon makers, and repairer, 644 Crockett; 545 Crockett; Beaumont, Texas, circa 1904–1914.

Feisel
F.T. Feisel and Co., blacksmith and wagon maker, 1509 Mission, San Francisco, CA, circa 1882–1890.

Feize
John Feize, carriage and wagon maker; Bristol, NV, circa 1884–1890.

Felber & Misfeldt
Wagon makers; Chippewa Falls, Wisconsin, circa 1885–1919.

Felsmann (see Kaiser & Felsmann)

Felton
John L. Felton, blacksmith and wheelwright, 300 W. 29th; Austin, Texas, circa 1902–1911.

Fenske
A. Fenske, wagon maker; Berlin, Wisconsin, circa 1865.

Fenske (see Nichols & Fenske)

Ferguson Bros.
Wagon makers; Beloit, Wisconsin, circa 1885–1919.

Ferguson & Hobson
Carriage makers; South Pueblo, Colorado, circa 1880–1890.

Fernand Manufacturing Co.
Built carriage parts, including the Fernand Quick-Shift Shaft Coupling; North East, PA, circa 1890–1910.

Ferrel
A. Ferrel & Son, carriage lines, 562–564 Main; Dallas, Texas, circa 1910.

Ferrel & Bandel
Carriage and wagon makers, 562 Main; Dallas, TX, circa 1905–1912.

Ferris (see Grant-Ferris Co.)

Ferry
Orrin P. Ferry worked on his own as a carriage and wagon maker before going into partnership with Henry S. Gorton. Around 1867, they built a new carriage making building. This new firm employed about 6 full time workers; New Woodstock, NY, circa 1860–1890's.

Fessmer & Breal
Blacksmiths and wagon makers, 413 Third; San Francisco, California, circa 1882–1889.

Fest
Henry Fest, blacksmith and wheelwright; also carriage and wagon manufacturing, corner of Laredo and Cevallos; San Antonio, Texas, circa 1887–1898.

Fettes
George N. Fettes, blacksmith and wagon maker; Cody, Wyoming, circa 1902–1908.

Fick (see Boellert & Fick)

Fiedler
M. Fiedler, wagon maker; Golden Lake, WI, circa 1879.

Fielding Brothers
George, Robert & Charles Fielding of New York, NY.

George, the son of ship carpenter Jeremiah Fielding, opened his first shop at 206 Houston Street in 1843. By 1846 or 1847, he was joined by brother Charles, and listed as a coach maker—near 4th Avenue and 27th Street—quite close to the John Stephenson shop.

Another brother, Robert Jr., joined the firm in 1855—about the same time they moved their business to 130 East 41st Street.

The Fielding brothers built the first of many circus vehicles in 1856, a combination band and advertising wagon for Lee & Bennett's circus of San Francisco, CA.

They were officially established as Fielding Brothers in 1859, and now known for their outstanding quality and craftsmanship of carriages and wagons.

Over the next 20 some years, the Fieldings would build a variety of circus wagons, band wagons, band chariots, tableau-dens, and cages for all of the major shows.

In 1883, the firm was reorganized as Fielding and Schuchman, after the death of George Fielding in 1882. The Fieldings moved to Broadway and 35th Street in 1885 or 86—and discontinued business within a year, circa 1843–1886.

Fien
L. Fien, wagon maker, 529 East 134th; New York, NY, circa 1899.

Fieweger
Julius Fieweger (and Sons after 1885), wagon makers; Menasha, Wisconsin, circa 1879–1903.

Fife
William Fife, blacksmith and wagon maker; Lyman, Idaho, circa 1905–1910.

Fife & Gaston
Carriages, buggies and wagons, 158 Elm corner of Market; Dallas, Texas, circa 1890–1900.

Fife & Miller
Carriages, wagons and buggies, 156–158 Elm corner of

Market, 247–249 Elm; Dallas, Texas, circa 1895–1910.

Fife & Miller
Carriage, buggy, wagon and phaeton dealers, W. J. Tackaberry, Mgr., 312 Houston; Ft. Worth, Texas, circa 1900–1910.

Filer
S. Filer, carriage maker, 7th between K and L; Sacramento, CA, circa 1855–1875.

Fillre
Alexander Fillre, carriage maker; Newfone, NY, circa 1850's.

Filmore
W.H. Filmore, carriage and wagon maker; Cherry Creek, Nevada, circa 1884–1890.

Findlay Buggy Co.
Buggy manufacturer; Findlay, OH, circa 1890–1910.

Fink
Lawrence Fink, wagon and horse-drawn truck manufacturer, 256 W. Houston; New York, NY, circa 1899.

Finklea
G. Finklea, carriages, buggies and wagons, 125 Main; Dallas, Texas, circa 1891–1900.

Finley
Thomas R. Finley, truck and wagon manufacturer, 520 West 43rd; New York, NY, circa 1899.

Finn
C. Magnus Finn, blacksmith and wheelwright, 817 Willow; Houston, Texas, circa 1900–1908.

Finn
Charles J. Finn, Cincinnati, Ohio, started in business in 1910, making carriages, wagons, buggies and surreys, as the John Finn Sons Co.

Finn
John Finn Sons, buggy manufacturer; Cincinnati, Ohio, circa 1880–1910.

Finnesey & Kobler
A well known manufacturer of carriages and wagons, located at Brown and 27th street; Philadelphia, PA. Specialized in fine commercial delivery vehicles, circa 1880–1900.

Finn Wagon Works
Rosita, CO, circa 1875–1880.

Firebaugh
W.H. Firebaugh & Co., carriage and wagon woodwork, 211–213 E. 6th; Austin, Texas, circa 1887–1895.

Firestone Tire & Rubber
One of several national firms that made a major contribution to the horse and buggy era; Akron, Ohio, circa 1890–1910.

(See more on this company and many others, in Volume 2 of Wheels Across America).

Firmin, Billings & Noe
Manufactured wagons, plows and farm implements; Madison, WI, circa 1850–1880.

Fish
A.J. Fish, wagon maker; Oxford, WI, circa 1879.

Fish Bros. & Co.
Originally organized as Fish and Buhl in 1866. Seven years later the name was changed to Fish Bros. & Co. Probably the second largest wagon factory in Racine, Wisconsin, circa 1866–1912.

Fishburn (see Speyer & Fishburn)

Fisher
Ezra Fisher was an early maker who owned and operated a long standing wagon making and repair shop on Farnham street; Cazenovia, NY, circa 1830's–1870's.

Fisher
Henry Fisher, wagon maker; Decora Prairie, WI, circa 1879–1885.

Fisher
In 1866, Horace Fisher started as clerk for the Robinson Wagon Co. in Cincinnati, Ohio, advancing to bookkeeper and then secretary. In 1888, Fisher became superintendent of its successor, The Standard Wagon Co., where he served for 27 years.

He then established his own business, the Fisher Carriage Co., (1893), on Crestline Avenue in Cincinatti, and worked for twenty more years, circa 1866–1913.

Fischer
J. & M. Fischer, wagon makers; Pittsburgh and Allegheny, PA., circa 1854–1870.

Fisher
L. Fisher, wagon maker; Berlin, Wisconsin, circa 1865.

Fisher Bros.
Carriage and wagon dealers; Angelica, Wisconsin, circa 1890–1910.

Fisher Mfg. Co., Ltd.
This firm built a number of attractive vehicles, including carriages, wagons and their Russian Portland Sleigh, a four passenger bob-runner sleigh, fitted with Fisher's Improved Patent Bobs.

They manufactured over 1,500 sleighs in 1888 alone; Homer, New York, circa 1880–1900.

Fisher (see Emerson & Fisher)
Fisher (see McMurray & Fisher Sulky Co.)
Fisher (see Wingett & Fisher)
Fisk (see Hadley & Fisk)

Fite
Charles Fite, maker of fine carriages; Southhampton, NY, circa 1890–1910.

Fitler (see Barnwell & Fitler)
Fitz
Charles R. Fitz, carriage and wagon maker; Southampton, Long Island, NY., circa 1890–1910.

Fitzgerald & Lenahan
Wagon makers, 127 King, New York, NY, circa 1899.

Fitzgibbon Bros.
Wagon makers; Monroe, Wisconsin, circa 1885–1915.

Fitzpatrick
I.N. Fitzpatrick, blacksmith and wheelwright, 610 Main Ave.; San Antonio, Texas, circa 1895–1906.

Fitzpatrick & Bowdoin
Blacksmiths and wheelwrights; also carriage and wagon manufacturers, Fredericksburg road near Garza; San Antonio, TX, circa 1887–1898.

Flaglor & Co.
Carriage makers; Wilmington, Delaware, circa 1880–1910.

Flandrau
A.S. Flandrau & Co., carriage dealer, also offered a number of other vehicles, including a coupe-rockaway; New York, N.Y, circa 1860–1910.

Flannery (see Dagnon & Flannery)

Flannigan Buggy Co.
Greenville, North Carolina, circa 1890–1910.

Fleming
G.W. Fleming, carriage and wagon manufacturer and dealer; Rathdrum, Idaho, circa 1908.

Flickner
P. Flickner, wagon maker; Delton, WI, circa 1879.

Flint
The Flint Gear and Top Co.; Flint, Michigan, circa 1890–1910.

Flint Road Cart Company
Established in 1886; name changed in 1896. (See Durant Dort Carriage Co); Flint, Michigan, circa 1886–1895.

Flint (see Tayler & Flint)

Florance
W.A. Florance, blacksmith and wagon maker, 282 Cedar Springs Ave.; Dallas, Texas, circa 1910.

Florance & Lynch
Blacksmiths and horseshoers, 160 Orange; Dallas, Texas, circa 1905.

Florance (see Wakeham & Florance)

Florence Wagon Works
Wagon manufacturer; Florence, Alabama, circa 1890–1910.

Flum
B. Flum, wagon maker; Philadelphia, PA., circa 1840's–1860.

Flynn
James Flynn, wagon and carriage maker, 19th Ward, New York, NY, circa 1850.

Flynn & Doyle
This Bantam, Connecticut firm manufactured carriages and wagons, including a number of commercial vehicles, circa 1890–1910.

Fogarty
James Fogarty, blacksmith and wheelwright, 1918 Provdence; Houston, Texas, circa 1900–1908.

Foos Manufacturing Co.
Built the Foos Scientific Steel Corn Harvester, also offered a wood-frame style called the Buckeye; Springfield, Ohio, circa 1890–1905.

Forbes Sleigh Co.
This company specialized in coaches and sleighs, building over 10,000 sleighs between 1885 and 1900; Westboro, Massachussets, circa 1880–1900.

Ford
D. Ford and Co., carriage and wagon makers; Milwaukee, WI, circa 1879.

Ford
P. Ford, wagon maker; West Branch, Wisconsin, circa 1865.

Forman (see Reed & Forman)

Forrest
C.W. Forrest, house, sign and carriage painter; ornamental work a specialty, West Side Plaza, frontingthe Southern Pacific R.R.; El Paso, Texas, circa 1882–1890.

Fort Smith Wagon Company
Known for their quality wagons, this Fort Smith, Arkansas firm built from hardwoods like hickory and white oak.

The company, circa 1880–1911, was bought out by John Deere Co.

Fortune
Thomas L. Fortune of St. Louis, Missouri invented a steam powered wagon with wheels eight feet high and twelve inches wide.

The inventor had it shipped to Atchison, Kansas by steamboat for a 4th of July trial run.

Fortune left his dreams and steam wagon behind in Atchison after two failed runs. The first run ended in a crash with a building. The second run did reach a speed of eight miles per hour, however the heavy vehicle sunk in the soft ground after it stopped, circa 1860.

Fosdick
Levi Fosdick, wagon maker; Lamartine, Wisconsin, circa 1865.

Foss
John F. Foss, carriage and wagon maker; Beloit, WI, circa 1879–1903.

Foster Carriage Co.
Buggy manufacturer; Cincinnati, Ohio, circa 1880–1910.

Foster & Arnett
Carriages and wagons; Trinidad, Colorado, circa 1882–1890.

Foster (see Stearns & Foster Co.)

Foulke
Edward H. Foulke manufactured carriage bodies and gears for the trade, 927 Market St.; Philadelphia, PA, circa 1870–1900.

Fountain
Ed Fountain, blacksmith and wagon maker; Georgetown, Colorado, circa 1880.

Fouts & Hunter Buggy Co.
Fouts and Bros. took over the livery business from Wm. H. Steward in 1864. Two years later Colonel William R Hunter became a partner to A.B. Fouts by buying out the interest of his brother.

While Fouts and Hunter were operating the livery business at Terre Haute (buying and selling horses and mules), Colonel Hunter would buy carloads of buggies from a Cincinnati factory, bring them to

Terre Haute and sell them at public auction.

He would also string them together, haul them to other towns in the area and sell them at auction.

In 1893 their business was destroyed by fire. When they rebuilt, they abandoned the livery business and concentrated on the carriage and vehicle trade.

They handled all classes of vehicles, making a specialty of Storm Top buggies of their own patent. They also were making the celebrated Mikado wagons—the result of much investigation and experiments. They sold thousands of these wagons. Colonel Hunter died in 1895. Following Hunter's death, A.B. Fouts took over as president.

Colonel Hunter's son, William A. Hunter, who was in the liverey business, sold his interest in that line, in 1901, to give full attention to Fouts & Hunter Carriage Mfg. Co. Upon the death of Mr. A.B. Fouts, William A. Hunter took over as president until the factory dissolved in 1917.

Fowler
A.C. Fowler, wagon maker; North Andover, WI, circa 1879–1903.

Fowler
James Fowler, blacksmith and wagon maker; Largo, Idaho, circa 1905–1910.

Fowler
J.T. Fowler, wagon maker; Mindoro, WI, circa 1879.

Fowler & Klatt
Wagon makers; Golden, Colorado, circa 1875–1882.

Fowler & Taylor
Blacksmiths and wagon makers; Golden, Colorado, circa 1882–1890.

Fowler (see Remington & Fowler)

Fox (see Walmer & Fox)

Francis
Howard B. Francis, carriage and wagon makers' material, 213 Houston; Ft. Worth, Texas, circa 1902–1908.

Frank
Lawrence Frank, blacksmith and wheelwright, 164 E. Church, and 2114 Church; Galveston, Texas, circa 1886–1894.

Frank
Philip Frank, wagon maker, 13 James Slip; New York, NY, circa 1899.

Frank Brothers
Manufacturers, agents, dealers and importers of carriages, farm and freight wagons, farm implements and more. This California-based business did a huge retail, wholesale, direct mail and catalog business throughout the west, 319–321 Market street; San Francisco, CA, circa 1870–1905.

They also had a store at 68–70 Front street; Portland Oregon.

Franklin
Franklin Wheel Co., buggy wheel manufacturer; Franklin, Ohio, circa 1890–1910.

Franklin Buggy Co.
Manufactured buggies, surreys, phaetons and rockaways. This company did a large wholesale business and advertised for dealers and agents throughout the United States; Columbus, OH, circa 1880's–1910.

Franklin Buggy Co.
Operated by A.H.S. Franklin, Barnesville, GA, circa 1890–1910.

Franklin Buggy Co.
Franklin, VA, circa 1890–1910.

Franz
Adam Franz, blacksmith and wheelwright, 231 Dawson; San Antonio, Texas, circa 1897–1905.

Franz (see Krog & Franz)

Franzke (see Hansen & Franzke)

Fraser
Thomas Fraser, blacksmith and wheelwright, 421 W. Main; Denison, Texas, circa 1887–1898.

Fraser (see Harrison & Fraser)

Frazier
R.S. Frazier, light carriage maker, 29 West Avenue; Lockport, NY, circa 1899.

Frazier
W.S. Frazier & Co., maker of carriages and wagons; Aurora, Illinois, circa 1890–1910.

Freasach
Wm. Freasach, wagon maker, residence, 9th between K and L; Sacramento, CA, circa 1855–1875.

Freauf
J.S. Freauf, blacksmith and wagon maker; Market Lake, Idaho, circa 1905–1910.

Frederick
Alexander, David and Wesley Frederick, buggy makers and coach trimmers, 14 Norlth Fifth Street; Mifflinburg, PA, circa 1860–1918.

Fredonia Carriage & Gear Co.
Manufactured mostly parts like bolts, couplings and gears to the carriage trade; Fredonia, PA, circa 1880–1910.

Freeman
S. Freeman & Sons built farm implements; Racine, Wisconsin, circa 1840–1920's.

Freeman (see Jucket & Freeman)

Freeport Carriage Co.
This Freeport, Illinois carriage, wagon and buggy builder was bought out around 1900 by Moline Plow Co. of Moline, Illinois, circa 1880–1900.

Freese
B. Freese, wagon maker; New Holstein, WI, circa 1879.

Freiburger
George Freiburger (and Sons after 1903), wagon makers; New London, Wisconsin, circa 1898–1919.

Freiberger
L. Freiberger, carriage and wagon maker; Antigo, Wisconsin, circa 1890–1910.

French
Ferdinand F. French, born in Pittsfield, NH (1843), moved to Boston at the age of 20. He was hired by William P. Sargent (see listing on William P. Sargent & Co.) to work as a carriage salesman. In 1871, he became a partner with Mr. Sargent.

William P. Sargent retired in 1885 and Ferdinand F. French was asked to reorganize the firm. This he did, as Ferd. F. French & Co., Ltd. Mr. French was installed as general manager and a member of the board of directors.

In 1890, the firm advertised that over 60,000 vehicles had been sold, and the company supplied vehicles to most of the wealthy and affluent of New England. A catalog of the same year, featuring foreign imports, boasted the Ferd. F. French & Co., Ltd. firm as the American represenative of Million, Guiet Et Cie (Million, Geiet & Co.) of Paris, France. They also represented many other artistic builders of France and several coach making firms of England. They carried a full line of sleighs, including the latest in Russian sleighs.

By this time Ferdinand F. French & Co., Ltd. was operating at five large and scattered locations—one in Saco, Maine, one in Merrimacport, Mass. and three in Boston.

In December of 1893, Ferdinand F. French left the company, quite suddenly. The exact reason was never made public. Charles W. Bradstreet, the original partner of William P. Sargent, was recalled from retirement to take control.

It was also made known at the time, that millionaire Joshua Montgomery Sears, Jr. was the real owner of Ferd. F. French & Co., Ltd.

Joseph Vendelin Boinay, who started as a carriage salesman, became the manager at the age of 29, and then the owner in 1905, when Joshua Montgomery Sears, Jr. died.

The Ferd. F. French & Co., Ltd. continued to manufacture carriages on a limited scale until 1915, and then repairing carriages and reselling used vehicles until 1917.

This closed an era of carriage building, which had begun some 69 years earlier with the formation of Sargent, Gunnison & Co. in the river village of Amesbury, in 1848.

French Carriage Co. (The)
Ferdinand F. French founded a new carriage company, in Boston, approximately 5 months after his sudden and unexpected departure from the Ferdinand F. French & Co., Ltd., (see Ferdinand F. French & Co., Ltd. listing) in what was commonly thought to be a dispute of some sort with management. It was revealed by a publication called *The Hub, one of the major trade publications of the day,* that the owner had not been French, as commonly believed, but was actually the Boston millionaire Joshua Montgomery Sears, Jr, quite possibly the wealthiest landowner in Boston.

This new company, *The French Carriage Co.*, was incorporated in Boston, and listed Daniel Lane of the Boston tailoring firm of Lane & Rowell as president and William H. Mills of the Standard Stave & Cooperage Co. in Boston as treasurer. Lane, Mills and Ferdinand F. French were listed as the board of directors.

They rented a five-story brick building as their repository at Kingston and Summer streets. This building offered a total of 15,000 square feet of repository space in the heart of downtown Boston—at a very prestigious location.

They prospered from the beginning, acting as sales agent for the fine carriages and sleighs manufactured by Henry Hooker & Co. of New Haven, Connecticut. Their catalogs stated that in addition to regular local business, they did a considerable mail-order business for carriages and sleighs to many foreign countries.

As the automobile began to replace the carriage, business for the horse-drawn vehicles continued to decline. By 1910, Boston business directories and advertisements no longer listed The French Carriage Company. The company was dissolved by October of 1911.

Ferdinand F. French died in 1917 at his home in Winchester, Mass. His body was cremated and his ashes buried beneath a tombstone engraved with only one word, French.

His obituary stated only that he was founder and president of The French Carriage Co. It made no mention of his association with the company which bore his name, or William P. Sargent & Co. It seems whatever happened back in 1893 was of such a bitter nature, that it caused him to denounce any association with the Ferd. F. French & Co., Ltd.

French
The J. & F. French company manufactured carriages and sleighs: Keene, NH, circa 1880–1900.

French (see Sprague & French)

Freutel
William Freutel (Jr. after 1898), wagon makers, circa 1879–1919.

Fried (see Lelh & Fried)

Friedgen
Matheus Friedgen, wagon and truck manufacturer, 441 West 37th; New York, NY, circa 1899.

Frisby & Smith
S.L. Frisby, blacksmith and wheelwright, 493 Elm, Dallas, Texas, circa 1897–1901.

Fritts (see Knox & Fritts)

Fritz
Peter Fritz, blacksmith and wheelwright, Georgetown road; Austin, Texas, circa 1887–1893.

Froelich
A. Froelich, carriage and wagon maker; Oshkosh, WI, circa 1879.

Froelich
Echert V. Froelich, blacksmiths and horseshoers, nw corner of 2nd and Grand Ave.; Dallas, Texas, 1905–1908, also 797 Grand Ave.; Dallas, Texas, circa 1908–1912.

Froelich
Richard Froelich, blacksmith and wagon maker, 797 Grand Avenue; Dallas, Texas, circa 1910.

Frontier Supply Co.
Dealer in agricultural implements; Kemmerer, WY, circa 1900–1908.

Frost
A.L. Frost, blacksmith and wagon maker; Marion, ID, circa 1905–1910.

Frost
F.J. Frost, carriage and wagon dealer and representative; Almond, Wisconsin, circa 1890–1910.

Frost & Wood Mfg. Ltd.
Sold bobsleds and sleighs manufactured by wagon makers in the United States, circa 1890–1920. They also manufactured all types of harvesting equipment, including the Champion land roller—and they offered several styles of mowers, including their Giant Mower, in their 1910 catalog; Smith Falls, Ontario, Canada.

Frost & Wood also sold the Kangaroo Gang Plow, built in the U.S. by Cockshutt Farm Equipment, Ltd.

Fry
Jason A. Fry, carriage maker; Saguache, CO, circa 1882–1889.

Fry
W.J. Fry, blacksmith, wheelwright and horseshoer, 108 S. Chaparral; Corpus Christi, Texas, circa 1910–1920.

Fuller Buggy Co.
Carriage, buggy and wagon maker—also produced an extensive line of sleighs and cutters; Jackson, Michigan, circa 1890–1910.

Fuller & Johnson Manufacturing Co.
Manufactured the New Eclipse Riding Plow. They also offered the Starks Force Drop Steel Corn Planter invented by Nils O. Starks in the 1880's. The company sold out to Madison Plow Co. around 1911; Madison, WI, circa 1840–1911.

Fulton
William T. Fulton Co., carriages, wagons and buggies, 363 Commerce; Dallas, Texas, circa 1910.

Fulton and Walker
Well known manufacturer of horse drawn delivery trucks, drays, wagons, ambulances and circuswagons. They also patented the complete design of some styles of their delivery wagons; Philadelphia, PA., circa 1890–1910.

Fulton & Walker Wagon Co.
Manufacturer of wagons and trucks, 229 Thompson; New York, NY, circa 1899.

Furhman
Frederick A. Furhman, wagon maker; Calumetville, Wisconsin, circa 1885–1911.

Gabert
Meyer Gabert and brother were carriage painters and trimmers, 308 Throckmorton; Ft. Worth, Texas, circa 1900–1908.

Gabert Brothers
Carriage painters and trimmers, 308 Throckmorton; Ft. Worth, Texas, circa 1905–1918.

Gackenbach
C.W. Gackenbach, carriage maker; Allentown, PA, circa 1880–1910.

Gage
B.F. Gage, carriage and commercial vehicle maker—including a coach and open style stage; Fisherville, Concord, New Hampshire, circa 1840's–1860's.

Gainsford Carriage Co.
Buggy manufacturer; Cincinnati, Ohio, circa 1880–1910.

Galbraith
H. Galbraith was a silver plater and manufacturer of carriage trimmings, 81 State Street; New Haven, CT, circa 1850's–1890.

Galdea
W.W. Galdea, buggy manufacturer; Cincinnati, Ohio, circa 1880–1910.

Gale Manufacturing Co.
Built farm equipment and implements, including the Albion Bean Harvester, the Daisy Hay Rake, (first built by Albion Manufacturing Company), and a number of plows like their rod-beam plow and the Big Injun riding plow; Albion, Michigan, circa 1870–1900.

Galeher
D.R. Galeher, carriage and wagon maker; Milwaukee, WI, circa 1879.

Galion Buggy Co.
Buggy makers; Galion, Ohio, circa 1870's–1910.

Gall
Fred H. Gall, blacksmith and wagon maker; Georgetown, Colorado, circa 1880–1885.

Gallagher
Bernard Gallagher, wagon maker, 222 Mission; San Francisco, California, circa 1882–1885.

Galloway
Wm. Galloway Co. of Waterloo, Iowa, manufactured a wide range of farm wagons, spreaders and implements, circa 1900–1930.

Galt & Tracy
This Rock Falls, Illinois company built the Galt Rotary Planter. This company was renamed Keystone Manufacturing Co. in 1880, circa 1860–1880.

Gananoque Carriage Co.
Manufactured a variety of carriages and other vehicles, like their Gananoque Sleigh; Gananoque, Ontario, Canada, circa 1880–1890.

Gannon
John Gannon, blacksmith and wagon maker; McCammon, Idaho, circa 1905–1910.

Garay & Telles
Blacksmiths, 612 S. Stanton; El Paso, Texas, circa 1906–1912.

Garcia
Juan Garcia, blacksmith and wheelwright, 104 N. Pecos; San Antonio, Texas, 1897–1898; and 920 San Fernando; San Antonio, Texas, circa 1900–1908.

Gardener
E.B. Gardener, wagon maker; Hingham, WI, circa 1879.

Gardner
M.V. Gardner, blacksmith and wagon maker, 10th, between J and K; Sacramento, CA, circa 1853–1865.

Gardner
Russell E. Gardner; St. Louis, Missouri, circa 1890–1910.

Gardner & Co.
Bruce Gardner, blacksmith; Afton, Wyoming, circa 1905–1910.

Gardner & Oliver
Blacksmiths and wagon makers; Grangeville, Idaho, circa 1905–1910.

Garing (see Clemens & Garing)

Garlington & Co.
C.F. Garlington, carriage and wagon manufacturer, 194–196 Commerce; Dallas, Texas, circa 1900–1910.

Garlington & Rodgers
Carriages, wagons and buggies, 198–200 Commerce; Dallas, Texas, circa 1900.

Garner (see Lane & Garner)

Garnich
Emil Garnich, wagon dealer and representative; Ashland, Wisconsin, circa 1890–1910.

Garrett
Robert N. Garrett, blacksmith and wagon maker; Garrett, Wyoming, circa 1902–1908.

Gaston Carriage Co.
Henry Gaston Carriage Co., carriages, wagons and buggies, 349–351 Elm; Dallas, Texas, circa 1910.

Gaston (see Fife & Gaston)

Gates Carriage Co.
Carriage and buggy builder; Bridgeport, Connecticut, circa 1890–1910.

Gault
Walter C. Gault, blacksmith and wheelwright, 609 San Felipe; Houston, Texas, circa 1900–1901.

Gausmann
William Gausmann Buggy Co., buggy manufacturer; Cincinnati, Ohio, circa 1880–1910.

Geary
George S. Geary, blacksmith and wagon maker; Silverton, Colorado, circa 1878–1885.

Gee
H.B. Gee, carriage and wagon maker; Canfield, Colorado, circa 1884–1890.

Geier
C. Geier, wagon maker; Grafton, Wisconsin, circa 1865.

Gembler
Louis J. Gembler, blacksmith and wheelwright; also carriage and wagon manufacturer, 431 W. Houston; San Antonio, Texas, circa 1887–1902.

George
J. George, wagon maker; Port Washington, Wisconsin, circa 1879.

George
William George, blacksmith and wagon maker, 3rd and Garfield and 211 Thornburg; Laramie, Wyoming, circa 1901–1910.

George (see Cook & George)

Gephart
George Gephart, wagon maker; Hayton, Wisconsin, circa 1885–1919.

Gerdle
Herman Gerdle, blacksmith and wagon maker; Big Horn, Wyoming, circa 1902–1908.

Gerhard Hardware Co
Carriage, wagon and buggy dealers, 410 Congress Ave., Tel. 32; Austin, Texas, circa 1893–1906.

Gerlach
S.F. Gerlach, blacksmith, wheelwright and wagon maker, 108–110 Main and 171 Lancaster Ave., se corner of 9th; Dallas, Texas, circa 1897–1910.

Gerleit & Grutzleman
Wagon makers, 176 East 119th; New York, NY, circa 1899.

Gerleit Bros & Ruschmann
Manufactured wagons, 304 West 143rd; New York, NY, circa 1899.

Gersdorf
Charles Gersdorf, blacksmith and wheelwright, 313 Chavez; San Antonio, Texas, circa 1897–1898; and corner of Zavala and Pecos; San Antonio, Texas, circa 1900–1906.

Gerstenslager Co.
Wooster, Ohio, circa 1890–1910.

Gerwin
C. Gerwin, wagon maker; Woodland, WI, circa 1879.

Getchell
Carriage factory; New London, Connecticut, circa 1890–1910.

Getts
G.W. Getts (and Son after 1885), wagon makers; Oregon, Wisconsin, circa 1879–1903.

Giambo (see Barbour & Giambo)

Gibbs
G.W. Gibbs & Co., carriage and wagon materials, 33–39 Fremont; San Francisco, California, circa 1888–1894.

Gibbs (see Bucher & Gibbs Plow Co.)

Gibson
C.W. Gibson, carriage maker; Saguache, Colorado, circa 1882–1887.

Gidcumb
Boston Gidcumb of 238–240 Commerce; Dallas, Texas was an agent and dealer in harness, buggies and wagons, circa 1890–1920.

In a few of their advertisements, the Gidcumb Company listed wagons manufactured by Luedinghaus-Espenschied Wagon Company of St. Louis, Missouri.

Gidcumb (see Clark & Gidcumb)

Giese
Charles Giese, carriage and wagon maker, 516 E. Douglas Ave.; Las Vegas, New Mexico, circa 1915.

Giese
Gustavus Giese, wagon maker; Menomonie, Wisconsin, circa 1885–1911.

Gies & Ladendorf
Wagon makers; Muscoda, Wisconsin, circa 1865.

Gifford
G.L Gifford, blacksmith and wheelwright, S. Flores and Mitchell; San Antonio, Texas, circa 1900–1907.

Gilbert
Carriage makers; Keelerville, Bucks County, PA, circa 1880–1910.

Gilbert
T.H. Gilbert, blacksmith and wagon maker, Pine Street; Leadville, Colorado, circa 1879–1890.

Giles
J.F. Giles, carriages, wagons and buggies, 249 Elm; Dallas, Texas, circa 1897–1905.

Gilg
J. Gilg, carriage and wagon maker, Milwaukee, WI, circa 1879.

Gill & Tatum
Blacksmiths and wheelwrights, 1325 W. Commerce; San Antonio, Texas, circa 1900–1910.

Gillespie
Charles H. Gillespie, successor to Parker & Gillespie, manufactured fine coach and carriage varnishes and paint, 554,556 W. 25th Street; New York, NY, circa 1870–1900.

Gilliland, Jackson & Co.
Manufactured a variety of farm implements, including an 1886 patented hay rake; Monroe City, Missouri, circa 1880–1900.

Gillingham & Sons
Wagon and carriage makers; Oshkosh, Wisconsin, circa 1885–1919.

Gimon (see Bazzlay & Gimon)

Gipson
G.W. Gipson, blacksmiths and horseshoers, 218 N. College Ave.; Dallas, Texas, circa 1908–1912.

Girton
Joseph Girton, builder of carriages, sulkeys and sleighs, also offered repair, paint and trim work. Girton advertised he would accept cash or country produce for his work; Lewisburg, PA., circa 1850–1870.

Glass (see Prouty & Glass Carriage Co.)

Gleeson
M.T. Gleeson was established in 1870. This firm manufactured first class coach, carriage and hearse lamps. They also offered a full line of coach and carriage mountings at wholesale and retail; 228–236 N. Fourth Street, Columbus, Ohio, circa 1870–1910.

Glenn & Ashford
Blacksmiths and horseshoers, 185 Caroline; Dallas, Texas, circa 1906–1912.

Glen Wagon Co.
Manufactured many styles of wagons and implements, including the Johnson Star manure spreader. The Glen firm used agents and jobbing houses throughout the midwest to market their products; Seneca Falls, NY., circa 1900–1920.

Glenwood Manufacturing Co.
This company built parts for carriage and sleigh makers, including hubs, spokes, bent and sawed fellows—also sleigh stock and harwood lumber; Glenwood, Wisconsin, circa 1880–1910.

Glessner (see Warder, Bushnell & Glessner)

Glick
A. Glick & Bros., wagon makers; Terre Haute, Indiana, circa 1858.

Glidden & Joy Varnish Company
This Cleveland, Ohio firm offered a full line of carriage and wagon paints and varnishes throughout the country, with branches in Boston, Chicago, Kansas City, Baltimore and St. Louis, circa 1850–1910.

Gline
J.C. Gline, wagon maker; Appleton, Wisconsin, circa 1865.

Globe Carriage Co.
Buggy manufacturer; Cincinnati, Ohio, circa 1880–1910.

Globe Plow Works
Successor's to the Davenport Plow Company, Globe offered a number of farm implements, like their Hercules Tricycle Sulky Plow; Davenport, Iowa, circa 1880–1910.

Gloeckner
F.M. Gloeckner, blacksmith and wheelwright; also carriage and wagon manufacturer, 217 Soledad, and 301 Soledad; San Antonio, Texas, circa 1887–1902.

Goad
W.E. Goad, blacksmith and wagon maker, 503 Elm; Dallas, Texas, circa 1910.

Goebel
M. Goebel, wagon maker; Elm Grove, WI, circa 1879.

Goetsch
August Goetsch (and Son after 1915), wagon makers; Franklin, Wisconsin, circa 1885–1915.

Goff
A.M. Goff, carriage and wagon maker; Marysville, CA, circa 1855–1875.

Goldammer
William C. Goldammer, wagon maker; Adell, WI, circa 1885–1919.

Golden
Lee J. Golden Carriage Co., manufacturer of buggies, phaetons, surries, spindle and spring wagons. First shop was on Liberty Street, later relocated to Water Street Harrisonburg, Virginia, circa 1890–1905.

Goldman
G.H. Goldman, carriage and wagon dealer and representative; Annaton, Wisconsin, circa 1890–1910.

Gombert
Lewis Gombert, wagon maker; LaSalle, NY, circa 1899.

Gonzales
Juan N. Gonzales, blacksmith and wheelwright, 1101 S. Laredo; San Antonio, TX, circa 1900–1908.

Goodrich
F.D. Goodrich and Co., wagon makers; Delavan, WI, circa 1879.

Goodrich
J.F. Goodrich & Co. manufactured a variety of buggies; including their number 7 triple surrey and number 4 buckboard, seating four persons back to back; New Haven, Conn., circa 1880–1910.

Goodrich
J.H. Goodrich, wagon maker, 110 Oregon, San Francisco, California, circa 1880–1890.

Goodrich
W.F. Goodrich, wagon maker; Emerald Grove, WI, circa 1879.

Goodyear Rubber
One of several national firms that made a major contribution to the horse and buggy era; Akron, Ohio, circa 1890–1910.

(See more on this company and many others, in Volume 2 of Wheels Across America).

Goold
James Goold & Co., circa 1804–1913, early manufacturer of carriages and sleighs.

Goold's career began in 1804 as an apprentice to coach makers William Clark and Jason Clapp.

Goold established his own shop in 1813. Over the next 100 years they built a wide variety of vehicles, including a swelled-body sleigh known as Albany cutters.

James Goold died at the age of 90, in 1879. His son and grandsons would continue the business until 1913; Albany, NY.

Gorham
M. Gorham, blacksmith and wagon maker, west 17th & Thomes; Cheyenne, WY, circa 1902–1908.

Gorman
J.B. Gorman, carriage painter, 1317 Market; San Francisco, California, circa 1888–1894.

Gorman
J.J. Gorman, carriage and wagon maker, 20th and Holladay, and 433 Blake; Denver, Colorado, circa 1878–1890.

Gorton
Henry S. Gorton was a long time carriage and wagon maker, who also joined in a partnership with carriage maker Orin P. Ferry in 1867; Cazenovia, NY, circa 1860–1890's.

Gosling
John W. Gosling Carriage Co., buggy manufacturer; Cincinnati, Ohio, circa 1880–1910.

Goss
J.C. Goss, wagon making and repairing; La Veta, CO, circa 1880.

Gotlieb (see Kock & Gotlieb)

Gottschalk
A.W. Gottschalk, buggy manufacturer; Cincinnati, Ohio, circa 1880–1910.

Gottsleben
Jacob Gottsleben manufactured light carriages, 31 Sullivan; New York, NY, circa 1899.

Gould
M.S. Gould, wagon maker; Emerald Grove, Wisconsin, circa 1865.

Gould
R.J. Gould started building steam fire-engines in Newark, NJ, circa 1865–1879. They offered five sizes, all designed by John "pop" Dennisson, an engine builder who was in business in Newark, NJ and Reading, PA. Gould constructed steamers for fire companies as far away as Mobile Alabama before selling his business, in 1875, to B.S. Nichols & Co. of Burlington, VT.

Mr. Nichols continued to build the same style engines, using the Gould patents and tools for three more years, giving up steam fire-engine building in 1879.

Gould
This Lake Grove, NY carriage and wagon maker built personal and commercial vehicles—including an Omnibus used to transport passengers at the Stony Brook, New York railroad station, circa 1890–1920.

Goulds, Austin & Caldwell Co.
Builders of commercial horse-drawn vehicles, including their line of road grading machinery. They advertised the Austin Steel Road Machines and other earth moving equipment.

This company was later known only as Austin Mfg. Co.; Chicago, Illinois, circa 1880–1915.

Goundrey Wagon Company, Ltd.
Makers of The Glen City Cart, advertised in the March 1891 *Carriage Monthly* trade journal as the finest finished and easiest riding cart on earth.

Goundrey also built fine road wagons, buggies and platform spring wagons; Watkins, NY, circa 1880–1910.

Gower (see Bagwell & Gower)

Grady
Michael Grady, wagon maker; Cazenovia, NY, circa 1855.

Graham
Minor T. Graham & Co., wagon factory, established around 1860 in Westport, Missouri. Graham started in the wagon business around 1858,

in partnership with A. Eberhart & Co. of Mishawaka, Indiana. This union was dissolved by March 1859.

The Graham wagon works incorporated all the various departments under one system: wheelwright, machine shop, lathe room, painting room and trim shop. In addition to the manufacture of wagons—they also built plows and other farm implements; St. Louis, Missouri, circa 1860–1870's.

Graham
Peter Graham, blacksmith and wagon maker; Black Hawk, Colorado, circa 1879–1890.

Graham
R. Graham, wagon maker; Mifflin, WI, circa 1879.

Graham
Robert Graham, wagon maker; Livingston, WI, circa 1885–1915.

Graham (see Baker & Graham)

Gramse (see Davis & Gramse)

Grand Avenue Carriage Factory
John S. Klapperich & Son, carriage and wagon makers, all kinds of repairing promptly attended to, No. 3 Grand Avenue; San Francisco, California, circa 1880–1890.

Grand Detour Plow Co.
This company was originally founded in 1837 by Major Andrus and John Deere, in the little town of Grand Detour, Illinois.

The partners soon went their separate ways, and the firm moved to Dixon, Illinois, in 1869.

Incorporated in 1879 as Grand Detour Plow Company, they would grow to offer dozens of styles, sizes and options on their popular implements. The Little Yankee sulky plow is just one of manuy designs they offered, before they were bought out in 1919, by J.I. Case Co.; Dixon, Illinois, circa 1837–1919.

Grandjean
S. Grandjean, wagon maker, I street, between 9th and 10th; Sacramento, CA, circa 1855–1875.

Grand Rapids Manufacturing & Implement Company
Built farm implements, including the Peare's Patent Orchard Gang Plow, a special designed gang plow for vineyards and orchards; Grand Rapids, MI, circa 1880's–1900.

Granger
J.W. Granger, wagon maker; Loveland, Colorado, circa 1884.

Granger (see Polk & Granger)

Grant-Ferris Co.
Manufactured farm implements; Troy NY, circa 1890–1900.

Grant (see Bull & Grant)

Granville
Joseph Granville, carriage painter, 25 Seventh; San Francisco, California, circa 1888–1900.

Graves
Blacksmith and wagon maker; Arvada, Colorado, circa 1880–1890.

Graves
L.C. Graves & Co. built carriages, sleighs and cutters; Springboro, PA., circa 1890–1910.

Gray
Samuel Gray, wheelwright; Saguache, Colorado, circa 1882.

Gray & Sons
William Gray Sr. emigrated from Roxborough, Scotland to Canada in 1853. Two years later, this blacksmith founded William Gray & Sons, circa 1855–1916, and began operations—building carriages and sleighs.

Eventually, this firm's factory and showrooms were housed in a huge three-story building. In their sixty-one years of operation, the production of buggies, carriages, sleighs and cutters numbered 283,456 units before switching their operation to the production of the automobile in 1916.

William Gray Sr. won many awards for his carriage designs. On a trip to Montreal in 1884, Mr. Gray was killed when he fell from a train. His sons, Robert—age 23—and younger brother James took over and ran the company.

Gray
William H. Gray of 27 Wooster, New York, NY, manufactured coaches, carriages, hearses, light and heavy wagons made to order. They also offered second-hand vehicles, circa 1850's–1870's.

Gray (see Atkinson & Gray)

Grede
George Grede and Bro., carriage and wagon makers; Milwaukee, Wisconsin, circa 1885–1919.

Green
Henry Green, blacksmith and wheelwright, 503 Preston Ave., Houston, Texas, circa 1900–1910.

Green
R.G. Green, wagon maker, 150 East 129th; New York, NY, circa 1899.

Green (see Printz & Green)

Green Bay Carriage & Wagon Co.
Carriage and wagon makers; Green Bay, WI, circa 1885–1915.

Greeninger
Adolph Greeninger, manufacturer and dealer of buggies, phaetons, carriages, driving carts, wagons; and repairing, 28–32 San Fernando Street; San Jose, California, circa 1888–1895.

Greeno
C.L. Greeno Co., buggy manufacturer; Cincinnati, Ohio, circa 1880–1910.

Greenwald (see Zwick, Greenwald & Co., Ltd.)

Greer
A.B. Greer, a builder of carriages, coaches and commercial vehicles, including a line of hearses; London, Ontario, Canada, circa 1890–1910.

Greer
Nat Greer, blacksmith; wagon and carriage maker; carriage painter and trimmer; carriage, wagon and buggy dealer, 110–114 W. Overland; El Paso, Texas, circa 1904–1914.

Greer
Simon Greer, blacksmith and wheelwright, east end of Howard; Houston, Texas, circa 1887–1888 and 708 Andrews; Houston, Texas, circa 1900–1910.

Gregg
Amos A. Gregg, carriage makers; Bustleton, 23rd ward; Philadelphia, PA, circa 1880–1910.

Gregg
Hamilton Gregg, blacksmith and wheelwright, 500 E. 13th; Austin, Texas, circa 1906–1912.

Gregg Carriage Co.
Makers of carriages and wagons, including their Kentucky Breaking Cart; Philadelphia, PA, circa 1880–1910.

Gregg & Hughes
Blacksmiths and wheelwrights, corner E. 6th and San Jacinto; Austin, Texas, circa 1885–1895.

Greif
E.M. Greif Carriage Co., buggy manufacturer; Cincinnati, Ohio, circa 1880–1910.

Grewell (see Richardson & Grewell)

Griffin
George S. Griffin, blacksmith and wheelwright; manufacturer of wagons, buggies, carriages and phaetons, 511 Colorado; also at 205 W. 5th; Austin, Texas, circa 1900–1918.

Griffin Buggy Co.
Griffin, GA, circa 1890–1910.

Griffin & Kirby
Blacksmiths and wheelwrights; carriage and wagon manufacturers, 511–513 Colorado; Austin, Texas, circa 1897–1913.

Griffis
Daniel F. Griffis, blacksmith and wagon maker, 167 K; Sacramento, CA, circa 1853–1865.

Griffis (see Hutchinson & Griffis)

Griffith
E.E. Griffith, blacksmith and wagon maker; Slack, Wyoming, circa 1901–1902.

Grim
F. Grim, carriage and wagon maker; Milwaukee, WI, circa 1865.

Grimm & Mallory
Blacksmiths and wagon makers; Lewiston, Idaho, circa 1905–1910.

Grimmer
Alfred W. Grimmer, wagon maker; Shawano, WI, circa 1865.

Grimmett (see Adams & Grimmett)

Griswold
G. Griswold & Co., blacksmiths and wagon makers, 7th, between J and K; Sacramento, CA, circa 1853–1865.

Grizzle (see Monschke & Grizzle)

Grohman
Martin Grohman, carriage and wagon maker; Athens, Wisconsin, circa 1890–1910.

Groo
H.H. Groo, blacksmith and wagon maker; Opal, Wyoming, circa 1901–1902.

Gropp
Gottfried A. Gropp, (possibly Grupp in 1885 and Graupp in 1901), wagon maker; Dousman, Wisconsin, circa 1865–1901.

Groton Carriage Co.
Manufactured road carts, buggies, carriages, cutters and sleighs. They built over 3,500 sleighs in the 1888–1889 seasons; Groton, NY, circa 1880–1910.

Gruber Wagon Works
Franklin H. Gruber (1835–1898) was the founder and proprietor of Gruber Wagon Works. He started out as a wheelwright and blacksmith apprentice under the guidence of his cousin John Henry at Henry's shop in Robesonia, Heidelberg Township, Pennsylvania.

Franklin was employed in the 1860's at his brother Isaac's buggy and spring wagon works in Mount Pleasant. He had another brother in Mount Pleasant, Erasmus, who operated a plow factory.

He eventually bought a farm, but continued to repair wagons and farm implements in his barn. In the early 1870's, Franklin built his first shop, across the road from the farm barn.

He added a two-story addition to accommodate requests for wagon and wheel repairs. Business continued to grow and in 1882, Franklin erected the Gruber Wagon Works just south of Pleasant Valley. The Gruber Wagon Works manufactured farm wagons, hayflats, wheel barrows, and specialty wagons designed to the customer's specifications.

Franklin H. Gruber had five sons, four of them joining him in the business and would assume control upon his death in 1898. His youngest son, Levi Franklin, became a Lutheran minister, served in Minneapolis, MN., and was later appointed President of the Lutheran Theological Seminary in Maywood, Illinois.

John W. (1860–1934) became a woodworker, and manager of the business following his father's death.

He selected the wood that would be cut and sawed for eventual use.

Adam (1864–1903) was the head of the paint department. He painted hundreds of Gruber wagons.

Jacob H. (1865–1944) became the master wheelwright. Records he kept indicate that he produced an average of 112 sets of four wheels per year. He also had a skill for watch and clock repairing, which he did at his home in the evenings.

George P. (1867–1941) performed the blacksmith duties. He "ironed" the wagons, made hand tools, and later made truck bodies.

In 1903, Adam was killed in a runaway horse accident. After that, John, George and Jacob took over the ownership and operation of the business, until their retirement in 1935. At that time, management of the business was transferred to John's son, Franklin P. Gruber.

Frank continued to operate the wagon works on a smaller scale, for repairs and specialty ordered wagons. In 1956, the final wagon built at the Gruber Wagon Works passed through its doors.

Frank Gruber finally closed the wagon works in 1972.

Grutzleman (see Gerleit & Grutzleman)

Gubchintzky
J. Gubchintzky, wagon maker; Kossuth, WI, circa 1879.

Guelph Carriage Top Co.
This Guelph, Ontario, Canada firm supplied carriage tops and related items to carriage builders throughout Canada and the United States, circa 1880–1900.

They also used a number of U.S. parts like Cately's patented Prop Springs from Cately & Ettling of Cortland, NY.

Guenther
A. Guenther, carriage and wagon maker; Milwaukee, WI, circa 1865.

Guerrero
I. Guerrero, Wyoming and New Braunfels Ave.; San Antonio, Texas, circa 1900–1910.

Guie
J.M. Guie, carriage maker, Newfone, NY, circa 1850's.

Guiles
O. Guiles, carriage maker; Silver Cliff, CO, circa 1880–1890.

Guilfoyle
Keran J. Guilfoyle manufactured light carriages, 233 West 50th; New York, NY, circa 1899.

Gulyas
Dan Gulyas, blacksmith and wagon maker; Horton, Wyoming, circa 1905–1910.

Gunderson
P. Gunderson, wagon maker; North Cape, WI, circa 1879.

Gunderson (see Olson & Gunderson)

Gundrum
John Gundrum, carriage and wagon dealer and representative; Addison, WI, circa 1890–1910.

Gunnison
C.E. Gunnison & Co. manufactured fine light carriages, like the Goddard buggies and the Stanhope Buggies; Merrimac, MA, circa 1870–1900.

Gunther & Braeuer
Wagon makers; Fond du Lac, Wisconsin, circa 1865.

Gurney
J.T. Gurney; patented and built the Gurney Cab; Boston, MA, circa 1870–1890.

Gurney
Wilson Gurney, carriage maker; Lee, NY, circa 1850's.

Gutelius
Daniel Gutelius, buggy maker, 603 Market Street; Mifflinburg, PA, circa 1880–1891.

Gutelius
Edwin Gutelius, buggy maker; Mifflinburg, PA, circa 1881.

Gutelius
H.A. Gutelius, buggy maker, fork of third and fourth streets (now the Woodlawn Cemetery), Mifflinburg, PA, circa 1900.

Gutelius
H.E. Gutelius, buggy maker; Mifflinburg, PA, circa 1870's–1880's.

Gutelius
J.T. Gutelius, buggy maker; Mifflinburg, PA, circa 1881.

Gutelius
Jacob Gutelius, buggy maker, south third and north side of Market streets; Mifflinburg, PA, circa 1855–1897.

Gutelius
John Gutelius & Sons (Charles, David F., Herbert L., John Wesley, and Joseph K.), buggy makers, circa 1876–1905, and later, Sarah Jane (daughter), circa 1905–1920, 527 Market Street; Mifflinburg, PA.

Gutelius
Thomas Gutelius, buggy maker, 358 Walnut Street; Mifflinburg, PA, circa 1855–1888.

Guthrie
Nehemiah Guthrie, blacksmith and wagon maker, 681 S Ervay; Dallas, Texas, circa 1910.

Guttroff
George Guttroff, wagon maker, 1233 Second Avenue; New York, NY, circa 1899.

Haas
A. Haas, blacksmith and wagon maker; McCammon, Idaho, circa 1905–1910.

Haas
Herman Haas, carriage and wagon dealers; Cheyenne, Wyoming, circa 1884–1890's.

Haas
H. Thomes Haas, blacksmith, carriage and wagon maker, sw corner 18th; Cheyenne, Wyoming, circa 1895–1896.

Haas (see McLean & Haas)
Haase (see McCall & Haase)
Haberer & Co.
Buggy manufacturer; Cincinnati, Ohio, circa 1880–1910.

Habhegers (see Haegers and Habhegers)
Habhegger
Theodore Habhegger, carriage and wagon maker; Milwaukee, WI, circa 1879–1911.

Hackman
Frederick Hackman, wagon maker; St. Louis, Missouri, circa 1850–1870.

Hackman (see Sherk & Hackman)

Hackney Wagon Co.
Wilson, N.C., circa 1890–1918.

Haddock
T.T. Haddock Carriage Co.; Cincinnati, Ohio, circa 1880–1903.

Hadley
Alfred Hadley, wagon maker; Glenbeulah, Wisconsin, circa 1865.

Hadley & Fisk
Carriage and wagon makers; Denver, Colorado, 1884–1890.

Hadley (see Taylor & Hadley)

Haegers and Habhegers
Wagon and carriage makers; Milwaukee, Wisconsin, circa 1865.

Haertt
T. Haertt, wagon maker; Mayville, Wisconsin, circa 1865.

Haffner
Frank Haffner, buggy manufacturer; Cincinnati, Ohio, circa 1880–1910.

Hagan
F. Hagan, blacksmith and wagon maker, 433 Blake; Denver, Colorado, circa 1880–1890.

Hageli
C. Hageli, wagon maker; New Glarus, Wisconsin, circa 1865.

Hagerstown Spoke & Beading Co.
Manufactured wheels, spokes, rims and hubs for carriages and wagons; Hagerstown, MD, circa 1870–1900.

Hahn
Francis Hahn built a variety of wagons in his shop, located south of Westport, including a Santa Fe Trail wagon, similar to the Conestoga-type wagon; Westport, Missouri, circa 1830–1860.

Haible & Butler
Carriage and sleigh manufacturer; Schenectady, NY, circa 1880's–1900.

Hairston
J.T.W. Hairston, carriages, buggies and wagons, W.M. Lea, trustee, 114 W. 2nd; Ft. Worth, Texas, circa 1890–1900.

Haldeman & Hohlbain
Carriage makers; New Britain, PA, circa 1880–1910.

Haldi
Peter Haldi, carriage and wagon maker, Altona, CO, circa 1884–1890.

Hale
J.W. Hale & Co., carriages, wagons and buggies, 203–205 Grand Ave.; Paris, Texas, circa 1890–1900.

Halfpenny
Milton Halfpenny, of Mifflinburg, PA, circa 1890–1920, built carriages, wagons and buggies, including a band wagon he made for the Swengel Band with the help of carriage maker Charles Hursh, in 1916.

Hall
A.B. Hall, blacksmith and wheelwright, ne corner of S. Ervay and Grand Ave., also 760–762 S Ervay and 629 Elm, also Holmes and 2 S Hickman; Dallas, Texas, circa 1897–1908.

Hall
S.C. Hall and Son, wagon maker; Columbus, WI, circa 1879.

Hall
William Hall, blacksmith and wagon maker, corner K and 8th; Sacramento, CA, circa 1853–1865.

Hall-Leeper Hardware Co
Carriages, buggies and wagons, 329 W. Main; Denison, Texas, circa 1899–1910.

Hall & Fox
Blacksmiths and wagon makers, corner of K and 8th; Sacramento, CA, circa 1853–1865.

Hall & Sanford
Carriage makers; Lee, NY, circa 1850's.

Hall (see Drew & Hall)

Hall (see Marlatts & Hall)

Hallenback
Darwin Hallenback, carriage maker; Whitestown, NY, circa 1850's.

Hallenbeck
E. Hallenbeck built carriages and sleighs. One of their popular designs was the New Hartford Jumper, as seen in the October 1866 issue of *New York Coachmakers Magazine*.

This style sold for $125; New Hartford, NY, circa 1860–1890.

Hallock
A.E. Hallock started manufacturing carriages in the 1870's. By 1881, Hallock had built a three story carriage factory near the Smithtown railroad station.

The firm continued to grow and Hallock took on a partner—C.B. Vail. They shipped their carriages throughout the region, circa 1870's–1900.

Halmgren (see Philman & Halmgren)

Haloma
G. Haloma, blacksmith and wheelwright, Govalle, R.F.D. No. 8; Austin, Texas, circa 1906–1912.

Ham
William Ham, wagon maker, 170 Walnut; Lockport, NY, circa 1899.

Hamblin
Edwin Hamblin, carriage and wagon maker; Clover Valley, Nevada, circa 1884–1890.

Hamilton
Green Hamilton, blacksmith and wheelwright, 610 Red River, and 704 E. 6th; Austin, Texas, circa 1893–1898. He later relocated to 606 Trinity, circa 1898–1911.

Hamilton
Samuel Hamilton, blacksmith and wheelwright, corner Neches and east 15th; Austin, Texas, circa 1889–1896.

Hamilton
Thomas G. Hamilton, blacksmith and wheelwright, 203 E 13th; Ft. Worth, Texas, circa 1904–1912.

Hamilton
William Hamilton, blacksmith and wheelwright, 412 Colorado; Austin, Texas, circa 1909–1916.

Hamilton & Son
Blacksmiths and wheelwrights, 950 Gladys Ave.; Beaumont, Texas, circa 1910–1920.

Hamilton (see Baker & Hamilton)

Hamilton (see Downing & Hamilton)

Hamlin
W. Hamlin, carriage maker; Mria, NY, circa 1850's.

Hamlin
William S. Hamlin, wagon maker; Sharon, Wisconsin, circa 1885–1919.

Hammes
Philip Hammes & Sons, wagon makers, Columbus and Saratoga; Utica, NY, circa 1899.

Hammond (see Arp & Hammond)

Hanaman
F. Hanaman, wagon maker; Columbus, Wisconsin, circa 1865.

Hancock Manufacturing Co.
J.H. Hancock, carriage manufacturer; Lynchburg, Virginia, circa 1911–1922.

Hand, McKinney & Massie
Carriages, wagons and buggies, 217–219 Polk and corner of 3rd, Amarillo, Texas, circa 1906–1916.

Hanford Wagon Works
Wagon and carriage maker who built vehicles for personal and commercial use; Unadilla, NY, circa 1890–1910.

Hanford (see Staples & Hanford)

Hanka
Frank Hanka, blacksmith and wagon maker, mining camp in Saguache county, elevation 8,500, tri-weekly stage to Villa Grove; Crestone, Colorado, circa 1883–1890.

Hanna
W.E. Hanna, blacksmith and wagon maker; Boise, Idaho, circa 1905–1910.

Hanna, Cowles & Co.
Carriage and wagon woodwork, 111 W. Main; Denison, Texas, circa 1887–1895.

Hannigan
Thomas Hannigan manufactured light carriages, 237 E. 63rd; New York, NY, circa 1899.

Hansen
C.J. Hansen, carriage and wagon manufacturer and dealer; Boise, Idaho, circa 1908

Hansen
J. Hansen & Son of Saugerties, New York were agents for the Milburn Wagon Company of Toledo, Ohio, circa 1880's–1910.

Hansen Wheel and Wagon Shop
Doug Hansen was born on July 2, 1958, the son of Richard Hansen, a craftsman who would rather work in his shop than tend the farm. Doug's mother had been raised on a farm in Letcher, South Dakota, and knew a great deal about horses—her real passion. In fact it was his mother's fascination with horses that would lead Doug into the wagon making trade.

He attended high school in nearby Mitchell, S.D., and went to the Mitchell Area Vocational School, where he took courses in general machine shop practices, metal working and welding. He wound up back on the farm, helping his parents.

One day his father, Richard Hansen , decided to buy a sawmill. It proved to be too small for the intended job. Doug decided he would try building one that was bigger. In addition to helping his father, it provided temporary work for him, as he sawed trees along the river bottom until the trees ran out.

By this time, he was becoming more interested in wheelwright work, and the building of wagons and other horse-drawn vehicles.

Today, Doug Hansen and his wife, Holly, have built an excellent wagon repairing and restoring business, which also offers new chuck wagons, hitch wagons and even stage coaches.

His mother had purchased some buggies at a local auction. She repaired the bodies and redid the trim but needed help with the wheels. She asked her son for his help. This was perhaps the challenge that started the Hansen Wheel and Wagon Shop.

Doug's grandfather, Lyle Shawd, had worked in a blacksmith shop as a young lad, and learned how to repair damaged wagon wheels. He found himself coaching and advising his grandson in the wheelwright trade.

Grandfather Lyle, as passionate as his daughter, about anything related to horsedrawn equipment, suggested to Doug that he pursue a career in wagon and wheel repair. Taking his grandfathers advice, he started to learn the tricks of the trade.

He started collecting old wagons, wagon parts and iron. He knew there were still an abundance of old vehicles scattered throughout the countryside in old barns. He talked to anyone who had a knowledge of this craft and researched what little literature he could find. The business prospered, especially the wheel repairing.

In addition to the chuck wagons and covered wagons, they now were offering a 6-mule Army escort wagon and the sheepherder's wagon, built to the buyer's special need and specifications. The shop also repaired and refurbished antique buggies and carriages.

Doug commenced researching old documents and any other historical materials on stagecoaches and their construction. His stagecoaches were always well-crafted, and well received.

Another source for business was when the draft horse community discovered the Hansen Wheel and Wagon Shop to be an excellent source for the manufacture of large hitch wagons, the type required for turning out four-up and six-up hitches. These large express wagons were once used as the heavy-duty trucks of their day, hauling heavy loads throughout America.

The Hansen Wheel and Wagon Shop enjoys well-earned success and is recognized for its excellent craftsmanship.

Hansen & Franzke
Carriage and wagon dealers and representatives; Antigo, Wisconsin, circa 1890–1910.

Hansom Cab
Not a company name, but a vehicle developed in England in the mid-1800's. Later in the century they were used in larger U.S. cities, mostly New York City. The addition of rubber tires by the early 1890's greatly improved the ride, circa 1830–1910.

Hanson Wagon Works
Andrew Hanson, carriage and wagon maker; Manitowoc, Wisconsin, circa 1885–1911.

Hanson
Christian J. Hanson, wagon maker; Tomahawk, Wisconsin, circa 1885–1903.

Hanson
Nels Hanson, blacksmith and wagon maker; Mackay, Idaho, circa 1905–1910.

Hanson
Nelson Hanson, wagon maker; Elk Mound, WI, circa 1879–1919.

Hanson (see Hilbert & Hanson)

Hanson (see Jackson & Hanson)

Hapgood Plow Co.
Manufactured farm implements, including the Piasa Bird Double Lift Gang Plow in the early 1900's; Alton, Illinois, circa 1880–1920.

Happy & Dockett
Blacksmiths and wagon makers; Lander, Wyoming, circa 1902–1908.

Harb & Vlan Ulzen
Manufacturer of saddles, collars, bridles, harness, whips, etc; Terre Haute, Indiana, circa 1858.

Harder
H. Harder, wagon maker; Beaver Dam, WI, circa 1879.

Harding & Russell
Blacksmiths and wagon makers; Sheridan, WY, circa 1901–1902.

Hardy
J.M. Hardy and Son, manufacturer of wagons, coaches, buggies and carriages, Beverley & Market streets; Stauton, Virginia, circa 1848–1929.

John Hardy's father, Charles W. Hardy, came from Leeds, England in the early 1800's and settled in Winchester, Virginia. His son Richard W. Hardy moved to Stauton in 1842 and opened a livery and stage coach business. Gradually this developed into a sideline business of building wagons, coaches, and buggies. Stauton was in the center of a network of stage lines, and business was thriving. Richard brought his younger brother John M. Hardy from Winchester to work with him in the business.

John showed from the start, a natural aptitude for tools and the mechanics of the trade. John, however, wanted more than just a trade—he wanted an education. So, at night he would study his books as thoroughly as he mastered his trade during the long days.

By 1848, he felt confident enough to establish his own business—a carriage shop in the same building where his brother had first gone into business. Now growing at an astonishing rate, the "Hardy" name had become synonymous with quality carriage making. These were the years when horse-drawn vehicles were the basis of transportation in America.

The Civil War years were hard on the Company, which was taken over by the Confederate Army.

When Sheridan came sweeping down the Shenendoah Valley, the buildings were all set afire and burned. When the flames died down, only one building remained standing—a brick building that fronted on Beverley Street. This was the building used as a nucleus to rebuild the plant.

During the comeback years for the South, the manufacture of vehicles was very important. Most all of the railroad transportation had been destroyed. Only by a horse-drawn conveyance could a person get anywhere and return. Business was definitely on the upswing.

In 1877 Mr. John Hardy fell and injured himself so severely that he was to become an invalid for many years. His son, Edward C. Hardy, then just a boy of 12, became a liason between his father's sick bed and the men at the factory.

In 1884, the senior Hardy made his son, who was just 17 at the time, a partner in his business. As business continued to grow, more buildings were added to the original little brick building.

In 1894, J.M. Hardy died and his partner-son, Edward C. Hardy bought out the interests of his sisters and brothers of the estate. But he left the firm name unchanged: "J.M. Hardy and Son"—Established 1848.

The automobile was rapidly replacing the horse and buggy in popularity and the demand was gradually shrinking to a mere trickle. He kept the business going until just two days before Christmas, in 1929, fire consumed the entire Stauton plant, except for the little brick building. A total of 127 vehicles in storage went up in smoke. Thus ending a long and continuous 81 years of American history.

Hare
Thomas Hare, of German ancestry, arrived in Marion, Iowa in 1839, becoming Marion's first blacksmith.

He was twenty years of age, and built one of the first homes.

In 1840, he made the irons for Marion's first sawmill. Later, he equipped the McCloud grist mill at McCloud's spring, towards Center Point.

In later years, he took up farming west of town. He died there in 1892, at the age of seventy-three years.

Harker Mfg. Co.
Buggy manufacturer; Cincinnati, Ohio, circa 1880–1910.

Harlis (see Williams & Harlis)

Harmeyer
E.F. Harmeyer, buggy manufacturer; Cincinnati, Ohio, circa 1880–1910.

Harmon (see Hanauer & Harmon)

Harness Machinery Co.
Montreal, Canada, circa 1890–1910.

Harper
J.D. Harper, sleigh and carriage maker; Christiana, PA, circa 1880–1900.

Harrell
Richard Harrell built several horse-drawn steam fire-engines in a short period of time, starting in 1869. The first was from the designs of John Nichols of the Grant Locomotive Works. Most of the plant was destroyed by fire, in 1871. Two units were salvaged and completed in the shops of Joseph Nussey & Co.

By 1874, the Harrell firm was out of business; Paterson, NJ, circa 1869–1874.

Harrington Co.
Peoria, Illinois, circa 1890–1910.

Harris
Anderson Harris Buggy Co., buggy manufacturer; Cincinnati, Ohio, circa 1880–1910.

Harris
Edward B. Harris, blacksmith and wheelwright, 212 E. 5th; Austin, Texas, circa 1900–1905.

Harris
J.F. Harris, blacksmith and wagon maker; Arco, Idaho, circa 1905–1910.

Harris
L.W. Harris, blacksmith and wagon maker; Boise, Idaho, circa 1905–1910.

Harris & Spiller
Blacksmiths, horseshoers and wheelwrights, Elm near Mill Creek; Dallas, Texas, circa 1886–1890's.

Harris (see Anderson and Harris Carriage Co.)

Harris (see Miller & Harris)

Harris (see Pomeroy & Harris)

Harrison
George W. Harrison, blacksmith and wheelwright, 513 E. 6th; 400 E. 5th; and 1114 Juniper, Austin, Texas, circa 1887–1918.

Harrison
H. Harrison, carriage and coach builders; Geneseo, NY, circa 1880–1900.

Harrison
Henry Harrison, blacksmith and wheelwright, 104 Congress Ave.; and 604 East Ave.; Austin, Texas, circa 1889–1911.

Harrison
J.P. Harrison, trustee, carriage and wagon material; Sherman, Texas, circa 1893–1900.

Harrison
Stephen Harrison was proprietor of the Harrison Carriage Factory, in Jersey, Ohio. This was one of the busiest industries in Licking County. The phaetons, buggies and platform spring wagons made here were sold to customers all over Ohio.

Harrison came to Jersey in 1843 and started the factory about 1850. He was also the first undertaker in Jersey. The factory was closed by F.E. Harrison on Oct. 12, 1926.

Harrison Wagon Works
William Harrison manufactured light and heavy farm wagons, including his "New Harrison Wagon". Their Grand Rapids, Michigan factory advertised, "one-horse wagons a specialty".

Harrison also had a branch office at the corner of 10th and Hickory streets in Kansas City, Missouri, managed by G.D. Webster, circa 1850–1920.

Harrison & Fraser
Blacksmith and wagon makers; Hayden, Colorado (county seat of Routt County, 200 miles nw of Denver), circa 1880–1890.

Harrison (see Lester & Harrison)

Hart
S.N. Hart, manufacturer of fine carriages; Hartford, CT, circa 1890–1910.

Hart Bros
Wagon makers; Lyons, WI, circa 1879.

Hartland
W.M. Hartland & Son of 4 Gold street: New York, NY, imported English colors and varnishes that were widely used by American carriage and wagon makers. One of their advertisements in an early trade magazine read "The Best Varnish is the Cheapest in the end". Their factory and chief office was located in Merton, Surrey, England.

They also had branch offices in Paris, France and Milan, Italy, circa 1850–1920.

Hartman
J.C. Hartman, carriage and wagon manufacturer, Dillon, between 11th and 12th; Cheyenne, Wyoming, circa 1908–1909.

Hartman's Carriage & Wagon Works
Carriage and wagon manufacturers; Boyertown, PA, circa 1880–1910.

Hartman Manufacturing Co.
Built farm implements in Vincennes, Indiana, circa 1900–1910.

Harton
Christian G. Harton, blacksmith, 1104 E. 6th; Austin, Texas, circa 1910–1920.

Hartwell
F. Hartwell, blacksmith and wagon maker; Canon City, Colorado, circa 1877 and 1879; also in Caribou, CO, circa 1878 and 1880.

Hartwell (see Makeley & Hartwell)

Harty
James Harty, blacksmith and wagon maker; Arco, Idaho, circa 1905–1910.

Harvey
John E. Harvey operated his carriage and wagon making shop in the rear portion of Crofoot and Doane's grocery store. His business card also read "general repairing a specialty", 754 S. Michigan Street; South Bend, Indiana, circa 1890–1910.

Harvey & Co.
Blacksmith and wagon maker; Black Hawk, CO, circa 1879–1889.

Harvey & Mull
Blacksmiths and wagon makers; Gillette, Wyoming, circa 1905–1910.

Harwood
R.B.Harwood, carriages, wagons and buggies, 751 Live Oak; Dallas, Texas, circa 1900–1910.

Harwood (see Wilcox & Harwood)

Hasdorff
W.R. Hasdorff, blacksmith and wheelwright, 512 Leal.; San Antonio, Texas, circa 1900–1912.

Haskell & Jones
This Albany, NY firm wasknown to have built one 5,000 lb. horse-drawn steam fire-engine in 1856, and sold it to the Albany Steel Co. of Troy, NY, circa 1866.

Hassett & Hodge
Formerly Jas. H. Hassett & Co., the new firm continued to build quality carriages and wagons of every style; Amesbury, MA, circa 1880's–1910.

Hatch
W.H. Hatch, blacksmith and horseshoer, 137 Ross Ave.; Dallas, Texas, circa 1908–1912.

Hathaway
E.E. Hathaway, carriage maker; Oriskany Falls, NY, circa 1899.

Hatley (see Whittet & Hatley)

Haupt
Jacob L. Haupt manufactured steam fire engines (see John Agnew); Philadelphia, PA, circa 1867–1875.

Havana Metal Wheel Co.
Manufactured metal wheels and related parts for the wagon industry; Havana, Illinois, circa 1890–1920's.

Havekotte
Louis Havekotte, buggy manufacturer; Cincinnati, Ohio, circa 1880–1910.

Haves
George Haves, carriage maker; Kirkland, NY, circa 1850's.

Hawks (see Turton & Hawks)

Haworth
James Haworth, carriage maker, corner of J and 4th; Sacramento, CA, circa 1853–1865.

Haworth & Sons Manufacturing Co.
George D. Haworth developed his first horse-drawn planter in the 1850's; Decatur, Illinois, circa 1850–1905.

Haworth, Eells & Co.
Carriage maker, Sacramento, CA, circa 1853–1865.

Haxton
Charles M. Haxton, carriage trimmer, corner 8th and L; Sacramento, CA, circa 1855–1875.

Hayden
Charles Hayden, wagon maker; Elroy, Wisconsin, circa 1885–1919.

Haydock
T.T. Haydock Buggy Co., buggy manufacturer; Cincinnati, Ohio, circa 1880–1910.

Haye
D. Haye, carriage painter and trimmer, 111 W. Commerce; San Antonio, Texas, circa 1897–1904.

Hayes
Calvin G. Hayes, wagon maker, 8th, between I and J; Sacramento, CA, circa 1853–1865.

Hayes
Charles Hayes, blacksmith and wagon maker; Meadows, Idaho, circa 1905–1910.

Hayes
Daniel D. Hayes manufactured an extension ladder truck for the fire fighting industry, circa 1882, (see American LaFrance Fire Engine Co.)

Hayes
John Hayes, manufactured wagons, carriages, buggies and sulkeys of every description. He also offered for sale, choice lots of hickory axles, hubs, dressed spokes and all kinds of carriage trimmings, corner 11th and J; Sacramento, CA, circa 1853–1865.

Hayes
J.S. Hayes, wagon maker, 116 Washington; San Francisco, California, circa 1882–1890.

Hayes Pump & Planter Co.
Eugenio K. Hayes started out in Kewanee, Illinois, but in 1886 moved and set up business in Galva, Illinois. Hayes planters were widely known and sold as The Original 4-wheel Planter. They claimed to have sold over 40,000 by the turn of the 20th century.

Hayes joined with three other companies to form Farm Tools, Inc. By the 1950's, only repair parts were available, as they were now under a division of Pittsburg Forgings Co. of Coraopolis, PA., circa 1880's–1950's.

Hayford (see Clifton & Hayford)

Hay Tool Manufacturing Co.

This Council Bluffs, Iowa company built various styles of sulky and push rakes. They were sold throughout the region and through distributors and jobbing outlets in St. Louis and Kansas City, circa 1880–1905.

Haywood
Haywood Wagon Co., carriage and wagon manufacturer, produced a variety of wagons, drays and delivery trucks. They contracted to the city of Newark for manufacturing dumping-garbage wagons; Newark, NY, circa 1890–1920.

This company also issued its own illustrated catalog.

Hazelwood & Johnson
Blacksmiths and wheelwrights, corner 1st St. and Congress Ave.; Austin, Texas, circa 1906–1910.

Hazelwood & McCown
Blacksmiths and wheelwrights, 102 W. 2nd; Austin, Texas, circa 1910–1913.

Hazlehurst (see Murray & Hazlehurst)

Healy & Co.
Carriage and wagon makers. New York, NY, circa 1880–1910.

Healey, Williams and Co.
This New York, NY firm produced a large number and variety of sleighs, carriages and other wheeled vehicles, out of their five-story factory, circa 1880–1900.

Heard & Smith
Blacksmiths and wheelwrights, 2207 East Ave.; Austin, Texas, circa 1912–1918.

Heath & Bennett
Blacksmiths and wagon makers; Buhl, Idaho, circa 1905–1910.

Heath (see Kent & Heath)

Heaton
A.E. Heaton, may have constructed one or more horse-drawn fire-engines; New York, NY, circa 1875.

Hebert & Demars
Wagon and carriage makers; Fort Atkinson, WI, circa 1879.

Hedges
Charles S. Hedges, carriage and wagon maker; Sag Harbor, NY, circa 1820–1830.

Hedrick
George William Hedrick Carriage Co., manufacturer of carriages, buggies, surreys, spring wagons, etc.; Dayton, Virginia, circa 1880–1911.

Heebner & Sons
Built threshers and other farm implements; Lansdale, PA., circa 1900–1920.

Hefner
H.J. Hefner & Son, blacksmiths and wheelwrights, 210 E. Houston; Sherman, Texas, circa 1899–1910.

Hegge Bros. Buggy Co.
Buggy manufacturer; Cincinnati, Ohio, circa 1880–1910.

Hehittenden
Sarveret Hehittenden, wagon and sleigh maker; Lysander, NY, circa 1850's.

Heidgen
Mathias Heidgen, wagon maker; Fort Howard, circa 1885–1898.

Heimbach
J.S. Heimbach, carriage and coach shop; New Berlin, PA., circa 1860–1880.

Hein (see Willie & Hein)

Heinl
Joseph Heinl & Sons, carriage and wagon makers; Milwaukee, Wisconsin, circa 1879–1915.

Heinlein
George Heinlein Carriage Co.; Covington, KY, circa 1890–1910.

Heinlein Foundry Co.
Manufacturer of hames; Columbus, Ohio, circa 1890–1910.

Heins & Anderson
Blacksmiths and wheelwrights, 312—25th; Galveston, Texas, circa 1890–1900.

Heins (see Peters & Heins)

V1-Heinzelmann Bros. Carriage Co.
The Heinzelmann brothers, John (President), William, Reginald and Fred operated this Belleville, Illinois company, circa 1857–1920. They made fine horse drawn carriages which were used throughout the United States.

Their storm buggy was so popular with country doctors, it took first prize at the 1904 World's Fair in St. Louis.

Heinzen
J. Heinzen, wagon maker; Woodville, WI, circa 1879.

Heise
William Heise, carriage and wagon dealer and representative; Alma, Wisconsin, circa 1890–1910.

Heiss
William A. Heiss, buggy maker, 531 Green Street (rear); Mifflinburg, PA, circa 1883–1931.

Heitkamp
Fred W. Heitkamp, wagon maker; Reedsburg, Wisconsin, circa 1885–1901.

Heitmann
F.W. Heitmann, blacksmith, carriage and wagon manufacturer supplies; and carriage and wagon woodwork, 113 Main; Houston, Texas, circa 1882–1901.

Held (see Roll & Held)

Helms
The Carriage Works, operated by Joe and Thomas Helms, manufactured wagons, carriages, etc.; North Dayton, Virginia, circa 1885.

Helms
W.T. Helms, sleigh and buggy builder Reiglesville, PA, circa 1880–1910.

Hench & Dromgold
Manufacturer of farm implements; York, PA., circa 1875–1900.

Henderson
Allen Henderson, blacksmith and wheelwright, 530 Orleans, circa 1906–1907, and at 2340 Railroad

Ave.; Beaumont, Texas, circa 1910–1920.

Henderson
Douglas Henderson, blacksmith and wagon maker, 610 Elm; Dallas, Texas, circa 1910–1920.

Henderson
G.W. Henderson, wagon maker; Unity, WI, circa 1879.

Henderson
M.P. Henderson & Son; Stockton, CA., circa 1880–1910.

This well known wagon maker was also famous for their Western Stage Wagons. They once built a freight wagon that weighed 6,515 pounds and carried 12 tons. The bed measured 20'x 5' with 5' front wheels and 1,800 pound, 8' rear wheels.

They also built vehicles for the U.S. government to convey tourist in the western parks.

Henderson
P.H. Henderson & Son, carriage company; Boston, Massachusetts, circa 1878–1903.

Henderson
T. Henderson, blacksmith and wheelwright, 1001 E 6th; Austin, Texas, circa 1887–1900.

Henderson Buggy Co.
Henderson, North Carolina, circa 1890–1910.

Henderson (see Craig & Henderson)

Henderson (see Pierson & Henderson)

Hendricks
Jacob Hendricks, buggy maker, 503 Chestnut Street; Mifflinburg, PA, circa 1855–1861.

Hendrickson
H.J. Hendrickson, carriage and wagon dealer and representative; Argyle, Wisconsin, circa 1890–1910.

Heney
E.N. Heney Company, carriage manufacturer; Montreal, Quebec, Canada, circa 1890–1910.

Heninger
J.H. Heninger, blacksmith and wheelwright, 916 W. Commerce; San Antonio, Texas, circa 1900–1908.

Henk
Casper Henk, carriage and wagon dealer; Abbotsford, Wisconsin, circa 1890–1910.

Henney Buggy Co.
This carriage and buggy builder from Freeport, Illinois was bought out by Moline Plow Co. of Moline, Illinois, in 1906, circa 1880's–1906.

Henning
Frank Henning, carriage and wagon maker; Raton, New Mexico, circa 1910–1920.

Henry
Isaiah Henry, buggy maker, 203 south fifth street; Mifflinburg, PA, circa 1866–1880's.

Henry & Adams
Blacksmiths and wheelwrights, 604 E. Belknap; Ft.Worth, Texas, circa 1905–1915.

Henry & Bell Hardware Co.
William Henry and R.E. Bell, carriage and wagon makers' material, 1615–1617 Main; Ft.Worth, Texas, circa 1904–1916.

Hensel
Henry Hensel, carriage maker; Rico, Colorado, circa 1880–1890.

Henshaw (see Kingsbury & Henshaw)

Henslee
Joseph M. Henslee, blacksmith and wheelwright, 722 Tremont; Galveston, Texas, circa 1900–1910.

Hensley
Gus Hensley, blacksmith, horseshoer, carriage and wagon maker, 219 Taylor, Phone 890, also 2116 BuchanaPhone 1443; Amarillo, Texas, circa 1910–1918.

Hentschel
Otto Hentschel, wagon maker, 549 West 14th; New York, NY, circa 1899.

Herbert
L. Herbert, blacksmith and wagon maker; Cavendish, Idaho, circa 1905–1910.

Herbrand Fifth Wheel Co.
Cincinnati, Ohio, circa 1880–1910.

Herbst
Fred Herbst, wagon maker; Sparta, Wisconsin, circa 1879–1885.

Hercules Buggy Co.
Buggy builders for Sears & Roebuck; Evansville, Indiana, circa 1890–1910.

Herdic
Herdic Phaeton Co.; Washington, D.C., circa 1870–1900.

Peter Herdic, owner of the company, invented and designed many of the public transportation vehicles that carry his name.

Herendeen Co.
Built farm implements; Geneva, NY., circa 1880's–1900.

Heritage
J.D. Heritage, carriage maker; Bustleton, 23rd ward; Philadelphia, PA, circa 1880–1910.

Hermann
J. Hermann, blacksmith, horseshoer and wheelwright, 840 Commerce; Dallas, Texas, circa 1886–1897.

Hermant
E.T. Hermant, wagon maker, Deerfield Corners, Oneida County, NY, circa 1899.

Hernandez
Benjamin Harnandez, blacksmith, 209 S. Piedras; El Paso, Texas, circa 1914–1920.

Herndon & Farley
Blacksmiths and wagon makers, Forney Ave. and 1 East Grand; Dallas, Texas, circa 1910.

Herold
Andrew F. Herold, wagon maker; Maiden Rock, WY, circa 1885–1898.

Herold
C. Herold, carriage and wagon maker, San Bruno near 26th; San Francisco, CA, circa 1888–1894.

Herrick (see Maloney & Herrick)

Herrington
Lewis J. Herrington, blacksmith and wagon maker, Larimer and 11th; Denver, Colorado, circa 1877–1887.

Herrmann
Joseph Jermann, blacksmith and wheelwright; also manufacturer of carriages, buggies, phaetons and wagons, 2 Ave. E. corner of East Houston; San Antonio, Texas, circa 1887–1898.

Herron (see Peters & Herron Dash Co.)

Hess
Louis Hess, wagon maker, 6 Gouveneur; New York, NY, circa 1899.

Hess
Paul Hess, blacksmith and wheelwright, 1215 Hamilton; Houston, Texas, circa 1900–1910.

Hess Spring & Axle Co.
Carthage, Ohio, circa 1890–1910.

Hess Spring & Axle Co.
Cincinnati, Ohio, circa 1890–1910.

Hess & Eisenhardt Co
Owners of the name and trade-mark of the Sayers & Scovil Co.; Cincinnati, Ohio.

Hessill & Leykom
Carriage and wagon dealers; Antigo, Wisconsin, circa 1890–1910.

Hettler (see Coultress & Hettler)

Heye
D. Heye, carriage painters and trimmers, 17 W. Commerce; San Antonio, Texas, circa 1887–1900.

Hickman-Ebbert Co.
Makers of the Ebbert farm wagon and other vehicles; Owensboro, Kentucky, circa 1890's–1920.

Hickman Peters Co. Inc.
Coldwater, TN, circa 1900.

Hickory Carriage and Buggy Co.
This shop was established around 1880, and later purchased by William Knapp, circa 1900. This Cincinnati, Ohio company specialized in the construction of light carriages, buggies, carts and wagons. Knapp operated the firm until it burned out in 1913.

At that time, William, and son Edwin J. Knapp, moved to Lawrenceburg, Indiana and started the Standard Vehicle Co., circa 1880–1913.

Hicks
B. Hicks, blacksmith and wagon maker, I, opposite public square; Sacramento, CA, circa 1853–1865.

Hicks
Frank Hicks, blacksmith and wagon maker, I, opposite public square; Sacramento, CA, circa 1853–1865.

Hicks
S.A. Hicks, blacksmith and wagon maker, 7th, between J and K; Sacramento, CA, circa 1853–1865.

Hicks
Samuel Hicks, blacksmith and wagon maker, I, opposite public square; Sacramento, CA, circa 1853–1865.

Hicks Bros.
Wagon makers, 349 West 48th; New York, NY, circa 1899.

Hicks (see Drew & Hicks)

Higgins Mfg. Co.
Buggy manufacturer; Cincinnati, Ohio, circa 1880–1910.

Higgins Mfg. Co.
Newport, Kentucky, circa 1890–1910.

Higginson
John L. Higginson, carriages, buggies and wagons, 115–121 N. Rusk Ave.; Denison, Texas, circa 1899–1910.

Highland Buggy Co.
Buggy manufacturer; Cincinnati, Ohio, circa 1880–1910.

Hilbert
George T. Hilbert, blacksmith and wheelwright, 197 Bryan; Dallas, Texas, circa 1898–1908.

Hilbert & Hanson
Blacksmiths and wheelwrights, 167 Camp; Dallas, Texas, circa 1897–1906.

Hildinger
John Hildinger, blacksmith and wheelwright, Mt. Bonnell road near creek; Austin, Texas, circa 1887–1896.

Hildinger & Son
Blacksmith and wheelwrights, 3000 Guadalupe; Austin, Texas, circa 1897–1918.

Hildinger, Schwinge & Hildinger
Blacksmiths and wheelwrights, 3000 Guadalupe; Austin, Texas, circa 1910–1920.

Hildreth Varnish Co.
Advertised as manufacturers of superfine coach varnishes and colors. Hildreth offered a variety of products to buggy builders throughout the region, 18 Broadway; New York, NY, circa 1870–1900.

Hilgres & Richmond
Blacksmiths and wagon makers; Clayton, New Mexico, circa 1900–1920.

Hiliger
W. Hiliger, wagon maker; Bloomer, WI, circa 1879.

Hill
Frank B. Hill, wagon maker, 3478 Third Avenue; New York, NY, circa 1899.

Hill
Richard Hill, wagon maker; Eagle, Wisconsin, circa 1865.

Hill & Moorlen
Hiram H. Hill and Frank Moorlen built two steam fire-engines, the first known as "Atlantic", was sold to the city of Augusta, and the sec-

ond smaller engine was sold to the city of Hallowell, Maine.

Both machines were marked with the letters Patented in the United States and Canada 1878; Augusta, ME, circa 1878–1880.

Hill (see Abbots & Hill)

Hillebrand
John Hillebrand, carriage, wagon, buggy and phaeton dealer, 319–323 Congress Ave.; Austin, Texas, circa 1887–1911.

Hillgar
F.G. Hillgar, carriage and wagon dealer and representative; Adell, Wisconsin, circa 1890–1910.

Hillin (see Murphy & Hillin)

Hillpot
J.A. Hillpot, blacksmith and wheelwright, 10th and Oak Cliff; Dallas, Texas, circa 1890–1900.

Hills Brothers & Wright
Carriages, wagons and harness, 152 N. Union; Pueblo, Colorado, circa 1880–1890.

Hilse
Frederick A. Hilse, blacksmith and wheelwright, 1017 San Felipe; Houston, Texas, circa 1900–1910.

Hilton
S. Hilton, carriage maker; Albany, NY, circa 1870–1900.

Hilton (see DeVoe & Hilton)

Himmelberger
Wagon manufacturer; Reading, PA., circa 1885–1905.

Hinckley & Drury
Their first steam fire-engine was built at the Boston Locomotive Works, in 1858. The exact number of engines they built is unknown, however of two that are documented, one was designed by J.M. Stone and named the "New Era"; the other a 10,500 lb. vehicle named "Rob Roy", but better known as "Mazeppa" #1.

The Mazeppa #1 was kept in active service until 1872 and was the last engine built by the Boston Locomotive Works; Boston, MA, circa 1858–1860's.

Hinks & Johnson
Manufacturers of carriages, coaches and hansom cabs; Bridgeport, CT, circa 1870–1910.

This company may also have built vehicles in New York.

Hirzel
Anton Hirzell, blacksmith and wagon maker, 715 west 22nd; Cheyenne, Wyoming, circa 1908–1909.

Hisey
J. Hisey, carriage maker; Pueblo, Colorado, circa 1882–1887.

Hissey
A.J. Hissey, wagon maker; Bear, WI, circa 1879.

Hobach (see Graves & Hobach)

Hobart
Hiram Hobart, wagon maker; Hingham, Wisconsin, circa 1865.

Hobbs
Blacksmith and wagon maker, 137 East 6th; Leadville, Colorado, circa 1881–1891.

Hobrick
August Hobrick, carriage and wagon dealer and representative; Ashippun, WI, circa 1890–1910.

Hobson (see Ferguson & Hobson)

Hochstettler Buggy Co.
Topeka, IN, circa 1890–1910.

Hock
Mrs. Katie Hock, wagon maker, 545 West 52nd; New York, NY, circa 1899.

Hodge
Paul Rapsey Hodge of New York, NY, completed the first steam fire-engine built in the United States, in 1841. (The first steam fire-engine ever built was in London in 1829, by George Braithwaite).

Tlhe Hodge engine was 13–1/2 feet long, and weighed about 15,000 pounds, and was first used by the Pearl Hose Co. #28 of New York city, circa 1841–1845.

Hodge & Buchholz
Wagon and carriage maker; Janesville, WI, circa 1865–1879.

Hodge (see Hassett & Hodge)

Hoeft
William Hoeft, wagon maker; Thiensvills, WI, circa 1885–1903.

Hoening
Augusta A. Hoening, wagon maker, 312 East 93rd; New York, NY, circa 1899.

Hoepfner & Wuest
Manufactured light carriages and wagons, 47 Bayard and 762 East 164th; New York, NY, circa 1899.

Hofer
J. Hofer, wagon maker; Waterford, WI, circa 1879.

Hoff
Albert Hoff, blacksmith and wagon maker; Elba, Idaho, circa 1905–1910.

Hoffer & Miller
Blacksmith and wagon maker; Lewiston, Idaho, circa 1905–1910.

Hoffman
Charles Hoffman, wagon maker, 1760 Second Avenue; New York, NY, circa 1899.

Hoffman
Frank K. Hoffman, wagon maker; Marion, Wisconsin, circa 1885–1911.

Hoffman
J. Hoffman & Son; New London, WI, circa 1879.

Hoffman & Co.
This company was primarily a wholesale manufacturer. They also sold many of their vehicles through mail-order catalogs; Albion, Indiana, circa 1890–1910.

Hofheinz
R.J. Hofheinz, carriages and wagons, 404 S. Flores; San Antonio, Texas, circa 1897–1910.

Hogan & Dilts
Wagon makers; Colorado Springs, Colorado, circa 1884–1894.

Hogerson Shop
Blacksmiths and wagon makers; Buffalo, Wyoming, circa 1900–1905.

Hoges
H.S. Hoges, blacksmith and wagon maker; Leland, Idaho, circa 1905–1910.

Hohlbain (see Haldeman & Hohlbain)

Hoier
C. Hoier, blacksmith and wheelwright, 202 Navarro; San Antonio, Texas, circa 1900–1912.

Holch
Charles Holch, wagon maker; Sparta, Wisconsin, circa 1865.

Holcher Bros. Buggy Co.
Crestline, Ohio, circa 1890–1910.

Holden
John Holden, blacksmith and wheelwright, carriage and wagon manufacturer, 204 W. Chestnut; Denison, Texas, circa 1893–1900.

Holden (see Rudd & Holden)

Holland
Daniel Holland, blacksmith and wheelwright, nw corner of Beckley Road and Ft. Worth Ave., also 118 McKinney Ave.; Dallas, Texas, circa 1900–1908.

Holland
Don A. Holland, blacksmith and wheelwright, 2800 Guadalupe; Austin, Texas, circa 1909–1916.

Holland
William Holland, blacksmith and wagon maker; Bancroft, Idaho, circa 1905–1910.

Hollenstein
John Hollenstein, wagon maker; Mayville, WI, circa 1885–1919.

Holler & Anderson Buggy Co.
Made its humble beginning at the rear of A.D. Holler's furniture store in Rock Hill, South Carolina in 1899. By 1892 it was incorporated as the Rock Hill Buggy Co. (see listing for Rock Hill Buggy Co.)

Hollopeter
Joseph Hollopeter, carriage and wagon maker; Lewisburg, PA., circa 1840–1860.

Holmes
Peter Holmes, blacksmith and wagon maker; Pueblo, Colorado, circa 1877–1890.

Holmes
William H. Holmes of New Woodstock, NY was a long timecarriage maker who was also involved in a hardware and grocery business with E.K. Jenkins of Cuba, NY; and another partnership with S.E. Morse, making carriages in New Woodstock, circa 1860–1880's.

Holmes & Arceneaux
Carriage manufacturers, and repairers, 764 College; Beaumont, Texas, circa 1906–1917.

Holmstrom
A.E. Holmstrom, blacksmith and wheelwright, 1607 Sabine; Austin, Texas, circa 1887–1900.

Holt Bros.
Carriage and wagon materials, 27–29 Beale and 30–32 Main; San Francisco, California, circa 1882–1894.

Holt Bros. Mfg. Co.
C.H. Holt was president, and later Mrs. S.A. Holt president of this New Hampshire wheel making company.

Established in 1865, their factory produced wheels, wheel making material and wagon woodwork. They advertised as "Makers of the Concord Wheels"; Concord, New Hampshire, circa 1865–1910.

Holt Manufacturing Co.
Manufacturer of wheels, wagons and carriages, (branch) 1104–1106 1st Ave; Spokane, Washington, circa 1905–1910.

Holt & Cochran
Blacksmiths and wheelwrights, 406 E. 7th; Austin, Texas, circa 1887–1900.

Holzman
Joseph Holzman, wagon maker; Mount Calvary, WI, circa 1885–1903.

Homer
C. Homer, blacksmith and wagon maker; Yuma, Arizona, circa 1884–1890's.

Homer Wagon Co., Limited
Manufactured a wide variety of wagon styles, including their Whitney road wagon. They also licensed a number of other parties to build their wagons; Cortland, NY, circa 1870–1910.

Homer (see Brockway, Homer)

Hommel (see Campbell & Hommel)

Hooker
Henry Hooker & Co. was incorporated in 1868, with Hooker as president and Edwin Marble as secretary. They would eventually become the largest and finest carriage manufacturing firm in New Haven, Connecticut.

Their manufacturing plant was five stories tall and covered an entire city block. They could turn out 25 of the finest and most elegant carriages every working day.

Advertisements claimed that the Hooker firm was *the largest and most complete carriage establishment in the entire world.* Hooker carriages were solidly built.

The French Carriage Co. was a very big distributor of the Hooker carriages and sleighs. (see listing on The French Carriage Co.).

Hooker advertisements also claimed to have produced over 200 completely different styles each year—and building "to order" over 175 styles of traps alone. No other company attempted anything on such a grand scale. Though he sold locally, the firm was classed as a wholesale manufacturer, circa 1868–1920.

Hoop
A.A. Hoop built carriages, buggies and sleighs in Mifflinburg, PA., circa 1880–1890.

Wheels Across America

Hoop
John Hoop, carriage and wagon manufacturer, 26 Preston; Houston, Texas, circa 1882–1892.

Hoop Brothers
Blacksmiths and wheelwrights; manufacturers of carriages, wagons, buggies and phaetons, 102 Preston Ave.; Houston, Texas, circa 1900–1910.

Hoop & Isaac
Blacksmiths and wheelwrights; carriage and wagon manufacturers, 21–26 W. Preston; Houston, Texas, circa 1887–1900.

Hoopes Bro. & Darlington
Hoopes Bro. & Darlington, established in 1866; West Chester, PA, manufacturers of excellent quality wheels, for every conceivable type of horse-drawn vehicle.

During 1876, at the Centennial Exhibition in Philadelphia, Hoopes Bros. & Darlington had been in business ten years. Their large display of many different size wagon and carriage wheels, hubs, both large and small, shafts, bent wood and rims drew much attention. For their exhibit, they won highest award with the following remarks, "It has been generally admitted that the wheels shown by Hoopes Bros. & Darlington have all the style about them that is possessed by those made in the workshops of our best carriage builders."

The company had over 100 competitors at one time. However, at the turn of the century when production was at its peak, the company maintained an agent and a wholesale house in London to handle the big English trade.

In 1896 there were 28,382 carriage and wagon makers in the United States—and an additional 10,316 carriage and wagon dealers.

In the early days, the company employed nearly 250 men. They had a morning steam whistle that called the employees to work, blowing once when they were to leave home and fifteen minutes later when they were to be at their places, ready to start the days work.

In 1904 the Hoopes Bros. & Darlington company had a capacity for making 40,000 sets of wheels a year.

This was an astonishing figure considering that they were only one of many large factories turning out wheels in America.

Over 100 years after the beginning, Thomas Hoopes, grandson of the founder, was still with the West Chester company—the last survivor of the large wheel making concerns.

Hoosier Drill
Hoosier Drill started building farm implements in Milton, Indiana before moving to Richmond in the early 1870's

This Richmond, Indiana company, circa 1860's–1929, offered a one and two-horse corn drill in the 1890's.

They, along with a few other firms, formed the American Seeding Machine Co., in 1903. They later became part of the Oliver Farm Equipment Co. in 1929.

Hooson
John Hooson, wagon maker; Ripon, Wisconsin, circa 1865.

Hoover
James M. Hoover, buggy maker, 212 Walnut Street; Mifflinburg, PA, circa 1887–1903.

Hoover Mfg. Co.
Avery, Ohio, circa 1890–1910.

Hoover Wagon Co.
George W. Hoover & Sons, carriage and wagon maker; York, PA., circa 1890–1910.

Hopkins
M. Hopkins, wagon maker, residence, 12th between H and I; Sacramento, CA, circa 1855–1875.

Hopkins (see Dael & Hopkins)

Hopp
Alfred A. Hopp, buggy maker, ne corner of Walnut and fourth streets; Mifflinburg, PA, circa 1903–1922.

Horan
T.E. Horan, carriages, buggies and wagons, 416 W. Main; Denison, Texas, circa 1893–1903.

Horn
T.E. Horn, carriages, buggies and wagons, 318 W. Main; Denison, Texas, circa 1893–1913.

Horn
W. Horn, carriage and wagon dealer and representative; Adell, Wisconsin, circa 1890–1910.

Hornback
J. Hornback, blacksmith and wagon maker; Fairplay, Colorado, circa 1877–1885.

Horner
C. Horner, blacksmith and wagon maker. Machine work of all kinds a specialty. Wagons, carriages and buggies made to order and repaired. Blacksmith work done with care and promptness, corner of Gila and Doten Streets; Yuma, AZ, circa 1882–1894.

Horst
Amos H. Horst was born in Ohio, May of 1908. He married in 1934 and farmed into the 1970's.

About 1973, Amos decided to build a closed-in buggy for himself. After he had his new buggy on the road, others saw it and wanted one just like it. So, over the next 8 or 9 years, Horst built approximately thirty-five buggy bodies. The last one was made about 1982.

Horton
L.B. Horton, blacksmith and wagon maker; Fairplay, Colorado, 1878 and Evans, Colorado, circa 1879–1880's.

Horton
Rosil Horton, wagon and blacksmith shop; Loveland, Colorado, circa 1880–1890.

Horton (see Hufman & Horton)

Hoshaw
E.D. Hoshaw, blacksmith and wagon maker; Dayton and Buffalo, Wyoming, circa 1900–1908.

Hoshaw & Rasmussen
Blacksmiths, carriage and wagon makers; Buffalo, Wyoming, circa 1905–1910.

Hoskins
Albert Hoskins, blacksmith and wagon maker; Clayton, Idaho, circa 1905–1910.

Hoten
V.A. Hoten, wagon and sleigh maker; Lafayette, NY, circa 1850's.

Hotz
Christoph Hotz's name was on a trade card with a Schuttler wagon on it which read: Wagon Manufactory—Schuttler & Hotz, Proprietors. Office located at 45 West Street (no city or state given), circa 1870–1880.

Houck
Alfred A. Houck, buggy maker; Mifflinburg, PA, circa 1876.

Hough
John Hough, carriage maker; Danboro, PA, circa 1880–1910.

Houghton
D.F. Houghton, wagon maker; West Salem, Wisconsin, circa 1865.

Houghton
Although not a carriage builder, George W.W. Houghton of New York, NY, made contributions to the industry that were paramount. Mr. Houghton, as editor of the Hub, a leading trade journal of the day, became a spokesman for the carriage industry.

Among his many accomplishments were his active membership in the carriage builders' national association, established in 1872, and his promoting the formation of a technical school for carriage workers.

With former Brewster & Company employee J.D. Gribbon as chief instructor, classes began in 1880, at the Metropolitan Museum of Art in New York, NY. The school and museum were first located at East 68th street and First avenue. Both moved to 34th street in 1881.

Houghton Sulky Co.
Marion, Ohio, circa 1890–1910.

Houk & Scott
Blacksmiths and wheelwrights, 467 Sabine Pass Ave.; Beaumont, Texas, circa 1910–1920.

House
M.E. House, blacksmith and wagon maker; Mountain Home, Idaho, circa 1905–1910.

House
S.N. House, blacksmith and wheelwright, 363–374 Commerce; Dallas, Texas, circa 1897–1901.

Houser
Peter Houser manufactured buggies, carriages and all classes of wagons on South Main Street; Kenton, Ohio, circa 1877.

Houston Carriage Co.
Carriages, wagons, buggies and phaetons, (see C.J. Stewart of Houston), 802 Commerce Ave.; Houston, Texas, circa 1900–1901.

Howard
Carriagesmith and horseshoer, repairing and jobbing neatly done and satisfaction guaranteed, 331 Lightstone Street; San Jose, California, circa 1882–1892.

Howard
John Howard, blacksmith and wheelwright, 611 Red River; Austin, Texas, circa 1903–1909.

Howard
R.L. Howard, circa 1850's–1870's, built farm implements, including an early line of mowers, after they acquired the Ketchem mower line in the 1850's.

Howard featured this and other designs in their 1860 catalog; Buffalo, New York.

Howard Buggy Works
Buggy makers; Ohio, circa 1870's–1900.

Howard Handle and Spoke Co.
Howard operated his shop in the Nittany Mountain region of Pennsylvania where he manufactured wheel parts for carriage and wagon makers, circa 1900–1915.

Howe & Baldwin
Blacksmiths and wagon makers; repairing, horse shoeing and general jobbers; James Howe and William Baldwin, proprietors; Raton, New Mexico, circa 1882–1890.

Hoyal
Andrew J. Hoyal built wagons for the California, Oregon Trail and the Santa Fe traders—and other southwest markets.

Before starting his own business, in the 1840's, he was part of the Hoyal & Bean Co.; Independence, Missouri, circa 1840–1860.

Hoyal & Bean
See Andrew J. Hoyal.

Hoyle
Arthur Hoyle, blacksmiths and horseshoers, Eagle Ford Rd and 2 N Ft. Worth Ave.; Dallas, Texas, circa 1905–1915.

Hoyle
R.E. Hoyle, blacksmith, wheelwright and wagon maker, 133 south Jefferson; 128 S Poydras; 258 Jackson; 190 Jackson, and 241 Young; Dallas, Texas, circa 1905–1910.

Hubbard
F. Hubbard, wagon maker; Sextonville, Wisconsin, circa 1865.

Hubbard & King
Blacksmiths, wheelwrights and horseshoers, 307 Mesquite; Corpus Christi, Texas, circa 1910–1920.

Hubert (see Kyle & Hubert)

Huden
Henry Huden, blacksmith and wagon maker, Los Angeles Street; Anaheim, CA, circa 1882–1890.

Huehner
August F. Huebner, blacksmith and wheelwright; carriage and wagon manufacturer, 2624 Mechanic; Galveston, Texas, circa 1888–1902.

Huefner
Paul Huefner, carriage and wagon dealer and representative; Alma, Wisconsin, circa 1890–1910.

Huettle
Ferdinand Heuttle, wagon maker; Dale, WI, circa 1879–1901.

Huffman (see Suydam & Huffman)

Hufman & Horton
Blacksmiths and wheelwrights, 905 Evans Ave.; Ft. Worth, Texas, circa 1900–1908.

Hugely
Martin Hugely, blacksmith and wheelwright, 520 E. 6th; Austin, Texas, circa 1887–1900.

Hughes
C.D. Hughes & Bros.; carriages, wagons and buggies; 116 S. Crockett; Sherman, Texas, circa 1893–1900.

Hughes
Hughes Buggy Co.; E.E. Hughes, President, Lynchburg, Virginia, circa 1903–1926.

Hughes
S.L. Hughes, blacksmith and wagon maker, 1200 Myrtle Ave.; El Paso, Texas, circa 1900–1915.

Hughes & Co.
Blacksmiths and wheelwrights, 168 Camp; Dallas, Texas, circa 1891–1902.

Hughes & Bose
Blacksmiths and wheelwrights, 165 Camp; Dallas, Texas, circa 1897–1906.

Hughes & Pratt
Wagon makers; Rockland, WI, circa 1879.

Hughes (see Boles & Hughes)

Hughes (see Gregg & Hughes)

Hull, Harris & Herron
C.C. Hull, William Harris, and J.J. Herron, circa 1890–1910.

Hummel
George H. Hummel, buggy maker, fork of third and fourth streets (now the Woodlawn Cemetery); Mifflinburg, PA, circa 1894.

Humphery
Fred Humphery, wagon maker; Shopiere, WI, circa 1865–1903.

Humphries (see Jackson & Humphries)

Hunn
William Hunn, blacksmith and wheelwright, 614 -26th; Galveston, Texas, circa 1893–1905.

Hunneman & Co.
Established in 1792 by William Cooper Hunneman, this firm built a world-wide reputation as a hand-pump fire-engine manufacturer.

The company was managed for many years by Samuel and William, the sons of William C. Hunneman.

By the mid-1850's, John C. (son of Samuel) and Joseph H. Hummeman had succeeded them.

They built their first steam fire-engine in 1866, under the direction of E.B. Jucket, their shop foreman. Several more machines were built before 1883, when the company went out of business; Boston, MA, circa 1792–1883.

Hunsinger
C. Hunsinger, wagon maker; Prairie du Chien, Wisconsin, circa 1865–1879.

Hunt
Frank D. Hunt, blacksmith and wagon maker; Dayton and Parkman, Wyoming, circa 1901–1910.

Hunt
George P. Hunt, carriage and wagon maker who also built two stage coaches as early as 1851, for use by John Adrient for the run from Marysville to Parks Bar and Long Bar. The ride to Parks Bar cost $4; Marysville, CA, circa 1850–1870.

Hunt
S.G. Hunt, blacksmith and wagon maker; Salida, Colorado, circa 1882–1890.

Hunt (see Pool & Hunt)

Hunter
B.J. Hunter, wagon maker; Springville, WI, circa 1885–1903.

Hunter
William Hunter, blacksmith and wagon maker; Kendrick, Idaho, circa 1905–1910.

Hunter (see Fouts & Hunter Buggy Co.)

Hunter (see Newman & Hunter)
Huntingburg Wagon Works Founded by Wm. Roettger, a blacksmith, and Mr. Propheter, a wheelwright, in Huntingburg, Indiana. They formed a partnership in 1874 and started a business making buggies, surreys, carts, wagons and pony vehicles.

Annual output at their peak was 10,000 units per year, circa 1874–1900's.

Huntington
Jacob R. (Jake) Huntington of West Amesbury, Massachusetts started building wagons and carriages In the mid-1800's, Huntington was one of the first to use assembly line production. In 1859, he moved his shop and workers to Cincinnati, Ohio, where he introduced this method of construction.

Eventually Huntington would return to West Amesbury and re-establish his successful carriage business, circa 1850–1900.

Hurd
H.F. Hurd & Co., blacksmith and wheelwright; carriage and wagon manufacturer, sw cormer of San Jacinto and Commerce, and ne corner of Travis and Commerce; Houston, Texas, circa 1882–1890's.

Hurlburt
G.R. Hurlburt, blacksmith and wagon maker; Pine Bluff, Wyoming, circa 1902–1910.

Hurlburt
L.J. Hurlburt, blacksmith and wagon maker; Pinebluff, Wyoming, circa 1901–1902.

Hurlburt Mfg. Co.
Carriage, wagon and sleigh builder; Racine Junction, Wisconsin, circa 1880–1890's.

Hurley
John H. Hurley, blacksmith and wagon maker, corner of K and 9th; Sacramento, CA, circa 1853–1865.

Hurley & Whitaker
Blacksmiths and wagon makers, corner of K and 9th; Sacramento, CA, 1853–1865.

Hursh
Charles A. Hursh, buggy maker, south fifth street north of Green; Mifflinburg, PA, circa 1887–1920.

Hursh
William D. Hursh, buggy maker, 240 Green street (rear); Mifflinburg, PA, circa 1880–1890.

Hursh
William H. Hursh, buggy maker, 429 Market Street (rear); Mifflinburg, PA, circa 1870–1890's.

Hurst
Alexander D. Hurst manufactured light carriages, 123 West 30th; New York, NY, circa 1899.

Hussey
Obed Hussey started out in Baltimore, Maryland, in the 1830's. This early inventor and implement maker later moved to Willmington, Delaware, where he developed and manufactured several styles of horse-drawn reapers and other farm equipment, circa 1830–1860's.

Hussey Mower & Implement Co.
Manufactured farm equipment, including their Hussey No-Pitman mower; Knightstown, Indiana, circa 1890's–1910.

Hutchins
C.N. Hutchins, blacksmith and wheelwright, 105 Orange; Dallas, Texas, circa 1891–1900.

Hutchinson
George C. Hutchinson, blacksmith and wagon maker, 167 K; Sacramento, CA, circa 1853–1865.

Hutchinson
W. Hutchinson, wagon maker; Mount Sterling, WI, circa 1879.

Hutchison Cut Leather Co.
Cincinnati, Ohio, circa 1880–1910.

Hutchinson & Griffis
Blacksmiths and wagon makers, 167 K; Sacramento, CA, circa 1853–1865.

Hutton
George Hutton; Richmond, Quebec, Canada, circa 1905.
Hutton built a caterpillar style horse-drawn truck that was patented in Canada and the United States.

Hy
E. Hy & Sons, sold out to Baldwin & Sibley; Lemars, Iowa, circa 1890–1899.

Hyde
J.L.Hyde, blacksmith; carriage and wagon maker; Canon City, Colorado, circa 1882–1890.

Hyde
William H. Hyde, wagons and agricultural implements, 3rd and Main; Pueblo, Colorado, circa 1875–1903.

Hyde & Ashby
Blacksmith and wagon makers; Canon City, Colorado, 1879 and Caribou, Colorado, circa 1880's.

Hyde & Kretschmer
Wagons and agricultural implements (see Peter Schuttler); Pueblo, Colorado, circa 1860–1890.

Hynds (see Elliott & Hynds)
Hysel
George Hysel, wagon maker; Rockton, WI, circa 1879–1903.

Illg
John Illg, Sr., blacksmith and wheelwright; also carriage and wagon manufacturer, 355 Dolorosa; San Antonio, Texas, circa 1887–1900.

Illg
John Illg, blacksmith and wheelwright, 605–613 Dolorosa; San Antonio, Texas, circa 1897–1902.

Illo (see Warden & Illo)
Implement Manufacturing Co.
Built the Davenport planter for a very short time; Davenport, Iowa, circa 1900.

Independent Harvester Co.
Manufactured farm implements, wagons and manure spreaders; Plano, Illinois, circa 1900–1930.

Indiana Buggy Co.
Elkhart, IN, circa 1890–1915.

Indiana Forging Co.
Indianapolis, Indiana, circa 1890–1910.

Indiana Lamp Co.
Surrey lamps; Connersville, Indiana, circa 1890–1910.

Indianapolis Dash Co.
Indianapolis, Indiana, circa 1890–1910.

Indian Forging Co.
Circa 1890–1910.

Ingram & Miller
Wagon makers; Tully, NY, circa 1850's.

International Carriage Co.
Manufactured carriages and sleighs, circa 1880's–1900.

International Harvester
Ohio, circa 1890–1910. (see more on International Harvester Co. in Wheels Across America Volume 2).

International Harvester Co. of America
Wagons, 101 Lincoln; Amarillo, Texas, circa 1920.

Ionia Wagon Company
This Ionia, MI, wagon manufacturer, established in 1880, would grow to be one of the largest of its kind in the state, producing over 12,000 wagons annually by the late 1890's. They also offered drays,

dump carts, floats and horse drawn log trucks.

The company is best known for their Bible Wagon, painted Prussian blue with aluminum striping and light red running gear, and their Capital Wagon, painted Sylvan green with aluminum striping and bright red running gear.

Both wagons were registered trade marks, circa 1880–1920.

Irby & Darr
Wagons, buggies and carriages; Dayton, NM, circa 1900–1915.

Irving
George Irving & Co. manufactured wagons, 209 West 18th, New York, NY, circa 1899.

Irving
L.A. Irving manufactured light carriages, 146 Lincoln Avenue; New York, NY, circa 1899.

Isaac
Joseph Isaac, blacksmith and wheelwright, manufacturer of carriages, wagons, buggies and phaetons, 108 Preston Ave.; Houston, Texas, circa 1900–1915.

Isaac (see Hoop & Isaac)

Iseli
Fred Iseli, blacksmith and wagon maker; Boise, ID, circa 1905–1910.

Isenberg
J.W. Isenberg, carriage maker; Pueblo, Colorado, circa 1882–1890.

Isham
H.L. Isham started building carriages, wagons and sleighs in the 1860's. By the 1870's, Isham joined Brundage to form Isham, Brundage & Co.; Plattsburgh, NY., circa 1860's–1870's.

Isham & Sturtevant
Wagon makers; Delavan, Wisconsin, circa 1865.

Israel
Solomon Israel, blacksmith and wheelwright, 2814 Broadway; Galveston, Texas, circa 1886–1894.

Ives
John A. Ives & Brother, later Ives & Son, built several sizes and styles of steam fire engines, including the popular crane-neck engine.

After nearly twenty years in the construction of steamers, Ives discontinued their business; Baltimore, MD, circa 1864–1884.

Jack
Arch Jack, blacksmith and wheelwright, 760 S. Ervay; Dallas, Texas, circa 1900–1910.

Jackson
A.A. Jackson, blacksmith and wagon work; Des Moines, New Mexico, circa 1915.

Jackson
Charles Jackson, blacksmith and wagon maker; Lewiston, Wyoming, circa 1902–1908.

Jackson
G.A. Jackson, blacksmith, 3201 Alameda Ave.; El Paso, Texas, circa 1905–1915.

Jackson
George C. Jackson, carriage maker, corner of J and 4th; Sacramento, CA, circa 1853–1865.

Jackson
George C. Jackson, wagon maker; Portage, Wisconsin, circa 1865–1898.

Jackson
H. Jackson, blacksmith and wagon maker, 503–2nd; Laramie, Wyoming, circa 1901–1906.

Jackson
J.F. Jackson, blacksmith and wagon maker; Grangeville, Idaho, circa 1905–1910.

Jackson
S. Jackson, blacksmith and wheelwright, 248 S. Lamar; Dallas, Texas, circa 1897–1905.

Jackson Bros.
Blacksmiths and wagon makers; Hailey, Idaho, circa 1905–1910.

Jackson Sleigh Co.
Offered a variety of sleigh styles; Jackson, Michigan, circa 1890–1910.

Jackson Wagons
This firm specialized in the construction of wagons, advertised as "The Light Running" Jackson wagon; Jackson, Michigan, circa 1870–1920.

Jackson & Baum
Carriage and wagon makers, 219 Walton, Syracuse, NY, circa 1899.

Jackson & Bowman
Blacksmiths and wheelwrights, 203 Cedar Spring; Dallas, Texas, circa 1898–1905.

Jackson & Hanson
Blacksmiths and wheelwrights, 282 S. Lamar; Dallas, Texas, circa 1891–1902.

Jackson & Humphries
Blacksmiths and wagon makers; Durango, CO, circa 1883–1890.

Jackson (see Gilliland, Jackson & Co.)

Jacobs
L.W. Jacobs, carriage maker, 225 Arch street; Philadelphia, PA, circa 1880–1910.

Jacobson
C. Jacobson, wagon maker; North Cape, WI, circa 1879.

Jager
John G. Jager manufactured light carriages, 255 West 31st; New York, NY, circa 1899.

Jahla
Joseph Jahla, wagon maker; St. Louis, Missouri, circa 1850–1870.

Jahn (see Rodstrom & Jahn)

Jahns
J.C. Jahns, carriage, buggy and wagon dealer, 815 Houston, Ft.Worth, Texas, circa 1896–1905.

Jaloma
J. Jaloma, blacksmith and wheelwright, se corner Utah and 4th; El Paso, Texas, circa 1898–1905.

James
J.D. James, blacksmith and horseshoer, Zangs Boulevard,

Trinity River; Dallas, Texas, circa 1905–1915.

James & Mayer Buggy Co.
Manufactured carriages, buggies and carts, including their #74 Dream Cart and #76 St. James Cart.

They also had a manufacturing plant in Ohio where they built a variety of vehicles, including their Dream Cart; Lawrenceburg, IN, circa 1880–1910.

Jameson
T.T. Jameson, wagon yards, 409 E. Belknap; Ft. Worth, Texas, circa 1896–1906.

Janacek Bros.
Carriage and wagon dealer and representative; Almond, Wisconsin, circa 1890–1910.

Janesville Carriage Works
Wagon and carriage makers; Janesville, WI, circa 1885–1915.

Janesville Machine Co.
Built a variety of implements, including the Prairie City Seeder. The firm was sold, in the early 1900's, to Samson Tractor Company; Janesvelle, Wisconsin, circa 1880–1900.

Janney Manufacturing Co.
Built implements and an early all-steel constructed husker-shredder; Ottumwa, Iowa, circa 1890–1910.

Janney (see Wicker & Janney)

Jaquith
L.S. Jaquith, wagon and carriage maker; Marion, Iowa, circa 1866–1879.

Jarrel
John U Jarrel, blacksmiths and horseshoers, 225 Grand Avenue, Dallas, Texas circa 1906–1912.

Jarrell
J.U. Jarrell, blacksmith and Horseshoer, 659 Commerce; Dallas, Texas, circa 1906–1912.

Jaufus
Wenzel Jaufus, carriage and wagon dealer and representative; Ashford, WI, circa 1890–1910.

Jeffers
William Jeffers was born in 1809, in the town of Milton, MA. Mr. Jeffers built a national reputation early on as a hand-pump fire-engine manufacturer. He offered two styles, known as "side strokes" and "double deckers". By the time he applied his full attention to the construction of steam fire-engines in 1861, the name William Jeffers was well known for quality and dependability; Pawtuckret, RI, circa 1861–1875.

Jeffers would go on to build over 60 machines, before he retired and sold his business to P.S. Skidmore of Bridgeport, CT. Mr. Skidmore constructed only eight more of the Jeffers steam fire-engines before a fire destroyed most of the patterns, in 1878, and he closed the business. William Jeffers died at his home in 1879.

Jenkins
E.H. Jenkins, blacksmith and wagon maker; Alwen, Wyoming, circa 1902–1908.

Jennings
N. Jennings, blacksmith and wheelwright; Sherman, Texas, circa 1893–1900.

Jensen
J. Jensen, wagon maker; Frank, WI, circa 1879.

Jensen
James F. Jensen, blacksmith and wagon maker; Garland, Wyoming, circa 1905–1910.

Jerald Sulky Company
The Jerald Sulky Company of Waterloo, Iowa, was one of the oldest builders of quality turf vehicles in the country.

The company was founded almost by accident in 1895. Samuel E. Jerald, (founder) was a cabinet maker in Osage, Iowa. Jerald built his first carriage for his own use. Many who saw and admired his work asked him to build one like it for them. He soon became widely known as a builder of fine carriages.

He developed and patented a racing sulky—known as the Petrola sulky. Business grew in three years time to the extent that better shipping facilities and access to raw materials was needed. In 1899 the business was moved to Waterloo, Iowa.

Samuel's son, Stanley E. Jerald, who had grown up in the business, took over when his father's health gave out. Stanley was president and general manager until his death in April of 1957.

During World War II, the Jerald Sulky Co. made thousands of field ambulance carriers for the Army.

Jerry
H.E. Jerry & Co., dealers in road wagons, carriages, concords, etc.; West Chazy, N.Y., circa 1890–1910.

Jewel Carriage Co.
Carriage manufacturer; Carthage, OH, circa 1890–1910.

Jewel Carriage Co.
Buggy manufacturer; Cincinnati, Ohio, circa 1880–1910.

Jewell
Oliver Jewell was born in Connecticut in 1776. This very early maker worked for years on his own and in other shops as a blacksmith and wagon maker.

Mr. Jewell died in Cazenovia, NY at the age of 90, circa 1790's–1840's.

Jewett
A.B. Jewett, wagon maker, Port Washington, Wisconsin, circa 1865.

Johansen (see Lindsay & Johansen)

Johns
Harrison Johns, blacksmith, horseshoer, and wagon maker, 136 S. Jefferson Ave.; Dallas, Texas, circa 1906–1912.

Johns
Israel Johns, blacksmith and wheelwright, 605 Neches; 505 E.

7th; and 715 Red River; Austin, Texas, circa 1895–1913.

Johns
Jack T. Johns, blacksmith and wagon maker; Artesia, New Mexico, circa 1906–1912.

Johns
L.B. Johns manufactured shifting carriage tops, complete with seat ready to fasten to body; located at the corner of Main and Barr Streets, Fort Wayne, IN, circa 1870–1900.

Johnson
Alexander Johnson, wagon maker; Camillus, NY, circa 1899.

Johnson
Butler Johnson, blacksmith and wheelwright, 394 South Park; Beaumont, Texas, circa 1910–1915.

Johnson
C.B. Johnson, carriage and wagon dealer and representative; Argyle, Wisconsin, circa 1890–1910.

Johnson
D.W. Johnson & Co. manufactured a variety of children's carriages, including horse and pony-drawn carriages and hand push styles; Hartford, CT, circa 1850–1900.

Johnson
E. Johnson, wagon maker; Portage, WI, circa 1879.

Johnson
Gus Johnson, blacksmith and wagon maker; Newcastle, Wyoming, circa 1901–1902.

Johnson
Henry Johnson, wagon and sleigh maker; Cicero, NY, circa 1850's.

Johnson
Henry J. Johnson, blacksmith and wheelwright, 1301 Dowling; Houston, Texas, circa 1900–1910.

Johnson
J.B. Johnson started out in 1859, building steam fire-engines in the shops of the Metropolitan Works in South Boston, MA. He soon moved over to the shops of McKay & Gallagher in East Boston. Here, he produced the steamers "Antelope" and the "William Chase" for the city's chief engineer.

Johnson moved for the last time, into the shops of Portland Co.'s Works, at Portland, ME., building nearly thirty machines before the end of his career, in 1869.

Mr. Johnson also is credited with the design and patent of an engine with a balance-wheel that would lay flat and spin around like a top; Portland, ME, circa 1859–1869.

Johnson
J.P. Johnson, wagon maker; Unity, Wisconsin, circa 1885–1915.

Johnson
John S. Johnson, blacksmith and wheelwright, Barton Spring road, 1511 S. Congress Ave. and 1216 S. Congress Ave.; Austin, Texas, circa 1898–1918.

Johnson
O.J. Johnson, wagon maker; Beloit, Wisconsin, circa 1879–1903.

Johnson
Peter Johnson, wagon maker; Franksville, WI, circa 1885–1911.

Johnson
R.F. Johnson Paint Co., Cincinnati, Ohio, circa 1880–1910.

Johnson
William Johnson, carriage and wagon maker, 12th and Front St.; Boulder, Colorado, circa 1877–1890.

Johnson & Co.
Blacksmiths and wheelwrights, 120 S. Rusk; Denison, Texas, circa 1893–1900.

Johnson & Spencer
Carriage makers; Salida, Colorado, circa 1882–1890.

Johnson (see Collins & Johnson)
Johnson (see Fuller & Johnson Manufacturing Co.)
Johnson (see Hazelwood & Johnson)
Johnson (see Hinks & Johnson)

Johnston
Daniel T. Johnston & Brothers, wagon makers; Pittsburgh, PA., circa 1850–1870.

Johnston Co.
Joe E. Johnston, carriages, wagons and buggies, sw corner of Elm, Jefferson and 135–137 Main; Dallas, Texas, circa 1910.

Johnston
Oscar Johnston & Co., blacksmiths and wheelwrights, Shell Road, Spindle Top; Beaumont, Texas, circa 1906–1912.

Johnston Harvester Co.
Manufactured tillage equipment, harvesting machines and other farm implements. Johnston bought out Richardson Manufacturing Co. in 1913 and began building the Easy Loader spreader.

They started out under the name of Johnston Huntley & Company in the 1840's, building their patented Cycloid mowers by the 1860's.

In the 1870's Johnston's Wrought Iron mower was popular, but by 1890 a new line, under the continental name, was being produced in large numbers.

Johnston became part of Massey-Harris in 1917; Batavia, NY., circa 1845–1917.

Johnston & McClain
Blacksmiths, wagon makers and carriage makers; Telluride, Colorado, circa 1883.

Johnston Transfer & Storage
Carriages, buggies and wagons, corner 105–107 N. Broadway; Dallas, Texas, circa 1891–1900.

Jones
Beverly A. Jones, blacksmith and wheelwright, 689 Elm; Dallas, Texas, circa 1898–1903.

Jones
D.C. Jones, blacksmith and wagon maker; Dixon, Wyoming, circa 1902–1910.

Jones
Isaac Jones, a Union County wagon maker also offered a full line of

lighter pleasure vehicles, including carriages, sulkeys and gigs; Lewisburg, PA, circa 1820's–1840's.

Jones
Lewis Jones (born 1799-died 1876) established his blacksmith and wagon making shop on the town square of Independence, Missouri, in 1827. Here he built a variety of wagons and farm implements. Jones also served as the government blacksmith for the Shawnee indian tribe.

It is not known how long Lewis Jones remained in the wagon business. He did find time for other business opportunities, including construction of the Nebraska House Hotel in Independence, Missouri (circa 1849) and for numerous trading trips to New Mexico and Mexico.

Jones
Phineas Jones & Co. was established in 1855. They advertised as manufacturers of the celebrated Jones Wheels; Newark, NJ, circa 1855–1905.

Jones
R. Jones, wagon maker; Watertown, WI, circa 1879.

Jones
Robert Jones, carriage and wagon maker; Brooklyn, N.Y., circa 1890–1900.

Jones
Silas Jones, carriage and wagon maker; Brinton, Utah, circa 1884–1890.

Jones
T.F. Jones, blacksmith; Burlington, Wyoming, circa 1905–1910.

Jones
Thomas Jones, carriage maker; Utica, NY, circa 1850's.

Jones
Tyson Jones Buggy Co.; Carthage, NC, circa 1890–1910.

Jones & Dahl
Blacksmiths and wagon makers; Dixon, Wyoming, circa 1900–1905.

Jones & Delaney
Blacksmiths and wagon makers, 131 S. Houston; Dallas, Texas, circa 1910.

Jones & Money
Blacksmiths and wheelwrights, carriage and wagon makers, 257 Wall; Beaumont, Texas, circa 1910–1915.

Jones & Smith
Wagon and carriage makers; Madison, Wisconsin, circa 1865.

Jones & Stelfox
Blacksmiths and wheelwrights;carriage and wagon makers, 201 W. 5th; Austin, TX, circa 1887–1890's.

Jones (see Clapp & Jones)
Jones (see Collins & Jones)
Jones (see Haskell & Jones)
Jones (see McGrath & Jones)
Jones (see Oler & Jones)

Jordan
Edward B. Jordan's business was established in 1868, successors to E.F. French. The Jordan firm built carriage roofs, sides, backs, and decks for broughams, coupes, rockaways and English hansom cabs. They also made tops and sides for delivery wagons and backs, sides and dashes for sleighs; 98 &100 Eleventh Avenue, New York, NY, circa 1868–1910.

Joubert & White
Carriage and wagon maker; Glens Falls, NY., circa 1870–1910.

Joy
C.B. Joy, blacksmith and wagon maker; Pueblo, Colorado, circa 1877–1890.

Joy (see Glidden & Joy Varnish Company)

Joyce
J.M. Joyce, blacksmith and wagon maker, 205 W 4th; Amarillo, Texas, circa 1910–1920.

Joyce (see Simpson & Joyce)

Jube
John P. Jube & Co.of 97 Bowery, New York, NY. Dealers in carriage goods, imported cloths and varnishes, circa 1870's–1900.

Jucket & Freeman
The "Northern Liberty" No. 8 was the first steam fire-engine built by this firm, at their shops on Hampden street, in 1869. This 8,500 lb. engine served for many years on the streets of Boston, including action at the great fire of November 9, 1872.

The business was discontinued in 1871, and their patterns were sold to Union Machine Company of Fitchburg, MA. This firm constructed several more machines from the Junket & Freeman designs, before going out of business.

Allen Supply Company acquired the patterns and built three more steamers; Roxbury, MA, circa 1869–1885.

Judkins
John B. Judkins Company, light vehicles; Merrimac, Massachusetts, circa 1890–1910.

Judson
A. Judson, carriage maker; Vernon, NY, circa 1850's.

Judson
A. Judson's Sons manufactured light carriages and wagons; Vernon, NY, circa 1899.

June
Seymour A. June, wagon and sleigh maker; Manlius, NY, circa 1850's.

Jung Carriage Co.
Jacob Jung, a German immigrant was a carriage maker by trade in the old country. He came to the United States in 1855 and established the Jung Carriage Co.

Jung wanted to provide a livelihood for his family and reliable transportation for settlers of the region; Sheboygan, Wisconsin, circa 1855–1890.

In 1890 his sons, Jacob Jr. and William, took over the successful business and operated it until 1917, when the advent of the automobile all but relegated the horse and buggy to history.

Jung Carriage Museum

Jacob Jung's grandson Wesley, who had spent childhood summers as an apprentice in the family's factory, (see Jung Carriage Co.) began collecting carriages in the 1930's "to preserve a lost art and fading heritage."

In 1963 his private collection became the core of the new "State Carriage Museum" created by the Wisconsin legislature. The Wesley Jung Carriage Museum opened to the public in 1968.

Today the museum exhibits popular modes of American-made transportation and work vehicles from the nineteenth and early twentieth centuries. With more than 100 horse-drawn and hand-operated vehicles, the collection ranks as Wisconsin's largest—and one of the largest in the nation.

Carriages range from commercial delivery wagons, fire wagons, sleighs, and a circus calliope—to children's play wagons and sleds.

Remarkable examples of the carriage-maker's craft include a Velvet Tobacco wagon and an umbrella-topped phaeton (both 1900), and a Silsby steam-powered fire pumper (1885).

Jungkurth

F.J. Jungkurth, carriage maker; Germantown, PA, circa 1880–1910.

Jungquist

William Jungquist, blacksmith and wagon maker; Rawlins, Wyoming, circa 1902–1908.

Kaiser

Paul Kaiser & Co., blacksmiths and wheelwrights; carriage painters and trimmers, 1826 Market; Galveston, Texas, circa 1900–1910.

Kaiser Buggy Co.

Henry Kaiser was born (1840) in Hesse, Germany. This is where he grew up and learned the buggy trade.

In 1859, he emigrated to America—first to Cincinnati and shortly thereafter to Kenton, Ohio.

He began the buggy business in 1864, on North Main Street; Kenton, Ohio. He manufactured buggies and light carriages.

With approximately 10 to 14 employees, the factory turned out 60/75 carriages per year. According to history records the firm made $10,000 in annual sales from selling and repairing carriages, phaetons and buggies. They advertised themselves as the Artistic Carriage Builders.

Eventually the business was carried on by his sons, under the firm name of Kaiser Motor Co. Four of six sons, Albert, Will, John and George remained in the business the longest.

The automobile stopped the popularity of the buggies. Before the final sale of the business, the company went from making and repairing buggies to selling automobiles, including the Tucker car in the 1950's.

Kaiser & Felsmann

Blacksmiths and wheelwrights, 2916 Broadway; Galveston, Texas, circa 1888–1894.

Kaizer

C. Kaizer, wagon and carriage maker; Cedar Grove, WI, circa 1879.

Kalamazoo Carriage & Wagon Co.

Manufactured carriages, wagons and sleighs; Kalamazoo, Michigan, circa 1880's–1910.

Kalamazoo Cart Co.

Manufactured and sold thousands of carts by the mid 1880's, including their Excelsior Drop-Bar Cart; Kalamazoo, Michigan, circa 1880–1900.

Kaltenbach

K. Kaltenbach, blacksmith and wagon maker; Georgetown, Colorado, circa 1880–1890.

Kamesch

Wenzel Kamesch, carriage and wagon dealer and representative; Antigo, Wisconsin, circa 1890–1910.

Kansas Manufacturing Company

Founded in 1874, this Leavenworth, Kansas company grew to become the largest wagon manufacturing firm in Kansas. By 1880, the company is said to have produced seven thousand wagons in one year. They built the famous Rocky Mountain freight wagon and the Leadville Quartz wagon.

Cyrus Townsend, son of Pittsburgh wagon maker Cyrus Townsend, served as general agent of the company.

A large number of their workers were convicts from the Kansas State Penitentiary, for which the company paid the state about 50-cents a day for each worker; Leavenworth, Kansas, circa 1874–1900.

Kansas Wagons

353 Wazee; Denver, Colorado, circa 1880–1890.

Kappe & Daab

Farm implement manufacturing company; Belleville, Illinois, circa 1880–1890.

Karis

Adam Karis, carriage and wagon maker; Arcadia, Wisconsin, circa 1890–1910.

Karling & Westlund

Blacksmiths, wheelwright and wagon makers; carriage, wagon and buggy dealer, 1605 Sabine; Austin, Texas, circa 1889–1894.

Kassinger

Jacob F. Kassinger, wagon maker; St. Elmo, Colorado, circa 1880–1890.

Kating

Kating and Son, wagon makers; Sheboygan, WI, circa 1879.

Katzner, Russell & Chase

This early firm specialized in road carts and other light vehicles; Marysville, CA, circa 1850's–1880's.

Kauffman Buggy Co.
Jacob Kauffman, founder of the Kauffman Co., was born in 1830 in Annville, Lebanon County, PA. He was apprenticed as a carriage body-maker at age 16, worked at his trade and in 1853 started a carriage factory at Jonestown, PA. About ten years later he sold out and moved to Ohio, settling first in Troy—and in 1869 moved to Miamisburg with his wife, five sons and one daughter. He started a carriage factory on North Main street, and made buggies that were considered the "Cadillac" of buggies.

His son William J. Kauffman was president of Enterprise Carriage Mfg. Co., also of Miamisburg.

Jacob died in 1903 and his pall bearers, at his request, were selected from factory employees, by whom he was greatly admired.

K.C. Buggy Co.
Buggy manufacturer; Cincinnati, Ohio, circa 1880–1910.

Kean & Lines
Builder of fine carriages and delivery wagons; New Haven, CT., circa 1870–1900.

Kearney
Dennis Kearney sr., wagon maker; Kenosha, WI, circa 1865.

Kearney (see Van Tassel & Kearner)

Kedenburg
J.P.A. Kedenburg manufactured light carriages and wagons, 335 East 46th; New York, NY, circa 1899.

Keefe (see Brinker & Keefe)

Keehn & Morris
Blacksmiths and wagon makers; Grand Junction, Colorado, circa 1881–1890.

Keeler
William Keeler, carriage maker; Hagersville and Keelersville, Bucks County, PA, circa 1880–1910.

Keene
A. Keene, wagon maker; Fulton, Wisconsin, circa 1865.

Keens
Harvey F. Keens. (see Kelk Carriage Works); Sedalia, MO, circa 1890–1925.

Kees (see Allison & Kees)

Keeser
William Keeser, carriage and wagon maker; Deming, New Mexico, circa 1884–1890.

Keim
George DeB. Keim was a dealer in carriage and coach trimming. They also did saddlery and harness work at 162 North Third Street; Philadelphia, PA, circa 1860's–1880's.

Kelk Carriage Works
Established in 1868 by Thomas Kelk, the company specialized in carriage production and advertised a full line of high grade spring vehicles. By 1889, the Kelk factory had grown to employ a number of craftsmen, including a young man from Canada named Harvey F. Keens. Mr. Keens would eventually be taken into partnership, and upon the death of Thomas Kelk, Harvey Keens became the sole owner.

1916 was the factories' peak production year, when over 750 carriages rolled out the door. The last carriage built by this company was in 1923, for an old country doctor. After that, little more than repair work was done in the Kelk & Keens shop, until it sold; Sedalia, Missouri, circa 1868–1923.

Keller
Ewald H. Keller, blacksmith and wheelwright; carriage, buggy, phaetons and wagon manufacturer and dealer; also carriage painters and trimmers, nw corner Throckmorton and W. 2nd; Ft. Worth, Texas, circa 1896–1906.

Keller
E.H. Keller, carriages, buggies and wagons; also carriage painters and trimmers, 404 W. Main; Denison, Texas, circa 1899–1910.

Keller
G. Keller, wagon maker; Sherwood, WI, circa 1879.

Keller
Henry Keller, wagon maker; Kansasville, WI, circa 1879–1919.

Keller
Martin Keller, blacksmith and wheelwright, 120 Nogalitos; San Antonio, Texas, circa 1897–1902.

Keller (see Mosehart & Keller)

Kellogg
Austin Kellogg manufactured wagons and sleighs; Lysander, NY, circa 1850's.

Kellogg
L.D. Kellogg, wagon maker; Readstown, WI, circa 1879–1911.

Kelly
J.K. Kelly, carriage maker; Pueblo, Colorado, circa 1882.

Kelly
John B. Kelly, blacksmith and wheelwright, Wood, bottom of Montgomery Ave. and Vine; Houston, Texas, circa 1887–1900.

Kelly
L. D. Kelly, wagon maker, 7th, between I and J; Sacramento, CA, circa 1853–1865.

Kelly (see Beedle & Kelly Co.)
Kelly (see Fassett & Kelly)
Kelly (see Knoulson & Kelly)
Kelly (see Laughlin & Kelly)

Kemp
James Kemp, farm implement manufacturing company; Kempton, Illinois, circa 1880–1900.

Kemp
John Kemp built carriages and sleighs; Detroit, Michigan, circa 1870's–1890's.

Kemp
Joseph S. Kemp's father came from England in 1838, married the following year, and settled on a farm south of Magog, Stanstead county, Province of Quebec, Canada.

Here, two years later, is where Joseph S. Kemp was born, July 4, 1841. At the age of seven years, Mr. Kemp began his off and on pursuit of education, until he reached the age of nineteen years.

He then gravitated to the trade that made him a successful manufacturer of manure spreaders. He talked his way into an apprenticeship, to learn the carpenter's trade, from a Mr. Fields at Derby, Vermont.

The next spring he went to Barton, Vermont and began carpentering. By 1866 he had returned to Canada to engage in the lumber business.

By September of that year he had married and moved to Portland Maine. He took some young carpenters with him—and they built and sold two houses.

Once again, he returned to his roots in Canada—and his first love, where he bought a farm. Unfortunately, he found out too late, the soil had been farmed to exhaustion.

He engaged in dairying and in feeding for beef, reasoning that this would be the best way to build up the exhausted soil. To spread the winter's make of manure was difficult work, time consuming and not very evenly spread.

In 1874, following out a line of thought that there could and ought to be built a machine to pulverize and spread manure evenly and in a measured quantity per acre, he rigged over an ox cart. This worked so well that a Mr. Allen, of Waterloo, Province of Quebec, wanted Kemp to build him a spreader. This he did in 1875.

It was the first practical spreader that was ever built. Within seven years from the building of the first spreader, Kemp had doubled the production of his farm.

In 1877 Kemp entered into a partnership for the manufacture of manure spreaders with a Mr. William Burpee of Derby, Vermont. In 1878 they built five machines in Canada and ten in Vermont. That same year, they made a contract with the Richardson Manufacturing Company of Worcester, Mass., to manufacture the spreaders under Kemp's patent, for a royalty of $5 each for the New England states.

Since this spreader was being so welcomed by New England farmers, Messrs. Kemp and Burpee decided to form a company to control the remainder of the United States.

After some Syracuse capitalists became interested in Mr. Kemp's patents, a corporation was formed under the laws of the State of New York. It was named The Kemp & Burpee Manufacturing Company.

For sixteen years Mr. Kemp and Mr. Burpee worked shoulder to shoulder until 1896, when Mr. Burpee died. Mr. Kemp remained with the firm until June, 1897, then he withdrew.

Now having time to make improvements, Mr. Kemp built the 20th Century Spreader and secured U.S. patents for it.

In 1900 Kemp closed an agreement with his son, W.I. Kemp, and Mr. John S. Lewis (who organized the J.S. Kemp Manufacturing Company) and they began manufacturing in Syracuse, N.Y.

On the last day of March they turned out their first 20th Century Spreader. At the date of the finishing of the first machine they had twenty-four more nearly done, and the next morning, April 1, 1900, their factory and all its contents were consumed in a fire.

Mr. John S. Lewis furnished the first cash deposit on which this company commenced business. Certainly nothing could have been more discouraging to any man than, after having invested his all, $3,500, to have it destroyed in one night by fire.

But Mr. Lewis was not discouraged, and he succeeded in making arrangements to start their business again at Newark Valley, New York. His unalterable conviction that the 20th Century Manure Spreader, as designed by Mr. J.S. Kemp, was a machine destined to score an unequivocal success, always spurred him on to renewed efforts. Business growth became so rapid and healthy, the company had to increase the capital stock. In 1903, they made still another increase and built a large and complete factory in Waterloo, Iowa, for the purpose of taking care of the trade west of the Mississippi River.

The J. S. Kemp Manufacturing Company became the largest and strongest manure spreader organization in the world, circa 1875–1930's.

Kemp
Henry E. Kemp & Co., dealers in carriages and wagons, also a line of agricultural implements by Emory L. Grant of Kenosha, Wisconsin. Business located on the west side of the plaza; Phoenix, AZ, circa 1888–1894.

Kempf
John Kempf, blacksmith and wagon maker; Genesee, Idaho, circa 1905–1910.

Kempton
Arthur E. Kempton, wagon maker; Markesan, Wisconsin, circa 1879–1919.

Kempton
Jason Kempton, blacksmith and wagon maker; Evans, Colorado, circa 1880–1890.

Kendall
In 1848, a new blacksmith began working in Marion, Iowa. Albert Kendall's original shop was on 11th street, between 7th and 8th avenues. During almost a century, and almost without interruption, the Kendall name has been, and still is, prominent in the business life of Marion, Iowa.

Albert Kendall and his wife, Sarah Higley were natives of West Granby, CT. They came to Linn County, Iowa with Sarah's two brothers in 1842.

Kendall
William Kendall, wagon maker; Neosho, WI, circa 1879.

Kennedy
Henry Kennedy, blacksmith and wagon maker; Juliaetta, Idaho, circa 1905–1910.

Kennedy
James Kennedy & Son manufactured wagons and trucks, 438 West 17th; New York, NY, circa 1899.

Kennedy & Risher
Blacksmiths and wheelwrights, 1107 E. 6th; Austin, Texas, circa 1898–1908.

Kennedy, Willing & Co.
Carriage and carriage goods, including harness and saddlery, 100–102 N. 3rd Street; Philadelphia, Pennsylvania, circa 1880–1900.

Kenner (see Ellis & Kenner)

Kennerly
Chesley Kennerly, blacksmith and wheelwright, 1004 E. 6th; Austin, Texas, circa 1893–1900.

Kent
M. Kent, wagon maker; Amherst, Wisconsin, circa 1879.

Kent & Heath
Blacksmith and wagon maker; Boise, Idaho, circa 1905–1910.

Kent & Schmidt
Blacksmith and wagon maker, 425 Larimer; Denver, Colorado, circa 1877–1880's.

Kentucky Wagon Manufacturing Co.
This Louisville, Kentucky firm built wagons at least into the 1950's, including their Old Hickory farm wagon of the 1920's. They also built a line of miniature wagons that could be pulled by a goat, circa 1880's–1950's.

Kenyon
J. Kenyon, blacksmith and wagon maker; Fletcher, Idaho, circa 1905–1910.

Kern
C. Kern, wagon maker; Beetown, Wisconsin, circa 1879.

Kern
C.J. Kern, wagon maker; Bagley, Wisconsin, circa 1885–1915.

Kern
Henry Kern, wagon maker; Potosi, Wisconsin, circa 1885–1903.

Kern
John Kern was a well known wagon maker and blacksmith. By the 1850's, he was building over 150 wagons per year.

Kern supplied the locals and contract freighters headed west; St. Louis, Missouri, circa 1840–1880.

Kern (see Schwartz & Kern)
Kerns (see Sellers & Kerns)
Kernegan (see King & Kernegan)

Kerr
David Kerr, wagon maker, 47–49 Beale; San Francisco, California, circa 1882–1890.

Kerr, Cunningham & Co.
Carriage and buggy builders; Rochester, NY, circa 1830's–1860.

Ketter Manufacturing Company
Specialized in the construction of delivery wagons, from light to heavy duty; Hanover, PA, circa 1850's–1915.

Ketterer
Charles P. Ketterer Co. manufactured wagons and trucks, 214 West 17th; New York, NY, circa 1899.

Ketterer
Philip Ketterer manufactured carriages, express and business wagons of all sizes, 90 Thompson; New York, NY, circa 1850's–1870's.

Kettner
August W. Kettner, wagon maker, 536 West 43rd; New York, NY, circa 1899.

Keuper
F. Keuper, wagon maker; Burlington, Wisconsin, circa 1865.

Keyes & Wilson
Manufactured light and heavy carriages, 372 Broome; New York, NY, circa 1899.

Keys
R.M. Keys, blacksmith and wagon maker; Menan, Idaho, circa 1905–1910.

Keyser & Rogers
Importers and manufacturers of carriage lamps, mountings, wrought bands; also linen cane work and four-in-hand furniture, 101 North Fourth Street; Philadelphia, PA, circa 1870–1900.

Keystone Carriage Co.
Mr. Albert Armstrong operated Keystone Buggy Co., in Cincinnati, Ohio, from 1889 to 1902, then sold out to the Columbus Vehicle Co.

Keystone Forging Co.
Built carriage and wagon accessories, including fifth wheels and their Standard Body Loops; Nothumberland, PA., circa 1890–1910.

Keystone Manufacturing Co.
Built farm implements and would eventually be purchased by International Harvester Co.; Sterling, Illinois, circa 1880–1905.

Keystone Manufacturing Co.
This Rock Falls, Illinois company started out as Galt & Tracy in the 1860's. After the name was changed to Keystone Mfg. in 1880, they began to carry a full line of implements, although the Galt Rotary Planter would remain part of their advertised line.

In 1904, they became part of the International Harvester Co., circa 1880–1904.

Keystone Paint and Filler Co.
Supplied paint and varnish to the carriage trade; Muncy, PA., circa 1890–1910.

Keystone Spring Works
Manufactured carriage, truck and wagon springs, including their patented Rib Cross Springs, Rib Side Springs and others.

Located at 13th and Buttonwood streets; Philadelphia, PA, circa 1870–1900.

Keystone Wagon Co.
Manufacturer of farm and delivery wagons; Reading, PA., circa 1890–1910.

Kidney
James Kidney Carriage Co., buggy manufacturer; Cincinnati, Ohio, circa 1880–1910.

Kilander & Rudd
Enterprise Carriage Co.; carriage, buggy and phaeton manufacturer; also carriage painters and trimmers, nw corner of Rusk and east 15th; Ft. Worth, Texas, circa 1900–1915.

Kilby
Alfred Kilby was credited with the construction of a track-laying truck; Dennysville, ME, circa 1902.

Kilgore-Peteler Company
Wheels; Minneapolis, MN, circa 1905–1910

Kiltner
E.C. Kiltner, wagon maker; Green Bay, WI, circa 1879–1903.

Kimball
C. P. Kimball, manufacturer of light vehicles, and credited with further developing and marketing the Portland Cutter; Portland, Maine.

Kimball also was a manufacturer of carriages, carriage delivery trucks and other commercial vehicles in Chicago, Illinois, circa 1860–1890.

Kimball
G.F. Kimball, carriage wheel manufacturer, located at 125 State Street; New Haven, CT, circa 1850's–1890.

Kimball
Peter Kimball introduced the Portland Cutter in 1816. This cutter had much straighter lines than the markedly rounded sides of the Albany Cutter introduced by James Goold; Portland, Maine, circa 1816–1840.

Kimball Bros.
Manufactured carriages, sleighs and wagons; Boston, MA., circa 1880's–1900.

Kimball & Co.
This San Francisco, CA. firm may have constructed one or more horse-drawn fire-engines, circa 1875.

Kimberlin Manufacturing Co.
R.P. Kimberlin Co. built farm implements, including their Iron Duke Harrow, 25 West Georgia street; Indianapolis, Indiana, circa 1870–1910.

King
Charles King worked as a wagon maker, blacksmith, volunteer fireman, stone mason and carpenter; Cazenovia, NY, circa 1845–1875.

King & Kernegan
Blacksmith and wagon maker, Del Norte, CO, circa 1880–1890.

King & Tetreault
Blacksmiths and wagon makers, Montezuma, CO, circa 1884–1890.

King (see Hubbard & King)

Kingman Plow Co.
Manufacturer of farm implements; Peoria, IL, circa 1900–1910.

Kingsbury & Henshaw
Carriage and wagon dealers and representatives; Antigo, Wisconsin, circa 1890–1910.

Kingsley
C. Kingsley, wagon maker; Wautoma, WI, circa 1879.

Kingsley (see English & Kingsley)

Kingston Buggy Co.
Kingston, N.C., circa 1890–1910.

Kingman Texas Implement Co.
Carriage, wagon and buggy manufacturer, se corner of Pacific Ave. and Houston; Dallas, Texas, circa 1910.

Kinker & Koelker
Buggy manufacturer; Cincinnati, Ohio, circa 1880–1910.

Kinnard Press Co.
Built agricultural implements, including a hay press equipped with a special attachment to a horse for its power.

The Kinnard firm reorganized as Kinnard-Haines Co. and entered the tractor manufacturing business; Minneapolis, MN, circa 1880–1920's.

Kinnear
J.A. Kinnear, blacksmith and wagon maker, south 3rd; Laramie, Wyoming, circa 1902–1908.

Kinnitt
P.M. Kinnitt, carriage and wagon manufacturer and dealer; Stanfield, Idaho, circa 1908.

Kinsey
W.J. Kinsey, 15th and Wazee, 15th and Wynkoop; Denver, Colorado, circa 1877–1887.

Kinsley
Edwin Kinsley (Kingsley-1915), wagon maker; Beloit, Wisconsin, circa 1885–1915.

Kipp
A. Kipp & Sons, manufacturer of truck wagons, carts and wagons; New York, NY., circa 1860–1870's.

Kipp
John L. Kipp manufactured wagons and trucks—some for export, 222 East 24th; New York, NY, circa 1899.

Kirby
Charles Kirby, blacksmith and wagon maker; Moorcroft, Wyoming, circa 1902–1910.

Kirby (see Griffin & Kirby)

Kircher
John Kircher & Sons, wagon makers, 702 East 12th; New York, NY, circa 1899.

Kircher
Louis H. Kircher, wagon maker, 615 East 12th; New York, NY, circa 1899.

Kirkland
G.W. Kirkland, Georgetown, Colorado, circa 1880's.

Kiser
Samuel Kiser, wagon maker, 9th, between J and K; Sacramento, CA, circa 1853–1865.

Kissick
Samuel Kissick, wagon maker; Pittsburgh, PA., circa 1835–1850.

Kitzmuller
M. Kitzmuller, carriage and wagon maker; carriage and wagon wheels; dealer in all kinds of carriage and wagon material, also in hard and soft wood lumber, 856–58 Howard; San Francisco, California, circa 1882–1890.

Kizer (see Leist & Kizer)

Klaber
Frederick Klaber, built and repaired wagons. With the help of eight men, he turned out over 70 wagons in 1860. Klaber died in 1866; Westport, Missouri, circa 1850–1866.

Klatt (see Fowler & Klatt)

Kleber
Ernest Kleber, wagon maker; Lodi, Wisconsin, circa 1865–1898.

Klein
William A. Klein, wagon maker; Lake Mills, WI, circa 1885–1919.

Klein & Daumeyer
Buggy manufacturer; Cincinnati, Ohio, circa 1880–1910.

Klobe Bros
(Kolbe-1911) Wagon makers; Eau Galle, WI, circa 1885–1919.

Klom
Klom & Thorpe Wagon Shop; Marion, Iowa, circa 1872.

Klopp
Philip Klopp & Son, buggy manufacturer; Cincinnati, Ohio, circa 1880–1910.

Klostermann
H. Klostermann, wagon maker; Morrison, WI, circa 1879.

Klotz
William Klotz, blacksmith and wagon maker; Fort Washakie, Wyoming, circa 1905–1910.

Kluever
Herman Kluever, carriage and wagon maker; Ashippun, Wisconsin, circa 1890–1910.

Klug
J.M. Klug, wagon maker; Whitewater, Wisconsin, circa 1885–1911.

Klumb
P. Klumb, wagon maker; Granville, WI, circa 1879.

Klumb
William Klumb, wagon maker; Kaukauna, WI, circa 1885–1919.

Klund
John Klund, wagon maker; Bloomer, WI, circa 1885–1919.

Knapp Plow Works
Manufactured wagons, plows and other farm implements; San Jose, CA, circa 1870's–1824.

Knight
A.A. Knight, wagon maker; Whitehall, WI, circa 1879.

Knight
A.E. Knight, wagon maker; Seneca, Wisconsin, circa 1865.

Knight & Co.
J.W. Knight, blacksmiths and implements; Dexter, New Mexico, curca 1915.

Knight Buggy Co.
John Robert Knight, owner, Franklin, Virgiaia; circa 1890–1916.

Knight & Page
Wagon makers; Waupaca, Wisconsin, circa 1879–1911.

Knoblaugh
A.L. Knoblaugh Co., buggy manufacturer; Cincinnati, Ohio, circa 1880–1910.

Knoblock (see Miller-Knoblock Wagon Co.)

Knoll
R. Knoll, wagon maker; Marcy, Wisconsin, circa 1879.

Knollhoff
John F. Knollhoff, wagon maker; St. Louis, MO, circa 1850–1870.

Knollhoff
W.W. Knollhoff, wagon maker; St. Louis, MO, circa 1850–1870.

Knoulson & Kelly
Known to have built one small horse-drawn steam fire-engine for the Troy Water Works, in 1875. The engine was on hand to be used, if necessary, on fires, but saw extensive use pumping out water mains; Troy, NY, circa 1875.

Knowles Steam Pump Works
Several styles and sizes of steam fire-engines were built by this firm and shipped to customers as far away as Egypt; Warren, MA, circa 1875–1890.

Knowlton
John Knowlton manufactured several horse-drawn steam fire-engines, including five machines for the Philadelphia Fire Department; Sharon Hill, PA, circa 1872–1880.

Knox
D. Knox, carriage maker; Rome, NY, circa 1850's.

Knox & Fritts
Blacksmiths and wheelwrights, 507 Main; Dallas, Texas, circa 1897.

Knuppel
William O. Knuppel, wagon maker, 223 West 34th Street; New York, NY, circa 1899.

Knutson
Christie Knutson, wagon maker; Berlin, Wisconsin, circa 1885–1903.

Knutson
J. Knutson, wagon and carriage maker; Manitowoc, WI, circa 1879.

Kobler (see Finnesey & Kobler)

Koch (see Carr & Koch)

Koch & Gotlieb
Blacksmith, carriage and wagon maker, 11th and Larimer; Denver, Colorado, circa 1879–1885.

Koehler
Emil Koehler, wagon maker; Bangor, Wisconsin, circa 1879–1915.

Koehler
Frank Koehler, wagon maker; Menomonee Falls, Wisconsin, circa 1885–1919.

Koehler
John H. Koehler, blacksmith and wheelwright, sw corner 27th and W. Mechanic, 2510 Strand, and 3610 H; Galveston, Texas, circa 1886–1894.

Koekler
J. Koekler, wagon maker; Watertown, WI, circa 1879.

Koelker (see Kinker & Koelker)

Koenig
Julius Koenig, wagon maker; Fillmore, WI, circa 1879–1903.

Koenig
Martin Koenig, wagon maker; Poniatowski, WI, circa 1885–1903.

Koenig
William Koenig, wagon maker, 237 St. Nicholas Avenue; New York, NY, circa 1899.

Koerble
John Koerble, Jr., carriage and wagon dealer and representative; Ackerville, WI, circa 1890–1910.

Koerner
Samuel Koerner, wagon maker, 67 Montgomery; New York, NY, circa 1899.

Koglmeier
Emeran E. Koglmeier, carriage-painter and trimmer; harness and saddlery, 200 S. Santa Fe; also 121 W. Overland; El Paso, Texas, circa 1900–1914.

Kohl
H.A. Kohl & Co., carriage and wagon dealers and representatives; Antigo, Wisconsin, circa 1890–1910.

Kokomo Rubber Co.
Rubber tires for vehicles; Kokomo, IN, circa 1890–1910.

The Kolb Wheelwrights

Kolb
George Michael Kolb (1744–1826), was a first generation wheelwright and wagon maker, New Hanover Township, Pennsylvania, circa 1765. His father was also George Michael Kolb, an immigrant (1709–1790) who came to America in 1738.

Kolb
George Kolb, (1775–1833), second generation wheelwright, circa 1795–1830.

Kolb
John Kolb, (1806–1878) was a third generation wheelwright and wagon maker, circa 1821.

Kolb
Joshua Lang Kolb, (1836–1887), fourth generation wheelwright and blacksmith, circa 1860's.

Kolb
William H.R. Kolb, (1860–1929), wheelwright, millwright and undertaker. This was the fifth and last generation of wheelwrights.

William was also a showman who put on plays at the old opera house in Pottstown, PA. William, as many other Americans of German ancestry did, changed his last name (from Kolb to Kulp) due to the xenophobia of many Americans during World War I.

The Kolb/Kulp Wheelwright Shop
The Kolb family wheelwright business started with George Michael Kolb in 1765 and ran continually until the death of William H.R. Kulp in 1929—a total of 164 years.

For 149 of those years (1780—1929) the business was located at the Church and Little Road area. This was part of Philadelphia County until 1784 when Montgomery County was created from part of Philadelphia County. These five generations of Kolb wheelwrights kept the wagon making art alive, from the English colonial period to the start of the automobile age.

With the onset of the Great Depression and the advancements made in automation and transportation—the horses, wagons, buggies and all attending equipment, hardware and supplies were rapidly fading from the American scene.

William's sons and grandsons showed no interest in ever reopening the shop. The equipment was sold during the depression.

That, however, is not the end of the story. Along came another generation (twins Richard and Robert Kulp). They grew up hearing family members talking about "The Shop".

Having spent a considerable amount of time and effort in researching the Kulp wagon making history, they established a part-time business making wheels and building detailed replicas of painted farm wagons. Today they can be found at:

Kulp Wheelwright Shop
2233 Little Road
Perkiomenville, PA
(Building Miniature Wagons)

Kolinsky & Wurster
Wagon and carriage manufacturer, 542 East 74th; New York, NY, circa 1899.

Kolling
William Kolling Carriage Co., buggy manufacturer; Cincinnati, Ohio, circa 1880–1910.

Koncsbach
N.C. Koncsbach, house, sign and carriage painter; Buena Vista, Colorado, circa 1882–1890.

Kopenhafer
George Kopenhafer, wheelwright; carriage and wagon maker; Denver, Colorado, circa 1883–1890.

Korber & Co.
J. Korber, wagons, vehicles and implements; also harness and saddlery; Albuquerque, New Mexico, circa 1900–1915.

Korn
L.C. Korn, blacksmith and wheelwright, 2902 Washington; Houston, Texas, circa 1900–1910.

Korn
Chester T. Korn Carriage Co., buggy manufacturer; Cincinnati, Ohio, circa 1880–1910.

Kovishty

A. Kovishty, (Zuni Indian), blacksmith and wagon maker on the Zuni Indian reservation in McKinley County, 45 miles south of Gallup, NM. The 1906 population was 1600, circa 1900–1910.

Kraft (see Smith & Kraft)

Krahn

August Krahn, wagon maker; Huilsburg, WI, circa 1879–1903.

Krakauer, Zork & Moye

Carriage, wagon and buggy dealers, 300–302 El Paso; also 117 San Francisco; El Paso, Texas, circa 1900–1911.

Kramer

E.M. Kramer Co. manufactured farm implements; Paxton, Illinois, circa 1890–1915.

Kramer

J. Kramer & Sons manufactured wagons and coal carts, 274 Henry; New York, NY, circa 1899.

Kramer

W. Kramer, wagon maker; Lone Rock, WI, circa 1879.

Kratz

Aaron Kratz was born on his fathers farm, July 9th, in 1832. Early on, he had an interest in the trade of blacksmith, and by his nineteenth birthday he had apprenticed himself out to a country blacksmith, to learn the trade. After two years of work without pay, young Aaron returned home, where his father built him a small shop on their family farm. Here he established a large local following and in just two more years, was able to build a larger two story shop. This was followed by an even larger three story factory, in 1857.

This factory was the first of its kind in Plumsteadville. The building was nearly 50 feet long and included a full basement. This area housed paints, varnishes, iron and other needed supplies for his rapidly expanding business—a business which soon reached the $100,000 annual income mark.

Mr. Kratz added an adjoining boarding house for his employees, and hired John R. Lear to run it. When it came to the shop, Aaron Kratz never hired a foreman. He would oversee all activities in the shop, and was known to pay by the piece, not by the hour. The Kratz employees liked this pay-by-the-piece work arrangement, and many of them worked until death or retirement age. One man worked for 47 years and others for 46, 44, 35, and two employees for 30 years.

Aaron Kratz was a very successful business man. Among his other ventures, he owned and operated a farm for profit—and to feed his workers. He also was involved with partners, in the Doylestown and Easton Street Railway Company; Plumsteadville, PA, circa 1851–1910.

Kratz

George Kratz, manufactured calliopes for circus wagons; Evansville, Indiana, circa 1875.

Kratzer Carriage Co.

Des Moines, Iowa, circa 1890–1910.

Kreamer

William Kreamer, wagon maker; Annaton, WI, circa 1865–1879.

Kreeb

John Kreeb, wagon maker, 385 First Avenue; New York, NY, circa 1899.

Kreis

James P. Kreis, buggy maker, north fifth street; Mifflinburg, PA, circa 1884–1892.

Kreisher & Brother

Buggy makers, Mifflinburg, PA, circa 1881–1892.

Krepser (see Everett & Krepser)

Kretchmer

Charles Kretchmer, blacksmith and wagon maker, 143 Union; Pueblo, Colorado, circa 1875–1912. This business was also know as Kretchmer & Nieuhaus, circa 1890–1900, and by 1903 operated as Kretchmer & Son.

Kretchmer

Frank Kretchmer, wagon maker; Pueblo, CO, circa 1893–1900

Kretchmer (see Hyde & Kretchmer)

Kreuger

F. Kreuger, wagon maker; Amherst, WI, circa 1879.

Kroeger

A.H. Kroeger Carriage Mfg. Co., buggy manufacturer; Cincinnati, Ohio, circa 1880–1910.

Kroeger

Charles Kroeger, wagon maker; Sheboygan Falls, Wisconsin, circa 1885–1919.

Krog & Franz

Blacksmiths and wheelwrights; also carriage and wagon manufacturer, corner of Houston and Nacogdoches; San Antonio, Texas, circa 1887–1900.

Kroh

C.Z. Kroh & Co. offered a large selection of tops and trimmings to the carriage trade; Toledo, Ohio, circa 1880–1910.

Krueger

C. Krueger, wagon maker; Watertown, WI, circa 1879.

Krueger & Stolzenburg

Wagon and carriage makers; Sheboygan, Wisconsin, circa 1885–1919.

Kruger & Wolf

Carriage and wagon makers; Madison, Wisconsin, circa 1865.

Krummbolz

Joseph Krummbolz, carriage and wagon maker; Arcadia, Wisconsin, circa 1890–1910.

Kubera (see Brach & Kubera)

Kuehl & Brothers

E. Kuehl and Brothers, blacksmiths and wagon makers, Chestnut St.; Leadville, CO, circa 1879–1880's.

Kuentzel

Albert Kuentzel, wagon maker; Lowell, WI, circa 1879–1903.

Kuhnle
William Kuhnle, manufacturer of buggies, carriages, express wagons and other work in this line, K Street, between 11th and 12th; Sacramento, California, circa 1882–1900.

Kunce
August Kunce, wagon maker; Merrimac, WI, circa 1885–1919.

Kunze
Max Kunze, blacksmith, horseshoer, and wagon maker, 892 Main; Dallas, Texas, circa 1908–1918.

Kurtz
John Kurtz, wagon maker; Fredonia, WI, circa 1879–1885.

Kurzynski Mfg. Co.
Buggy manufacturer; Cincinnati, Ohio, circa 1880–1910.

Kutenruth
C. Kutenruth, carriage and wagon maker; Blumenau, Colorado, circa 1884–1890.

Kyle & Osborne
Blacksmiths and wheelwrights, Texas Ave., between Main and Travis; Houston, Texas, circa 1882–1888.

Kyle & Hubert
Blacksmiths and wheelwrights, 715 Texas Ave.; Houston, Texas, circa 1900–1910.

Laage
C.H. Laage, carriage and wagon materials, 216 Mission; San Francisco, California, circa 1888–1894.

Laake
H. Laake, wagons, Colorado, circa 1890–1910.

LaBelle Wagon Works
B.F. Moore was president and A.L. Moore vice-president of this early wagon manufacturing company—specializing in farm and freight wagons; Fond du Lac, Wisconsin, circa 1870–1900.

Lack
H.R. Lack, manufacturer of wagons and carriages; horseshoeing and general jobbing, Main street; Woodland, CA, circa 1888–1894.

Lackey
P. Lackey, wagon maker; Westfield, WI, circa 1879.

Lacks
Gottlieb Lacks, carriage and wagon manufacturer and dealer; Boise, Idaho, circa 1908.

LaCrosse Plow Co.
Founded in 1865, this LaCrosse, WI company, circa 1865–1929, was well known in the tillage implement business. The LaCrosse Hustler Sulky Plow is just one of the numerous styles they offered in the early 1900's.

They were taken over by the Allis–Chalmers company in 1929.

LaCrosse Wallis Carriage Co.
Manufactured carriages and sleighs; LaCrosse, Wisconsin, circa 1880–1900.

Ladd (see Downie & Ladd)

Ladendorf (see Gies & Ladendorf)

Lail Supply Co. Inc.
James T. Lail, president, and David B. Cole, secretary, offered farm implements, wagons, vehicles, harness, saddlery and blacksmithing; Cimarron, New Mexico, circa 1915.

Laine
D.M. Laine, maker of wagons and carts, including a line of dog carts; Philadelphia, PA, circa 1890–1910.

Lake & Spaugh
Blacksmiths and wheelwrights, 629 Elm; Dallas, Texas, circa 1891–1900.

Lambert (see Pratt & Lambert)

Lame
J.W. Lame, blacksmith and wheelwright, ne corner E. 14th and San Bernard; Austin, Texas, circa 1906–1912.

Lame & Bonte
Blacksmiths and wheelwrights; carriage and wagon manufacturers, 604 East Ave.; Austin, Texas, circa 1895–1905.

Lamere
Jerry Lamere, wagon maker; Egg Harbor, Wisconsin, circa 1885–1915.

Lamont
J. Lamont, wagon and carriage maker; Madison, WI, circa 1879.

Lancaster
C. Lancaster, wagon maker; Union Center, WI, circa 1879.

Lancaster
James Austin Lancaster Co., manufactured carriages, sleighs and wagons, including their No. 102 "Lancaster Station Wagons."

They were also wholesale manufacturers of carts, pony traps and miniature vehicles; Merimac, MA, circa 1880–1910.

Lander
Michael Lander, wagon maker, 727 Eleventh Avenue; New York, NY, circa 1899.

Lane
Thomas W. Lane, vehicle manufacturer; Amesbury, MA, circa 1890–1910.

Lane
W.T. Lane, blacksmith and wagon maker; Fort Bridger, Wyoming, circa 1902–1910.

Lane & Garner
Carriage makers; West Philadelphia, PA, circa 1880–1910.

Lang
A.J. Lang, carriage trimmers; Ogden City, Utah, circa 1884–1890.

Langanhan
A. Langanhan, carriage and wagon dealer; Ableman, Wisconsin, circa 1890–1910.

Langdon
George W. Langdon worked in the Moeller Brothers shop and is credited with the invention of a machine to apply gold leaf to the wood carvings on circus wagons. Baraboo, Wisconsin, circa 1890–1920.

Langdon (see Brady, Langdon & Briggs)

Lange
F.W. Lange, blacksmith and wheelwright; also carriage, wagon, buggy and phaeton manufacturer, 293 E. Commerce, and 353 E. Commerce; San Antonio, Texas, circa 1887–1902.

Lange
F.W. Lange, blacksmith and wheelwright, 353 E Commerce; San Antonio, Texas, circa 1897–1902.

Langly & Coleman
Blacksmiths and wagon makers, 302 Tyler; Amarillo, Texas, 1900–1910.

Lanham & Robinson
Blacksmiths and wheelwrights, 1609 Guadalupe; Austin, Texas, circa 1897–1905.

Lansing Binding Co.
Lansing, MI, circa 1890–1910.

Lansing Wagon Works
Manufactured Lansing wagons and Clark buggies. They also offered carriage runner conversion kits; Lansing, MI, circa 1890–1915.

Lanyon
Robert Lanyon, wagon maker; Mineral Point, WI, circa 1865.

Lanz
Andrew Lanz (and Sons-1901), wagon maker; Monroe, Wisconsin, circa 1879–1919.

Lapeer Steel Axle Co.
Lapeer, MI, circa 1890–1910.

LaPorte Carriage Co.
J.J. Parkhurst, President, builders of carriages and sleighs; LaPorte, Indiana, circa 1880's–1911.

Laramie Coal Co.
Dealers in agricultural implements, 310–1st; Laramie, Wyoming, circa 1900–1908.

Lare
George P. Lare, blacksmith and wagon maker, 353 Wazee; Denver, Colorado, circa 1881–1890.

Larendon
Edwin Larendon, carriage, wagon, buggy and phaeton dealer, 1301–07 Franklin Ave.; Houston, Texas, circa 1900–1910.

Lariviere
P.A. Lariviere was known for his so-called Canadian patterns and Russian style sleighs. Lariviere designed and patented a turn-out seat used in carriages and sleighs; Montreal, Canada, circa 1870's–1900.

Larrabee
G.N. Larrabee, blacksmith and wagon maker; Moscow, Idaho, circa 1905–1910.

Larrabee (see Sturtevant-Larrabee Co.)

Larsen
John J. Larsen, wagon maker; Maiden Rock, Wisconsin, circa 1885–1919.

Larson
A. Larson, wagon maker; New Lisbon, WI, circa 1879.

Larson
J. Larson, wagon maker; Wild Rose, WI, circa 1879.

Larson
J.O. Larson, carriage and wagon maker, Aurora, Utah, circa 1884–1890.

Larson (see Smedbron & Larson)

Lasgo
Michael, Lasgo, wagon maker, 327 East 107th; New York, NY, circa 1899.

Las Vegas Carriage Works
East Douglas Ave.; Las Vegas, New Mexico, circa 1890's–1910.

Lathrop
H.L. Lathrop, carriage, buggy and wagon dealer, 605 Main; Ft. Worth, Texas, circa 1896–1906.

Latta
Moses Latta designed and built one of the first successful steam fire-engines, in 1852, named "Uncle Joe Ross". This engine weighed nearly 22,000 lbs. and required four horses, ridden artillery style, to pull it.

The firm built several more engines, including the "Citizens' Gift" (purchased by the city with money raised by citizen donations) before being sold to Lane & Bodley, in 1863. The new owners built seven or eight more vehicles before selling out in 1868, to Ahrens Manufacturing Co.; Cincinnati, OH, circa 1852–1868.

Lauder
M.R. Lauder, carriage painters and trimmers, 103 Camp; Dallas, Texas, circa 1897–1905.

Lauersdorf
F. Lauersdorf, wagon maker; Hustisford, WI, circa 1879.

Lauersdorf
W. Lauersdorf, wagon maker; Watertown, WI, circa 1879.

Laughlin
J.R. Laughlin, blacksmith, wheelwright and horseshoer, 318 Staples; Corpus Christi, Texas, circa 1910–1920.

Laughlin & Kelly
Dealers in carriage lights and hardware; Antigo, Wisconsin, circa 1890–1910.

Laurence & Townsen
Carriage makers, 19th Ward; New York, NY, circa 1850.

Lausen
A.A. Lausen, blacksmith and wheelwright, 279 E. Mechanic and 19th; Galveston, Texas, circa 1886–1890.

Lauteman
J. Lauteman, wagon maker; Fairplay, Wisconsin, circa 1865.

Law
William B. Law, blacksmith and wheelwright, 1306–1308 Houston; Ft. Worth, Texas, circa 1905–1910.

Law & Bussey
Blacksmiths and wheelwrights, 1701 E. 1st; Ft. Worth, Texas, circa 1905–1915.

Lawrence
E. Lawrence, wagon maker; Ironton, WI, circa 1879.

Lawrence
George Lawrence, a master wood carver from New York, NY, worked on circus wagons built by Sebastian Wagon Works, circa 1860–1890.

Lawrence, Bradley & Pardee
Successors of the famed James Brewster, this group of three carriage, sleigh and buggy builders would not remain in partnership for long. First, in 1868, the original Brewster partner John R. Lawrence sold his interest to Bradley and Pardee. In 1871, Pardee sold out to Bradley who would eventually sell the property to A.T. Demarest & Company.

Under Demarest, the factory grew to employ over 100 workers, building both carriage and automobiles, before closing business in 1915, 61–67 Chapel street; New Haven, CT, circa 1850's–1870's.

Lawrenceburg Buggy Co.
Buggy manufacturer; Lawrenceburg, IN, circa 1890–1910.

Laws
James D. Laws & Son, carriage maker; Holmesburg, PA, circa 1880–1910.

Laymen
Michael Abraham Layman, proprietor of M.A. Layman Carriage Factory, manufacturer of carriages, surries, buggies, etc.; Dayton, Virginia, circa 1911–1917.

Lea
H.G. Lea & Sons, carriage makers. They specialized in the construction of road carts; Nevada, OH, circa 1880–1900.

Leach
Joseph Leach, carriage maker; New York, NY.

Leader
Jacob Leader was born in 1814 near the Conestoga River Valley in Lancaster County, Pennsylvania. Leader started working in the wagon making trade there at age 17. By 1834 he had moved to Pittsburgh, then on to St. Louis, Missouri the next year.

A few more moves were in store for Jacob Leader, including two trips to Illinois. On one of those trips, in 1839, he was married.

He finally settled down in Independence, Missouri to become the head of Robert Weston's wagon making division, circa 1814–1860.

Leatherwood & Rowell
Blacksmiths and wagon makers, Maple Ave. and 1 north Turtle Creek; Dallas, Texas, circa 1910.

Lebkicker
Alphred Lebkicker was a carriage and buggy builder; Mifflinburg, PA., circa 1850's–1870's.

Lee
Luncefield Lee came to the Shenandoah Valley from East Virginia and settled in the vicinity of McGaheysville. Sometime around 1850, Luncefield Lee began to operate a wagon making shop.

A few years later he moved to Port Republic where he set up a factory to manufacture wagons. Some of the new machinery was driven by horsepower. His factory in East Rockingham was the most up-to-date at that time, circa 1850–1870's.

Lee & Larned
Wellington Lee was the inventor and his partner, Mr. Larned designed and built steam fire-engines to be drawn by hand or horse.

Their first machine was constructed at the Novelty Works in New York Clity, 1856. They did an extensive business manufacturing several more engines over the next thirteen years; New York, NY, circa 1856–1869.

Leech
George Leach, wagon maker; Delavan, Wisconsin, circa 1865.

Leeland
L. and S. Leeland, wagon makers; Alma, WI, circa 1879.

Leeper (see Hall-Leeper Hardware Co.)

Leeper, Lingo & Co.
Carriage and wagon woodwork, 100–104 E. Main, and 230 W. Main; Denison, Texas, circa 1887–1900.

Lefferts
E.C. Lefferts invented a wagon spring that enabled an old-style farm wagon to be turned into a spring wagon in very short order. The rights to Lefferts' invention was sold to A.E. Hallock, for wider distribution; Long Island, NY, circa 1880.

Lehmann
Adam Lehmann, wagon maker; Beaver Dam, circa 1879–1911.

Leibel
H. Leibel, wagon maker; New Cassel, Wisconsin, circa 1885–1915.

Leicher
Adam Leicher, wagon maker; Loganville, WI, circa 1879–1885.

Leip
J.H. Leip, blacksmith and wagon maker; Junction, Idaho, circa 1905–1910.

Leippe
Jacob A Leippe's Sons manufactured shafts and rims for carriage and wagon makers throughout the region; Reading, PA, circa 1880's–1910.

Leist & Kizer
Wagon makers, Front Street; Cincinnati, OH, circa 1845–1870's.

Leiting
T.A. Leiting, wagon maker; Kenosha, WI, circa 1879–1885.

Leitzman
Charles Leitzman, blacksmith, and wagon maker, 400 West 2nd, Leadville, Colorado, circa 1880–1881, also 305 East 7th and corner of Elm and Leiter; Leadville, Colorado, 1883–1890.

Leitzman & Boellert
Blacksmiths and wagon makers; Black Hawk, CO, circa 1879–1880.

Leiva
P. Leiva, blacksmith and wheelwright, 115 S. Pecos; San Antonio, Texas, circa 1897–1905.

Lelh & Fried
Carriage makers; Allentown, PA, circa 1880–1910.

Lemke
August Lemke, wagon maker; Wausau, Wisconsin, circa 1879–1901.

Lemmer
R. Lemmer & Co., carriage and wagon maker; Staten Island, NY, circa 1870–1900.

Lenahan (see Fitzgerald & Lenahan)

Lenfesty (see Treat & Lenfesty)

Lengert
George Lengert & Sons, specialized in commercial delivery wagons; Philadelphia, PA., circa 1890–1900.

Lenhart
F.J. Lenhart, blacksmith and wagon maker; Green River, Wyoming, circa 1900–1910.

Lennon
John Lennon, blacksmith and wagon maker; Riverside, Wyoming, circa 1901–1902.

Lennox
E.E. Lennox, carriage painter and trimmer, 302 W. Weatherford; Ft. Worth, Texas, circa 1900–1910.

Lenz
Ehlert Lenz & Co., wagon maker; Fond du Lac, Wisconsin, circa 1879.

Lenz
William Lenz, wagon maker; Oakfield, WI, circa 1885–1911.

Leonard
Hiram Leonard, wagon maker; Clay, NY, circa 1850's.

Leonhardt
William Leonhardt, wagon builder; Baltimore, MD, circa 1870–1900.

Lepper & Moase
Wagon makers; Fond du Lac, Wisconsin, circa 1865.

Leroy
H.C. Leroy, wagon maker; Loyal, WI, circa 1879.

LeRoy Plow Co.
Building farm implements; LeRoy, NY, circa 1890's–1940.

Leslie (see McCall & Leslie)

Lester & Harrison
Blacksmiths and wagon makers; Hill, Idaho, circa 1905–1910.

Lester (see Waterhouse & Lester)

Leuty & Yeaman
Blacksmiths and wagon makers; Burley, Idaho, circa 1905–1910.

Leverich (see Wade & Leverich)

Levy
J. Levy & Bros., dealers in carriages, buggies, and phaetons, 2216–2224 Church; Galveston, Texas, circa 1886–1902.

Levy
Max Levy, wagon maker, 126 Attorney; New York, NY, circa 1899.

Lewis
F.L. Lewis, blacksmith and wagon maker; Hyattville, Wyoming, circa 1901–1902.

Lewis
J.A. Lewis, wagon yards, 505 W. Weatherford; Ft. Worth, Texas, circa 1896–1906.

Lewis
J.C. Lewis & Co., carriage and wagon dealers and representatives; Antigo, Wisconsin, circa 1890–1910.

Lewis
J.H. Lewis Wagon Co., buggy manufacturer; Cincinnati, Ohio, circa 1880–1910.

Lewis
J.W. Lewis Wagon Co., buggy manufacturer; Cincinnati, Ohio, circa 1880–1910.

Lewis
Walter Lewis, carriage painters and trimmers, 230 Commerce; Dallas, Texas, circa 1898–1910.

Lewis
W. G. Lewis, wagon maker; Del Norte, Colorado, circa 1880, also Colorado Springs, Colorado, 1882–1890.

Lewis
William Lewis, wagon maker; Sheboygan Falls, WI, circa 1865.

Lewis, Oliver & Phillips
Manufactured wrought iron wagon hardware for all the major wagon companies throughout the country, including Studebaker Brothers and many more.
  By 1880 they would employ nearly 700 men and turn out hardware for 90,000 wagons per annum; Pittsburgh, PA., circa 1870–1900.

Lewis Spring & Axle Co.
Jackson, MI, circa 1890–1910.

Lewis & Swalm
Blacksmiths and wagon makers; Lander, Wyoming, circa 1902–1908.

Lewis (see Mitchell & Lewis)

Lewis (see Thomas & Lewis)

Leykom (see Hessill & Leykom)

Libbey
George A. Libbey, blacksmith and wagon maker; Georgetown, Colorado, circa 1880–1890.

Licht
J. Licht, wagon maker; Rubicon, WI, circa 1879.

Licklighter
John H. Licklighter, wagon maker; Port Republic, Virginia, circa 1866.

Lietmeyer
Frank Lietmeyer, buggy manufacturer; Cincinnati, Ohio, circa 1880–1910.

Light
Andrew Light manufactured wagons, and also advertised Dearborn carriages for sale; St. Louis, Missouri, circa 1820–1840.

Lighthall
A.C. Lighthall, carriage and wagon maker; 336 Blake; Denver, Colorado, circa 1879–1890.

Lighthall (see McDonough & Lighthall)

Lilla
F. Lilla, wagon maker; Dodge, WI, circa 1879.

Lincoln
J.H. Lincoln, wagon maker; Montfort, WI, circa 1885–1898.

Lind & Solberg
Wagon makers; Viroqua, Wisconsin, circa 1885–1898.

Linde
John Linde, wagon maker; Beaver Dam, WI, circa 1885–1903.

Linder (see Loftus & Linder)

Lindsay & Johansen
Blacksmiths and wagon makers; Montpelier, Idaho, circa 1905–1910.

Lindsey
Samuel Lindsey, blacksmith and wagon maker; Fairplay, Colorado, circa 1878–1880's.

Lindstrom
I. Lindstrom, blacksmith and wagon maker, 1800 Eddy; Cheyenne, Wyoming, circa 1900–1905.

Lines
Thomas D. Lines built light carriages, 131 Gifford; Syracuse, NY, circa 1899.

Lines (see Kean & Lines)
Lines (see Peck & Lines)

Ling
Horace Ling, carriage and wagon maker Denver, Colorado, circa 1884–1890.

Ling & Levoy
In 1857 a Mr. William Ling and Mr. Levoy formed a partership called the Ling & Levoy Carriage Co. in Middletown, Ohio.

When Mr. Levoy retired, D.H. VanSickle came into the business and it became Ling & Van Sickel.

Some years later, a rubber tire plant was added so that rubber tires could be put on vehicles used on the city streets, circa 1857–1900.

Lingo (see Leeper, Lingo & Co.)

Lininger & Metcalf
Carriage dealers; Omaha, Nebraska, circa 1890–1910.

Linke
W.H. Linke, wagon maker; Hillsboro, WI, circa 1885–1903.

Linstroth Wagon Co.
Manufactured a variety of wagons; St. Louis, Missouri, circa 1900–1940's.

Lints
John Lints manufactured wagons and sleighs; Clay, NY, circa 1850's.

Lion Buggy Co.
Buggy manufacturer; Cincinnati, Ohio, circa 1880–1910.

Lippert
Max Lippert, wagon maker, 415 East 23rd; New York, NY, circa 1899.

Lippey (see Muffer & Lippey)

Lippleman Carriage Co.
Buggy manufacturer; Cincinnati, Ohio, circa 1880–1910.

Lippoldt & Simpson
Carriages, Pearl Street; Boulder, Colorado, circa 1883–1890.

Lipps
John Lipps, blacksmith and wheelwright, near nw corner East Overland and Stanton, and 508 South El Paso; El Paso, Texas, circa 1898–1905.

Litchfield Manufacturing Co.
Built various farm implements, including a popular line of manure spreaders; Waterloo, Iowa, circa 1900–1940's.

Little
John P. Little furnished material for seats, stuffing and upholstery; Picture Rock, PA., circa 1900–1910.

Little
William Little was a carriage maker; Amesbury, MA., circa 1800–1820's.

Lloyd
D. Lloyd, blacksmith and wagon maker; Gifford, Idaho, circa 1905–1910.

Lockett
B. Lockett, blacksmith and wheelwright, 216 E. Lamar; Sherman, Texas, circa 1895–1905.

Loe
Nils Loe, wagon maker; Soldiers Grove; WI, circa 1879–1901.

Loeser
John N. Loeser, wagon maker, 28 East 134th; New York, NY, circa 1899.

Loftus & Linder
Wagon maker, 115 Front; Rome, NY, circa 1899.

Logan
David Logan, blacksmith and wheelwright, 714 E. Houston; San Antonio, Texas, circa 1897–1902.

Lombard
A.F. Lombard, carriage and wagon dealer and representative; Arnott, Wisconsin, circa 1890–1910.

Long
Henry Long, wagon maker; Jackson County, Missouri, circa 1850–1860.

Long
William Long, blacksmith and wheelwright, 504 San Pedro Ave.; San Antonio, Texas, circa 1897–1904.

Long, Black & Alstatter Co.
This Hamilton, Ohio firm manufactured farm implements, mostly cultivators, and was considered a pioneer in the tillage implement business; circa 1870's–1920's.

They may have later been known as Long & Alstater Co.

Long & Silsby
Built sleighs and carriages; Albany, NY, circa 1880–1900.

Longwell's Transfer & Carriage Co.
Blacksmiths and carriage, wagon and buggy makers; carriage painters and trimmers, 116–120 San Francisco; El Paso, Texas, circa 1904–1914.

Longwell (see Ballinger & Longwell)

Lonsdale & Enright
Manufactured light carriages, 110 Mulberry; Syracuse, NY, circa 1899.

Lord & Poll
Carriage and wagon makers; Sheridan, WY, circa 1902–1910.

Lorenzo's Carriage Shop
A. H. Lorenzo, carriage and wagon maker, 423 Grand Ave.; Las Vegas, NM, circa 1900–1915.

Lothrop
John J. Lothrop, blacksmith and wagon maker, 1505 Vallejo; San Francisco, CA, circa 1882–1890.

Lott
Rueben B. Lott, blacksmith and wheelwright, 1107 E. 6th; 714 E. 6th; and 509 E. 7th; Austin, Texas, circa 1900–1918.

Loud Bros.
Manufacturer of heavy and enclosed vehicles—also built a variety of sleighs; Merrimac, MA, circa 1880–1910.

Loudermilk
George W. Loudermilk, funeral director, fine ambulances, funeral cars and carriages, 463–465 Main St., corner Harwood, Main 293, Hack Stand, Main 38, best equipped establishment in the south; Dallas, Texas, circa 1901–1908.

Loughridge
J.M. Loughridge, carriage maker; Silver Cliff, Colorado, circa 1882–1890.

Louis
J.H. Louis Carriage & Wagon Co. of Cincinnati, Ohio, circa 1890–1910.

Loungen (see Tucker & Loungen)

Lovatt
George A. Lovatt, blacksmith and wagon maker; New Fork, Wyoming, circa 1902–1908.

Love
W.E. Love, buggies, surreys, phaetons, express, delivery and laundry wagons, also buggy tops, and shafts, 173 Elm Street; Dallas, Texas, circa 1900.

Lowell Cutter Co.
Manufactured sleighs and cutters; Lowell, Michigan, circa 1889–1920.

Lown
William Lown, carriage and sleigh maker; Troy, NY, circa 1870–1900.

Lowrey
Joseph L. Lowrey, mechanical engineer and inventor, started working on the design of a horse-drawn steam fire-engine as early as 1842. It wasn't until 1855 that he would receive a contract to build his engine from the Board of Underwriters of Pittsburgh. One more was completed in 1857; Pittsburgh, PA, circa 1842–1857.

Luckenbach
F.E. Luckenbach, blacksmith and wheelwright, 2004 N. New Braunfels Ave.; San Antonio, Texas, circa 1900–1910.

Luckenbach & Rausch
Blacksmiths and wheelwrights, 512 Ave. D; San Antonio, Texas, circa 1897–1904.

Ludlam & Smith
Carriage makers, 18th Ward, New York, NY, circa 1850.

Ludtke
Gottlieb Ludtke, wagon maker; Princeton, WI, circa 1885–1903.

Luedinghaus-Espenschied Wagon Co.
Two of the foremost names in the construction of freight and farm wagons in this country; St. Louis, MO, circa 1880–1920.

Lull Carriage Co.
Carriage, wagon and sleigh maker—including commercial vehicles. This firm was also known as Lull & Skinner Co. at some point; Kalamazoo, MI, circa 1890–1910.

Lund
Andrew W. Lund, wagon maker; River Falls, WI, circa 1885–1919.

Lundbeck
P. Lundbeck & Brothers, blacksmiths and wheelwrights, 213 W. 6th; Austin, Texas, circa 1887–1900.

Lundbeck (see Pompee & Lundbeck)

Lupfer
J. Lupfer, carriage and wagon maker; Sheboygan, WI, circa 1879.

Luth Carriage Co.
Fred L. Luth, Superintendent, buggy manufacturer; Cincinnati, Ohio, circa 1880-1923.

Luth (see Ratterman & Luth)

Lyles, Tulloss Hardware Co.
Carriages, wagons and buggies, 511 Polk; Amarillo, Texas, circa 1910–1920.

Lynch (see Florance & Lynch)

Lynchburg Carriage Co
D.M. Higginbotham and G.E. Shaner manufactured carriages; Lynchburg, IN, circa 1923–1926.

Maas
August Maas, wagon maker; Thiensville, WI, circa 1885–1901.

MacGowan Carriage Co.
Buggy manufacturer; Cincinnati, Ohio, circa 1880–1910.

Mackey (see Burkart & Mackey Mfg. Co.)

Mackh
Matthew Mackh, wagon maker, 531 West 21st; New York, NY, circa 1899.

MacPherson
Myron Emmet MacPherson was a truly great circus artist of Baraboo, Wisconsin. He was employed by Ringling Brothers of Baraboo, WI.

With the decline of skilled wood carvers, circus owners turned to painted scenes as a means of decorating their wagons. Fairy tales, animals, landscapes, biblical scenes and portraits of circus owners were popular themes at the time.

Although most artist rarely signed their work, MacPherson on occasion did slip an inconspicuous "Mac did it" onto his painted panels, circa 1905–1920.

Madison
Calvin H. Madison, carriage painters and trimmers, 1173 Angelina; Austin, Texas, circa 1910–1920.

Madison
Eugene W. Madison, blacksmith and wheelwright, 1009 E. 11th; Austin, Texas, circa 1900–1910.

Madison Plow Co.
Started building plows in 1880. Soon after, they became part of Fuller & Johnson Manufacturing Co.

Madison Plow reappeared in 1911 when Fuller & Johnson went into the gasoline engine business.

Madison Plow Co. would offer a line of farm implements, including their new Eclipse Sulky Plow, for several more years, circa 1880–1920.

Magedanz
Edward Magedanz jr., wagon maker; Duplainville, Wisconsin, circa 1911–1919.

Magedanz
William Magedanz, wagon maker; Duplainville, Wisconsin, circa 1885–1903.

Magill & Bryden
Carriages and wagons; Denver, Colorado, circa 1882–1890.

Maginn
E.J. Maginn, carriage and wagon maker; Denver, Colorado, circa 1884–1890.

Magner
F.W. Magner, carriage and wagon manufacturer and dealer; Boise, Idaho, circa 1908.

Maguire & Spudig
Blacksmiths and wagon makers; Gallup, New Mexico, circa 1900–1915.

Maigatter
Frederick Maigatter, wagon maker; Kewaunee, Wisconsin, circa 1885–1901.

Maile
Gottlieb Maile, wagon maker, 220 West 100th; New York, NY, circa 1899.

Majors & Russell
Messrs. Major & Russell operated a wagon making business in Westport, Missouri. In 1858, they sold their shop to M.T. Graham and his business partner, A. Eberhart & Co. of Mishawaka, Indiana, circa 1840–1858.

Makeley & Hartwell
Blacksmiths and wagon makers; Canon City, CO, circa 1879–1890.

Makitta
Solomon Makitta, blacksmith, wheelwright and horseshoer, Leopard, corner of Sam Rankin; Corpus Christi, Texas, circa 1913–1919.

Mallard (see White & Mallard)

Mallery (see Castree-Mallery Co.)

Mallett
F. Mallett, balcksmith and wagon maker; Durango, Colorado, circa 1884–1890.

Mallory (see Grimm & Mallory)

Malmberg
John A. Malmberg, wagon maker, 1161 First Avenue; New York, NY, circa 1899.

Malon
John Malon, carriage maker; Newfone, NY, circa 1850's.

Malone
D.R. Malone Buggy Co., carriage, buggy and wagon dealer, 115 W. Weatherford; Ft. Worth, Texas, circa 1896–1906.

Maloney
William Maloney, carriage maker, 15th and Wewatta; Denver, Colorado, circa 1880–1890.

Maloney & Herrick
Blacksmiths and wagon makers; Coeur d'Alene, Idaho, circa 1905–1910.

Manchester
S.G. Manchester, wagon maker; Oxford, Wisconsin, circa 1885–1903.

Manchester
T.A. Manchester, wagon maker; Excelsior, Wisconsin, circa 1885.

Manchester Wagon Factory
Sole owner, Cyrus Townsend, formerly of Towsend & Radle, started out as a blacksmith in the 1830's. By 1841 he had his own wagon factory with a warehouse on St. Clair Street in Pittsburgh, PA where they would advertise the manufacture of carriages, sleighs, wagons and carts.

Townsend's Manchester Wagon Factory is credited with selling more wagons to the southwest and Sante Fe traders than any other Pittsburgh maker of his time, including several Mexican traders who paid for their wagons in gold.

In 1854, Townsend sold his business to the firm of Phelps, Carr & Co. and retired, circa 1830's–1854.

Mandt
T.G. Mandt Co. made wagons, sleighs and bobsleds. The Mandt company sold out to Moline Plow Co. in 1906.

Moline Plow would continue to build "The Genuine T.G. Mandt Wagon" for several more years; Stoughton, Wisconsin, circa 1865–1906.

Mann
O. Mann, wagon maker; Wyocena, WI, circa 1879.

Mann Saddlery Co.
Emil Mann, wholesale, retail, repair of buggies, wagons, harness, saddlery and farm implements, 213–215 West Copper Ave.; Albuquerque, New Mexico, circa 1910–1920.

Mann & Nelson
Blacksmiths and wagon makers; Coeur d'Alene, Idaho, circa 1905–1910.

Manning
Thomas Manning Jr. & Co. started out in the repair and rebuilding business in Cleveland, OH. This firm also manufactured a variety of styles and sizes of steam fire-engines over the years.

At one time the streets of Cleveland had more than ten of their machines in use, circa 1886–1900.

Mansfield
S.G. Mansfield, blacksmith and wheelwright, 118 Camp, also sw corner of North Akard and Jackson, and 145 South Akard; Dallas, Texas, circa 1897–1910.

Mansfield Machine Works
Over 50 fire-engines were constructed by this firm, before 1900. Their first, was completed in 1883, based on the patents granted them, June 14, 1881; Mansfield, OH, circa 1881–1900.

Mansur (see Deere & Mansur Co.)

Mansur & Tebbett's Implement Co.
Manufacturer of wagons, buggies, and carriages, their main plant was in St. Louis, MO, circa 1877–1901. They started out buying buggies from other manufacturers and selling them to local customers.

In 1891, they established a buggy facctory of their own. It became known as the Sunlight Factory because of the numerous tall windows on all four sides of the building. They had branches at 168 S. Lamar and at 149–151 Elm in Dallas, Texas, circa 1891–1901.

Mansur & Tebbetts was purchased by John Deere Plow Co. in 1901, and by 1913 was incorporated under the name of Reliance Buggy Co.

Manville (see Dodge & Manville)

Marchall
G.T. Marchall, carriage and wagon manufacturer and dealer; Franklin, Idaho, circa 1908.

Marcow
John Marcow, wagon maker; Marytown, WI, circa 1885–1903.

Margedent (see Bentel & Margedent Co.)

Markel
Peter Markel made wagons and sleighs; Salina, NY, circa 1850's.

Marker
James Marker, wagon maker; Viola, Wisconsin, circa 1885.

Markert
Robert Markert, buggy manufacturer; Cincinnati, Ohio, circa 1880–1910.

Markerud
H. Markerud; wagon maker; Ettrick, Wisconsin, circa 1879.

Markle
J. Markle, wagon maker; Waukesha, Wisconsin, circa 1879.

Marlatts & Hall
Plow and wagon manufactures; Pittsburgh, PA., circa 1835–1850.

Marlborough's Sons
Carriage and buggy builders; Brooklyn, NY, circa 1880.

Marmion
J.B. Marmion, blacksmith and wheelwright, 1802 Providence; Houston, Texas, circa 1900–1901.

Maroa Manufacturing Co.
Built farm implements; Maroa, Illinois; circa 1910–1915.

Marrette
Nicholas Marrette, carriage and wagon dealer and representative; Appleton, WI, circa 1885–1919.

Marseilles
Marseilles Manufacturing Co. of Marseilles, Illinois. Early builder of corn shellers and other farm implements. Established in 1859, they would grow to offer the largest line of shellers in the country by 1895. Marseilles was aquired by John Deere in 1911, circa 1859–1911.

Marsh Harvester Co.
C.W. and W.W. Marsh began to design and build harvester equipment as early as the 1850's. They established the Marsh Harvester Co. in 1868 to manufacture farm implements; Sycamore, IL, circa 1858–1890.

Marsh
Isaac M. Marsh, one of the first carriage makers in this area, also operated as Marsh & Nolan. Their shop was later occupied by John F. Schwiebert's Richmond Wagon Works, located on Richmond road; Richmond, NY, circa 1880–1910.

Marshall
A.P. Marshall & Co. was a firm that built carriages and sleighs designed by Mr. Marshall, a skilled draftsman and artist. A sample of his talent can be seen in a pen and ink sketch, in an August 1882 issue of *The Hub*, a major trade publication of the day, showing Marshalls Round-Back Portland Cutter; Lancaster, New Hampshire, circa 1870's–1900.

Marshall
J. Marshall, blacksmith and wheelwright, 221 E. Mulberry; Sherman, Texas, circa 1893–1900.

Marshall
S. Marshall, blacksmith and wagon maker, J, between 10th and 11th; Sacramento, CA, circa 1853–1865.

Marshall & Nye
Blacksmiths and wagon makers, J, between 10th and 11th; Sacramento, CA, circa 1853–1865.

Marske
Albert H. Marske, wagon maker; Whitewater, WI, circa 1885–1915.

Martell
John Martell, carriage and wagon materials, 623 Sacramento, San Francisco, California, circa 1888–1894.

Marten
J. Marten, wagon maker; Manitowoc Rapids, WI, circa 1879.

Martin
A.O. Martin, blacksmith and wagon maker; Lyon, Idaho, circa 1905–1910.

Martin
John Martin, blacksmith and wagon maker, 511–2nd and 400–3rd; Laramie, WY, circa 1901–1908.

Martin
John Martin, blacksmith and wheelwright, 1501 Throckmorton; Ft. Worth, Texas, circa 1904–1906.

Martin
M.D. Martin Carriage Works of York, PA was a manufacturer of wagons and carriages, circa 1890–1910.

Martin
P.N. Martin, wagon maker; Fairchild, WI, circa 1879.

Martin
Raymond M. Martin was born in Elkart County, Indiana in 1951. He moved to Dayton, VA in 1970. He worked for a few months at the Mill Cabinet Shop, Inc.

In 1971, he started making cabinets on his own,. He was surprised to see the people of Dayton were still using the old-style open buggies and surries. He built several closed buggies—Indiana style—for local customers.

By 1979, Ray had made molds that allowed him to make buggy bodies out of ABS plastic.

In 1980, Ray decided to get out of the woodworking business, so he sold his shop and moved to the Spring Creek area to try his hand at dairy farming.

Martin
Thomas Martin, carriage maker; Trinidad, CO, circa 1882.

Martin Bros.
Carriage and wagon dealers; Angelica, Wisconsin, circa 1890–1910.

Martin, Pennell & Co.
Built carriages and sleighs; Portland, Maine, circa 1880's–1900.

Martin & Torry
Blacksmiths and wagon makers, 1602 Mission; San Francisco, California, circa 1882–1885.

Martin (see Durr, Martin & Co.)

Martin (see Eklund & Martin)

Martinson
Oscar E. Martinson, blacksmith and wheelwright; carriage painter and trimmer; also carriage, wagon, buggy and phaeton manufacturer and dealer, 300 W. Weatherford, and ne corner of Rusk and E. Belknap; Ft. Worth, Texas, circa 1900–1915.

Martinson (see Schmitt & Martinson)

Marvin
Charles Marvin was a carriage painter in the A.E. Hallock shop; Smithtown, NY, circa 1880–1900.

Marx
George B. Marx manufactured wagons and horse-drawn trucks, 410 East 13th; New York, NY, circa 1899.

Maschek & Cameron
Blacksmiths and wheelwrights, Shell road near Spindle Top; Beaumont, Texas, circa 1906–1907, also a shop on Guffey; Beaumont, Texas, circa 1910–1915.

Mason
A.G. Mason, wagon maker; Beaver Dam, WI, circa 1879.

Mason
F.C. Mason & Co., sleighs; St. Johns, Michigan, circa 1890–1910.

Mason
James C. Mason, wagon maker and blacksmith: Jackson County, Missouri, circa 1850–1860.

Mason
R.W. Mason, blacksmith and wagon maker; Colorado Springs, CO, circa 1878–1880's.

Mason
W.T. Mason, wagon maker; Sparta, Wisconsin, circa 1865.

Mason Stable Co.
Manufactured hansom cabs and heavy carriages, 50 East 69th; New York, NY, circa 1899.

Mason & Black
Carriage and wagon manufacturers, blacksmiths and wheelwrights, 14–16 Commerce; Houston, Texas, circa 1882–1890.

Mason (see Nourse & Mason Co.)

Mason (see Sorber & Mason)

Massey-Harris Co.
Manufactured farm implements and related equipment. They bought J.I. Case Plow Works in 1928; Toronto, Ontario, Canada, circa 1900–1940.

Massey-Harris Harvester Co.
This Batavia, NY company, circa 1900–1940's, was based in Toronto, Ontario, Canada—and entered the U.S. market after the acquisition of Johnson Harvester Co. in 1917.

Massie (see Hand, McKinney & Massie)

Massuere
W.P. Massuere & Co., carriage and wagon dealers and representatives; Arcadia, Wisconsin, circa 1890–1910.

Mast
P.P. Mast Buggy Co., manufacturer of buggies; Springfield, Ohio, circa 1890–1910.

Mast
P.P. Mast & Co., established in 1854, built farm implements, including their No. 4 Buckeye Sunbeam cultivator.

They joined with others in 1903 to form American Seeding Machine Co.; Springfield, Ohio, circa 1865–1903.

Masters
William Masters, wagon maker; Elroy, Wisconsin, circa 1879–1898.

Masury
John W. Masury & Son; offered coach paints and varnish from their New York and Chicago locations, circa 1870–1910.

Mathai & Son
Blacksmiths and wagon makers, Mission near 29th; San Francisco, California, circa 1882–1890's.

Mathews
I.B. Mathews, carriage maker; Centreville, PA, circa 1880–1910.

Matias
Romero Matias, blacksmith and wagon maker; Clyde, New Mexico, circa 1906–1916.

Mattern
Jacob Mattern, wagon maker, 215 West 53rd; New York, NY, circa 1899.

Matterson & McLaughlin
Wagon makers; Eureka and Manawa, Wisconsin, circa 1879.

Matthews
A.B. Matthews & Son, blacksmiths and wagon makers; Boise, Idaho, circa 1905–1910.

Mathews (see Randall & Mathews)

Mattox
William Mattox, blacksmith and wagon maker; Parkman, Wyoming, circa 1905–1910.

Maugg
John Maugg, blacksmith and wagon maker; Keuterville, Idaho, circa 1905–1910.

Maurer
C. Maurer, wagon maker; Richfield, WI, circa 1879.

Maurer
F.X. Maurer Co. built farm implements; Spencer, Iowa, circa 1900–1920.

Mauser
A. Mauser and Bro. Carriage Works, operated their own stitching and paint shops in separate buildings from the main carriage works; McEwensville, PA., circa 1890–1920.

Mautz
J.E. Mautz, blacksmith and wagon maker; Idaho Falls, Idaho, circa 1905–1910.

Maxey
John J. Maxey, carriage maker, 196 15th; Denver, Colorado, 1878–1879, also 355 Wazee; Denver, Colorado, circa 1881–1890's.

Maxon
Nelson Maxon, carriage maker; Augusta, NY, circa 1850's.

Maxwell
R.E. Maxwell, blacksmith and wheelwright, 201–203 E. Belknap; Ft. Worth, Texas, circa 1904–1916.

May
Henry May, blacksmith and wheelwright, 190 Leonard; Dallas, Texas, circa 1900–1910.

Mayer & Carolus
Blacksmiths and wheelwrights; and carriage and wagon manufacturer, 296 S. Alamo; San Antonio, Texas, circa 1887–1900.

Mayer (see James & Mayer Buggy Co.)

Mayer (see Weaver & Mayer)

Maytag Co.
This well known home appliance company started out building a variety of farm equipment; Newton, Iowa, circa 1900–1920.

McAfee (see Farrell & McAfee)

McAlister
W. McAlister, blacksmith and wheelwright, Ewing Ave. east end of 13th and Oak Cliff; Dallas, Texas, circa 1891–1900.

McAlister & Sons
W.M. McAlister, blacksmith and wheelwright, Lancaster Ave. between 9th and 10th; Dallas, Texas, circa 1897–1905.

McAnulty
S.E. McAnulty, blacksmith and wagon maker; Buffalo, Wyoming, circa 1901–1910.

McArthur
R.A. McArthur, blacksmith and wagon maker; Luther, Idaho, circa 1905–1910.

McAuliff (see Corbett & McAuliff)

McAvoy
A. McAvoy & Son built road wagons and a dozen different styles of road carts; Racine, Wisconsin, circa 1880's–1900.

McAvoy & Noonan
Carriage and wagon makers; Racine, WI, circa 1879.

McCabe, Young & Co.
Designed and constructed a number of unusual custom delivery wagons; St. Louis, MO, circa 1880–1900.

McCain (see Wilkinson & McCain)

McCall Manufacturing Co.
N.H. McCall also served time as manager of the Hay Tool Manufacturing Company. The McCall company of Macon, Missouri built farm implements that were sold throughout the midwest by most of the major machinery distributors; Macon, Missouri, circa 1890's–1920.

McCall & Haase
Carriage Manufacturing Co.; St.Louis, Missouri, circa 1874–1898.

McCall & Leslie
Blacksmiths and wagon makers; Bonners Ferry, ID, circa 1905–1910.

McCallum Steel Wheel Wagon Co.
This firm manufactured its own line of wagons and steel wagon wheels; Aurora, Illinois, circa 1880's–1910.

McCallum (see Philips, McCallum & Baker)

McCegua
William McCegua manufactured wagons, coaches, carriages, carts, drays and horse-drawn trucks. He changed his last name to McKee sometime before 1850. From his shop, located on seventh street in Pittsburgh, PA, circa 1839–1870, he

supplied his local customers with a wide variety of vehicles and also built wagons for those engaged in trade on the Santa Fe trail, circa 1839–1870.

McChesney
R.A. McChesney & Son, wagon makers; Brewerton, NY, circa 1899.

McClain (see Johnston & McClain)

McClary
James McClary of McClary & Brow, K street between 9th and 10th; Sacramento, CA, circa 1855–1875.

McClary & Brow
Wagon makers, K street between 9th and 10th; Sacramento, CA, circa 1855–1875.

McClaskey
R. McClaskey, blacksmith and wagon maker; Sheridan, Wyoming, circa 1901–1902.

McClellen (see Shaw & McClellen)

McComb & Newell
Carriage and wagon makers; Austin, Nevada, circa 1884–1890.

McCormick Harvesting Co.
A manufacturer of farm implements, and considered the leader in the reaper business. They also built King of the Meadow all-steel hay rakes; Chicago, IL, circa 1860–1902.

McCown
John L. McCown, blacksmith and wheelwright, 107 Congress Ave. and 119 Congress Ave.; Austin, Texas, circa 1909–1925.

McCown (see Hazelwood & McCown)

McCrillis
J.B. McCrillis and Son built carriages and sleighs; Portland, Maine, circa 1880's–1900.

McCrumb Bros.
Blacksmiths and wagon makers; Midvale, Idaho, circa 1905–1910.

McCullough
B.S. McCullough, blacksmith and wheelwright, 2901 Harrisburg road; Houston, Texas, circa 1900–1910.

McDaniel
Phillips McDaniel made sleighs and wagons; Salina, NY, circa 1850's.

McDaniel & Burrows
Blacksmiths and wheelwrights, 1500 W. Bond.; Denison, Texas, circa 1887–1900.

McDonald
A. McDonald, carriage and wagon maker; Cherry Creek, Nevada, circa 1884–1890.

McDonald
P.H. McDonald, blacksmith and wheelwright, 400 Nolan; San Antonio, Texas, circa 1900–1910.

McDonald (see Bradford & McDonald

McDonnell
P.S. McDonnel & Co., blacksmith and wheelwright; manufacturer of carriages, wagons, buggies and phaetons, 1712 Congress Ave.; Houston, Texas, circa 1900–1910.

McDonough & Lighthall
J.R. McDonough, blacksmiths and wagon makers, 421 Blake; Denver, Colorado, circa 1878–1880's.

McDonough (see Everett & McDonough)

McEachon (see Oswald & McEachon)

McFarlan
J.B. McFarlan Carriage Co., circa 1890–1910.

McFarlan Carriage Co.
This carriage manufacturer was known for their extra fancy vehicles; Kansas City, KS, circa 1890's–1920.

McFarland
Marcus D.L. McFarland, blacksmith, wheelwright and wagon Maker, 207 E. 5th; and 404 E. 7th; Austin, Texas, circa 1887–1913.

McFarlin
J.F. McFarlin, blacksmith and wagon maker; Denver, Idaho, circa 1905–1910.

McGee & Rathjen
Blacksmiths, wagon makers and repairing; Aztec, New Mexcio, circa 1906.

McGill (see Robinson, McGill Harness Co.)

McGilvray
Archie McGilvray, blacksmith and wheelwright, E. 5th, 1/2 mile east of city limits, andBastrop road, 3 mile east of Montopoils Bridge; Austin, Texas, circa 1912–1918.

McGoldrick & Witt
Blacksmiths and wheelwrights; and carriage and wagon manufacturers, 218 N. Flores; San Antonio, Texas, circa 1887–1888.

McGough
John McGough, wagon maker; Eau Claire, Wisconsin, circa 1865.

McGowen
Patrick McGowen, wagon maker, 9th, between J and K; Sacramento, CA, circa 1853–1865.

McGrath & Jones
Blacksmiths and wagon maker; Casper, Wyoming, circa 1900–1910.

McGuffy Brothers
Dealers in agricultural implements; Cody, WY, circa 1900–1910.

McGuire
John McGuire, blacksmith and wagon maker; Dempsey, Idaho, circa 1905–1910.

McInturff
William McInturff, blacksmithing, wagon and coach maker; Timberville, Virginia, circa 1885.

McInturff (see Whitesides & McInturff)

McIlhenney
J.M. McIlhenney, blacksmith and wheelwright, 598 Ross Avenue and 133 S. Jefferson; Dallas, Texas, circa 1891–1899.

McIlwayn
Neal McIlwayn, coach and wagon maker; Pittsburgh and Allegheny, PA, circa 1840–1870.

McIver-Patterson Vehicle Co.
Carriage, wagon and buggy dealers, 107 San Francisco; El Paso, Texas, circa 1900.

McKay
William McKay, blacksmith and wagon maker; Central City, Colorado, circa 1881.

McKay & Alexander
Carriage painters and trimmers, 783 Elm; Dallas, Texas, circa 1908.

McKee (see Price, McKee & Co.)

McKenzie
K.F. McKenzie, blacksmith and wagon maker; Clearwater, Idaho, circa 1905–1910.

McKillip
Charles McKillip, wagon maker, 190 K, corner 7th; Sacramento, CA, circa 1853–1865.

McKinney
John McKinney, carriage and wagon manufacturer and dealer; Salmon, Idaho, circa 1908.

McKinney (see Hand, McKinney & Massie)

McKinnon Dash & Hardware Co., Ltd.
This company, with factories in Syracuse and Buffalo, NY; Troy and Cincinnati, OH; and St. Catharines, Ontario, Canada built mostly dashes and fenders.

They purchased the dash department from Peters Dash Co. in 1899. This was a company with a capacity for making 500,000 buggy dashes per year. This newly purchased machinery was distributed among the factories at Syracuse and Buffalo, NY, and Troy, Ohio.

This company also manufactured wholesale carriage, cart, buggy and wagon parts for makers in the U.S. and Canada, circa 1880–1910.

McKnight Transfer, Livery & Sales Co.
Carriage painters, trimmers, wagons and buggies, 612 Polk; Amarillo, Texas, 1909; also Carriage Lines, 104–120 Taylor; Amarillo, Texas, circa 1909–1920.

McLane
Mr. McLane was a wagon maker from Whitewater, WI, circa 1879.

McLaughlin
M. McLaughlin, livery and feed, wagon and blacksmith shop; Fairplay, Colorado, circa 1882–1890.

McLaughlin Carriage Co.
Robert McLaughlin, 1836–1921, a pioneer of the Canadian vehicle industry, was born in the family homestead near the village of Tyrone, Ontario, Canada.

Robert's father, John McLaughlin, a cobbler from Northern Ireland, emigrated to this country in 1832. Five years later, he settled onto 100 acres of virgin forest land in Durham County, near Tyrone.

After his marriage to Mary Smith of Enniskillen, Robert received title to 50 acres of his father's land.

There he built a house and a large driving shed, where he set up a small workshop.

In 1867, despite his lack of technical training, he built two cutters in his driving shed. He had a natural skill in using wood-working tools, and began making axe handles, neck yokes and whiffletrees for neighbors. His business prospered and in 1869 he moved to Enniskillen and started The McLaughlin Carriage Works.

The business continued to expand so rapidly that in 1877, he moved again, this time to Oshawa.

In 1892, he took his sons, Robert Samuel and George William into partnership. An older son, with a degree in chemistry, settled in Toronto, founding J.J. McLaughlin Limited, inventor of the Canada Dry Ginger Ale formula.

In December 1899, the factory was totally destroyed by fire, but Robert McLaughlin, with the help of his two sons, Sam and George, began a new era in a new and larger plant. Incorporated in 1901, they were soon turning out twenty-five thousand vehicles per year, and became the largest carriage works in the British Empire.

The company continued to make horse-drawn vehicles until 1915. In 1921, Robert McLaughlin died, at the age of eighty-five.

McLaughlin (see Matterson & McLaughlin)

McLean & Haas Carriage and wagon makers, Fond du Lac, WI, circa 1879.

McLeod
William McLeod, wagon, carriage, and blacksmith shop; Buena Vista, CO, circa 1882–1890.

McMahon (see Crane & McMahon)

McMellon (see Wollman & McMellon)

McMillan
N. McMillan, blacksmith and wheelwright, 226 S. Oregon; El Paso, Texas, circa 1898–1909.

McMillan Bros.
Carriage and wagon dealers; Angelica, Wisconsin, circa 1890–1910.

McMitchell
A. McMitchell, wagon maker, corner 7th and K; Sacramento, CA, circa 1855–1875.

McMurray & Fisher Sulky Co.
Makers of the Double Axle Sulky, patented December 23, 1890, and advertised as "The Best Sulky in the World".

This firm did a substantial retail and wholesale business; Marion, OH, circa 1880–1915.

McNalley
J.D. McNalley, blacksmith and wheelwright, 26 Franklin; Houston, Texas, circa 1882–1895.

McNalley
M. McNalley, blacksmith and wheelwright, 50–52 Congress; Houston, Texas, circa 1882–1895.

McNamara
James McNamara & Sons manufactured wagons, Orlin Avenue and Lowmede Place; New York, NY, circa 1899.

McNaughton (see Munro & McNaughton)

McNeel
J.M. McNeel, blacksmith and wheelwright,1104 S. Flores; San Antonio, Texas, 1897–1898; and 110 Champ; San Antonio, Texas, circa 1898–1910.

McRay (see Brigham, McRay & Co.)

McSherry
D.E. McSherry & Co. manufactured farm equipment and implements, including the McSherry Broadcast Seeder and the McSherry Grain Drills; Dayton, OH, circa 1880–1920.

McSherry Manufacturing Co.
Built farm implements; Middletown, Ohio, circa 1880–1920.

McVaw
D. McVaw manufactured and sold, retail or wholesale, their McVaw's patented buggy and buck wagon. McVaw also built other vehicles, springs, gears and bodies; 8 East Main Street, Louisville, KY, circa 1870–1900.

McWilliams
Blacksmith and wagon maker; Minidoka, Idaho, circa 1905–1910.

McWilliams (see Buxton & McWilliams)

Meincke
Frederick Meincke, wagon maker; Prescott, WI, circa 1879–1901.

Meincke
John Meincke, carriage and wagon maker; Milwaukee, WI, circa 1879.

Meiser
Henry Meiser, wagon maker, 230 East 122nd; New York, NY, circa 1899.

Meisner
Charles Meisner, wagon maker, 210 West 28th; New York, NY, circa 1899.

Meister
A. Meister, manufacturer of buggies, carriages, express wagons and all other work in this line. Repairing of all kinds done with neatness and dispatch, 9th Street, between I and J; Sacramento, CA, circa 1882–1885.

Meitzner
Herman Meitzner, wagon maker, Kingsbridge Road and West 162nd; New York, NY, circa 1899.

Melarkey
David Melarkey, blacksmith and wagon maker, J, between 13th and 14th; Sacramento, CA, circa 1853–1865.

Melarkey (see Rippon & Melarkey)

Melas
Frank Melas, blacksmith and wheelwright; also carriage and wagon manufacturer, corner of Morales and N. San Saba; San Antonio, Texas, circa 1887–1900.

Melas
Louis Melas, blacksmith and wheelwright, 301 Morales; San Antonio, Texas, circa 1897–1902.

Melbourne Buggy Co.
Melbourne, Kentucky, circa 1890–1910.

Melburn & Co.
Lafayette A. Melburn established Melburn & Co. in 1877. They manufactured carriages and wagons, 486 Larimer and 584–586 Holladay; Denver, Colorado, circa 1877–1910.

They were also known as Colorado Carriage Works—and advertised for sale—fine carriages, buggies, express and delivery wagons, all built with Melburn's Patent Spring, which they claim enabled them to manufacture each vehicle from $10 to $18 less than other first class springs on the market at that time.

Melendez
Juan Melendez, blacksmith, 600 S. Ochoa; El Paso, Texas, circa 1910–1920.

Meller & Behr
Blacksmiths, 317 Santa Fe; El Paso, Texas, circa 1909–1919.

Mellon
M.J. Mellon, wagon maker, L, between 8th and 9th; Sacramento, CA, circa 1853–1865.

Mendenhall
W.K. Mendenhall, carriage, wagon, buggy and phaeton dealer, 6 San Jacinto; Houston, Texas, circa 1887–1900.

Menick & Weber
Wagon and carriage makers; Milwaukee, Wisconsin, circa 1865.

Mensch
O.P. Mensch, buggy maker, fork of third and fourth streets (now the Woodlawn Cemetery); Mifflinburg, PA, circa 1881.

Mentzlaff
Henry Mentzlaff, wagon maker, Richfield, WI, circa 1885–1915.

Merkel (see Schaeffer, Merkel & Co.)

Merkle
W.H. Merkle, carriage and wagon maker; Breckenridge, Colorado, circa 1883–1890.

Merric
T. Merric, carriages, wagons and buggies; Sherman, Texas, circa 1893–1900.

Merrick
E.V. Merrick & Son of Philadelphia, PA manufactured three steam fire-engines, the last in 1859, was built for the Weccacoe Engine Company #19 Volunteer Fire Dept. of the city of Philadelphia, circa 1858–1859.

Merritt
Lon Merritt, blacksmith and wagon maker; Bedford, Wyoming, circa 1900–1910.

Mersick (see English & Mersick)

Merts & Riddle
This Ravenna, Ohio firm, circa 1831–1926, was originally known as Clark Carriage Company, established in 1831. The name changed to Merts & Riddle Coach and Hearse Company in 1861 when it was purchased by brothers-in-law Charles Merts and Henry W. Riddle. Mr. Merts was a fine wood worker and tool maker. He also was able to supervise the shop while his partner, Mr. Riddle, spent most of his time on the road as the company salesman.

Their shop employed some of the foremost wood carvers and craftsmen of the day, doing all of the work by hand in the Ravenna factory.

Charles Merts sold out his share of the business in 1891 to Riddle, and the company name was changed to Riddle Coach and Hearse. By the time the firm began to manufacture motorized vehicles it was known only as Riddle Manufacturing Co.

The firm offered a full line of motorized hearses and ambulances from about 1912 until the factory closed in 1926. Over the years, many famous people were carried to their graves in a Riddle hearse, including two presidents, McKinley and Harding, and a cowboy named Roy Rogers, who was buried from a restored Riddle hearse in 1998.

Meserole
John G. Meserole, carriage painter and trimmer, over 409 Rusk; Ft. Worth, Texas, circa 1905–1915.

Meserole Bros.
Carriage painters and trimmers, 405 Elm; Dallas, Texas, circa 1897–1910.

Messerly
John Messerly, wagon maker, corner of Wolf and German Streets; Harrisonburg, Virginia, circa 1850.

Messinger
S.S. Messinger & Son manufactured horse-drawn and horse powered farm equipment; Tatamy, PA, circa 1870's–1900.

Metcalf
L. Metcalf, wagon maker; Galina, Colorado, circa 1884–1890's.

Metcalf (see Lininger & Metcalf)

Metropolis Bending Co.
Cleveland, OH, circa 1890–1910.

Metz
E. Metz, carriages, wagons and buggies; Sherman, Texas, circa 1893–1903.

Metzger
J.M. Metzger, wagon shop; Fort Collins, Colorado, circa 1881–1890's.

Metzner
Charles Metzner, wagon maker; Fort Atkinson, WI, circa 1879–1885.

Meungras
Mr. Meungras made wagons and sleighs: Camillus, NY, circa 1850's.

Meyer
Anton Meyer, blacksmith and wheelwright, 1427 S. Laredo; San Antonio, Texas, circa 1897–1907.

Meyer
F. Meyer, wagon maker; Rock Springs, WY, circa 1879.

Meyer
Fred Meyer & Son, carriage and wagon dealer and representative; Ableman, Wisconsin, circa 1890–1910.

Meyer
George Meyer & Co. manufactured heavy carriages, 228 East 63rd; New York, NY, circa 1899.

Meyer
Henry W. Meyer of Cincinnati, Ohio made carriages of every description—wagons, harness and accessories—on paper, making catalogs for the manufacturers, circa 1890's–1950. At the age of 16 he began an eight year run at the F.C.H. Manns Co., first as an apprentice, to learn the illustrating of vehicles.

At the age of 26, Meyer went into business for himself, establishing Meyer Engraving.

He retired in 1950 and in 1965 he authored the book—*Memories Of The Buggy Days*.

Meyer
J. Meyer, wagon maker; Paoli, WI, circa 1879.

Meyer
Joseph F. Meyer Co., blacksmith, carriage and wagon manufacturers supplies; and carriage and wagon woodwork, 28–32 Franklin; Houston, Texas, circa 1882–1890—and later as blacksmiths and carriage makers supplies, and carriage, wagon, buggy and phaeton dealer, 806–812 Franklin Ave.; Houston, Texas, circa 1890–1910.

Meyer & Bros.
Wagon makers, Terre Haute, Indiana, circa 1858.

Meyer (see James & Meyer Buggy Co.)

Meyer (see Mueller & Meyer)

Meyers
William Meyers, blacksmith and wagon maker; Kendrick, Idaho, circa 1905–1910.

Meyers Brothers
Carriage makers; Pueblo, Colorado, circa 1882–1890's.

Meynig
Henry M. Meynig, blacksmith and wheelwright, se corner of west Postoffice and 26th, and bottom of Church and Winnie, and 614—29th; Galveston, Texas, circa 1886–1902.

Meza
U.G. Meza & Son, blacksmiths, wheelwrights and horseshoers, 612 Broadway; Corpus Christi, Texas, circa 1910–1920.

Miami Rubber Co.
Cincinnati, Ohio, circa 1880–1910.

Michaels
John H. Michaels Wagon Co.,

buggy manufacturer; Cincinnati, Ohio, circa 1880–1910.

Michie
J.W. Michie, blacksmith and wagon maker; Meridan, Wyoming, and later as blacksmiths and carriage makers supplies, and carriage, wagon, buggy and phaeton dealer, 806–812 Franklin Ave.; Houston, Texas, circa 1890–1910.

Michigan Buggy Co.
This company not only built carriages and buggies, they also had produced over 20,000 sleighs by the early 1890's. They built 5,000 sleighs in the 1888–1889 season alone; Kalamazoo, Michigan, circa 1880–1910.

Michigan Cutter Co.
This firm manufactured sleighs in a variety of styles and designs, producing over 25,000 vehicles in the 1889–1890 season alone; Lowell, Michigan, circa 1880–1900.

Michler
Herman A. Michler, wagon maker; Fond du Lac, Wisconsin, circa 1885–1919.

Michler
O.F. Michler, wagon maker; Fond du Lac, Wisconsin, circa 1919.

Michler
William Michler, wagon maker; Fon du Lac, Wisconsin, circa 1915.

Middleton
M.M. Middleton, carriage and wagon dealer and representative; Argyle, Wisconsin, circa 1890–1910.

Middleton Buggy Co.
Middletown, Ohio, circa 1890–1910.

Middleton & Dukes
Blacksmith and wagon makers, Loveland, Colorado, circa 1882.

Mier Carriage & Buggy Co.
Ligonier, IN, circa 1890–1910.

Mierswa
C. Mierswa, wagon maker; Oshkosh, WI, circa 1879–1898.

Mierswa
D. Mierswa, wagon maker; Oshkosh, WI, circa 1879.

Mierswa
G. Mierswa, wagon maker; Oshkosh, WI, circa 1879.

Mifflinburg Body & Gear Co.
Horace Orwig, president and manager; buggy maker, (merged with the Mifflinburg Body Co.), northwest corner of Walnut and eighth streets; Mifflinburg, PA, circa 1911–1917.

Mifflinburg Body Co.
William F. Sterling, president, followed in 1931 by Oren Sterling, buggy maker, (results of a merger of the Mifflinburg Buggy Co. and the Mifflinburg Body & Gear Co.), northwest corner of Walnut and eighth streets; Mifflinburg, PA, circa 1917–1944.

Mifflinburg Buggy Co.
Partnership of Harry F. Blair, Robert S. Gutelius and Alfred A. Hopp, buggy makers, 358 Walnut street; Mifflinburg, PA, circa 1897–1903, Corporation: 1903–1917.

Mikado Wagons
See Fouts & Hunter Buggy Co.

Milburn
George Milburn & Co. were the successors to A. Eberhart & Co. Milburn employed over 100 men by the late 1860's. His shop was located near the St. Joseph river, a likely power source for this large factory; Mishawaka, Indiana, circa 1860's–1890's

Milburn Wagon Co.
Carriage, wagon, buggy and phaeton dealer, Tel. 206, 407 E. 6th; Austin, Texas, circa 1887–1900.

Milburn Wagon Co.
Carriages, buggies, phaetons and wagons, 40 Soledad, 10–12 W. Houston, M.V. Cumins, manager; San Antonio, Texas, circa 1887–1888.

Milburn Wagon Company
Manufactured a full line of carriages and buggies, farm wagons and commercial vehicles. In addition, they built the Milburn Hollow-Axle Wagon; Toledo, Ohio.

They offered a full line of vehicles at their branch office in Memphis, TN, circa 1870–1920's.

Miles
Edmund Miles owned and operated the E. & M. Miles blacksmith and carriage shop, with his brother Manley Miles, at 28 Albany street. They also built a fair amount of wagons and sleighs; Cazenovia, NY, circa 1820's–1850's.

Miles Bros.
Makers of the New Standard varnish brush, 102 Fulton St.; New York, NY, circa 1860–1900.

Milhaupt
Conrad Milhaupt, wagon maker; Appleton, WI, circa 1885–1915.

Mill
A.E. Mill, wagon maker; Mount Sterling, WI, circa 1879.

Miller
A. Miller, blacksmith and wheelwright; Idaho Springs, Colorado, circa 1883–1890.

Miller
C.F. Miller, blacksmith and wheelwright, 601 S. Presa.; San Antonio, Texas, circa 1897–1907.

Miller
Daniel B. Miller, buggy maker, southwest corner of Walnut and north fifth street; Mifflinburg, PA, circa 1870–1918.

Miller
F.W. Miller Manufacturing Co., made a number of implements, including the Miller's Bean Harvester; LeRoy, NY., circa 1880–1900.

Miller
George B. Miller & Son Mfg. Company of Waterloo, Iowa, circa 1890–1930, built a variety of farm equipment, including the Robinson Spreader acquired through the purchase of Robinson Spreader Co. of Vinton, Iowa—around 1920.

Miller
George C. Miller, who is credited with building the first wagons for sale in Cincinnati, came to this city

in 1812 from his native New Jersey as a blacksmith. He worked hard for the next 12 years, and in 1824 bought out his employer, Jacob Williams.

In his shop this same year, Miller constructed the first steel-spring jig (a light one-horse carriage with a single pair of wheels).

During the next 50 or so years, Miller's carriage business flourished. His factories produced landaus with glass and leather tops, coaches, side-bar wagon, sulkies, buggies and most every type of conveyance.

Miller's success enticed other wagon builders to Cincinnati. The demise of the buggy industry died a slow death. Miller said, "Although the death of an individual business is not uncommon, the demise of an industry is somewhat rarer." It is usually the result of the customers no longer needing or wanting your product. It took several factors, like better roads and automobiles, to complete the end of an era.

Miller
H.K. Miller, wagon maker; Georgetown, CO, circa 1883–1890's.

Miller
J.I. Miller, wagon maker; West Point, WI, circa 1879.

Miller
J. Miller, wheelwright; Mancos, CO, circa 1883–1890.

Miller
John G. Miller, buggy maker, 429 Market street; Mifflinburg, PA, circa 1872–1905.

Miller
Solomon B. Miller, buggy maker, 429 Market street (rear); Mifflinburg, PA, circa 1878–1900.

Miller
William Miller, wagon maker; Oconomowoc, Wisconsin, circa 1885–1903.

Miller
W.J. Miller & Sons, wagon makers; Genoa Junction, Wisconsin, circa 1879–1898.

Miller Bros.
Manufactured all styles of light and heavy carriages, buggies, wagons, landaus, broughams, cabriolets and rockaways. They also featured their Elcho Hunting Car in a number of advertisements, corner of Hill and Market Street; Amesbury, MA, circa 1870's–1910.

Miller Bros. Manufacturing
C.A. and J.H. Miller builders of the celebrated Miller road cart; Spring Valley, Illinois.

Miller Buggy Shop
Andy Miller, proprietor, wheelwright and carriage restoration; Bloomfield, Iowa.

Andy and his wife, Bev, operate a shop restoring buggies, carriages and antique automobiles. They use only traditional materials—real leather, horse hair, excelsior and they nail with trimmers tacks. They do not allow vinyl, foam rubber or staple guns. They have restored old vehicles and built new ones this way for many years, and are still in business today.

Andy revealed the two oldest horseless carriages restored were both made by the Chicago Motor Vehicle Co. in 1895. They have also restored an 1879 Roberts Electric vehicle, said to be the oldest operating electric vehicle in the world. The oldest truck they have restored, was a 1908 REO.

Miller Carriage Co.
Buggy manufacturer; Cincinnati, Ohio, circa 1880–1910.

Miller Hardware & Lumber Co.
Carriage and wagon dealer and representative; Alma Center, Wisconsin, circa 1890–1910.

Miller & Barbian
Blacksmiths and wheelwrights, rear 114 Commerce; Dallas, Texas, circa 1900.

Miller & Harris
Blacksmiths and wagon makers; Farmington, New Mexico, circa 1900–1915.

Miller-Knoblock Wagon Co.
Made street sprinkler wagons, also had factory in South Bend, IN, 390 Hudson; New York, NY, circa 1899.

Miller & Parton
Blacksmiths and wagon makers; Hagerman, Idaho, circa 1905–1910.

Miller (see Aultman, Miller & Co.)
Miller (see Bowden & Miller)
Miller (see Casey & Miller)
Miller (see Click & Miller)
Miller (see Fife & Miller)
Miller (see Hoffer & Miller)
Miller (see Ingram & Miller)
Miller (see Seiberling & Miller Co.)

Miller (see Womack & Miller) Milligan (see Stevens & Milligan)

Mills
James Mills, blacksmith and wagon maker; Evanston, Wyoming, circa 1900–1910.

Milton
John Milton, wagon maker; Mineral Point, circa 1865.

Milwaukee Harvester Co.
This company started building reapers and other farm equipment in the 1850's. Incorporated in 1884, they built the Milwaukee Corn Binder, a line that was carried well into the 1920's.

By 1902, they had merged with some other firms to form International Harvester Co.; Milwaukee, Wisconsin, circa 1850–1902.

Milwaukee Hay Tool Co.
Built huskers and shredders; Milwaukee, WI, circa 1890–1910.

Minch
J. Minch, wagon maker; Ahnapee, WI, circa 1879.

Miner
Rafael Miner, blacksmith, 613 Broadway; El Paso, Texas, circa 1910–1920.

Miner
Tom L. Miner, blacksmith and wagon maker, 307 S. Stanton; El Paso, Texas, circa 1904–1916.

Miner
W.A. Miner, dealer in carriages, buggies, and wagons, also livery, sale and feed stables; Greeley, Colorado, circa 1884–1890.

Minneapolis Harvester Works
Built farm equipment and implements; Minneapolis, MN, circa 1870–1900.

Minnesota Carriage & Sleigh Co.
Established in 1887, they produced a full line of sleighs, carriages and buggies; St. Paul Park, Minnesota, circa 1887–1910.

Minnick
William Minnick, blacksmith and wagon maker; Broadway, Virginia, circa 1850.

Minor & Rosas
Blacksmiths and wheelwrights, E. Overland, bottom of Utah, Stanton; El Paso, Texas, circa 1898–1903.

Minor & Stevens
Manufactured carriages at 72 Walker Street; New York, NY., circa 1850's–1870's.

Mireur
Joseph Mireur, carriages and vehicles, 409 Mewquite; Corpus Christi, Texas, circa 1910–1920.

Misfeldt (see Felber & Misfeldt)

Mishawaka Plow Co.
Built farm equipment; Mishawaka, Indiana, circa 1880–1900.

Mishawaka Wagon Co.
This company employed a network of dealers and agents to help distribute their wagons across the country; Mishawaka, Indiana, circa 1880–1920.

Mitchell
Henry Mitchell, carriage and wagon maker, sold his wagon factory to Edward Bain (1855) in Kenosha, Wisconsin. He then moved to Racine and established the Mitchell Wagon Co., circa 1855–1915.

Mitchell
John S. Mitchell, blacksmith and wheelwright, 209 Lancaster Ave.; Dallas, Texas, circa 1898–1903.

Mitchell
P.R. Mitchell Co., buggy manufacturer; Cincinnati, Ohio, circa 1880–1910.

Mitchell
William Mitchell, wagon maker; Cuba City, WI, circa 1885–1903.

Mitchell Wagon Co.
Manufactured wagons and other farm implements; Des Moines, Iowa, circa 1890–1920. Later became part of J.I. Case Plow Co.

Mitchell Wagon Co.
The largest wagon factory in Racine, Wisconsin, was started by Henry Mitchell in 1855. They later became the Mitchell & Lewis Co.

Mitchell Wheel Co.
Buggy wheel manufacturer; Miamisburg, Ohio, circa 1890–1910.

Mitchell & Lewis Co.
Established in 1832 and for a while known as Mitchell Wagon Co. of Racine, Wisconsin. They made a huge number of wagons, including covered wagons. They advertised their wagons as "Monarch of the Road".

By 1915, the company is again listed as Mitchell Wagon Co.; and by 1918 Mitchell wagons were being manufactured by John Deere Wagon Co. of Moline, IL, circa 1832–1918.

Mittendorf Mfg. Co.
Manufactured implements and tillage equipment; Hermon, Missouri, circa 1900–1920.

Moase (see Lepper & Moase)

Moat
Robert Moat, blacksmith and wagon maker; Fairplay, Colorado, circa 1881–1890.

Model Carriage & Harness Co.
Carriage manufacturer; Cincinnati, OH, circa 1890–1910.

Modie
John Modie of Independence, Missouri built wagons for local customers and advertised wagons suitable for the Oregon, California and Sante Fe trails, circa 1840–1860.

Moeller Wagon Works
Henry Moeller Sr. and his sons Corwin and Henry Jr. built circus wagons for their first cousins, the Gollmars and the Ringlings.

The Moeller wagon shop was located on third street in Baraboo, Wisconsin, circa 1880–1920's.

Moeller & Thuerer
Wagon makers; Baraboo, WI, circa 1879.

Moen
A.J. Moen, wagon maker; Westby; WI, circa 1885–1911.

Moffat
G. Moffat, wagon maker; DePere, Wisconsin, circa 1879.

Moldenhauer & Damm
Wagon and carriage makers; Eau Claire, Wisconsin, circa 1885–1915.

Moline Plow Co.
Built plows, planters and other implements, starting in 1861. Bought out the T.G. Mandt Co. of Stoughton, WI in 1906. This wholly owned subsidiary was known as the Mandt Wagon branch of Moline Plow Co.; Moline, Illinois.

They developed a number of new designs and sold thousands of their popular lines of equipment, like the Gretchen Planter, around 1900. The Flying Dutchman and Bismark trade mark were two of their more popular lines before WW I.

The firm continued to expand their carriage and wagon line with the purchase of Freeport Carriage Company (1900) and Henney Buggy Company (1906), both from Freeport, Illinois. They also began marketing Crescent wagons and Wisconsin steel-wheel farm trucks.

Moline Plow joined other firms in 1929 to form the Minneapolis-Moline Power Implement Co.; Moline, Illinois, circa 1861–1929.

Moline Wagon Co.
This Moline, Illinois firm, established in 1854, manufactured wagons and other road vehicles, circa 1854–1910.

They were bought out by John Deere & Company in 1910.

Molitor Bros.
Wagon and carriage makers; Fond du Lac, WI, circa 1879–1885.

Molitor
M. and M. Molitor, carriage and wagon makers; Fond du Lac, Wisconsin, circa 1898–1919.

Moll
John Moll, carriage and wagon maker; Allenton, Wisconsin, circa 1890–1910.

Molter
Charles Molter, carriage painter, 1112 Mission; San Francisco, California, circa 1888–1894.

Molzen
Peter Molzen, wagon and truck maker, 357 West 26th; New York, NY, circa 1899.

Monarch Buggy Co.
Buggy manufacturer; Cincinnati, Ohio, circa 1880–1910.

Monarch Carriage Goods Co.
Cincinnati, Ohio, circa 1890–1910.

Money (see Jones & Money)

Monmouth Plow Co.
Known for their lightweight plows and implements; Monmouth, Illinois, circa 1890's–1930.

Monning
Harry Monning, buggy manufacturer; Cincinnati, Ohio, circa 1880–1910.

Monpetit
J.B. Monpetit Carriage Shop, maker of carriages, wagons and other horse drawn vehicles; Plains, Montana, circa 1890–1910.

Monroe
J. Monroe, wagon maker; Appleton, WI, circa 1879.

Monschke Co.
Blacksmith, carriage and wagon makers, 643–645 Elm; Dallas, Texas, circa 1910.

Monschke & Grizzle
Carriage painters and trimmers, 643–645 Elm; Dallas, Texas, circa 1905–1915.

Monschke (see Benson & Monschke)

Monschke (see Thofern & Monschke)

Montgomery Ward & Co.
This early retail and wholesale giant, like Sears, Roebuck & Co., took advantage of their wide spread outlet stores and widely distributed mail order catalogs, to offer everything needed for home, farm and ranch, including horse-drawn implements, buggies and wagons; Kalamazoo, Michigan, circa 1890–1910.

(See more on this firm and many others in Volume 2 of *Wheels Across America*).

Moon Brothers
St. Louis, MO, circa 1890–1910.

Mooney
Wheelwright and livery stables, I street between 5th and 6th; Sacramento, CA, circa 1850–1860.

Moore
A.I. Moore (or) I.M. Moore, carriage painter; New York, NY, circa 1870–1900.

Moore
Archibald Moore, blacksmith and wheelwright, sw corner of Fulton and Velasco; Houston, Texas, circa 1900–1910.

Moore
David Moore, carriage and wagon maker; Colorado Springs, Colorado, circa 1882–1890.

Moore
Enoch Moore, wagon maker; Jackson County, Missouri, circa 1850–1860.

Moore
Lewis Moore & Co. manufactured wagons and trucks, 20 Clarke; New York, NY, circa 1899.

Moore
Oscar Moore, blacksmith and wheelwrights, 511 E. 5th; Austin, Texas, circa 1910–1920.

Moore
R.G. Moore, wagon maker; Centralia, WI, circa 1879.

Moore
William Sterling Moore; Batavia, Ohio, circa 1890–1910.

Moore & Rawlins
Carriages, wagons and buggies, agent Troy Pivot, Axle Farm Wagons, 271 Elm; Dallas, Texas, circa 1897–1915.

Moore & Son
John M. Moore, blacksmith and wagon maker, 15th and Wazee; Denver, Colorado, circa 1880, also hard wagon carriage and hardwood lumber, 197 15th; Denver, Colorado, circa 1881–1890.

Moorlen (see Hill & Moorlen)

Morehouse
Daniel Morehouse manufactured wagons and sleds: Lysander, NY, circa 1850's.

Morgan
C.W. Morgan, blacksmith, wheelwright, agricultural implements and maker of fine carriages, phaetons, buggies and spring wagons,

1712–1722 Thomes street; Rawlins, Wyoming, circa 1872–1910.

Morgan
D.S. Morgan & Co. manufactured farm equipment, reapers, and tillage implements. They built farm implements early on as Seymour & Morgan and may very well have operated the oldest reaper factory in the world; Brockport, NY, circa 1840–1900.

Morgan
J.R. Morgan, blacksmith, carriage and wagon maker, Spring St. and Central; Colorado City, Colorado, 1877; Central City, Colorado, 1879, Castle Rock, Colorado in 1880, and Irwin Colorado, 1881. (Mining town in Gunnison, known as Ruby Camp 30 miles northwest of Gunnison).

Morgan & Son
Blacksmiths, horseshoers, and wagon makers, se corner North Akard and Patterson Ave. and 233 Camp; Dallas, Texas, circa 1910.

Morgan & Williams
Wagon makers; Racine, WI, circa 1879.

Morgan (see O'Connor & Morgan)

Morgan (see Seymour & Morgan)

Moritz
Joseph Moritz, wagon maker; Taycheedah, Wisconsin, circa 1865.

Morrill (see Osgood, Morrill, Bird & Schofield)

Morris
Albert B. Morris, blacksmith, wheelwright, horseshoers, and wagon maker, 684 Ross ave., and 288–290 Hall; Dallas,Texas, circa 1900–1910.

Morris
Isaac P. Morris was known to have constructed three steam fire engines. His most noted was one built in 1859 from a design of Alexander McCausland for Engine Company #17 of Philadelphia, named the "Good Will". This engine saw constant use until capsized and destroyed in an 1888 accident, Philadelphia, PA, circa 1859–1870.

Morris
J.A. Morris, carriage maker; Bucksville, PA, circa 1880–1910.

Morris
J.R. Morris' Son, carriage and wagon woodwork, 49–51 Main; Houston, Texas, circa 1887–1900.

Morris
S.A. Morris, blacksmith and wheelwright, Barton Springs road; Austin, Texas, circa 1900–1912.

Morris & Currin
Carriage makers; Recene, Colorado, circa 1882–1895.

Morris (see Keehn & Morris)

Morris (see Morse & Morris)

Morrison
J.M. Morrison, carriage painter, 417–22nd; San Francisco, California, circa 1888–1894.

Morrison
John Clinedinst Morrison was born near Stanardsville, Green County, Virginia, July of 1834. He moved to Harrisonburg in 1854 and rented one of the old Braithwaite shops where be began making wagons and buggies.

John C. Morrison's Carriage Works, manufacturer of top and open buggies, two-wheel carts, rockaways and spring wagons, also all repairing work, corner of W. Market and German Sts.; Harrisonburg, Virginia.

Morrison
Thomas Corcoran, Sr. manufactured carriage lamps in Cincinnati, Ohio, circa 1900–1910.

Morrison
W.A. Morrison, blacksmith and wagon maker; Anaheim, California, circa 1882–1885.

Morrison Manufacturing Co.
Built farm implements and tillage equipment like their Lenhart Sulky Plow. The company changed their name, in the early 1900's, to Fort Madison Plow Co.; Fort Madison, Iowa, circa 1890–1920.

Morrison & Corcoran
Manufacturers of carriage, coach and hearse mountings; including the M. & C. detachable dash rail. They also offered gold, silver and nickel plating; Cincinnati, Ohio, circa 1870's–1900.

Morrow-Thomas Hardware Co.
Carriages, wagons and buggies, 312–314 Polk; Amarillo, Texas, circa 1905–1920.

Morsback
Graf Morsback, buggy manufacturer; Cincinnati, Ohio, circa 1880–1910.

Morse
Silas E. Morse established his carriage and carriage bent works manufacturing business in 1850, with partners Ralph Bell and James L. Savage in Cazenovia, NY. These partners split up after five years. Morse then joined another local craftsman, William H. Holmes in a new partnership.

Morse would make several more moves and changes in business partners, including his nephew and another carriage maker, Erastus Seymour, before settling down for good, in New Woodstock, NY to run his own S.E. Morse & Co., circa 1850–1880's.

Morse Spring Co.
Manufactured the Morse Compensating Spring Cart; Trumansburg, NY, circa 1880–1910.

Morse & Morris
Wagon makers; Waupun; WI, circa 1879.

Morse & Peterson
Blacksmiths and wagon makers; Lander, Wyoming, circa 1901–1902.

Mortenson
N.C. Mortenson, carriage and wagon maker; Box Elder, Utah, circa 1884–1890's.

Mortenson
N.C. Mortenson, carriage and wagon maker; Brigham City, Utah, circa 1884–1890's.

Mosehart & Keller
Blacksmiths and wheelwrights; carriage trimmers and painters; carriage, wagon, buggy and phaeton manufacturer and dealers, 1302–1304 Franklin Ave.; Houston, Texas, circa 1900–1910.

Moseman
C.M. Moseman & Brother, carriage makers and dealers; New York, NY, circa 1870–1910.

They also offered a full line of harness and saddlery in their 1890 illustrated catalog.

Moss
Collins Moss, buggy maker; Mifflinburg, PA, circa 1876.

Moss
Daniel Moss, buggy maker, 605 Chestnut street; Mifflinburg, PA, circa 1862–1880.

Moss
Daniel B. Moss, buggy maker, 615 Chestnut street, Mifflinburg, PA, 1877–1899, also, fork of third and fourth streets, circa 1899–1910.

Moss
George Moss, buggy maker, 525 Chestnut street, 1866–1889 and, 14 north fifth street (second floor of Frederick buggy shop); Mifflinburg, PA, circa 1899–1903.

Moss
James Moss, buggy maker, 617 Chestnut street; Mifflinburg, PA, circa 1860's–1890.

Mosse (see Tignor & Mosse)

Mossman
Henry Mossman, wagon maker; Muscoda, WI, circa 1885–1911.

Motley
James Motley, carriage and wagon maker, 388 Wazee; Denver, Colorado, circa 1878–1890.

Mourlot
Charles Mourlot, wagon maker, 250 West 27th; New York, NY, circa 1899.

Mowe
Louis Mowe, wagon maker; Stevens Point, Wisconsin, circa 1865.

Moye (see Krakauer, Zork and Moye)

Moyer
Harvey A. Moyer was a carriage and wagon maker. In addition, they manufactured a variety of carriage parts and equipment, including the Gold Medal runabout gear and the Moyer Hub Borer.

The latter was able to bore a set of four wheels in less than a minute, according to their advertisement, 259 Wolf; Syracuse, NY, circa 1870–1910.

Moyer Carriage Co.
Rochester, New York, circa 1890–1910.

Moyers
F.B. Moyers, carriage and wagon maker; Conejos, Colorado, circa 1884–1890.

Mt. Carmel Axle Works
Manufactured springs, axles and their Ives Patented Tree. They were established in 1833 by Frederic Ives; New Haven, CT, circa 1833–1900.

Mt. Vernon Iron Works
Manufactured farm equipment and implements in association with C.G. Cooper & Co.; Mt. Vernon, OH, circa 1880–1900.

Muckle
The H.A. Muckle Manufacturing Company was established in 1887. They built carriages, wagons and over 10,000 sleighs, by 1900; St. Paul Park, MN, circa 1887–1910.

Mueller & Meyer
Carriage and wagon makers; Milwaukee, Wisconsin, circa 1865–1879.

Muffer & Lippey
Carriage makers, 49–51 Marlow Street; New York, NY, circa 1890's.

Muir
J.C. Muir, carriage and wagon dealer and representative; Arcadia, Wisconsin, circa 1890–1910.

Mulcahy
Edmund Mulcahy, wagon maker, 713 East 12th; New York, NY, circa 1899.

Mull (see Harvey & Mull)

Mullarky
P. Mullarky, wagon maker; DePere, WI, circa 1879.

Muller
Adolphus Muller was a carriage and sleigh maker who offered a number of original designs, like their six passenger Extension-Top Sleigh displayed in an September 1877 issue of The Hub, a major trade publication of the day; New York, NY, circa 1860's–1890.

Mulligan (see Winchester & Mulligan)

Mulready
Thomas Mulready, wagon maker; Pueblo, Colorado, circa 1881–1890.

Mummer (see Wilson & Mummer)

Munch
M. Munch, wagon maker; Weyauwega, WI, circa 1879.

Muncie Jobbing & Mfgr. Co.
Manufactured carriage-trimming material; Muncie, IN, circa 1880–1900.

Munckton
G.A. Munckton, carriage and wagon makers, Oakland Ave. and 2 South Montrose; Dallas, Texas, circa 1910–1920.

Munckton Bros.
Blacksmiths, wheelwrights, and horseshoers, 688 Ross Ave. and 221 N.Akard corner of Camp, also 178–180 N. Akarad; Dallas, Texas, circa 1891–1908.

Mundt
J. Mundt, wagon maker; Fond du Lac, WI, circa 1879.

Munn
A.F. Munn, blacksmith, carriage and wagon maker; Colorado Springs, CO, circa 1877–1880's.

Munroe-McIntosh Carriage Co.
Carriage manufacturer; Alexandria, Ontario, Canada, circa 1890–1910.

Munro & McNaughton
Blacksmith and wagon makers; Teller, Colorado, circa 1882–1890.

Munzesheimer
Louis Munzesheimer, blacksmith and wheelwright, 212–214 N. Akard; Dallas, Texas, circa 1900.

Murdock
James Murdock Jr. manufactured brass signs and name plates for carts, carriages and wagons; 52 Longworth St., Cincinnati, OH, circa 1870–1900.

Murphy
B.F. Murphy, blacksmith and wagon maker; Boise, Idaho, circa 1905–1910.

Murphy
James Murphy, blacksmith and wagon maker; Grangeville, Idaho, circa 1905–1910.

Murphy
Joseph Murphy was born in 1805 in Ireland. Of all the St. Louis wagon makers, he is by far the best known today.

After serving his apprenticeship (1819–1825) under Daniel Caster, a St. Louis wagon maker, he then worked a short time for Samuel Mount, Edward Harrington, James Earl and John B. Hunt.

Murphy established his own shop June 22, 1826, and would grow to employ about 25 men and produce over 400 drays and wagons a year.

Murphy turned over the business to his sons in 1888 and retired.

Before his death (around 1901) Joseph Murphy built a reputation as a painstaking master craftsman, turning out a superior product and making him the foremost St. Louis wagon manufacturer, circa 1826–1901.

Murphy & Hillin
Blacksmiths, 305 S. Oregon; El Paso, Texas, circa 1909–1914.

Murray
Wilbur H. Murray Carriage Co., buggy manufacturer; Cincinnati, Ohio, circa 1880–1910.

Murray
William A. Murray Spring Co., Cincinnati, Ohio, circa 1880–1910.

Murray & Hazlehurst
This firm built six steam fire-engines. The first in 1858, for the Washington Engine Company #13, Volunteer Fire Dept., and their last, built and shipped to Savannah, GA in 1860, named "Thom's King". Worthington of New York designed all of their pumps; Baltimore, MD, circa 1858–1860.

Murray (see Nichols & Murray)

Musser
Harold Musser worked in the hardware and carriage trimming business as a young boy in his father's shop. Musser would later run his own business supplying hardware and carriage trimming supplies; Mifflinburg, PA., circa 1870–1890.

Musser & Bernard
Blacksmiths and wagon makers, 424 West Chestnut; Leadville, CO, circa 1880–1890.

Myers
Andrew Myers, wagon maker, Main St.; Georgetown, Colorado, circa 1877, 1879 and 1881–82., and in Golden, Colorado, circa 1878.

Myers
M.H. Myers, wagon maker; Black Earth, WI, circa 1879.

Myers & Bros.
Wagon makers; Terre Haute, Indiana, circa 1858.

Myers Hardware & Saddlery Co.
Carriage, wagon and buggy dealers, Charles Bonnell, Manager; also agricultural implements, harness and saddlery, 310 S. El Paso; El Paso, Texas, circa 1906–1918.

Myers and Drumheller
Wagon makers; Port Republic, Virginia, circa 1872–1887.

Naegelin
William Naegelin, blacksmith and wagon maker; Animas City, Colorado, circa 1879–1890.

Nash
Duane H. Nash manufactured agricultural equipment; Millington, NJ, circa 1880–1910.

National Carriage Co.
Buggy manufacturer; Cincinnati, Ohio, circa 1880–1910.

National Hardware Co.
Cincinnati, Ohio, circa 1880–1910.

National Wheel Co.
Manufactured wheels for every style and size of vehicle, producing over 75,000 sets a year by 1890; Jackson, MI, circa 1880's–1910.

Naw
Andrew Naw, blacksmith; and carriage and wagon maker, California Street; Socorro, New Mexico, circa 1884–1890's.

Naylor
John Naylor, blacksmith and wagon maker; Blackfoot, Idaho, circa 1905–1910.

Neafie (see Reanie & Neafie)

Neal
G.W. Neal, blacksmith and wagon maker; Elmoro, Colorado, 1879–1883. (206 miles South of Denver and 4 miles from Trinidad).

Neal & Bolser
Manufacturers of a very expensive line of vehicles; Amesbury, MA, circa 1890–1910.

Neale
W.R. Neale, blacksmith and wagon maker, Alamosa, Colorado, circa 1884–1890.

Needham
R.J. Needham, wagon maker; Stockbridge, WI, circa 1879–1903.

Neff
E. Neff, carriage and wagon dealer and representative; Antigo, Wisconsin, circa 1890–1910.

Negelin Brothers
Blacksmiths and wagon makers; Durango, Colorado, circa 1884–1890's.

Neil
G.G. Neil, blacksmith, 18th and Eddy street; Cheyenne, Wyoming, circa 1892–1893.

Neil (see Books & Neil)

Neis
V.F. Neis, was a blacksmith and wagon maker; Recene, Colorado. This was a mining town in Sumit County, 20 miles from Leadville on the 10 mile extension of the Denver & Rio Grand R.R. Neis also served Kokomo, a mining camp, population of both camps 800, altitude 10,500, one weekly paper, 18 miles to Leadville and 25 miles to Breckenridge, circa 1881–1889.

Nelson
Abe Nelson Leather Co. of Cincinnati, Ohio, circa 1880–1910.

Nelson
Albert Nelson, blacksmith and wagon maker; Georgetown, CO, circa 1880–1890.

Nelson
C. Nelson, blacksmith and wagon maker; Archer, ID, circa 1905–1910.

Nelson
Charles O. Nelson, blacksmith and wheelwright, W. Strand, bottom of 25th, 26th; Galveston, Texas, circa 1886–1890's.

Nelson
J.J. Nelson, carriage and wagon dealer; Amherst, Wisconsin, circa 1890–1910.

Nelson
John Nelson, carriage and wagon maker; Antigo, Wisconsin, circa 1890–1910.

Nelson
L. Nelson, blacksmith and wagon maker, South 2nd; Leadville, Colorado, circa 1880–1890.

Nelson
N. Nelson, wagon maker; Cazenovia, WI, circa 1879–1885.

Nelson
Thomas Nelson, blacksmith and wheelwright, 3216 Ave. I; Galveston, Texas, circa 1893–1900.

Nelson (see Mann & Nelson)

Neubauer
J.W.H. Neubauer, carriage and wagon maker; Oshkosh, WI, circa 1879.

Nevil
Zachary L. Nevil, blacksmith and wheelwright, sw corner Barton Springs and Fredericksburg road; Austin, Texas, circa 1910–1918.

Newark
The Newark Coach Lamp Mfg. Co. of New Jersey, circa 1890–1910.

Newark Machine Co.
Built the Victor Double Huller, a clover huller and threshing machine—also offered the Miller Spreader; Newark, Ohio, circa 1880–1910.

New Conklin Wagon Co.
This quality wagon manufacturing company built a series of vehicles and was known for special 14-spoke front and 16-spoke rear wheels; Olean, NY, circa 1860's–1900.

Newell (see Demerritt & Newell)

Newell (see McComb & Newell)

New Haven Spring Co.
Manufactured springs and axles for wagons and carriages; New Haven, CT, circa 1850's–1890.

New Haven Wheel Co.
Established in 1845, this firm manufactured a full line of wheels, spokes, rims, hubs, spring bars, sawed felloes, whiffletrees and seat sticks.

They also manufactured Sarven's Patent Wheel, 148–152 York Street; New Haven, CT, circa 1845–1910.

New Idea Spreader Co.
Manufactured farm implements including manure spreaders and the New Idea Harvest Wagon. They sold their spreader under the NISCO trademark for several years; Coldwater, Ohio, circa 1900–1950. They also built a line of hay tools and rakes, after the purchase of Sandwich Manufacturing Co.

Newkirk
J. Newkirk, wagon maker; Shopiere; WI, circa 1879.

Newman & Hunter
Blacksmith and wagon maker; Longmont, CO, circa 1878–1881.

Newman (see Welbers & Newman)

Newnes
Richard Newnes, wagon repair shop; Dillon, Colorado, 1884 and wagon maker; Frisco, Colorado, circa 1883–1890.

Newnom
George H. Newnom, blacksmith and wheelwright, 711 Red River; Austin, Texas, circa 1900–1910.

New Process Manufacturing Co.
Built farm implements; Lincoln, Nebraska, circa 1890–1910.

Newton
Charles H. Newton, wagon maker, 5th, between I and J; Sacramento, CA, circa 1853–1865.

Newton Carriage Co.
Most of this firm's business was wholesale. They manufactured large quantities of vehicles for other distributors and jobbers; Kalamazoo, Michigan, circa 1880–1900.

Newton Wagon Co.
Built a full line of farm wagons untill the company was bought out

by Emerson-Brantingham of Rockford, Illinois, around 1911; Batavia, Illinois, circa 1880–1911.

New York Transfer Co.
Makers of carriages, coaches, cabs and a line of stagecoaches; New York City, circa 1870–1890.

Neyman
V.E. Neyman, blacksmith and wagon maker; Albion, Idaho, circa 1905–1910.

Nichol
Thomas. J. Nichol Co., builder of steam calliopes for the circus and carnival trade; Cincinnati, Ohio, circa 1900–1920.

Nicholas
D.P. Nicholas & Co. manufactured hansom cabs, 215 West 53rd; New York, NY, circa 1899.

Nicholas (see Bunz & Nicholas)

Nichols
B.S. Nichols & Co. was a steam fire-engine manufacturer. Nichols purchased the company of R.J. Gould in 1875, buying the entire rights, patents, tools, etc. They continued to build the Gould style engines uintil going out of business in 1879; Burlington, VT, circa 1875–1879.

Nichols
J. Nichols, wagon maker; White Creek, WI, circa 1879.

Nichols & Fenske
Wagon makers; Berlin, Wisconsin, circa 1865.

Nichols & Murray
W.M Nichols and Perry Murray, blacksmithing, carriage and wagon manufacturing and repairing. Coach and carriage painting and trimming promplty and neatly done, corner of Montezuma and Madison Streets; Phoenix, Arizona, circa 1888–1894.

Nichols & Shepard
Built threshers from around the turn of the century, then merged with others in 1931 to form the Oliver Farm Equipment Company; Battle Creek, Michigan, circa 1900–1931.

Nicholson
D. Nicholson, coach and wagon maker; Pittsburgh and Allegheny, PA., circa 1840–1870.

Nickedemus
Joseph Nickedemus, blacksmith; Marion, Iowa, 1864–1893.

Nicklos
John Nicklos, blacksmith and wagon maker; Arapahoe Agency, Wyoming, circa 1900–1905.

Nicolaisen & Stuhr
Blacksmiths and wagon makers, 408–412 west 16th; Cheyenne, Wyoming, circa 1895–1910.

Nieling
Martin Nieling, wagon maker; Little Chute, WI, circa 1879–1885.

Nielsen Brothers
Carriage manufacturing, horseshoeing and general blacksmithing shop. Silver medal received for the best display of hand-made horseshoes at the State Fair of California in 1881. Located on 10th Street, between J and K; Sacramento, California, 1882–1898.

Nissan Wagon Co.
Tycho Nissen was born in Denmark in 1732. He came to Charlestown, North Carolina in 1770. The following year he went to Bethania and worked as a wagon maker on and off until his death in 1789.

His son, Christian Nissen left wagon making to others and was a farmer who probably wished his son John Philip Nissen had stayed home and worked the farm too.

But John Philip Nissen was a boy with a mechanical talent. He tinkered with the family wagon. By the time he was in his early teens, John Philip Nissen had built a wagon of his own.

In 1834, he moved to the area that would later be known as the Winston-Salem area. There he built a log shed high on a hill. The Nissen Wagon Works trace back to that log shed.

J.P. Nissen worked for the Confederacy during the Civil War, making supply wagons and gun carts for Lee and Johnson. The Nissen wagon was as well known and as highly thought of as the famous Studebaker wagons.

Nissen always insisted on the best quality of materials and workmanship, and when his boys—George E. and William M. Nissen—took over the works shortly after the Civil War they continued to build the finest crooked bed wagons that man and materials combined could make.

Will Nissen is remembered as a giant of a man, who was soft spoken and even tempered. He dropped out of school at an early age to apprentice in J.P.'s wagon works. When he eventually headed the company, they were producing 50 wagons a day—some 15,000 a year.

Will wasn't a church goer, but was a Christian man in every sense.

He was remembered as a man who was "Will" to his men, ate lunch with and pitched horshoes after lunch with them, and generally took care of his men. It was said he pioneered the industrial retirement plan. When his workers got too old to perform their tasks, Will would keep them on doing handy work around the factory.

In 1919 the Nissen Wagon Works burned to the ground. Instead of laying off—Will hired one outside man to head up construction—then put his own crew of over 200 men to work, building a bigger and better facility. This, for a period of four months before production resumed.

The end of an era came when the family tradition, which began with Tycho Nissen in 1770, ended in 1925, with the sale of the business.

Noake
H.P. Noake, carriage and wagon manufacturer, blacksmith and horseshoer, California Street, Socorro, NM, circa 1888–1894.

Noake
H.P. Noake, carriages, wagons, buggies, implements and harness, 111–115 W. Overland; also black-

smith and carriage maker; carriage painter and trimmer, 200–210 W. Overland; El Paso, Texas, circa 1898–1911.

Noake
Harry P. Noake, blacksmith, wheelwright, wagon and carriage maker; carriage, wagon and buggy dealer; sw corner S. Santa Fe and W. Ovrerland; El Paso, Texas, circa 1904–1918.

Noakes
T.J. Noakes, blacksmith, wheelwright and horseshoer, 414 William; Corpus Christi, Texas, circa 1910–1920.

Noblet
Peter Noblet, wagon maker, I between 9th and 10th; Sacramento, CA, circa 1855–1875.

Noe (see Firmin, Billings and Noe)

Nolan
J.H. Nolan & Son, built carriages for all occasions; Denison, Texas, circa 1893–1911.

Nolt
Elam H. Nolt, custom manufacturing and repair work; Ephrata, PA., circa 1970.

Nolt
Leroy N. Nolt was born in June of 1949, in Lancaster County, PA. In 1970 he moved to Rockingham County, Virginia, where he met and married Linda Showalter in 1972.

He was employed by the Burkholder Buggy Shop near Dayton until the end of 1978. He then went into the buggy making business on his own, in rural Bridgewater, VA.

Noonan (see McAvoy & Noonan)

Nordling & Taylor
Blacksmiths and wagon makers; Moscow, Idaho, circa 1905–1910.

Norman Buggy Co.
Griffin, GA, circa 1890–1910.

Norris
C.B. Norris, wagon maker; Hammond, WI, circa 1879–1901.

Norris
George H. Norris, blacksmith and wagon maker; Morrison, Colorado, circa 1882–1890.

North River Agricultural Works
This New York, NY firm manufactured farm equipment and implements, including their one-horse non-riding Swift's Improved Lawn Mower, in the mid-1860's. They also offered one of the earliest sulky plows—the Fisher Patent Premium Lever Plow—invented by Samuel Fisher of West Windsor, NJ, circa 1860–1880.

Northrup
H.W. Northrup, wagon maker; Alma Center, WI, circa 1879.

North Side Wagon Yard
Wagon yards, 208 N Tyler; Amarillo, Texas, circa 1900–1920.

Northwestern Manufacturing Co.
Manufacturer of carriages, wagons and sleighs. They had built nearly 20,000 sleighs by 1900; Fort Atkinson, WI, circa 1880–1920.

Northwestern Sleigh Co.
Designed and built wagons, carriages and sleighs. They offered a number of fine cutters—like their No. 8 "Minnesota Chief" with Chapman Shifting-bar, also their No. 40 light combination wagon and No. 81 buggy with side-bar double cross springs, Fowler street; Milwaukee, Wisconsin, circa 1870's–1905.

Norton
F.W. Norton, wagon maker, Elm St.; Leadville, CO, 1881–1898.

Norton
Philo P. Norton, wagon maker; Cazenovia, NY, circa 1830's–1857.

Norwegian Plow Co.
This firm manufactured the Honest Abe Sulky Plow in the 1880's; Dubuque, Iowa, circa 1880–1900.

Nostrand
Robert H. Nostrand of Long Island, NY. (see East Williston Cart Company).

Nott Fire Engine Co.
Manufacturer of fire equipment; Elmira, N.Y, circa 1890–1910.

Nourse & Mason Co.
Manufactured farm implements, including their Kirby mowers. They also used some Ketchum patents in their mowing machine line, including the Davis Improved mower. They were also known as Ruggles, Nourse & Mason.

By the mid 1860's the firm was taken over by Ames Plow Company—also from Boston, MA., circa 1850's–1866.

Nova Scotia Carriage Co.
This carriage manufacturer was established in 1868 and did well until 1908, when the automobile became more popular. They ultimately went out of business by 1917; Kentville, Nova Scotia, circa 1868–1917.

Novelty Carriage Works
Anthony McAvoy and Morris Noonan organized the Novelty Carriage Works in Racine, Wisconsin, 1874. They built buggies and light road wagons for many years, circa 1874–1900.

Novelty Carriage Works
Carriage maker; Wilmington, DE, circa 1880–1910.

Noyes Carriage Co.
Manufacturer of carriages, buggies, wagons and sleighs, and when the buggy business slowed due to the coming of the automobile, the Noyes Carriage Co. went into the making of House Trailers; Elkhart, Indiana, circa 1890–1915.

Nuevenberg
John Nuevenberg, carriage and wagon dealer and representative; Athens, Wisconsin, circa 1890–1910.

Nuges
F. Nuges, wagon maker, 3 Macdougal; New York, NY, circa 1899.

Nunier
M. Nunier & Co., wagon makers; Sherwood, WI, circa 1879.

Nussbaumer
Adolf Nussbaumer, carriages, wagons and buggies, 213 Gaston Ave.; Dallas, Texas, circa 1900.

Nye
Levi Nye, blacksmith and wagon maker, J, between 10th and 11th; Sacramento, CA, circa 1853–1865.

Oakfield Agricultural Works
Manufactured farm implements and other equipment; Oakfield, NY, circa 1890–1910.

O'Bannon (see Reynolds & O'Bannon)

Oberdorf
E. Curtis Oberdorf, buggy maker, 242 Market street (rear); Mifflinburg, PA, circa 1900–1905.

Oberdorf
Henry G. Oberdorf, started out as a carpenter, then began buggy making, northeast corner of Walnut and second streets; Mifflinburg, PA, circa 1880–1890.

O'Brian
John O'Brian, wagon maker, with G.J. Overshiner, 4th, between I and J; Sacramento, CA, circa 1853–1865.

O'Brien
J.H. O'Brien, wagons; Boulder, Colorado, circa 1882–1890.

O'Brien Brothers Mfg. Co.
Carriage manufacturers; Tiffin, OH, circa 1890–1910.

O'Connell
William O'Connell, blacksmith and wagon maker; Kemmerer, Wyoming, circa 1901–1910.

O'Connor
James O'Connor manufactured carriage name plates, steel stamps, letters and figures, 141 W. 5th Street; Cincinnati, Ohio, circa 1870–1900.

O'Connor & Morgan
Blacksmiths and wheelwrights, rear 160 N. Akard; Dallas, Texas, circa 1891–1900.

O'Donnell
Tom O'Donnell, blacksmith, wagon maker and repairer for Charles Closson Livery in Santa Fe, New Mexico, circa 1900–1910.

Oertel
F.A. Oertel, wagon maker; Praire du Sac, WI, circa 1879–1885.

Ogden
John Ogden, carriage and wagon makers; Milwaukee, WI, circa 1865.

Ogden Carriage Co.
Carriage Manufacturer; Ashland, Ohio, circa 1870–1900.

Ogden (see The Cary-Ogden Co.)

Ogdon
W.C. Ogdon & Sons, carriage, wagon makers and blacksmiths; Marysville, CA, circa 1850's–1870's.

Ogle
B.J. Ogle, wagon maker; Lawson, Colorado, 1878; Leadville, Colorado, 1878; Lake City, Colorado, circa 1879–1884.

O'Harra & Brothers
J.T. O'Harra & Brothers, wagon makers and blacksmiths; Colorado Springs, Colorado, circa 1882–1890.

Ohio Carriage Co.
Under the direction of H.C. Phelps, company president, this firm operated factories in two Ohio cities, Cincinnati and Columbus. They manufactured over 200,000 vehicles under the "Split Hickory" trade mark, between 1899–1913.

Ohio carriage dealt exclusively with retail customers through an extensive direct mail order business, circa 1880–1920.

Ohio Cultivator Co.
Well known farm implement and cultivator manufacturer, founded by Harlow C. Stahl in 1878—sales included the Ohio Spreader line in the 1920's, and later its new Famous Ohio Spreader in 1935; Bellevue, Ohio, circa 1878–1940's.

Ohio Seat Co.
Cincinnati, Ohio, circa 1880–1910.

Ohio Steel Wagon Co.
Manufactured wagons and other farm vehicles—including their own steel wheels; Wapakoneta, Ohio, circa 1900–1910.

Ohio Tanning Co.
Cincinnati, Ohio, circa 1880–1910.

Ohlsen
The Ohlsen Wagon Company, builders of some of the first practical circus calliopes.

Established 1864, they were builders of general heavy duty, spring wagons of all shapes and sizes. It was said they had built for Barnum, Cole, Forepaugh, Robinson and the Sells Brothers and all of the principal showman of the day.

William Kirkup & Son was a brass foundry and Vanduzen & Tift was a bell founder. These two Cincinnati firms were most likely the sources for the instruments in the Olhlsen-built wagons; Cincinnati, Ohio, circa 1864–1920.

Ohnemus & Son
R. Ohnemus & Son, blacksmiths, wagon makers and Gasoline engines; Carlsbad, New Mexico, circa 1900–1915.

O'Kelley
C.L. O'Kelley, blacksmith and wagon maker; Culdesac, Idaho, circa 1905–1910.

Okerland
P. Okerland, blacksmith and wagon maker, Francisco between Powell and Mason; San Francisco, California, circa 1882–1895.

Oldenburg
William Oldenburg, carriage and wagon makers; Lander, Wyoming, circa 1901–1910.

Older
W.H. Older, wagon maker; Packwaukee, WI, circa 1879.

Olds Wagon Works
Manufactured several styles of wagons, including the Olds Wagon and

the Old Reliable Olds Wagon; Fort Wayne, IN, circa 1890–1910.

Olds & Short
Blacksmiths; Douglas, Wyoming, circa 1905–1910.

Oler & Jones
Blacksmiths and wheelwrights, 375 Washington; Beaumont, Texas, circa 1900–1915.

Oliver
J.G. Oliver, blacksmith and wagon maker; Buffalo, Wyoming, circa 1902–1908.

Oliver
R.H. Oliver, carriage and wagon maker; Buffalo, Wyoming, circa 1905–1910.

Oliver Case & Co.
Built wagons and farm implements; Westport, Missouri, circa 1870–1900's.

Oliver Chilled Plow Works
James Oliver, through his numerous patents, built one of the foremost plow companies in the world. Over his long and successful career, Oliver perfected his chilled plow design, using a special alloy of iron. Eventually in 1929, Oliver, along with others, would form the Oliver Farm Equipment Co.; South Bend, Indiana, circa 1880's–1929.

Oliver (see Gardner & Oliver)

Oliver (see Lewis, Oliver & Phillips)

Olmstead
O.L. Olmstead, wagon maker; Neenah, WI, circa 1879.

Olmstead
P.E. Olmstead, carriage and wagon manufacturer; Marion, Iowa, circa 1871.

Olson
Andew J. Olson, blacksmith, carriage and wagon maker, corner Wyoming & 1st Sreet; Shoshoni, Wyoming, circa 1906–1907.

Olson
John Olson, blacksmith and wagon maker; Dickey, Idaho, circa 1905–1910.

Olson & Gunderson
Manufactured wagons, 261 Tenth Avenue; New York, NY, circa 1899.

Oneida Carriage Works
This firm's business, located on Cedar Street in Oneida, NY, was mostly a manufacturer for the wholesale trade.

They offered carriages, surreys, buggies and road wagons; and shipped their product to a large number of agents, dealers and retail stores, circa 1880–1910.

O'Neil
John O'Neil, a carriage, coach, wagon and sleigh maker, operated his business out of the old John Williams woolen mill; Cazenovia, NY, circa 1880–1920.

O'Neil Implement Co.
Built farm equipment under the Flying Swede name, including the Flying Swede Terror and other implements; Marseilles, Illinois, circa 1910–1920's.

Oppenheimer
Aaron J. Oppenheimer & Co. manufactured light carriages, 204 East 24th; New York, NY, circa 1899.

Opperman
Charles Oppermann, blacksmith and wheelwright; also carriage and wagon manufacturer, sw corner of Nogolitos and Cevallos; San Antonio, Texas, circa 1887–1900.

Orchard & Bros.
Wagon makers; Lamartine, WI, circa 1879.

Ordway
W. Ordway, carriage maker with Hayworth, Eells & Co.; Sacramento, CA, circa 1853–1865.

Orendorff (see Parlin & Orendorff Co.)

Orendorff (see Parlin & Orendorff Implement Co.)

O'Rourke
John T. O'Rourke, blacksmith and wagon maker, 207 Mesa Ave.; El Paso, Texas, circa 1904–1918.

Orr
C.M. Orr, blacksmith and horseshoer; also manufacturer of carriages, wagons and buggies, 149 N. College Ave.; Dallas, Texas, circa 1910.

Orr
John W. Orr, engraver and superior draftsman, offering his work to the carriage makers, 75 & 77 Nassau Street: New York, NY, circa 1850–1900.

Orris (see Eberly & Orris Co.)

Orrville Machine Co.
Manufactured the New Combined Champion; Orrville, Ohio, circa 1875–1900.

Ortego
Santiago Ortego, blacksmith and wheelwright, E. 5th, 1 mile of Comal; Austin, Texas, circa 1905–1915.

Ortiz & Co.
Wagons, harness and saddlery, Albuquerque, New Mexico, circa 1906–1916.

Ortiz
Tony Ortiz, blacksmith, harness and saddlery, 2nd and Copper; Albuquerque, New Mexico, circa 1910–1920.

Orwig
Samuel Orwig, buggy maker; Mifflinburg, PA, circa 1855.

Osborne
D.M. Osborne & Co. built the Osborne Columbia Corn Harvester and other farm equipment.

Established in 1862, after an earlier venture in 1855 with W.A. Kirby building the Kirby Mower.

Osborne went on to manufacture a full line of farm implements beforethey were bought out by International Harvester, circa 1903–1905.

I.H. later sold the Osborne line to Emerson-Brantingham, in 1919, and in turn, this firm was purchased by J.I. Case in 1928; Auburn, NY, circa 1855–1928.

Osborne
R.F. Osborne & Co., wagon and carriage material, 751 Market St.; San Francisco, California, circa 1882–1890's.

Osborne
W.B. Osborne, agent for Mitchell and Lewis wagons; Loveland, Colorado, circa 1882–1890.

Osborne (see Kyle & Osborne)

Osgood
G.W. Osgood, Morrill, Bird & Schofield, vehicle manufacturers, also built a number of sleighs and cutters; Amesbury, MA, circa 1880–1910.

Osgood
L. Osgood, wagon maker; Jordan Center, WI, circa 1879.

Osman & Woodside
Carriage manufacturers; Bucyrus, OH, circa 1890–1910.

Ostertag
John Ostertag, wagon maker; Weyauwega, Wisconsin, circa 1865.

Oswald & McEachon
Wagon makers, 59 Elm; Lockport, NY, circa 1899.

Otis
A.L. Otis, wagon maker; Hudson, WI, circa 1879.

Otis
E. Otis, blacksmith and wagon maker; Ledarhill, New Mexico, circa 1906–1913.

Otis
G.W. Otis, wagon maker; Hudson, WI, circa 1879.

Otto
William Otto, blacksmith and wagon maker; Boulder, Colorado, circa 1878–1890.

Over
Ewald Over manufactured farm implements, including their 3-in-1 roller, pulverizer and stalk cutter; Indianapolis, IN, circa 1880's–1900.

Overman Carriage Co.
Buggy manufacturer; Cincinnati, Ohio, circa 1880–1910.

Overshiner
G.J. Overshiner, blacksmith and wagon maker, 4th, between I and J; Sacramento, CA, circa 1853–1865.

Overshiner & Cochran
Carriage makers, J street between 12th and 13th; Sacramento, CA, circa 1850–1860.

Owens (see Scholes & Owens)

Owensboro Ditcher & Grader Co.
Built earth-moving equipment, including the Martin All-Steel Ditcher and other horse-drawn commercial graders; Owensboro, Kentucky, circa 1890–1930.

Owensboro Wagon Co.
Manufacturer of wagons, trucks, and drays. Produced their #8 catalog, circa 1913, showing The Owensboro dray and wagons; Owensboro, KY, circa 1890–1920.

Owensboro Wheel Co.
Buggy wheel manufacturer; Owensboro, Kentucky, circa 1890–1910.

Owsley
Roy R. Owsley, carriage painter and trimmer, 409 Rusk; Ft. Worth, Texas, circa 1905–1910.

Owsley
S.H. Owsley, wagon maker; Wellington, Wisconsin, circa 1865.

Oxford Buggy Co.
Carriage and wagon manufacturer located in Oxford, North Carolina and Henderson, North Carolina, circa 1890–1910.

Oyler
George K. Oyler Manufacturing Co. of St. Louis, Missouri built farm implements and other horse-drawn farm equipment, circa 1860–1900.

Paananen
John Paananen, blacksmith and wagon maker; Diamondville, Wyoming, circa 1902–1910.

Pacific Coast Home Supply Ass'n.
Established in 1888, this company became one of the largest of its kind on the west coast. Their catalog #123 of 1897 made available almost anything you could need for home, farm or ranch. Everything from buggies and bailing wire to windmills and wagons.

They advertised that their goods could be shipped anywhere and offered correspondence in all languages, 13 Front street; San Francisco, CA, circa 1888–1905.

Padgitt
The Tom Padgitt Company was established in Bryan, Texas in 1867.

Padgitt built one of the foremost harness and saddle making shops in the country. The company expanded to several locations, namely Bryan, Waco, Austin and Dallas, Texas.

All the Padgitt stores offered a full line of carriages, buggies, wagons and more, circa 1867–1920's.

Padgitt Bros. Co.
Established in the 1870's by Jesse D. and William C. Padgitt as a saddle and harness shop.

The Padgitts quickly grew to offer a full line of wagons and carriages, while also acting as agents for several major vehicle manufacturers like Babcock, Moyer, Hynes, Cunningham and others.

The sons of William C. Padgitt, Charles and Tomas, continued the business into the 1940's—242–246 Commerce Street; Dallas, Texas.

Page
L.E. Page, wagon and carriage maker. All kinds of blacksmithing and wood work done at short notice. All work guaranteed, corner

of 3rd and Allen streets; Tombstone, Arizona, circa 1888–1894.

Page Brothers Buggy Co.
Marshall, Michigan, circa 1890–1910.

Page (see Knight & Page)

Paggi
Michael Paggi, blacksmith, wheelwright; carriage, and wagon makers, 501–507 Neches; Austin, Texas, circa 1887–1911.

Paggi
Carriage and wagon manufacturer and carriage, wagon, buggy and phaeton dealer, 419–421 E. 6th; Austin, Texas, circa 1887–1907.

Paine
Allen Paine & Son was established in 1823, offering a full line of carriage goods, 2 South Liberty Street; Baltimore, MD, circa 1823–1900.

Painter
C.F. Painter, blacksmith and wagon maker; Diamondville, Wyoming, circa 1900–1905.

Painter
W.A. Painter, blacksmith and wagon maker; Bloomington, Idaho, circa 1905–1910.

Paige & Warren
Blacksmiths and wheelwrights, 218 College Ave., Dallas, Texas, circa 1891–1900.

Palm (see Wilder & Palm)

Palmer
Charles H. Palmer, Jr., vehicle manufacturer; Amesbury, MA, circa 1890–1910.

Palmer
Charles L. Palmer wagon maker; Marshall, WI, circa 1885–1919.

Palmer
Delbert E. Palmer, wagon maker; Marshall, WI, circa 1879–1919.

Palmer
J. Palmer, wagon maker; Viroqua, WI, circa 1879.

Palmer
R. Palmer, carriage and wagonmaker; Cedar City, Utah, circa 1884–1890.

Palmer (see Baldwin & Palmer)

Palmer & Doucet
Manufacturers of heavy and enclosed vehicles; Merrimac, MA, circa 1890–1910.

Pannier
E.G. Pannier (and Son-1919) wagon makers; Chippewa Falls, Wisconsin, circa 1879–1919.

Panther City Hardware Co.
Carriages, buggies, wagonsand phaetons, 115–117 Houston; Ft. Worth, Texas, circa 1904–1918.

Papst
Herman Papst, blacksmith and wagon maker; Lookout, Idaho, circa 1905–1910.

Pardee
William H. Pardee, carriage and wagon maker; Appleton, WI, circa 1879.

Pardee (see Lawrence, Bradley & Pardee)

Park
Thomas Park, blacksmith and wagon maker, Maple St.; Leadville, CO, circa 1880–1890.

Parker
Albert J. Parker, blacksmith and wheelwright, ne corner Barton Springs road; South Austin, Texas, circa 1910–1916.

Parker Buggy Co.
B.E. Parker, buggy maker of Suffolk, Virginia, circa 1890–1907. Parker Buggy Co. was taken over by Knight Buggy Co. in 1907.

Parker & Gillespie
Makers of fine coach and carriage varnish and paint; New York, NY, circa 1860's.

Parker & Sanger
Blacksmiths and wagon makers; Ketchum, Idaho, circa 1905–1910.

Parlin & Orendorff Co.
Established in 1842 by William Parlin, offering a full line of implements—including the famous Canton Clipper plows, Canton Disc plows, Sulky plows, cultivators and corn planters; Canton, Illinois, circa 1842–1919.

Mr. Parlin died in 1891. International Harvester purchased Parlin & Orendorff in 1919 and would continue to sell their design for years.

Parlin & Orendorff Implement Co.
Dealers for the main plant in Canton, Illinois, they offered carriages, buggies and wagons, 101 Lincoln; Amarillo, Texas, circa 1916, and 110–114 Commerce, 145–158 Elm corner of Jefferson, William M. Robinson, manager; Dallas, Texas, circa 1891–1910.

Parren & Davis
Blacksmiths and wagon makers; Boulder, Colorado, circa 1880–1890.

Parrish
John H. Parrish, blacksmith and wheelwright, Decatur Ave.; Ft. Worth, Texas, circa 1905–1910.

Parritt
George T. Parritt, wagon maker; Beaver Dam, WI, circa 1879.

Parry
Joseph L. Parry was a designer, inventor and factory superintendent at the Reanie & Neafie steam fire-engine company; Philadelphia, PA, circa 1857–1880.

After Reanie & Neafie ceased operations in 1870, Mr. Parry continued to build fire engines for S.W. Landell & Co. and one final engine at the Philadelphia Hydraulic Works.

Parry
Parry Manufacturing Co.; Indianapolis, Indiana, circa 1890–1920. Like to many others, they advertised themselves as "The largest Carriage factory in the World."

Parton (see Miller & Parton)
Pasche
F. Pasche, carriage painters and trimmers, 705 Ave. B; Houston, Texas, circa 1897–1907.
Passmore & Son
Carriage repairs, 414 South 2nd, Albuquerque, NM, circa 1915.
Patch
A.H. Patch manufactured farm machines—like his Black Hawk corn sheller. Patch died in 1909, circa 1875–1909.
Pate
C.W. Pate, blacksmith and wheelwright, 105 S. Houston; Dallas, Texas, circa 1897–1904.
Paterson
P.N. Paterson, carriage and wagon dealer; Amherst, Wisconsin, circa 1890–1910.
Paterson
W.A. Paterson Company, carriage manufacturer; Flint, Michigan, circa 1869–1910.
Pattee Plow Co.
Built many farm implements including their popular Jenny Lind cultivator, The High Grade, The Busy Bee, The New Departure, and the Patte combine; Monmouth, Illinois, circa 1900–1940.
Patterson
A.H. Patterson, blacksmith and wagon maker; Fort Collins, Colorado, circa 1880–1890.
Patterson
C.R. Patterson & Co., buggy manufacturer; Greenfield, Ohio, circa 1890–1910.
Patterson (see Pullen & Patterson)
Patton
J.W. Patton, wagon maker; Ceddes, NY, circa 1850's.
Patton
N.C. Patton, blacksmith and wheelwright; carriage, buggy and wagon manufacturer; Sherman, Texas, circa 1893–1900.

Patton
William L. Patton & Co., manufacturer of wagon covers, tents, awnings, ore sacks, etc., 352–354 Lawrence Street; Denver, Colorado, and 220 Washington Street; Chicago, Illinois, circa 1882–1900.
Paulat
E. Paulat, wagon maker, 432 East 18th; New York, NY, circa 1899.
Payson (see Perrin, Payson & Co.)
Peabody Buggy Co.
Buggy maker; Fostoria, OH, circa 1890–1910.
Peachey Bros.
Wagon makers; Beaver Dam, WI, circa 1879.
Peafau Buggy Co.
Melbourne, Kentucky, circa 1890–1910.
Pearce
Ora Pearce made wagons and sleighs; DeWitt, NY, and Clay, NY, circa 1850's.
Pearson (see Doney & Pearson)
Pease
Pease Manufacturing Co. of Racine, Wisconsin. Built farm implements, circa 1890–1900.
Pease
Samuel Pease, manufacturer of heavy and enclosed vehicles; Merrimac, MA, circa 1890–1910.
Peaslen
O.B. Peaslen, blacksmith and wagon maker, 2020 Polk, San Francisco, California, circa 1882–1890.
Peck & Avery
Manufactured wagons and sleighs; Lysander, NY, circa 1850's.
Peck & Lines
Carriage and cart makers from Bridgeport, Connecticut, circa 1890's–1910.
Peerless Buggy Co.
Owensboro, Kentucky, circa 1890–1910.

Peers
Thomas L. Peers, blacksmith and wagon maker; Independence, Missouri., circa 1850–1860.
Pekin Wagon Co.
This company has roots going back to 1849. They manufactured a wide variety of wagons and farm vehicles, including the Pekin wagon; Pekin, Illinois, circa 1849–1930's.
Pellet
E. Pellet, wagon maker; Waukesha, WI, circa 1879.
Pena
S. Pena Jr., blacksmith and wheelwright, 804 N. San Marcos; San Antonio, Texas, 1897–1898; and 531 Delgado; San Antonio, Texas, circa 1900–1910.
Pena
Simon Pena, blacksmith and wheelwright; also carriage and wagon manufacturer, 235 S. Laredo, and 321 W. Nueva; San Antonio, circa 1887–1902.
Pennell (see Martin, Pennell & Co.)
Pennfuld
Mather Pennfuld, carriage maker; Utica, NY, circa 1850's.
Pennington
Alonzo Pennington, blacksmith and wheelwright, 606 Trinity; Austin, Texas, circa 1897–1903.
Pennington
Z.T. Pennington, blacksmith and wheelwright, 503 W. Railroad; Ft. Worth, Texas, circa 1900–1910.
Pennington & Son
Blacksmiths and wheelwrights, 606 Trinity; Austin, Texas, circa 1900–1910.
Peppard
Samuel Peppard, of Oskaloosa, Kansas, was known for his attempt at building a windwagon, although not as fortunate as Andrew J. Dawson, also from Oskaloosa.

Peppard's craft was destroyed about sixty miles short of Denver, Colorado, circa 1860.

Perkins
Charles Perkins, wagon maker; Ripon, Wisconsin, circa 1865.

Perkins
J.B. Perkins, wagon maker; Waupaca, WI, circa 1879.

Perkins
Nathaniel C. Perkins, blacksmith, and wheelwright, 2217 Odin Ave.; Houston, Texas, circa 1900–1910.

Perkins Brothers
Blacksmiths and wheelwrights, South Austin; Austin, Texas, circa 1887–1895.

Perkins & Campbell Co.
Buggy manufacturer; Cincinnati, Ohio, circa 1880–1910.

Perlewitz Bros.
Carriage and wagon makers; Algoma, Wisconsin, circa 1890–1910.

Perrin, Payson & Co.
Carriage and coach paint and varnish makers; New York, NY, circa 1870–1910.

Perry
P.W. Perry, wagon maker; Arena, WI, circa 1879.

Perry (see Birdsall, Waite & Perry Mfg. Co.)

Perry (see Webb, Taylor & Perry)

Perschke
William Perschke, wagon maker, W. Boulevard and 119th; New York, NY, circa 1899.

Peru Plow & Implement Co.
Manufactured all types of farm equipment—everything from plows to wagons.
   They developed a large trade in carriages, surries and buggies; Peru, Illinois, circa 1880–1910.

Peteler (see Kilgore-Peteler Co.)

Peters Buggy Co.
Columbus, Ohio, circa 1890–1910.

Peters Carriage Co.
Columbus, Ohio, circa 1890–1910.

Peters
Peters Dash Co.; manufacturer of buggy dashes. Claimed they had the capacity of turning out 500,000 buggy dashes per year; Columbus, Ohio, circa 1890–1910.

Peters
Thomas A. Peters, blacksmith and wheelwright, 314 W. 13th; Ft. Worth, Texas, 1904–1905, also 248 W. 13th; Ft. Worth, Texas, circa 1906–1912.

Peters
W. Peters, wagon maker; Johnson Creek, WI, circa 1879.

Peters & Heins
Wagon makers, 612 East 63rd; New York, NY, circa 1899.

Peters & Herron Dash Co.
Dashers, fenders, etc.; Columbus, Ohio, circa 1890–1910.

Peterson
A.P. Peterson, carriage and wagon dealer and representative; Ashland, WI, circa 1890–1910.

Peterson
C. Peterson, blacksmith and wagon maker, 307-First; Laramie, Wyoming, circa 1901–1902.

Peterson
H. Peterson, blacksmith and wagon maker; Alcova, Wyoming, circa 1902–1908.

Peterson
H.A. Peterson, blacksmith and wagon maker; Heyburn, Idaho, circa 1905–1910.

Peterson
I. Peterson, wagon maker; Osseo, WI, circa 1879.

Peterson
J. Peterson, wagon maker; Hortonville, WI, circa 1879.

Peterson
Jesse Peterson, wagon maker; Menomonee, Wisconsin, circa 1865.

Peterson
P.E. Peterson, wagon maker; Briggsville, WI, circa 1879.

Peterson (see Morse & Peterson)

Peton
Lewis Peton, wagon maker, 7th, between I and J; Sacramento, CA, circa 1853–1865.

Petree (see Farthing, Petree & Co.)

Petrie
Amos A. Petrie, wagon maker; Mauston, WI, circa 1885–1919.

Pettigrew
H.C. Pettigrew & Co., carriages, buggies and phaetons, 110–112 Houston; Ft. Worth, Texas, circa 1904–1918.

Pettits
Asa Pettits, wagon maker, between J and K; Sacramento, CA, circa 1853–1865.

Pevernitz
Frank Pevernitz, wagon maker; Kewaunee, Wisconsin, circa 1865.

Pfeiffer
Albert Pfeiffer, wagon maker, 311 Avenue B; New York, NY, circa 1899.

Pfeiffer
Frederick Pfeiffer, wagon maker, 17 Vestry; New York, NY, circa 1899.

Pfile
John F. Pfile, blacksmith and wagon maker, 675 Brannan, San Francisco, CA, circa 1882–1897.

Phelan
J.J. Phelan, blacksmith and wagon maker; Colorado Springs, Colorado, circa 1880–1890.

Phelps, Carr & Co.
Wagon makers; Pittsburgh and Allegheny, PA., circa 1854–1870.

Phelps (see Speyer & Phelps)

Phelps (see Zeller, Phelps & Swift)

Philipson
Thomas Philipson, wagon maker; Fox Lake, Wisconsin, circa 1879–1919.

Phillips
H.W. Phillips, blacksmith and wagon maker; Lyman, Wyoming, circa 1905–1910.

Phillips
J.E. Phillips, blacksmith and wagon maker; Encampment, Wyoming, circa 1900–1908.

Phillips
J.H. Phillips, wagon maker; Brandon, Wisconsin, circa 1865.

Phillips
K.P. Phillips, carriage maker, Porter, NY, circa 1850's.

Phillips
T. Phillips, wagon maker; Leon, WI, circa 1879.

Philips, McCallum & Baker
Carriage painters and trimmers, 301–303 S. Oregon; El Paso, Texas, circa 1905–1915.

Phillips (see Lewis, Oliver & Phillips)

Philman & Halmgren
Manufactured wagons, 238 East 85th; New York, NY, circa 1899.

Phipp
A.W. Phipp, blacksmith and wagon maker; Evanston, Wyoming, circa 1900–1905.

Phoenix Carriage Co.
Buggy manufacturer; Cincinnati, Ohio, circa 1880–1931.

Phoenix Coach Works
Carriage maker; Philadelphia, PA, circa 1880–1910.

Pias (see Caruthers & Pias)

Pickarska
Joseph Pickarska, blacksmith and wagon maker; Emida, Idaho, circa 1905–1910.

Piedmont Wagon & Mfg. Co.
Issued an illistrated catalog with samples of their wagons, trucks and drays; Hickory, NY, circa 1900–1915.

Pierson & Henderson
Blacksmiths and horseshoers, 610 Elm; Dallas, Texas, circa 1908.

Pierson & Shacklett
Blacksmiths and wheelwrights, 610 Elm; Dallas, Texas, circa 1900–1910.

Pieters
Joseph Pieters, wagon maker; Burlington, WI, circa 1865–1879.

Pieters Bros.
Wagon makers, Burlington, Wisconsin, circa 1865–1919.

Pigott
M. Pigott, blacksmith and wheelwright; also carriage, wagon, buggy and phaeton manufacturer, 203 Soledad; San Antonio, Texas, circa 1887–1890.

Pigott
W. M. Pigott, blacksmith and wheelwright, 139–143 Main Ave.; San Antonio, Texas, circa 1897–1908.

Pike
John T. Pike, carriage maker, corner of L and 4th; Sacramento, CA, circa 1853–1865.

Pine, Riling & Wheeler
Blacksmiths and wagon makers, East 2nd; Leadville, Colorado, circa 1880–1890.

Pinneo & Daniels Wheel Co.
Dayton, Ohio, circa 1890–1910.

Pioneer Manufacturing Co.
Manufactured carriages, wagons and sleigh parts. Offered a special conversion kit adjustable to fit any carriage, buggy or light delivery wagon. This device would allow one vehicle to change from wagon to sleigh. In 1888 the kit sold for $5, plus freight; Columbus, Ohio, circa 1870–1890.

Pioneer Pole & Shaft Co.
Manufacturer of buggy shafts and poles; Piqua, Ohio, circa 1890–1910.

Pipkorn
Fred Pipkorn, wagon maker; Freistadt; WI, circa 1879–1903.

Piqua Wagon Co.
They built the Piqua wagon and a few other styles of vehicle. Annual wagon sales reached 2,000 vehicles by the mid-1890's; Piqua, Ohio, circa 1890–1905.

Pittman
Roy Temple Pittman, carriage maker in the Good Mill area of Rockingham County Virginia, circa 1900.

Pitts
H.A. Pitts & Sons Mfg. Co., manufacturers of the Chicago Pitts separators, and other farm implements; Chicago, IL, circa 1875–1900

Pitts Agricultural Works
Manufactured farm implements, including water wagons and coal wagons; Buffalo, NY, circa 1880's–1910.

Plano Harvester Co.
Manufactured farm implements, including the Jones Lever Binder in 1881, developed by William H. Jones. They also built the Jones Chain-Drive mower.

Plano merged with others in 1902 to form International Harvester Co.; Plano, Illinois, circa 1881–1902.

Plants Manufacturing Co.
Established in 1842, Plants grew to become one of the largest suppliers of carriage bolts, hinges and fastners in the world, with factories in two cities; Plantsville, CT and New Haven, CT, circa 1842–1900.

Platt (see Adriance, Platt & Co.)

Platt and Townsend
Ezra M. Stratton, a carriage maker from New York and publisher of "The New York Coachmaker's Magazine", served as an apprentice to Charles Townsend and Mr. Platt (1824 to 1829) in this early Connecticut carriage shop. (see Ezra M. Stratton), circa 1820–1850.

Plumbe
J.F. Plumbe, wagon and carriage material, 25 Second; San Francisco, California, circa 1882–1895.

Plymouth Foundry & Machine Co.
Manufactured farm machines and implements, including the Plymouth Hero steel beam plow; Plymouth, Wisconsin, circa 1880–1900.

Politz
F. Emil Politz, blacksmith and wheelwright, 2005 Houston Ave.; Houston, Texas, circa 1900–1910.

Polk & Granger
Carriages, buggies, phaetons and wagons, 210–212 Soledad; San Antonio, Texas, circa 1887–1900.

Poll (see Lord & Poll)

Pollard Co.
C.L. Pollard, wagons and farm implements; Espanola, New Mexico, circa 1900–1915.

Pollard
Charles H. Pollard, blacksmith and wheelwright, 107 W. 5th; Austin, Texas, circa 1905–1915.

Polley
H.C. Polley made light carriages and wagons: Skaneateles, NY, circa late 1800's.

Pollock
J. Pollock, wagon maker; Lancaster, WI, circa 1879.

Pollock & Co.
Manufactured parts for wholesale to carriage and buggy builders, including the Behlen Boot, advertised as the King of Buggy Boots; 322 Main Street, Cincinnati, OH, circa 1880's–1910.

Pomeroy
R.W. Pomeroy, carriage and wagon maker; Denver, Colorado, circa 1884–1890's.

Pomeroy & Harris
Wagon and carriage makers, 224 12th; Denver, Colorado, circa 1883–1890's.

Pomeroy's El Paso Transfer Co.
Blacksmiths and wagon makers; carriage painters and trimmers, 300–308 S. Oregon; El Paso, Texas, circa 1905–1910.

Pommer
C. Pommer, blacksmith and wheelwright, 226 Cantegral, and 278-1/2 Live Oak, also 266 Thomas Ave.; Dallas, Texas, circa 1891–1905.

Pompee
Adolph Pompee, carriage and wagon maker, 213 W. 6th; Austin, Texas, circa 1887–1890's.

Pompee & Lundbeck
Blacksmiths and wheelwrights, 213 W. 6th; Austin, Texas, circa 1887–1890's.

Pontiac Buggy Co.
Manufacturer of surreys, buggies, phaetons and road wagons; Pontiac, Michigan, circa 1890–1910.

Pool
James Pool was born in Virginia. He worked in various jobs and locations. From 1830 to 1833 he was a gunsmith and blacksmith at the Delaware Agency in Kansas.

Pool served as the blacksmith of Neosho Sub-agency in 1841, and later moved to Independence, Missouri where he worked a few years before moving on to New Mexico. Around 1849, he opened a wagon repair and blacksmith shop in Santa Fe, New Mexico, circa 1830–1860.

Pool Brothers
In 1845, Harris Pool started a small carriage shop on the corner of Franklin and Cherry Streets, in Kenton, Ohio. He operated the shop for about four years before moving to California.

His brother, William, succeeded him, and he was subsequently joined by another brother, John. They became partners, circa 1845–1880's.

Pool & Hunt
Starting in 1858, this Baltimore, MD firm built fourteen steam fire-engines in their ten years of business (1858–1868). One of the largest units served for over thirty years at the Washington Engine Company #14, a Philadelphia, PA. volunteer fire department.

Pool (see Desmond & Pool)

Poro
Edward Poro, blacksmith and wagon maker; Elo, Idaho, circa 1905–1910.

Porter
E.A. Porter & Bros. manufactured farm implements and the Porter Corn Thresher; Bowling Green, Kentucky, circa 1890–1905.

Porter (see Chester & Porter)

Port Huron Engine-Thresher Co.
Built threshers, engines and other horse drawn farm equipment; Port Huron, Michigan, circa 1895–1915.

Portsmouth Cart Co.
An 1890's advertisement from this cart manufacturing company reads—They Go Fast and Ride Easy; Portsmouth, OH, circa 1880–1910.

Portsmouth Wheel Company
Manufacturer of every size and style of carriage and wagon wheels; Portsmouth, OH, circa 1870–1910.

Post
E. J. Post & Co., wagons and implements, Albuquerque, New Mexico, 1900–1920.

Post Bros. Buggy Co.
Columbus, Ohio, circa 1890–1910.

Post & Crawford
Wagon makers; Lakewood, New Mexico, 1900–1910.

Potter
C.F. Potter, carriage painter, Manzanares Ave.; Las Vegas, New Mexico, 1895–1905.

Potter
Warren Potter, blacksmith and wagon maker; Cottonwood, Idaho, circa 1905–1910.

Pottle
Benjamin Pottle, wagon maker; Shullsburg, Wisconsin, circa 1865.

Potts
Isaac Potts, wagon maker; Philadelphia, PA., circa 1840's–1860.

Poullain
William H. (Bill the Horseshoer) Poullain, blacksmith and wheelwright, 262 Fannin and 658 Main; Beaumont, Texas, 1905–1915.

Powers
D.L. Powers, carriage and wagon maker; Georgetown, Colorado, circa 1877–1879; also a carriage and wagon shop, Fort Collins, Colorado, circa 1878–1883.

Powers
D.S. Powers, wagon maker, Fort Collins, CO, circa 1884–1889.

Powers (see Scott & Powers)

Poyen
John S. Poyen & Co. dealt in carriage goods and hardware; including a full line of cloths, patent leather, lamps, canopies and much more; Merrimac and Amesbury, MA, circa 1860–1910.

Praen
John Praen, wagon maker; Columbus, Wisconsin, circa 1865.

Pratt
A.L. Pratt & Co. of Kalamazoo, Michigan—makers of the Pratt's Perfection Cart, circa 1880–1900.

Pratt
D.G. Pratt's firm specialized in one-man road wagons. They offered a full line of log and lumber trucks, also farm, express and delivery wagons. Harness was available for all vehicles sold by Pratt; 34 Broad St., Boston, MA, circa 1880–1910.

Pratt
William Pratt, wagon maker; Markesan, Wisconsin, circa 1865.

Pratt & Anderson
Wagon makers; Fort Collins, Colorado, circa 1884–1890.

Pratt & Chase
Established in 1882, this company built a variety of vehicles—carriages, buggies and over 20,000 cutters and sleighs, by 1890; Coldwater, Michigan, circa 1882–1900.

Pratt & Lambert
Manufacturers of fine coach and carriage paint & varnishes, 110 John Street; New York, NY, circa 1880–1900.

Pratt (see Hughes & Pratt)

Pratt (see Raynolds, Devoe & Pratt)

Pratt (see Winans, Pratt & Co.)

Preffer
John Preffer, carriage and wagon maker; Berthoud, Colorado, circa 1884–1890.

Prehn
Thomas Prehn, wagon maker; Newtonburg, Wisconsin, circa 1865.

Pretlow Buggy Co.
Mr. W.M. Weede; Franklin, VA, circa 1910–1915.

Pretchett (see Adam & Pretchett)

Price
Edward Price, wagon maker; Mauston, Wisconsin, circa 1865.

Price
Frank Price, blacksmith, horseshoeing and maker of carriages and heavy mine carts, 261 Warren Avenue; Cripple Creek, Colorado, circa 1900–1930.

Price
F.S. Price, wagon dealer; Tyler Hill, PA, circa 1890–1910.

Price
J.W. Price, blacksmith and wheelwright, 1212 S. Congress Ave.; S. Austin, Texas, circa 1898–1906.

Price, McKee & Co.
They operated a wagon manufacturing shop in the Missouri State Penitentiary at Jefferson City, Missouri. Their production exceeded 100 wagons a year, circa 1840's–1880's.

Price & Shaw
Designed, manufactured and sold carriages and sleighs throughout the United States and Canada; St. John, New Brunswick, Canada, circa 1870's–1900.

Price (see Eaton & Price)

Pride
W.H. Pride, wagon maker; Avoca, WI, circa 1879.

Prine
F.B. Prine, blacksmith and wagon maker; Lapwai, Idaho, circa 1905–1910.

Printz & Green
Carriage makers; Holmesburg, 23rd ward, Philadelphia, PA, circa 1880–1910.

Prochazka (see Bolles & Prochazka)

Proll
Justus Proll, blacksmith and wheelwright; also a carriage and wagon manufacturer, 421 6th, and corner of Sixth and Elm; San Antonio, Texas, circa 1887–1898.

Prouty
David Prouty & Co. built a line of implements like the Michigan Double Plough; Boston, MA, circa 1850's–1890.

Pryne
Aron Pryne, wagon and sleigh maker; Lysander, NY, circa 1850's.

Puffet
Charles Puffet, wagon and sleigh maker; DeWitt, NY, circa 1850's.

Pugh
Day Pugh started a blacksmith shop in the late 1840's on Columbus Street; Kenton, Ohio.

Shortly thereafter, Francis Meyer erected a two-story building next to Pugh and opened a wagon shop. In a short time Pugh bought the factory from Myers and continued the manufacturing of carriages and wagons for about four years. He than abandoned the business, and C.C. Drake carried it on for a short time, circa 1848–1860.

Pullen & Patterson
Wagon makers; Argyle, Wisconsin, circa 1865.

Pulliam
S.W.W. Pulliam; prop., Enterprise Carriage Works; carriage, wagon, buggy and phaeton dealer, 604 East Ave.; Austin, Texas, circa 1900–1910.

Pulver
Hiram Pulver, wagon maker, I, opposite public square; Sacramento, CA, circa 1853–1865.

Pulver Bros.
Wagon makers; Victory, WI, circa 1879.

Purdum
N. Purdum & Co.; Chillicothe, Ohio, circa 1890–1910.

Pursch
A.E. Pursch, blacksmith and wheelwright, 2402 S. Flores; San Antonio, Texas, circa 1897–1906.

Pursel (see Wall & Pursel)

Pytel
J.L. Pytel, blacksmith and wheelwright; and carriage and wagon manufacturer, S. Flores near Fair Grounds; San Antonio, Texas, circa 1887–1902.

Queen City Carriage Co.
Buggy manufacturer; Cincinnati, Ohio, circa 1880–1910.

Queen City Forging Co.
Cincinnati, Ohio, circa 1880–1910.

Queen City Top Mfg. Co.
Buggy tops; Cincinnati, Ohio, circa 1880–1910.

Queen City Varnish
Makers of high grade colors, varnishes and japans—established in 1845 and incorporated in 1890—this firm offered a wide variety to the coach and carriage painters; Cincinnati, OH, circa 1845–1915.

Quimby
J.M. Quimby & Co. manufactured light and heavy carriages, 232 Fifth Avenue, New York, NY. They also had a factory in Newark, NJ, circa 1890's.

Quinlan (see Chambers, Bering, Quinlan Co.)

Quinn
J.F. Quinn, blacksmith and wheelwright, 602 W. Market; San Antonio, Texas, circa 1897–1906.

Quinn
G.W. Quinn, blacksmith, wheelwright, horseshoer, and wagon maker, corner of Grand and 2nd Ave., also 167 Camp; Dallas, Texas, circa 1900–1910.

Quinsler (see Edmond & Quinsler)

Quintana
Manuel Quintana, blacksmith and wagon maker, 317 E. 7th; El Paso, Texas, circa 1900–1905.

Quintana & Espinosa
Blacksmiths, 613 Utah; El Paso, Texas, circa 1905–1918.

Raaser
Fred Raaser, blacksmith and wheelwright, 120 S. Jones; Ft. Worth, Texas, circa 1904–1912.

Rachofsky
M. Rachofsky, blacksmith, wheelwright, horseshoer, and wagon maker, 160 N. Akard; Dallas, Texas, circa 1897–1910.

Racine-Sattlery Co.
Manufactured a full line of vehicles, including farm wagons. They were formerly known as Racine Wagon & Carriage Co.; Racine, WI, circa 1880–1916.

They also manufactured and sold plows, planters and tillage equipment at their outlet in Springfield, Illinois.

They sold part of their company to Montgomery Ward in 1916.

Racine Sattlery Co.
Carriages, wagons and buggies, nw corner Elm and Houston; Dallas, Texas, circa 1890–1916.

This was one of many outlets for the main plant in Racine, Wisconsin.

Racine Wagon & Carriage Co.
Organized in 1886, making a full line of vehicles, including farm wagons. In 1890 they merged with Racine-Sattlery Co.; Racine, Wisconsin, circa 1886–1890.

Radkey
Stephen B. Radkey, blacksmith and wheelwright; carriage and wagon manufacturer; carriage, buggy, wagon and phaeton dealer; carriage painters and trimmers, 505–511 Colorado; Austin, Texas, circa 1898–1910.

Radle (see Townsend & Radle)

Raffauf
Anton Raffauf, wagon maker, 727 West Dominick; Rome, NY, circa 1899.

Rainey
J.D. Rainey, blacksmith; carriage and wagon maker; Golden, Colorado, circa 1880–1890.

Raish
Charles Raish, carriage and wagon maker, was attributed with making the first top buggy in Marysville in 1854—and selling it for $500, which was quite a sum for those days; Marysville, CA, circa 1853–1870.

Ralph
J. Ralph, carriage and wagon maker; Dodgeville, WI, circa 1879.

Ramakers
L.C. Ramakers, blacksmith and wheelwright, 12 N. 20th, between Ave. A and Brick wharf; Galveston, Texas, circa 1889–1894.

Rambo & Specht
Established in 1865, this firm manufactured varnish and paint for agricultural implements; and the coach, carriage and wagon trade.

At times, they also used the El Dorado trade mark, 981 N. 2nd Street; Philadelphia, PA, circa 1865–1910.

Ramsdell
Isaac Ramsdell, wagon maker; Paris, NY, circa 1899.

Ramsey
James T. Ramsey, blacksmith and wheelwright, 705 Prairie Ave.; Houston, Texas, circa 1900–1910.

Ranck
John Jefferson Rank was a wagon and carriage maker. He served as an apprentice to William H. Blind, before opening his own shop with his brother Samuel C. Ranck; New Columbia, PA., circa 1850–1870.

Randall
George Randall, blacksmith and wagon maker; Bruneau, Idaho, circa 1905–1910.

Randall
James V. and W. Randall, carriage maker; Newtown, Bucks County, PA, circa 1880–1910.

Randall
J.D. Randall Co., makers of stitching and harness machinery, and carriage leather dies and punches; Cincinnati, Ohio, circa 1890–1910.

Randall
S.G. Randall was an early inventor of farm equipment; Providence, Rhode Island, circa 1855–1880.

He received a patent in 1859 for a grain seeder and disc harrow while still living in New Braintree, MA.

Randall & Mathews
Carriage makers; Centerville, PA, circa 1880–1910.

Random
James Random, wagon maker, Terre Haute, Indiana, circa 1858.

Rasmussen
H.O. Rasmussen & Co., wagon makers, 630 East 144th; New York, NY, circa 1899.

Rasmussen (see Hoshaw & Rasmussen)

Ratcliff
P.W. Ratcliff, blacksmith; Dayton, Wyoming, circa 1905–1910.

Rathjen (see McGee & Rathjen)

Ratliff & Watland
Sioux City, Iowa, circa 1890–1910.

Ratterman & Luth
Buggy manufacturer; Cincinnati, Ohio, circa 1880–1923.

Ratterman (see Baxter, Byrn & Ratterman)

Rausch (see Luckenbach & Rausch)

Rauschenberger
William Rauschenberger, wagon maker; Reeseville, WI, circa 1879–1919.

Rawdon
T.M. Rawdon, blacksmith and wheelwright,133 S. Jefferson; Dallas, Texas, circa 1900.

Rawlins (see Moore & Rawlins)

Raynolds, Devoe & Pratt
Dealers in paints, oils, and stripers for the carriage and wagon trade, 106–108 Fulton Street; New York, NY, circa 1850–1900.

Reanie & Neafie
In 1857, this firm employed Joseph L. Parry as their designer, inventor and factory superintendent, to oversee all steam fire-engine construction. Under his supervision, they grew into one of the most successful companies in Pennsylvania.

Reanie & Neafie discontinued business in 1870. Mr. Parry built four more engines at the shops of S.W. Landell & Co. and his last engine at the Philadelphia Hydraulic Works; Philadelphia, PA, circa 1857–1870.

Redfield
W. Redfield, wagon maker; Hamlin, WI, circa 1879.

Reber Wagon Works
Wagon manufacturer; Centerport, PA., circa 1880's–1900.

Reed
Daniel Reed, wagon maker; Syracuse, NY, circa 1850's.

Reed
D.C. and H.C. Reed built a variety of farm implements, including what they called "the first successful spring-tooth harrow"; Kalamazoo, Michigan, circa 1870–1900.

Reed
James W. Reed, wagon maker; Remsen, NY, circa 1899.

Reed
Martin G. Reed, buggy maker; Mifflinburg, PA, circa 1876.

Reed
Samuel Reed, carriage and wagon maker; Trinidad, Colorado, circa 1880–1890.

Reed & Forman
Manufactured buggies and sleighs; Poughkeepsie, New York. circa 1880–1900.

Reel
Oren I. Reel, carriage painters and trimmers, 126 Patterson Ave.; Dallas, Texas, circa 1898–1908.

Regalado
Narciso Regalado, blacksmith, 305–1/2 S. Stanton; El Paso, Texas, circa 1910–1920.

Reherd
William Reherd was born in York County, Pennsylvania in 1804, moved to Harrisonburg, Virginia when he was 20 years old. Within six years he had established his own shop, where he did a combination of blacksmithing and wagon making until 1851. He then bought a farm a couple of miles east of Harrisonburg and ran a sawmill, circa 1824–1851.

Reiber & Renner
Wagon makers, 616 West 25th; New York, NY, circa 1899.

Reidenbach
Peter Reidenbach manufactured wagons and trucks, 164 Eldridge; New York, NY, circa 1890's.

Reina
A. Reina & Co., carriage and push cart manufacturer, 163 Worth; New York, NY, circa 1899.

Reiner
J. Reiner, carriage and wagon maker; Madison, WI, circa 1879.

Reinmuller
Henry Reinmuller & Son, wagon makers, 521 West 47th; New York, NY, circa 1899.

Reisner
B.A. Reisner, blacksmith and wheelwright; carriage and wagon manufacturer, 21, 23, 26 Preston; and 13–15 Commerce; Houston, Texas, circa 1882–1890's.

Reliable Carriage Works
Blacksmiths and wheelwrights; carriage, wagon, buggy and phaeton dealers, 108 N. Rusk; Ft. Worth, Texas, circa 1905–1906.

Reliance Buggy Co.
St. Louis, MO, circa 1890–1910.

Relyea
S.B. Relyea offered saddles, harness and carriage trimmings, 4th street, between I and J; Sacramento, CA, circa 1855–1875.

Rember
William Rember, blacksmith and wagon maker; Hailey, Idaho, circa 1905–1910.

Remington
J.C. Remington, blacksmith and wagon maker, 1st and Ford St.; Gold Hill, Colorado, circa 1877–1885.

Remington & Fowler
Blacksmith and wagon makers; Golden, Colorado, circa 1879–1885.

Renner (see Reiber & Renner)

Rentchler Drill Co.
Built farm implements; Belleville, Illinois, circa 1880–1890.

Rentfrow (see Dickenson & Rentfrow)

Renwick
J.W. Renwick, manufacturer of carriages and commercial vehicles; New York, NY, circa 1890–1910.

Repsom
H. Repsom, wagon maker; Marshall, Wisconsin, circa 1865.

Retsnider
William D. Retsnider, carriage maker; Doylestown, PA, circa 1880–1910.

Reuland
Mathias Reuland, wagon maker; Baraboo, WI, circa 1879–1901.

Reuss
L. Reuss, blacksmith and wheelwright; also carriage and wagon manufacturer, 602 Live Oak; San Antonio, Texas, circa 1887–1896.

Rex Buggy Co.
Connersville, Indiana, circa 1890–1910.

Reynolds
C.M. Reynolds, wagon maker; Mifflin, WI, circa 1879.

Reynolds
William G. Reynolds & Co. manufactured carriage and sleigh parts, including solid foot and adjustable dashes or fenders; Columbus, OH, circa 1880–1900.

Reynolds & O'Bannon
Blacksmiths and wheelwrights, 204 N. Lamar; Dallas,Texas, circa 1891–1900.

Rhein
W.H. Rhein & Co., dealers in agricultural implements; Lander, Wyoming, circa 1900–1908.

Rhoades-Carmean Buggy Co.
Marshalltown, Iowa, circa 1890–1910.

Rhody & Weber
Carriage, buggy and wagon dealers, 418–420 E. 6th; Austin, Texas, circa 1905–1915.

Rice
T.W. Rice, carriage and wagon maker; Milwaukee, WI, circa 1879.

Richards
George Richards, wagon maker: Philadelphia, PA, circa 1840's–1860.

Richards
Samuel Richards, blacksmith; Clark, Wyoming, circa 1905–1910.

Richards Auto Painting Co.
Carriage painters, trimmers and carriage lines, 204–207 W 6th; Amarillo, Texas, circa 1913–1916.

Richardson
W.C. Richardson, carriage maker; Salida, CO, circa 1882–1890.

Richardson
W.H. Richardson, carriage, wagon, buggy and phaeton dealer; carriage and wagon woodwork, 401 E. 6th and corner of Trinity; Austin, Texas, circa 1893–1911.

Richardson
W.H. Richardson, blacksmith and wagon maker, 808 west 27th and Eddy and 18th; Cheyenne, Wyoming, circa 1870–1900.

Richardson Manufacturing Co.
This Worcester, MA firm built farm implements, including their Worcester-Kemp spreaders, under license of the Kemp company patents. Richardson used numerous jobbing houses throughout the midwest. They sold their spreader line to Johnston Harvester Co. of Batavia, NY in 1913, circa 1890–1913.

Richardson & Grewell
Wagon makers and blacksmiths; Loveland, CO, circa 1882–1883.

Richardson (see Zane & Richardson)

Richmond Wagon Works
John F. Schweibert (see Isaac M. Marsh), previously of the same location; Richmond, NY.

Richmond (see Hilgers & Richmond)

Rickards (see Campbell & Rickards)

Riddle (see Merts & Riddle)

Rider
George Rider, wagon maker; Jackson County, Missouri, circa 1850–1860.

Ridings
J.G. Ridings, carriage and wagon makers, 518–520 Tyler; Amarillo, Texas, circa 1905–1915.

Reipe (see Tegetmeier & Riepe)

Riesner
B.A. Riesner, blacksmith and wheelwright; manufacturer of carriages, wagons, buggies and phaetons, 813–819 Commerce; Houston, Texas, circa 1900–1910.

Riker (see Walborn & Riker)

Riley
J.W. Riley, blacksmith and wagon maker; Ferdinand, Idaho, circa 1905–1910.

Riling, Warner & Co.
Carriage and wagon makers, 104 E. 2nd; Leadville, Colorado, circa 1883–1890.

Ringrose
J.T. Ringrose, carriage and wagon dealer and representative; Alma Center, WI, circa 1890–1910.

Rio Grand Painting & Trimming Co.
Carriage painters and trimmers, 308 S. Florence; El Paso, Texas, circa 1910–1920.

Rippon
Charles Rippon of Rippon & Melarkay. K. betweem 13th and 14th; Sacramento, CA, circa 1853–1865.

Rippon & Melarkey
Blacksmiths and wagon makers, J, between 13th and 14th; Sacramento, CA, circa 1853–1865.

Rishel
George W. Rishel, buggy maker; Mifflinburg, PA, circa 1881–1886.

Rishel
John Rishel, buggy maker, 544 Chestnut street (rear); Mifflinburg, PA, circa 1870–1883.

Risher
A. Ford Risher, blacksmith and wheelwright, 817 E. 7th; and 603 Trinity; Austin, Texas, circa 1910–1918.

Risher
Rufus Risher, blacksmith, wheelwright and wagon maker, 1106 E. 11th; 1203 E. 6th; 511 E. 5th; and 1195 Chicon; Austin, Texas, circa 1889–1913.

Risher
William E. Risher, blacksmith, wheelwright and wagon maker, 604 East Ave., 802 E. 6th; 716 E. 6th; and 817 E. 7th; Austin, Texas, circa 1887–1910.

Risher (see Kennedy & Risher)

Risse
John Risse, blacksmith and wagon maker; Evans, Colorado, 1877 and La Veta, Colorado, circa 1877–1880's.

Ritter
James R. Ritter, buggy maker, 317 Walnut street (rear); Mifflinburg, PA, circa 1915.

Ritter (see Voigt & Ritter)

Riverside Carriage Works
Carriage manufacturer; Warren, OH, circa 1890–1910.

Roach
I.L. Roach, blacksmith and wagon maker; Encampment, Wyoming, circa 1905–1910.

Robb
Samuel Robb owned his own shop in New York, NY.

A master wood-carver, Samuel Robb would oversee wood carvings on many of Sebastian Wagon Co.'s circus wagons, tableau wagons, band wagons and cages, circa 1860–1890.

Robbins
L.D. Robbins, wagon maker; Mount Vernon, WI, circa 1865.

Robert
Isan Robert, blacksmith and wagon maker, 113 Leit; Leadville, Colorado, circa 1881–1890.

Roberts
A. Roberts, carriage and wagon maker; Manitowoc, WI, circa 1879.

Roberts
F. S. Roberts, carriage and wagon works, blacksmithing, wood work, painting and trimming, corner 110–114 Elm and Houston Streets; Dallas, Texas, circa 1897–1910.

Roberts
George D. Roberts, carriage and wagon dealer and representative; Algoma, Wisconsin, circa 1890–1910.

Roberts
R. and William Roberts, wagon makers; Hazel Green, Wisconsin, circa 1865.

Roberts & Case
Carriage and wagon manufacturers, 62 Broadway; New York, NY, circa 1890's.

Roberts, Case & Spring
Offered for sale, carriages and wagons manufactured by numerous makers. They also were agents for Fish Bros. Wagon Company of Racine, WI.

This firm also sold dock timber, pine and hardwood lumber, 58–60 Broadway; New York, NY, circa 1880's–1910.

Roberts, Thorp & Co.
Manufactured a variety of farm equipment. They first started in 1848 as Cox & Roberts in Belleville, Illinois.

Cyrus Roberts moved to Three Rivers, Michigan in 1855 where they built horse-drawn farm equipment as Roberts, Thorp & Co. (Incorporated in 1875).

This firm also built some railroad specialties; Three Rivers, Michigan, circa 1848–1890.

Robertson Bros.
Wagon makers; Patch Grove, Wisconsin, circa 1865–1885.

Robertson Carriage Co.
Carriage and wagon maker; Denver, Colorado, circa 1883–1890.

Robertson & Doll
Carriage Company, N. Robertson, president and manager, H.C. Doll, secretary and treasurer, corner Arapahoe and 14th; Denver, Colorado, circa 1888–1894.

Robertson & Doll
Carriages, H.C. Doll, manager, 379–381 Arapahoe; Denver, Colorado, circa 1882–1890's.

Robins
P. Robins, carriage maker, corner J and 13th streets; Sacramento, CA, circa 1855–1875.

Robinson
Charles A. Robinson, blacksmith and wagon maker; Meeteetse, Wyoming, circa 1901–1902.

Robinson
George Robinson, blacksmith and wagon maker, J, between 12th and 13th; Sacramento, CA, circa 1853–1865.

Robinson
Samuel M. Robinson, blacksmith and wheelwright, 1418 S. Main; Ft. Worth, Texas, circa 1900–1910.

Robinson
The Robinson Manufacturing Co.; Freeport, IL, circa 1890–1910.

Robinson Bros.
Blacksmiths and wagon makers; Franklin, Idaho, circa 1905–1910.

Robinson Spreader Company
Manufactured a unique design, wide-spread beater spreader, unlike others on the market at that time. George B. Miller and Son continued to market this design after the Robinson factory closed; Vinton, Iowa, circa 1900–1915.

Robinson Wagon Company
This Cincinnati, Ohio company, circa 1866–1888, manufacturer of wagons, would later become the Standard Wagon Company.

Robinson & Vanderbelt
This early carriage and sleighbuilding company employed two well known craftsmen. They were Abraham Efner, who took credit for designing the first rounded back swell-body cutters, and in 1832, George R. Groot was the first to build the exaggerated goose-neck sleigh fronts; Albany, NY, circa 1820's–1860.

Robinson (see Lanham & Robinson)

Robinson, McGill Harness Co.
Shelbyville, Tennessee, circa 1890–1915.

Rock Falls Manufacturing Co.
Built wagons, carriages and hearses; Rock Falls, Wyoming, circa 1880–1910.

Rock Hill Buggy Co.
Originally known as Holler & Anderson Buggy Co. in 1889. It was located at the rear of A.D. Holler's furniture store in Rock Hill, South Carolina.

It was incorporated as the Rock Hill Buggy Co. in 1892. By 1905, J.G. Anderson was president and general manager.

The Rock Hill Buggy Co. made every type of wagon, buggy, and farm and delivery wagon. In 1905 a complete buggy was made, painted, trimmed, packed and shipped every twenty-five minutes. This record held until 1912.

The sale of buggies began to decline by 1919, and practically ceased by 1920.

Rock Island Plow Co.
A major manufacturer of plows and other farm implements with an extensive line of cultivators. This Rock Island, Illinois firm, circa 1855–1937, offered a light-weight balanced design—easy on the horses.

Rock Island also sold the Great Western spreaders from Smith Mfg. Co. beginning in 1911, and introduced their Model B spreader, about 1920. This firm may have started out as Tate & Buford around 1855.

A number of Rock Island advertisements in the early 1880's show B.D. Buford & Co. implements, i.e. Buford's 1883 Walking Spring Cultivator, Defiance Cultivator and the Buford Blackhawk—all available through Rock Island Plow Co.

Also in the 1880's, D.B. Buford & Co. advertisements show that the Rock Island Plows are available through them.

The Rock Island Plow Co. was sold to J.I. Case Co. in 1937.

Roderick Lean Manufacturing Co.
Built an extensive line of farm tillage equipment, including what might have been the original leverless cultivator. The company had a long run—founded in 1870 by Roderick Lean and merged with others in 1930 to form Farm Tools, Inc.; Mansfield, Ohio, circa 1870–1930.

Rodgers
C. Rodgers, carriage and wagon maker; Cheyenne, Wyoming, circa 1884–1890.

Rodgers
C.W. Rodgers, blacksmith, carriage and wagon maker, 501 west 17th, Cheyenne, Wyoming, circa 1902–1910.

Rodgers
E. Rodgers, carriage maker with Haworth, Eells & Co.; Sacramento, CA, circa 1853–1865.

Rodgers
Richard Rodgers, manufacturer of wagons, buggies, sulkies, express wagons and agricultural implements. They also did blacksmithing and repairing, 17th and Thomes; Cheyenne, Wyoming, circa 1872–1896.

Rodgers (see Garlington & Rodgers)

Rodriguez
G.M. Rodriguez, blacksmith, 425 S. Oregon; El Paso, Texas, circa 1910–1920.

Rodriguez
Jesus Rodriguez, blacksmith and wheelwright, 102 W. 2nd; Austin, Texas, circa 1905–1915.

Rodreguez (see Estrada & Rodriguez)

Rodstrom & Jahn
Blacksmiths and wheelwrights; carriage painters and trimmers; carriage, buggy, wagon and phaeton manufacturers and dealers; carriage and wagon makers' material; Ft. Worth Carriage Works, 409 Rusk; Ft. Worth, Texas, circa 1900–1915.

Roedel
Frank A. Roedel, 317 west 16th; Cheyenne, WY, circa 1902–1910.

Roedler
Charles Roedler, wagon maker, 520 West 30th; New York, NY, circa 1899.

Roehm & Davison
Carriage and wagon materials, Cecil Warner, manager, 109 California, San Francisco, California, circa 1888–1894.

Rogers
Amadee B. Rogers, wagon maker, 1923 Boston Road; New York, NY, circa 1899.

Rogers
Charles W. Rogers, blacksmith and wagon maker, 17th and Thomes; Cheyenne, Wyoming, circa 1900–1908.

Rogers
J.H. Rogers Carriage Co. manufactured light carriages at a factory in Springfield, MA. and sales at 1634 Broadway; New York, NY, circa 1899.

Rogers Mfg. Co.
Produced sleighs and carriages; Mason, Michigan, circa 1885–1900.

Rogers Grocer Co.
Wagon yard, 600 E. Belknap; Ft. Worth, Texas, circa 1896–1906.

Rogers (see Keyser & Rogers)

Rohr
Jacob Rohr, Sr. & Co., makers of wagons, barouches, carryalls, buggies, riding and burden carriages, etc., and repair work of all kinds done on short notice.

Born in Fredrick County Maryland in 1782, Rohr, at age 16, moved to Harrisonburg, Virginia where he operated his business for many years, circa 1798–1860's.

He died in Harrisonburg in 1866.

Rohr
Joseph T. & Alfred C. Rohr, Proprietors of a carriage shop, east side of German (now Liberty) Street; Harrisonburg, Virginia, circa 1866.

Rojas
Porfirio Rojas, blacksmith, wheelwright and wagon maker, 309 S. Kansas; El Paso, Texas, circa 1900–1914.

Roland Buggy Co.
W.W. Rowland and son, S.K. Rowland, buggy makers; Sumter, South Carolina, circa 1910–1920.

Roll & Held
Wagon maker, 402 East 25th; New York, NY, circa 1899.

Rollan
Felix Rollan, wagon maker, Del Norte, Colorado, 1877–1884, also in Elkhorn, CO, circa 1880.

Romaine
John Romaine, wagon maker, 215 Cherry; New York, NY, circa 1899.

Rome Spring Wagon Co.
Wagon and carriage makers; Rome, NY, circa 1890's.

Romig
William F. Romig, buggy maker, Mifflinburg, PA, circa 1900.

Ronstadt
The F. Ronstadt Co.—This well known Arizona maker operated one of the largest saddle, carriage and wagon manufacturing businesses in the southwest. They were also agents and dealers in farm implements.

One early Ronstadt advertisement read "Makers of the Arizona Bone Dry Wagons". They had their own paint shop, blacksmith shop, machine shop, basement stock room, hardware and saddle shop and harness and trim shop. They also maintained a full display of vehicles in a sales show room and second floor repository.

As the company moved into the motor vehicle business they added an auto garage and repair shop. All of this was supplied by a separate company-owned warehouse located near the S.P.R.R. railroad tracks; Tucson, AZ, circa 1880–1930.

Roper
H.L. Roper, blacksmith and wagon maker, also manufacturer of mining ore carts; Lake Valley, New Mexico, 1906. Over $3,000,000 in silver has been taken from the mines of this small town, (pop. 150), circa 1900–1912.

Rosas
S. Rosas, blacksmith and wheelwright, 304 Monterey; San Antonio, Texas, circa 1900–1910.

Rosas (see Minor & Rosas)

Rose
Jonathan Rose, carriage maker; Westmoreland, NY, circa 1850's.

Rose
J.W. Rose & Co., carriage and wagon manufacturer, 202–204 Main; Houston, Texas, circa 1882–1890.

Rose
Walton Rose, wagon maker, 164 West 16th; New York, NY, circa 1899.

Rosenberg
Nelson Rosenberg, wagon maker, First Avenue; New York, NY, circa 1899.

Rosenthal Corn Husker Co.
Made only ensilage cutters and huskers. Their 1896 model was called the Big Cyclone; Milwaukee, Wisconsin, circa 1890–1925.

Rosette & Beaty
Blacksmiths and wheelwrights; carriage and wagon makers, carriage painters and trimmers; also wagon, carriage, buggy and phaeton

dealer, 511 Colorado; and 505–507 Colorado; Austin, TX, circa 1887–1898.

Roth Brothers
Carriages and wagon makers; Fort Collins, CO, circa 1883–1890.

Roth
E.D. Roth, carriage and wagon maker; Fort Collins, Colorado, circa 1884–1890.

Rouse (see Stevens & Rouse)

Roush
George W. Roush, buggy maker; Mifflinburg, PA, circa 1855.

Roush
Joseph Roush was a carriage and buggy builder; Mifflinburg, PA., circa 1850's–1870's.

Rowe
John Rowe, blacksmith and wagon maker; Georgetown, Colorado, circa 1880–1890.

Rowell (see Leatherwood & Rowell)

Rowland Buggy Co.
Sumter, S.C., circa 1890–1910.

Rowland (see Beggs & Rowland)

Rowland (see Ward & Rowland)

Rowley (see Coleman, Eskridge & Rowley)

Royer Brothers
Buggy makers, 500 Walnut street (rear); Mifflinburg, PA, circa 1900.

Royer Wheel Co.
Manufactured every style of wheel and hub, including their Rouse Band and compressed narrow banded hub; Cincinnati, Ohio, circa 1880–1910.

Rucker
D.H. Rucker, Brigadier General, U.S. Army, credited with the design and development of the Rucker Ambulance which saw extensive use during the latter years of the Civil war, circa 1860–1870.

Rudberg
Albert Rudberg, blacksmith and wagon maker; Idaho Springs, Colorado, circa 1883–1890.

Rudd
Ole Rudd, blacksmith and wheelwright, 108 Throckmorton; Ft. Worth, Texas, circa 1905–1910.

Rudd & Holden
Carriage and wagon makers; Oshkosh, WI, circa 1879.

Rudd & Spencer
Blacksmiths, wagon makers and gunsmiths; Canon City, Colorado, circa 1882–1890.

Rudd (see Kilander & Rudd)

Rude Bros Manufacturing Co.
Started out building farm implements in the blacksmith shop on the family farm, circa 1868–1940.

By the early 1870's they were established in Liberty and incorporated in 1881. They built an extensive line of cultivators and other farm implements, including what they claimed to be the "best wood beam cultivator in the world".

They also built the Mascot Sulky Hay Rake and a wide variety of Indiana implements. Sometime after 1900, Rude Bros. mostly built manure spreaders: Liberty, Indiana, circa 1868–1940.

The firm became part of General Implements in the 1930's and only repair parts were sold by B.F. Avery Company in the 1940's. Rudy Elmer Rudy, buggy maker, 200 Market street (rear); Mifflinburg, PA, circa 1900.

Rugg
R.H. Rugg, wagon maker; Brodhead, Wisconsin, circa 1865.

Ruggles (see Nourse & Mason)

Rumely
M. Rumely Co. changed its name to Advanced Rumely Thresher Company around 1914. They built threshers and other implements; La Porte, Indiana, circa 1890–1920.

Rummel
Gustav Rummel, blacksmith and wheelwright; also carriage and wagon manufacturer, 214 Acequia; San Antonio, Texas, circa 1885–1900.

Rumsey Mfg. Co.
Established in 1887, they built buggies, wagons and sleighs; Milwaukee Junction, Detroit, Michigan, circa 1887–1910.

Rumsey Manufacturing Co.
Manufactured horse-drawn fire equipment, including a hand-drawn hose carriage.

Four-wheeled hose carriages were known as the "spider", while the two-wheeled hose carriages were called "jumpers"; Seneca, NY, circa 1870–1900.

Running
A. Running, wagon maker; Colfax, WI, circa 1879.

Ruschmann (see Gerleit Bros. & Ruschmann)

Ruser
Ferdinand Ruser & Sons, wagon makers, 1410 Park Avenue; New York, NY, circa 1899.

Russell
Joseph Russell was a carriage and sleigh builder who offered several styles, including the Russell's Portland Cutter; Portland, Maine, circa 1870–1890.

Russell
L.W. Russell, carriage and wagon maker; Boulder, Colorado, circa 1884–1890.

Russell
M.B. Russell, blacksmith, wheelwright and horseshoer, 519 Schatzel; Corpus Christi, Texas, circa 1910–1920.

Russell Grader Mfg. Co.
Manufacturer of road equipment; Minneapolis, MN., circa 1920–1930.

Russell (see Harding & Russell)

Russell (see Katzner, Russell & Chase)

Ryan
John Ryan, blacksmith and wagon maker; Boise, Idaho, circa 1905–1910.

Ryan
Patrick Ryan, blacksmiths and wagon makers, 205 Fillmore; Amarillo, Texas, circa 1900–1910.

Rynes
C. Rynes, wagon maker; Oconto, WI, circa 1879.

Sabath
F.E. Sabath, blacksmith and wheelwright, 21–23 and 26 Preston; Houston, Texas, circa 1882–1890.

Safety Shredder Co.
Built farm equipment and advertized "No More Loss of Hands" for their shredder in 1903; New Castle, Indiana, circa 1890–1910.

Saidler
William Saidler Jr. & Bros. manufactured wagons and trucks, 429 West 17th; New York, NY, circa 1899.

Sames
Peter Sames was a buggy and sleigh maker; Rockford, Illinois, circa 1890–1910.

Sammis
F.G. Sammis, carriage and harness shop; Huntington, NY, circa 1840–1860.

Sammis & Cornelius
Blacksmiths, wagon and carriage makers; New York, NY, circa 1870–1900.

Sander
A.J. Sander, wagon maker; Midway, WI, circa 1879.

Sanders
Adolphus M. Sanders (and Son—1901), wagon makers; Reedsburg, WI, circa 1879–1915.

Sanders
C. Sanders, blacksmith and wagon maker; Otto, Wyoming, circa 1902–1910.

Sandford & Dunn
Wagon makers; Waterville, NY, circa 1899.

Sandquist
Nelson P. Sandquist, Jr. manufactured wagons and trucks, 1745 First Avenue; New York, NY, circa 1899.

Sandwich Manufacturing Co.
This early Sandwich, Illinois farm equipment manufacturing company was founded by Agustus Adams in 1867. Adams had moved to Sandwich in 1857 from Elgin, Illinois, where he had set up one of the first iron foundries, in 1840.

The Sandwich Manufacturing Co. built shellers and other horse-drawn equipment until they were absorbed by New Idea Company, in the 1930's, circa 1840–1930.

Sanford
C. Sanford provided the painting and lettering work in the A.E. Hallock shop; Smithtown, NY., circa 1880–1900.

Sanford (see Hall & Sanford)
Sanger (see Parker & Sanger)
San Juan Stores
Wagons, implements and Repairing; Texas, circa 1906–1911.

Sargeant
D.F. Sargeant & Sons of Geneseo, Illinois manufactured buggies, carts and carriages, circa 1880–1900.

Sargeant
W.P. Sargeant, dealer in agricultural implements; Lusk, Wyoming, circa 1900–1905.

Sargent
George W. Sargent, carriage and wagon dealer; Abrams, Wisconsin, circa 1890–1910.

Sargent
Nelson Sargent, blacksmith and wagon maker; Carbon, Wyoming, circa 1900–1908.

Sargent
William P. Sargent & Co. evolved from a humble beginning. William Sargent's grandfather, Joshua, had been a carpenter in South Amesbury, Massachusetts (or, as it was commonly referred to—River Village) for many years. He became associated with a Mr. Michael Emery, a chaise maker, who had recently moved his chaise manufacturing to the river village from West Newberry. He built a factory here and continued the chaise building business.

Ebeneezer Fullington was manufacturing carriage bodies and sleigh woodwork just west of Emory's shop. In 1823, he took on a young lad named William A. Gunnison for a seven year apprenticeship. He served an additional three years as a journeyman. Gunnison than began to manufacture carriages. However, he had very little capital, and his total investment was a large factory building, a large storage building and his home, next door.

Joshua Sargent's son, Patten Sargent, was born in 1793, in West Amesbury. He entered into a five year apprenticeship in the trade of silver-plating carriage parts. Upon completion of his apprenticeship, he moved to the River Village and built a building for the manufacture and sales of carriages and selling carriage hardware and trimmings, and for his silver plating work.

In 1824, William Henry Haskell entered the employ of Patent Sargent as a silver-plater at 14 years of age.

William Phillip Sargent, the eldest son of Patten Sargent, was born in Amesbury in 1819. By the age of 17, he was apprenticed to the trade of carriage building in his father's factory.

Patten Sargent was made a bank director in Salisbury and felt he did not have the time to run the carriage business, so he sold it to William H. Haskell. Two years later, Haskell took William P. Sargent, age nineteen, into partnership with him.

A couple of years later, Patten repurchased the business (May 1840) and ran it with his two sons,

William P. and Henry Sargent, as Patten Sargent & Sons until 1851.

A fire erupted in the paint shop in October of that year and consumed ten buildings in all. The factory was never rebuilt. Again, Patten turned his attention to banking and politics.

Just three years prior, young William P. Sargent had formed a second partnership with William A. Gunnison as Sargent, Gunnison & Co., taking William H. Haskell as a partner.

They opened a repository in Boston (1851) for the sale of carriages and sleighs. Eventually Sargent would move to Boston to take charge of the repository.

By 1862, having seen Patten Sargent, William H. Haskell and William A. Gunnison depart the carriage business in River Village for various reasons, William P. Sargent formed a partnership with Charles W. Bradstreet. In 1871, he took his son, Horace M. Sargent and Ferdinand F. French into partnership. French had come to the company as a salesman in 1863. Horace lasted with the company for only 10 years. Bradstreet died in 1908.

With the rapid expansion of business, the company seemed to be always looking for more or larger buildings. They had several locations in Boston and one in Saco, Maine.

Patten Sargent died in August of 1883. A year and a half later, William P. Sargent's wife, Hannah, died. At this time, William decided to retire from the business and Ferdinand F. French was called to take charge of business.(See Ferdinand F. French). In June of 1885, the firm was reorganized as Ferd. F. French & Co., Ltd.

William P. Sargent died February 17, 1888. At his funeral, the Rev. Dr. Duryea commented on the large number of carriage makers in attendence, attesting to the character and honesty of William P. Sargent, in his dealings with people.

Sarven

James D. Sarven was the inventor of the Sarven Patent Wheel, (see New Haven Wheel Co. and Woodburn & Scott), circa 1850.

Saul (see Sebastian Wagon Co.)

Saunders

Virginus L. Saunders operated a wagon making shop in Mt. Crawford, Virginia—after the Civil War.

Saxton

J. Saxton, wagon maker, resided over Dick's store; Las Vegas, New Mexico, circa 1895–1900.

Sayers & Scovil Co.

As a young man, William A. Sayers moved from Greenfield, Ohio to Cincinnati, in 1876. He wanted to demonstrate his talent as a carriage designer and builder with the J.W. Gosling Company.

With his ambition and talent, young Sayers soon opened his own shop at 8th and Sycamore, with A.R. Scovil as his bookkeeper and partner, circa 1880–1919.

Their first carriage was sold at an auction, held at the 5th Street Horse Market for $100 with an order for ten more at the same price. That was the start of carriage and buggy production for Sayers & Scovil.

When the Company introduced a line of "Young Men's Buggies," production eventually increased to over 500 vehicles per year.

Sayers & Scovill moved to a large 100,000 sq. ft. plant on Colerain Avenue in 1887. Here they continued to enjoy a flourishing business until the plant was damaged by fire in 1919.

For the next 25+ years, the Company operated from temporary quarters in the Haberer building and then from a large plant at Gest and Summer Streets. In 1945 the Company moved into its new modern factory at Rossmoyne, Ohio.

The Sayers & Scovil name and trade-mark is now owned by the Hess & Eisenhardt Company.

Schacht Buggy Co.

Buggy manufacturer; Cincinnati, Ohio, circa 1880–1910.

Schaeffer, Merkel & Co.

Wagon manufacturers; Fleetwood, PA, circa 1890–1910.

Schanding

Peter Schanding, carriage and wagon dealer and representative; Ashland, WI, circa 1890–1910.

Schanze

John Schanze, carriage and wagon manufacturer, spring and light wagons a specialty, corner of 6th Avenue and Mechanics' Street; Emporia, Kansas, circa 1882–1890.

Scheer

Jacob Scheer was one of the largest wagon makers in St. Louis, Missouri—second only to Joseph Murphy. By 1850, the Scheer firm was producing over 200 wagons a year, circa 1840–1880.

Scheidler

Charles Scheidler, wagon maker, 352 West 53rd; New York, NY, circa 1899.

Schenbach

C.F.A. Schenbach, carriage, wagon and sleigh maker; New York, NY, circa 1890–1910.

Schenck

Matthias Schenck, wagon maker; Dundee, WI, circa 1879–1903.

Scheu (see Buob & Scheu)

Schiffers

Peter Schiffers, blacksmith and wheelwright; also carriage and wagon manufacturer, 740 Austin, and 902 Austin; San Antonio, Texas, circa 1887–1905.

Schindler

Henry Schindler, wagon maker; New Glarus, Wisconsin, circa 1865.

Schlage

Herman Schlage, carriage and wagon dealer and representative; Ashippun, WI, circa 1890–1910.

Schlichenmeier
William Schlichenmeier, blacksmith and wheelwright, 310 E. Commerce; San Antonio, Texas, circa 1897–1902.

Schmidlin & Driscoll
Manufactured coach lamps at 135 Mercer Street; New York, NY, circa 1850's–1870's.

Schmidt
A. Schmidt, carriage and wagon maker; Madison, WI, circa 1879.

Schmidt
A.C. Schmidt, manufacturer of wagons and carriages, Grand Ave. and 7th St.; Las Vegas, New Mexico, circa 1895–1905.

Schmidt
Frederick D. Schmidt, Sr., blacksmith and wheelwright; carriage and wagon manufacturer, and carriage painters and trimmers, 523–24th, and 2402 Church; Galveston, Texas, circa 1886–1902.

Schmidt
George Schmidt of Cincinnati, Ohio operated his carriage and wagon works on Sycamore street, starting in the late 1800's.

They were best known for the beautiful circus wagons he built for Forepaugh Sells circus and Barnum, Bailey & Hutchinson shows, circa 1890–1910.

Schmidt
Louis Schmidt, wagon maker, 66 Clinton; New York, NY, circa 1899.

Schmidt
P.C. Schmidt, wagon maker; Barton, Wisconsin, circa 1865.

Schmidt (see Kent & Schmidt)

Schmitt
A.R. Schmitt, blacksmith and wheelwright; also carriage and wagon manufacturer, 621 Ave. B; San Antonio, Texas, circa 1880's–1905.

Schmitt
John Schmitt, wagon maker, 62 Grove; New York, NY, circa 1890's.

Schmitt
Peter Schmitt, wagon maker, 54 Tompkins; New York, NY, circa 1899.

Schmitt & Martinson
Manufacturer of carriages, buggies and wagons, 401 W. Weatherford; Ft.Worth, Texas, circa 1896–1908.

Schneider
George Schneider, carriage and wagon dealer and representative; Addison, WI, circa 1890–1910.

Schneider
H. Schneider, wagon maker; Reeseville, WI, circa 1879.

Schneider & Ackerman
Wagon makers, 518 East 15th; New York, NY, circa 1899.

Schnelt
Jacob Schnelt Jr., wagon maker; Pendleton, NY, circa 1899.

Schnoer
A. Schnoer, wagon maker; Gasport, NY, circa 1899.

Schofield (see Osgood, Morrill, Bird & Schofield)

Scholes & Owens
Blacksmiths; Cody, Wyoming, circa 1905–1910.

Scholl
Julian Scholl & Co., maker of wagons and other commercial vehicles; New York, NY, circa 1890–1910.

Schrack
C. Schrack & Co.; manufacturers of coach and carriage paints and varnishes.

They were established in 1816 and advertised themselves as the oldest varnish house in America, 152 & 154 North Fourth Street; Philadelphia, PA, circa 1816–1900.

Schram
Charles Schram, carriage and wagon dealer and representative, Alderly, WI, circa 1890–1910.

Schreffler
George F. Schreffler, buggy maker; Mifflinburg, PA, circa 1876.

Schubert
George Schubert, blacksmith and wheelwright, Brooklyn heights; Ft. Worth, Texas, circa 1905–1915.

Schubert Bros Gear Co.
Established in 1888 and incorporated in 1897, this company offered a full line of carriages and wagon gear for sale at retail or wholesale.

They also manufactured surries, buggies, wagons, carts, automobile bodies, tops and trimmings of all kinds; Oneida, NY, circa 1888–1920.

Schubert, Rushing & Shaw
George Schubert, P.O. Rushing and S.S. Shaw, blacksmiths and wheelwrights, se corner of east 1st and Sylvania Ave.; Riverside, Texas, circa 1904–1912.

Schuchman
George Schuchman, wagon maker, 134 East 41st; New York, NY, circa 1899.

Schukraft
William Schukraft & Sons, makers of express and delivery wagons, drays and brewer's trucks; Chicago, Illinois, circa 1890–1910.

Schuldt
George Schuldt, blacksmith and wheelwright, Bonham, and 761 Liberty Ave.; Beaumont, Texas, circa 1906–1911.

Schulte
G.B. Schulte Sons Co., buggy manufacturer; Cincinnati, Ohio, circa 1880–1910.

Schulte
J.E. Schulte & Co., blacksmiths; Casper, Wyoming, circa 1905–1910.

Schultz Wagon Co.
Manufacturer of fine wheeled vehicles, including circus wagons; Dalton, Ohio, circa 1880–1910.

Schulz
Frank Schulz, carriage painters and trimmers, 19 North; San Antonio, Texas, circa 1887–1900.

Schulz (see Topperwein & Schulz)

Schumacher
Christian Schumacher, wagon maker, 423 West 39th; New York, NY, circa 1899.

Schumacher
G. Schumacher, blacksmith and wheelwright, 125 Fredericksburg road; San Antonio, Texas, circa 1897–1902.

Schumacher
John Schumacher, wagon maker, 530 West 55th; New York, NY, circa 1890's.

Schumann (see Benedict & Schumann)

Schuttler
Peter Schuttler, a native of Germany, established his wagon shop in 1843, at 22nd and Rockwell Streets; Chicago, Illinois. He advertised his wagons as "The Old Reliable".

By the mid-1850's he had a factory with 100 workers producing over 120 wagons per month. The Schuttler factory built a variety of vehicles, including large freight wagons, circa 1843–1900.

Schuttler wagons were popular in the west, and were sold by other wagon shops, like Hyde & Kretschmer of Pueblo, Colorado.

Schwab & Smith
Blacksmiths and wagon makers; Afton, Wyoming, circa 1902–1908.

Schwaeble
Matthias Schwaeble, wagon maker, 106 Lawrence; New York, NY, circa 1899.

Schwalbe
William Schwalbe, wagon maker; Hartford, WI, circa 1879–1903.

Schwartz & Kern
Carriage makers; Coopersburg, PA, circa 1880–1910.

Schwarz
Conrad Schwarz, carriage, wagon, buggy and phaeton dealer, 603–605 Preston Ave.; Houston, Texas, circa 1900–1910.

Schweickert
Mr. Julia F. Schweickert, dealer of agricultural implements, carriages and other vehicles, 317 west 16th; Cheyenne, WY, circa 1892–1905.

Schweitzer
John Schweitzer & Co. manufactured buggies; Hamilton, Ohio, circa 1890–1910.

Schweninger
J. Schweninger, wagon maker, 141 Elm, Leadville, Colorado, circa 1884–1890.

Schwenk
Abraham Schwenk, carriage maker; Norristown, PA, circa 1880–1910

Schwinehart
J. Schwinehart was a carriage and wagon maker, operating out of his brick shop at the corner of Market and Union streets; New Berlin, PA., circa 1843–1860's.

Schwinge (see Hildinger, Schwinge & Hildinger)

Schwoob
George W. Schwoob, blacksmith and wagon maker; Cody, Wyoming, circa 1900–1908.

Schwoob
H.H. Schwoob, blacksmith and dealer in agricultural implements; Cody, Wyoming, circa 1905–1910.

Scientific Farming Machinery Co.
This company built farm implements and equipment, including some designed by Guy E. Lincoln; Minneapolis, MN, circa 1900–1925.

Scioto Buggy Co.
Ohio, circa 1890–1910.

Scobie
David Wiley Scobie, originally from Scotland, came to Cambridge, Wisconsin, where he learned blacksmithing from Fred Ford. In 1861, Scobie enlisted to fight in the Civil War. Upon his return, he resumed working in Ford's blacksmith shop, which he eventually bought and named The D.W. Scobie WagonFactory.

Scobie made harrows and farm wagons, especially hay wagons, buggies, sleighs, and other agricultural implements.

In late 1891, a fire partially destroyed his business. In the fall of 1892, he built the brick and stone building which still stands today, in Cambridge, Wisconsin.

Scobie employed eight to twelve men, making a specialty of hay wagons, harrows and sleighs. For these three items, he held three separate patents. He also continued to manufacture other vehicles and implements.

D.W. Scobie continued his business until 1902, when ill health forced him to give it up. He died in 1913, and the shop was sold to the Simondson brothers.

Scott
R.D. Scott & Co. was a carriage and sleigh builder; Pontiac, Michigan, circa 1890–1910.

Scott
Robert B. Scott, wagon maker; Philadelphia, PA., circa 1840's–1860.

Scott
William Scott, wagon maker, 48 Watts; New York, NY, circa 1899.

Scott & Bros.
Wagon makers; Terre Haute, Indiana, circa 1858.

Scott & Powers
Blacksmith and wagon maker; Fort Collins, Colorado, circa 1881–1890.

Scott (see Bean & Scott)
Scott (see Bryden & Scott)
Scott (see Houk & Scott)
Scott (see Woodburn & Scott)
Scott (see Woy & Scott)
Scovill (see Sayers & Scovill)

Scranton Axle Company
Produced axles and carriage parts; Lancaster, PA, circa 1890–1910.

Scrimshire
W.B. Scrimshire, carriages, buggies and phaetons, 210–214 W. 2nd; Ft. Worth, Texas, circa 1904–1911.

Scrimshire & Bobo
Carriage, wagon, buggy and phaeton dealers, 114 Throckmorton; Ft. Worth, Texas, circa 1905–1915.

Scudder
Timothy Scudder was a highly skilled artist and portrait painter. He developed a first class carriage painting business. Working out of his own shop, Scudder painted vehicles for private customers and also free-lanced for many local carriage makers. A few vehicles were built or assembled from prefabricated parts and sold in his shop. Mr. Scudder also found time to make a profit from his interest in photography. Huntington, NY., circa 1880–1900.

Search Manufacturing Co.
This company built a line of threshers and horse powered tread machines; Sheboygan Falls, Wisconsin, circa 1880's–1900.

Searls
The Searls Manufacturing Co., makers of whip sockets, over 250 styles; Newark, N.J, circa 1890–1910.

Sears, Roebuck & Co.
This national firm produced and distributed countless numbers of everyday products for home, business, farm and ranch, including farm implements, buggies, carriages and wagons. Making use of their vast array of outlet stores and catalogs, this firm made a huge impact on the number of vehicles manufactured and sold during the horse and buggy days; Chicago, Illinois.

(See more on this company and many others in Volume 2 of *Wheels Across America*).

Seaton & Whiffen
Wagon makers; Janesville, Wisconsin, circa 1865.

Sebastian Wagon Co.
In the early 1850's Jacob Sebastian was listed as a wheelwright at 218 Third avenue, across the street from his home at 211 Third avenue in New York, NY. Here he made commercial wagons, light carriages, wheels and iron parts for vehicles. Around 1858, he set up a partnership with Louis Saul, at 700 Third avenue. When his partner changed his name from Saul to Saal, so did the firm to "Sebastian and Saal." They would grow and expand to 700, 702 and 704—Third avenue,

Between 47th & 48th street in Manhattan. Here they built wagons of every description—including painting, trimming and repairing. In 1874, the partners separated, with Sebastian expanding again, taking over 204, 206, 208 and 210 East 43rd street. Here they started building heavy wagons, wagon trucks, brewers wagons and, by 1878, circus wagons.

Jacob Sebastian died September 18, 1884. The next few years would see a major reorganization, changing the company name to Sebastian Manufacturing Company in 1885; with the majority of the new owners being brewing companies.

Although other commercial vehicles were being constructed, their specialty would now be brewers wagons and circus wagons.

August 19, 1893, the company name was changed to Sebastian Wagon Company. Over the years, many detailed and elaborate circus wagons were built in their shops.

With the help of Samuel A. Robb, a master wood carver, they constructed—the "twin lions" telescoping tableau for Barnum & Bailey circus; the 22 foot-long Pocahontas Columbus bandwagon for Pawnee Bill Wild West Show. One of the largest parade wagons ever built was a ten ton, 28 foot monster, the Two Hemispheres for Barnum & Bailey in 1903, circa 1850–1920.

Sechler
Mr. D.M. Sechler apprenticed in the carriage building trade as early as 1835 in Milton, PA.

Around 1877, he moved to Cincinnati, Ohio and established Sechler & Co., manufacturer of carriages, buggies, phaetons, surreys, runabouts, spring wagons, two-wheeled carts, and two and four passenger slat wagons for oil field service.

A Mr. John C. Endebrock, who started with the company at age 14 and worked his way up to Secretary, tells the following story:

Our greatest experience while in the carriage business came with our entry into the foreign field, where we eventually became the world's largest exporter of horse drown vehicles.

Our next great experience came with our entry into the trailer industry. It was a case of beginning from scratch for almost nothing was known about trailers. We designed the TRAILMOBILE and patented the automatic coupler now used on trailer trucks. We changed our name from the Sechler & Co. to the Trailmobile Company. In 1950 the Trailmobile Co. was sold to the Pullman Co. and continued under the name Trailmobile Inc., a wholly owned subsidiary; Cincinnati, Ohio, circa 1877–1920.

Sechler Carriage & Implement Co.
D.M. Sechler built wagons, carriages and other farm implements, including the Black Hawk corn planter, in Moline, Illinois, circa 1870–1930. Although Sechler Carriage & Implement Co. were associated with Cincinnati, Ohio and Moline, Illinois, they employed countless agents, jobbers, dealers and retail-wholesale outlets around the country. A few of these were in Dallas, Chicago and St. Louis.

A portion of their implement line may have been aquired in 1903 by American Seeding Machine Co. and the rest sold to Ohio Cultivator Company after Sechler went out of business in the 1920's. Ohio Cultivator continued to build these planters for many years, circa 1877–1920's.

Sedvorowski
A. Sedvorowski, wagon maker; Germania, WI, circa 1879.

Seffel
Stephen Seffel, blacksmith and wheelwright; also carriages, phaetons, buggies, and wagons, on East Crocket; San Antonio, Texas, circa 1887–1900.

Seiberling & Miller Co.
Manufactured farm implements and other equipment, including their Standard Senior mower; Doylestown, Ohio, circa 1895–1905.

Seidel Buggy Co.
Carriage and buggy builder, offered an extensive line of vehicles through their catalogs; Richmond, Indiana., circa 1880–1920.

Seidelman
George L. Seidelman, blacksmith and wheelwright, 701 Mechanic; Galveston, Texas, circa 1893–1902.

Seiler
A.J. Seiler, carriage and wagon maker; Arlington, Wisconsin, circa 1890–1910.

Seislove
George Seislove manufactured all kinds of carriage and sleigh wood bendings, top bows and basswood panels; 620 & 622 Linden Street, Allentown, PA, circa 1880's–1910.

Seixas
Eugene E. Seixas, blacksmith and wheelwright; dealers in carriages, buggies and phaetons; manufacturer of carriages and wagons, 2322 Postoffice; Galveston, Texas, circa 1886–1894.

Sell (see Burns & Sell)

Sellars
Lon Sellars, wagons, 500 Tyler; Amarillo, Texas, circa 1912–1920.

Sellers & Kerns
Carriage makers; Whitehallville, Bucks County, PA, circa 1880–1910.

Senours Manufacturing Company
This Chicago, Illinois firm offered a variety of paint, stain, varnish, and glazes for the carriage trade. They advertised as Senours Superfine Carriage Paint, circa 1880–1910.

Session
Byron Session, blacksmith; Byron, Wyoming, circa 1905–1910.

Setley
George W. Setley operated his blacksmith shop in the same building as carriage maker George Conner, at west fourth and Bieber streets; Williamsport, PA., circa 1890–1915.

Severson
Sever Severson, successor to W. Elliott & Co., blacksmithing, horseshoeing, carriage and wagon making, and automobile repairing, 1812 Eddy Street; Cheyenne, Wyoming, circa 1900–1920.

Seymour
Erastus Seymour, carriage, sleigh and wagon maker, operated his business out of the old John Williams woolen mill; Cazenovia, NY, circa 1870–1904.

Seymour & Morgan
This early Brockport, NY firm built a number of reapers, mowers and other horse-drawn farm equipment, including the famous New Yorker reaper.

They also manufactured reapers for the McCormick Company before the latter moved to Chicago, circa 1840–1870's.

Shacker (see Wilson & Shacker)

Shacklett (see Pierson & Shacklett)

Shadel
Reuben Shadel, wagon maker, corner K and 8th; Sacramento, CA, circa 1853–1865.

Shadle
R. Shadle, carriage maker with Haworth, Eells & Co.; Sacramento, CA, circa 1853–1865.

Shaffer
George Shaffer operated the Singer Glen Carriage Works. It was a blacksmith shop and carriage factory, located in the village of Singer Glen, Virginia, circa 1885–1890.

Shaler
Michael D. Shaler, wagon maker; Lowell, NY, circa 1899.

Shannon
C.L. Shannon, blacksmith and wagon maker; Caldwell, Idaho, circa 1905–1910.

Shannon
Joseph Shannon, blacksmith and wagon maker; Cuprum, Idaho, circa 1905–1910.

Sharer
Q. Sharer, carriage and wagon maker; LaCrosse, Wisconsin, circa 1865.

Sharkey
The J.T. Sharkey company offered a number of vehicle designs, including several carriages in their 1890's company catalog; Taunton, MA, circa 1890–1910.

Sharp
H.M. Sharp, carriage and wagon maker; Beloit, WI, circa 1879.

Shattell
Edward Shattell, blacksmith and wagon maker; Cataldo, Idaho, circa 1905–1910.

Shatz
F. Shatz, wagon maker; Cedarburg, Wisconsin, circa 1865.

Shaw
Henry C. Shaw, blacksmith and wheelwright, 518 E. 6th; and 1203 E. 6th; Austin, Texas, circa 1893–1911.

Shaw
P.H. Shaw was a carriage and sleigh builder who offered a number of stylish vehicles, including Shaw's Four-Passenger Albany Sleigh as seen in the September 1876 Hub, a popular trade magazine; Albany, NY, circa 1870–1900.

Shaw
Sumner S. Shaw, blacksmith and wheelwright, 1st and Sylvania; Riverside, Texas, circa 1905–1910.

Shaw
Z. Shaw, wagon maker; Roxbury, WI, circa 1879.

Shaw & McClellen
Carriage and wagon makers; Jackson County, Missouri, circa 1850–1860.

Shaw (see Price & Shaw)

Shaw-Wells Co.
Dealers in wagons and carriages, 324 Main Ave.; Spokane, Washington, circa 1905–1910.

Shawk
Abel Shawk was a former partner of Moses Latta, the famous Cincinnati, Ohio steam fire-engine builder.
    Shawk designed and built five of his own, starting in 1855; Cincinnati, OH, circa 1855–1860.

Sheets & Cosman
Blacksmiths, wheelwrights; carriage and wagon manufacturers, carriage painters and trimmers, 431–433 Jackson; Dallas, Texas, circa 1891–1910.

Sheldon Axle Co.
Manufactured carriage and wagon axles and hardware; Wilkes-Barre, PA, circa 1890–1910.

Shell
George Shell operated his own shop as a buggy maker; Mifflinburg, PA, (1880–1890), before taking the position of paint shop foremen at the Mifflinburg Buggy Company, circa 1880–1920.

Shelly
William Shelly, wagon maker; Janesville, Wisconsin, circa 1865.

Shelton
George J. Shelton, blacksmith and wheelwright, 212 E. 5th and 509 E. 5th; Austin, Texas, circa 1910–1922.

Sheman (see Dow, Sheman & Co.)

Shepard
Francis W. Shepard, wagon maker, 852 Jackson Avenue; New York, NY, circa 1899.

Shepard
J.A. Shepard & Sons, wagon and truck maker; New York, NY, circa 1880–1910.
    They built one of the largest freight wagons or freight trucks ever, and named it Thunder. It weighed over 7 tons and required six horses to move while empty, and up to 50 horses—when fully loaded.
    The wheels are said to have weighed 3,000 pounds each. The vehicle was so large it was assembled in the street in front of the Shepard Shops.
    The wagon was used to move machinery, huge blocks of stone, etc.

Shepard (see Nichols & Shepard)

Sheppard Iron Works
This firm is known to have built several steam fire-engines, mostly of the horizontal style; Buffalo, NY, circa 1865–1875.

Sherin & Bro.
Carriage and wagon makers; Milwaukee, WI, circa 1879.

Sherk & Hackman
Carriage makers in Cumberland County, building a variety of quality vehicles, including an auto-top surrey. This type surrey was used to transport participants to the 120th anniversary of President Lincoln's Gettysburg Address; Carlisle, PA., circa 1880–1910.

Sherman Implement Co.
Carriage and wagon maker, 112 S. Crockett; Sherman, Texas, circa 1895–1915.

Sherwin Williams
Cleveland, Ohio, circa 1890–1910.

Shields
J.H. Shields & Co., manufacturer of wagons, buggies, carriages, etc.; Amesbury, MA, circa 1890–1910.

Shinick
T.J. Shinick, wagon maker, Copper and 2nd; Albuquerque, New Mexico, circa 1900–1910.

Shoenbeck
August S. Shoenbeck, carriage and wagon dealer and representative; Ableman, WI, circa 1890–1910.

Short
J.W. Short, blacksmith and wagon maker; Boise, Idaho, circa 1905–1910.

Short
Orville H. Short, carriage and sleigh maker; Syracuse, NY, circa 1880–1900.

Short (see Olds & Short)

Shriner
B.W. Shriner, blacksmith and wagon maker; Kooskia, Idaho, circa 1905–1910.

Shufelt
J.H. Shufelt, carriage painter; Santa Fe, NM, circa 1906–1912.

Shuler
The W.S. Shuler Spring Co. of Amsterdam, N.Y., circa 1890–1910.

Shupe
John Shupe, blacksmith and wagon maker; Montpeilier, Idaho, circa 1905–1910.

Shupp
W.H. Shupp, carrriage and wagon factory, 147–149 Bridge St.; 156 Bridge St., and 1337 Bridge St. (1900); Las Vegas, New Mexico, circa 1882–1900.

Sibley
W.H. & F. Sibley were carriage, wagon and sleigh builders; Westboro, MA, circa 1880–1900.

Sibley (see Baldwin & Sibley)

Side Delivery Buncher Co.
Farm implements; Toledo, Ohio, circa 1890–1910.

Sides (see Danels & Sides)

Siefert & Faber
Carriage and wagon dealers and representatives; Alma Center, Wisconsin, circa 1890–1910.

Sievers & Erdman
Manufacturer of elegent landaus, coaches and broughams. At one

time they employed 150 skilled mechanics. They were first located at Brush and Woodbridge, but a few years later moved to ne corner of Jefferson and Beaubien; Detroit, Michigan, circa 1875–1910.

Silsby
William Silsby, wagon maker, 199— J; Sacramento, CA, circa 1853–1865.

Silsby Mfg. Co.
This was one of the foremost manufacturers of steam fire pumps and horse-drawn fire equipment. Horace C. Silsby, born in 1817 in Connecticut, established the "Island Works" in 1845, producing various pumps and equipment.

In 1856, he formed Silsby, Mynderse & Co., with partners Edward Mynderse and John Shoemaker. Here, with the help of other well known inventors, like M.R. Clapp (inventor of the Clapp & Jones engine and a drop-tube boiler); and Birdsall Holly (inventor of a rotary steam cylinder), they built the first "Silsby" steamer, a 9,500 lb. experimental engine named "Neptune". Silsby's second engine, named "Long John", saw much improvement, but still employed the horizontal boiler, a design used until the development of the vertical boiler, in 1860.

In 1857, the city of Chicago purchased "Little John" for a reported $5,000, and put it to good use for many more years.

Horace C. Silsby, circa 1845–1891, joined Ahrens of Cincinnati, OH; Button of Waterford, NY; and Clapp and Jones of New York, to form the "American Fire Engine Co."; Seneca Falls, NY.

Silsby (see Long & Silsby)
Silverthorn
S. Silverthorn, wagon maker; Iola, WI, circa 1879.

Silvertson
H. Silvertson, wagon maker; Cylon, Wisconsin, circa 1865.

Simmang
Carl Simmang, blacksmith and wheelwright; also carriage and wagon manufacturer, sw corner of N. Walnut and Burleson; San Antonio, Texas, circa 1887–1900.

Simmang
W.F. Simmang, blacksmith and wheelwright; also carriage and wagon manufacturer, 608 W. Commerce; San Antonio, Texas, circa 1887–1900.

Simmons (see Border & Simmons)
Simmons
J.E. Simmons, carriage maker; Sedgwick, CO, circa 1882–1890.

Simon
August Simon, blacksmith and wheelwright; also carriage and wagon manufacturer, 296 South Alamo; San Antonio, Texas, circa 1887–1900.

Simondson Bros.
Wagon makers; Cambridge, Wisconsin, circa 1910–1920.

Simons
Henry Simons was a wagon maker who built and shipped vehicles to South America, Mexico, West Indies and others; Philadelphia, PA., circa 1840's–1860.

Simons, Coleman & Co.
This carriage and wagon maker of Philadelphia, PA was known for an impressive feat in 1857. In conjunction with the Wilson, Childs & Co., also of Philadelphia, they produced 550 wagons in about five weeks for the U.S. Army's Utah Expedition, circa 1850–1870.

Simpers
T.W. Simpers, wagon maker; Philadelphia, PA., circa 1840's–1860.

Simpson
Frank Simpson, wagon maker; Independence, MO, circa 1840–1850.

Simpson
John S. Simpson, carriage, wagon, buggy and phaeton dealer; and carriage and wagon woodwork, 308–310 E. 6th; Austin, Texas circa 1900–1911.

Simpson Carriage Co.
James B. Simpson, carriages, buggies and wagons, J.W. McManus, manager, 145–147 Elm; Dallas, Texas, circa 1891–1905.

Simpson & Joyce
Blacksmiths and wagon makers, 203 W 4th; Amarillo, Texas, circa 1900–1910.

Simpson (see Lippoldt & Simpson)
Singer Glen Carriage Works
Blacksmith and carriage factory; Singer Glen, Virginia, circa 1885–1890. (See George Shaffer listing).

Sinnigson
James Sinnigson, blacksmith and wheelwright, 602 Navasota; Austin, Texas, circa 1910–1920.

Sintgenich
E.B. Sintgenich, manufactured only one horse-drawn steam fire-engine; Rochester, NY, circa 1872.

Sior & Trousch
Wagon makers, 444 West 53rd; New York, NY, circa 1899.

Sivertson
John Sivertson, carriage and wagon maker; Amherst, Wisconsin, circa 1890–1910.

Sixel
G. Sixel, wagon maker; Centreville, WI, circa 1879.

Skandia Plow Co.
Building plows and implements; Rockford, Illinois, circa 1880–1900.

Skeel
Gilbert Skeel, wagon maker; Pine River, WI, circa 1879–1885.

Skell
M. Skell, wagon maker; Pine River, Wisconsin, circa 1865.

Skinner-Russell Co.
Louisville, Kentucky, circa 1890–1910.

Slack
J.E. Slack, blacksmith and wagon maker; Colorado Springs, Colorado, circa 1879–1880's.

Slack
W.D. Slack built wagons, carriages, buggies and sleighs at his shop at 6th and St. Louis streets; Lewisburg, PA, circa 1870–1880's.

The Slack shop closed in the 1880's, after his death.

Slater & Cronce
Carriage makers; Frenchtown, NJ, circa 1880–1910.

Slaughter
C.C. Slaughter, carriages, wagons and buggies, office over 247 Main; Dallas, Texas, circa 1900.

Slaughter (see Watkins and Slaughter)

Sloan
David Sloan, coach and wagon maker; Pittsburgh and Allegheny, PA, circa 1840–1870.

Sloan
M.C. Sloan of Bloomburg, PA was a carriage and buggy builder, circa 1870–1910.

Sloan (see Brown, Sloan & Alexander)

Slocum
O.H. Slocum, wagon and sleigh maker; Onendaga, NY, circa 1850's.

Slusser
John K. Slusser, blacksmith and wheelwright, 1317 S. Congress Ave.; Austin, Texas, circa 1910–1918.

Small
C.W. Small, carriage and wagon maker; Bryn Maur, PA, circa 1890–1910.

Smalley
B.H. Smalley, dealer in carriages and other vehicles, 18th and O'Neil; Cheyenne, WY, circa 1900–1905.

Smart (see Biddle & Smart)

Smasal
John Smasal, blacksmith and wheelwright; also carriage and wagon manufacturer 2 North; San Antonio, Texas, circa 1887–1900.

Smedbron & Larson
Carriage and wagon makers, also dealers in carriage lights and trimming; Arkdale, Wisconsin, circa 1890–1910.

Smith
Edward Smith, wagon maker, 1722 Thomes; Cheyenne, Wyoming, circa 1906–1907.

Smith
Edward Smith, fine varnish; Chicago, Illinois, circa 1890–1910.

Smith
Edward Smith & Co., established in 1827, manufactured fine varnishes and coach colors, 147 Times building; New York, NY, circa 1827–1900.

Smith
Elias Smith, blacksmith and wagon maker; Fairview, Wyoming, circa 1902–1908.

Smith
Ervin Smith and Company prepared oak and hickory for the carriage trade at their bending works in York, PA, circa 1890–1910.

Smith
George Smith, blacksmith and wagon maker; Lardo, Idaho, circa 1905–1910.

Smith
G.H. Smith, blacksmith and wagon maker; Montrose, Colorado, circa 1883–1890.

Smith
Harry Smith, blacksmith and horseshoer, 304 Exposition Ave.; Dallas, Texas, circa 1905–1912.

Smith
Henry J. Smith made wagons and light carriages; Elbridge, NY, circa 1899.

Smith
Jackson G. Smith & Sons; Barnesville, Georgia, circa 1865–1910.

Smith
James A. Smith & Co. manufactured agricultural equipment, including Wheelers Combined Reaper & Mower, patented by Cyrenus Wheeler Jr.; Ancaster, Ontario, Canada, circa 1870–1880's.

Smith
James Smith built commercial vehicles—including fire fighting equipment. First known as a hand fire-engine builder—Smith entered the field of steam fire-engine builders during the Civil War period.

His machines were designed to be drawn by horse or by hand, and he sold several in the area of New York city before abruptly going out of business for reasons unknown; New York, NY, circa 1850–1870.

Smith
J.G. Smith, blacksmith, horseshoer and wheelwright, 305 Boll; Dallas, Texas, circa 1886–1890.

Smith
John C. Smith of Smith & White, coach, sign and ornamental painters, 115 K, between 4th and 5th; Sacramento, CA, circa 1853–1865.

Smith
John E. Smith, blacksmith and wagon maker; Monument, Colorado, circa 1883–1890.

Smith
Jos. N. Smith manufactured a full line of dash rails, seat rails and handles for carriage, sleigh and coach makers. They also offered the sale of name plates; 14 &16 Macomb Street, Detroit, MI, circa 1880–1900.

Smith
J.T. Smith, carriage and sleigh maker was known for building a line of closed-body sleighs like Smiths' Booby Sleigh, sometimes called the Booby Hut and one of the finest and costliest sleighs for private use; Boston, MA, circa 1870's–1900.

Smith
P.L. Smith, wagon maker; Janesville, Wisconsin, circa 1865.

Smith
Samuel B. Smith, a dealer in carriage goods; shafts, poles, seats, axles,

springs and assorted carriage parts, 238 Chapel Street; New Haven, CT, circa 1850–1900.

Smith
W.H. Smith manufactured wagons, trucks and coal carts, 454 West 14th; New York, NY, circa 1899.

Smith
William Smith, blacksmith and wagon maker; Shoshone Agency, Wyoming, circa 1895–1910.

Smith
William Smith of Port Jefferson, New York, circa 1830–1869, operated a blacksmith and wagon shop for nearly 40 years, before retiring to California in 1869.

Smith Manufacturing Company
This firm produced an extensive line of farm implements under the name Great Western. Eventually this line of equipment came under control of the Rock Island Plow Co.; Chicago, Illinois, circa 1890–1911.

Smith-Eggers Co.
Buggy manufacturer; Cincinnati, Ohio, circa 1880–1910.

Smith-Howard Co.
Blacksmiths' and carriage makers' supplies, 110–112 Travis; Houston, Texas, circa 1900–1910.

Smith & Barlows
Manufacturers of bent felloes and every style and description of bent materials for carriage, wagon and sleigh wood work.

This firm was owned and operated by Horace Smith, Daniel S. Barlow and William H. Barlow; Bridgeport, CT, circa 1850–1890.

Smith & Bulian
Blacksmith and wheelwright, 1610 Guadalupe; and 1507 Guadalupe; Austin, Texas, circa 1909–1913.

Smith & Eilenberger
Blacksmiths and wheelwrights, 1311 N. Main; N. Ft.Worth, Texas, circa 1905–1915.

Smith & Kraft
Wagon makers, 449 East 77th; New York, NY, circa 1899.

Smith & Sons
Jackson G. Smith & Sons was a pioneer buggy factory in Barnesville, Georgia, circa 1890–1910. It was originally known as Smith and Summers, until J.G. Smith bought out Mr. Summers.

Smith & Sons
Carriages, wagons and buggies, nw corner of Main and Broadway; Dallas, Texas, circa 1910.

Smith & White
Coach , sign and ornamental-painters, and coach trimmers, 115 K Street, between 4th and 5th; Sacramento, CA, circa 1853–1865.

Smith (see Campbell & Smith)
Smith (see Davis & Smith)
Smith (see Deibler & Smith)
Smith (see Frisby & Smith)
Smith (see Heard & Smith)
Smith (see Jones & Smith)
Smith (see Ludlam & Smith)
Smith (see Schwab & Smith)
Smith (see Williams & Smith)
Smith (see Worden & Smith)

Sneed
James Sneed, carriage and wagon maker; Marysville, CA, circa 1855–1875.

Snell
William Snell, blacksmith and wagon maker; Ranchester, Wyoming, circa 1902–1908.

Snider
W.L. Snider, blacksmith and wagon maker; Merna, Wyoming, circa 1902–1908.

Snodgrass
Wagon makers; Terre Haute, Indiana, circa 1858.

Snodgrass
John Snodgrass, blacksmith and wagon maker; Golden, Colorado, circa 1879–1880's.

Snodgrass
S.W. Snodgrass, dealer in carriages and buggies, also coach trimming, harness and sadddlery. They also advertised for sale—the Derby brand of gears and springs; Mifflinburg, PA, circa 1870–1890's.

Snow
W.K. Snow, carriages, wagons and buggies, 291 San Jacinto; Dallas, Texas, circa 1900.

Snow & Rodger
Makers of cutters and wagons; Van Buren, NY, circa 1850's.

Snyder
Daniel W. Snyder, buggy maker; Mifflinburg, PA, circa 1881–1890.

Snyder
E. Snyder, carriage and wagon maker; Central City, Colorado, circa 1879–1880's.

Snyder
J.H. Snyder, blacksmith and wagon maker; Athol, Idaho, circa 1905–1910.

Snyder
William and A.J. Snyder, dealers in carriage and coach trimmings, also harness and saddlery; Philadelphia, PA, circa 1860–1880.

Solberg (see Lind & Solberg)

Somboty
Emery Somboty, blacksmith and wagon maker; Horton, Wyoming, circa 1902–1910.

Sonner
William Sonner, wagon maker, 408 West 52nd; New York, NY, circa 1899.

Sorber & Mason
Carriage makers; Monroe Village, PA, circa 1880–1910.

Sorley
W.B. Sorley, carriage and buggy Manufacturer, Fannin betweenPreston and Prairie; Houston, Texas, circa 1882–1895.

Sorrow
Joseph Sorrow, blacksmith and wagon maker; Grangeville, Idaho, circa 1905–1910.

Sosule
W.G. Sosule, wagon maker, residence 10th street between I and J; Sacramento, CA, circa 1855–1875.

Souix City Iron Works
Makers of carriages and wagons; Souix City, SD, c1890–1910.

Soult
Franklin Soult, carriage painter and trimmer, was the son of Nathan A. Soult, a local blacksmith and wagon maker.

Franklin worked on his own and in several other shops around New Woodstock and the Cazenovia area, including J.L. Darling's carriage shop and McCabes's blacksmith shop; Cazenovia, NY, circa 1866–1890's.

Soult
Nathan A. Soult, blacksmith and wagon maker, also worked for a short time in the shops of J.L. Darling and Frank Soult; Cazenovia, NY, circa 1848–1870.

Southard
Blacksmith and wagon maker; Trinidad, Colorado, circa 1880.

South Bend Chilled Plow Co.
Manufactured farm implements, mostly plows. Some of their plows were designed by W.L. Casaday, like the Garland Riding Plow, the Casaday High Lift Gang Plow, and the Casaday Foot-Lift Sulky Plow. The firm became part of Vulcan Plow Company in the 1920's and later merged with others into Farm Tools, Inc; South Bend, Indiana, circa 1870–1930.

South Bend Wagon Co.
This firm devoted their entire factory to the exclusive manufacture of wagons, including farm wagons, freight wagons, plantation wagons, log trucks and farm carts; South Bend, Indiana, circa 1870's–1910.

Southcotte
G.B. Southcotte, wagon maker; Colorado Springs, Colorado, 1879–1880; Del Norte, Colorado, 1880; Loveland, Colorado, circa 1882 and Manitou, Colorado, circa 1883–1887.

Southern Carriage Co.
Buggy manufacturer; Cincinnati, Ohio, circa 1880–1910.

Southern Rock Island Plow Co.
Manufacturer and dealers in implements, machinery, vehicles, farm wagons, etc. F.A. Head, president, A.B. Taber, vice president, and F.B. Jones, secretary, were dealers in carriages, wagons and buggies, nw corner of Elm and Houston; Dallas, Texas, circa 1897–1910.

Soward
J.F. Soward, blacksmith and wagon maker; Boise, Idaho, circa 1905–1910.

Sown
David J. Sown made wagons and sleighs; Lysander, NY, circa 1850's.

Spalding
S.W. Spalding was a carriage, coach and sleigh maker; Bingham-ton, NY, circa 1850's–1880's.

Spanjer Bros. Woodcarving Co.
The Spanjer brothers designed and built many fancy and elaborate figures, scrolls and letters for circus wagons of all types; New York, circa 1870–1920.

Spannhake
John Spannhake, wagon maker, 206 East 47th; New York, NY, circa 1899.

Sparks (see Weston & Sparks)
Spaugh (see Lake & Spaugh)
Spears' Axle Co.
Located at the corner of Main, Water and 27th Streets, they manufactured buggy, carriage and wagon axles; Wheeling, West Virginia, circa 1880–1910.

Specht (see Rambo and Specht)
Speer
Alexander Speer & Sons manufactured their own special designed Hillside Plow and other horse-drawn implements; Pittsburgh, PA, circa 1870's–1900.

Spelling
Broemforter Spelling Co., buggy manufacturer; Cincinnati, Ohio, circa 1880–1910.

Spencer
J.L. Spencer & Co., carriage and sleigh maker; Oneida, NY, circa 1880–1900.

Spencer
John Spencer Co., carriage, wagon, buggy and phaeton dealer, 1304 Houston; Ft. Worth, Texas, circa 1905–1910.

Spencer (see Johnson & Spencer)
Spencer (see Rudd & Spencer)
Spengler
P.H. Spengler, blacksmith and wheelwright, 1449 N. Flores; and 108 Fredericksburg road; SanAntonio, Texas, circa 1900–1910.

Speyer & Fishburn
Carriage makers; Denver, Colorado, circa 1883–1890.

Speyer & Phelps
Carriages and wagons, 280–282 20th; Denver, Colorado, circa 1884–1890.

Spiller (see Harris & Spiller)
Spokes
Branson, MO, circa 1890–1910.

Sprague
E.R. Sprague, wagon maker; Orfordville, Wisconsin, circa 1865.

Sprague Mowing Machine Co.
Founded by William Sprague in the 1860's, Sprague designed and built mowing machines and other equipment; Providence, Rhode Island, circa 1860's–1880's.

Sprague & French
Carriage and buggy builders; Norwalk, Ohio, circa 1890–1910.

Spreyer & Phelps
Carriage and wagon makers; Denver, Colorado, circa 1884–1890.

Spring (see Roberts, Case & Spring)

Sproule
Harper Sproule, blacksmith, carriages and wagon maker; Raton, New Mexico, circa 1906–1912.

Spudig (see Maguire & Spudig)

Staacke
A.F. Staacke, carriages, buggies, phaetons and wagons, 27 Soledad; San Antonio, Texas, circa 1887–1900.

Staacke
Staacke Brothers, carriages and wagons, 133–135 W. Commerce; Houston, Texas, circa 1897–1902.

Stade
Henry Stade, specialized in the trade of trimming carriages and buggies; Appleton, Wisconsin, circa 1890–1910.

Stalcup
Frank Stalcup, blacksmith and wagon maker; Otto, Wyoming, circa 1901–1902.

Standard Carriage Goods Co.
Manufacturers of fine carriage and coach trimmings; Cincinnati, OH, circa 1880's–1910.

Standard Ditching Machine Co.
Built commercial horse-drawn equipment related to road construction; St. Louis, MO, circa 1880–1900.

Standard Harrow Co.
Built and patented the Peterson Corn Harvester in 1890. They also produced the Standard spreaders, using the Kemp design; Utica, NY, circa 1890–1910.

Standard Oil Cloth Co.
New York, NY, circa 1890–1910.

Standard Varnish Works
Grand Rapids, Michigan, circa 1890–1910.

Standard Vehicle Co.
This was one of the few horse-drawn vehicle businesses to survive the introduction of the automobile into the market. The Knapp's built carriages for a variety of commercial uses, including Walt Disney Inc., and the original Broadway production of Oklahoma.

The firm closed shortly after the death, in 1957, of Edwin Knapp; Lawrenceburg, IN, circa 1914–1957.

Standard Vehicle Co.
Pontiac, MI, circa 1890–1910.

Standard Wagon Co.
A Mr. Burrows was president of Standard Wagon Co., manufacturer of carriages, wagons, and buggies, Cincinnati, Ohio, circa 1880-1910.

They also had branch offices in Atlanta, Albany, Chicago and Dallas, Texas. They once sent an entire trainload of carriages to their branch in Dallas, Texas.

Stanley
Joseph S. Stanley, blacksmith and wheelwright; manufacturer of carriages, buggies and phaetons, 1400 Rusk; Ft.Worth, Texas, circa 1904–1905, and then at 1015 Rusk; Ft.Worth Texas, circa 1905–1915.

St. Anthony Hill Sleigh & Carriage Works
This firm offered a wide variety of vehicles; St. Paul, Minnesota, circa 1880–1900.

Staples & Hanford
New York, NY, circa 1890–1910.

Star Tank Co.
Built farm implement equipment, including water tanks on steel farm truck wagons; Goshen, Indiana, circa 1900.

Star Wagon Co.
Manufacturer of wagons, buggies, carriages, phaetons, and farm equipment, George Greene, proprietor, 12th Avenue SE; Cedar Rapids, Iowa, circa 1866–1895.

Stauss
E. Stauss, blacksmith and wheelwright, 601 S. Presa.; San Antonio, Texas, circa 1900–1910.

Stauss
Julius Stauss, carriage and wagon maker; Milwaukee, Wisconsin, circa 1865.

Staver Carriage Co.
Manufactured a full line of carriages and buggies; Chicago, Illinois, circa 1890–1920.

Staver & Abbott
Manufactured carriages, wagons and nearly 10,000 sleighs, by 1890; Chicago, Illinois, circa 1880–1900.

Steadman
E. Steadman, wagon maker; Fayetteville, NY, circa 1899.

Stearns & Foster Co.
Buggy manufacturers; Cincinnati, Ohio, circa 1880–1910.

Steele (see Carver & Steele Manufacturing Co.)

Steese
Thomas Steese, buggy maker, 106 Market street (rear); Mifflinburg, PA, circa 1870–1903.

Steffian-Krakauer Hdw. Co.
A carriage, wagon and buggy dealer, 300–302 El Paso; El Paso, Texas, circa 1898–1906.

Stehwein (see Doebert & Stehwein)

Steideman
Henry Steideman, wagon maker; St. Louis, Missouri, circa 1850–1870.

Stein
Albert Stein, blacksmith and wagon maker; Glenn's Ferry, Idaho, circa 1905–1910.

Stein
Charles W. Stein, carriage and wagon materials, 265 Stevenson; San Francisco, California, circa 1882–1894.

Stein Double Cushion Tire Co.
Akron, Ohio, circa 1890–1910.

Steiness
L. Steiness, blacksmith and wheelwright, 352 Washington; Houston, Texas, circa 1882–1890's.

Stelfox (see Jones & Stelfox)

Stephens
Thomas Stephens, carriage maker; Applebachsville, Bucks County, PA, circa 1880–1910.

Stephens & Bozarth
Blacksmiths and wagon makers; Juliaetta, Idaho, circa 1905–1910.

Stephenson
John Stephenson; New York, NY, circa 1830–1880.

Stephenson became known as the nation's foremost builder of the Omnibus, with customers from as far away as New Zealand. Probably the largest Omnibus ever built was drawn by up to ten horses and capable of transporting 120 passengers.

This same vehicle was later motorized by George Schlitz of Brooklyn, New York. Schlitz installed a Knox-Martin tractor and operated it as a picnic-excursion bus.

John Stephenson also built a number of band wagons and band chariots for the circus and flat foot shows.

Stevens
A.E. Stevens & Co., a wheel manufacturing company established in 1850. Their office and factory was located at 9–15 Union street; Portland, Maine.

They manufactured wood hubs, and additionally—under patents—manufactured the Sarven and the Warner wheels, circa 1850–1930.

Stevens
A.W. Stevens Co. made huskers and other farm equipment. They began their business in 1842 at Genoa, NY. By 1878 the Stevens company had moved to Auburn, NY where they would grow and expand their implement line.

Around 1898, the firm finally settled in Marinette, Wisconsin, circa 1842–1910.

Stevens
H.G. and H.W. Stevens, manufacturer of heavy and enclosed vehicles; Merrimac, MA, circa 1890–1910.

Stevens
Thomas C. Stevens, blacksmith and wagon maker, Main Street; Trinidad, Colorado, circa 1880–1890.

Stevens & Milligan
Blacksmith and wagon maker; Georgetown, Colorado, circa 1880.

Stevens & Rouse
Livery, feed and Herdic coaches; Colorado Springs, Colorado, circa 1882–1887.

Stevens (see Allerton & Stevens)

Stevens (see Minor & Stevens)

Stevens (see Wilber, Stevens & Co.)

Steward
William H. Steward, blacksmith and wheelwright; carriage manufacturer and repairer, 659 Main; Beaumont, Texas, circa 1906–1912.

Stewart
A.F. & S.C. Stewart built wagons and other commercial vehicles—including a hand-drawn fire hose cart; Rochester, NY, circa 1890–1910.

Stewart
A.T. Stewart, blacksmith and wagon maker, 43 Union; Pueblo, Colorado, circa 1884–1890.

Stewart
C.J. Stewart, agent for all kinds of carriages, top and open buggies, wagons, harness and horses; repairing and jobbing, and carriage exchange, 484 Curtis Street; Denver, Colorado, circa 1881–1900.

Stewart
C.J. Stewart, proprietor of Houston Carriage Co., blacksmiths and wheelwrights; manufacturer of carriages, wagons, buggies and phaetons, 802–804 Commerce; Houston, Texas, circa 1900–1915.

Stewart
Francis H. Stewart, carriage, wagon, buggy and phaeton dealer, 111 Fannin; Houston, Texas, circa 1900–1915.

Stewart
J.S. Stewart, blacksmith and wagon manufacturer, Greenwood between 5th and 6th; Pueblo, Colorado, circa 1884–1900.

Stilger
John W. Stilger, wagon maker, 137 West 61st; New York, NY, circa 1899.

Stimson, Valentine & Co.
This firm supplied varnish and coatings to the carriage trade, 36 India Street; Boston, MA, circa 1850–1900.

Stinson
Edward B. Stinson Co., wheel manufacturer; Baltimore, MD, circa 1880–1900.

Stitzer
John S. Stitzer, buggy maker; Mifflinburg, PA, circa 1841–1845.

Stivers
Rufus M. Stivers built light and heavy carriages and sleighs; New York, NY, circa 1870's–1900.

Stivers
William Stivers, carriage maker, 17th Ward; New York, NY, circa 1850's.

Stivers & Tilton
Carriage and buggy makers; New York, NY, circa 1880–1910.

St. Marys Wheel and Spoke Co.
With Thomas A. White as president and his son, J.C. White, superintendent—this St. Marys, Ohio firm became one of the foremost wheel manufacturing companies in the U.S. Specializing in heavy, massive-style wheels, they supplied all the big circuses and major wagon builders.

Lightweight wheels were decorated with spokes that had designs lathe turned into the wood, then painted bright colors. Others used doughnut shaped panels of wood bolted to the spokes. These panels were scrolled and fluted, then painted in flashy designs.

Wheels with bolted panels were vulnerable to damage and soon gave way to the famous "sunburst" wheels.

These wheels were made by cutting flutes into the side of each spoke, then a wedge-shapped piece of pine was firmly inserted. The top edge of this wedge, or sometimes called a web, was cut with a different design. They were then painted red, white, blue, orange and yellow. As the wheel revolved the effect was a sunburst-like flash of color, circa 1880–1940.

Stock
August Stock, wagon maker, 152 East 35th; New York, NY, circa 1899.

Stockton
W. Stockton, blacksmith and wagon maker; Newcastle, Wyoming, circa 1905–1910.

Stoddard
J.C. Stoddard of the American Steam Music Company, has been generally credited with being one of the earliest inventors of the steam calliope; Worcester, Massachusetts.

The earliest United States calliope patent, was issued to him in October of 1855. Stoddard's patent for a poppet valve was so good that, after his patent protection expired in 1872, many others adopted this type of valve.

Stoddard Manufacturing Co.
Built farm equipment, including the Climax disc harrow, and the Beck side-delivery hay rake; Dayton, Ohio, circa 1880–1900.

Stoeber
William Stoeber, wagon maker, 707 Elton Avenue; New York, NY, circa 1899.

Stoelling
O. Stoelling, wagon maker; Bergholtz, NY, circa 1899.

Stogsdill (see Beeman & Stogsdill)

Stokes
J. Stokes, carriage maker; Pueblo, CO, circa 1882–1890's.

Stokey (see Dagnal & Stokey)

Stokey & Webster
Henry L. Stokey, blacksmiths and wheelwrights, 589 Ross Avenue; Dallas, Texas, circa 1900–1910.

Stolzenburg (see Krueger & Stolzenburg)

Stone
Crandal Stone & Co., built top joints for vehicles; Binghampton, New York, circa 1890–1910.

Stone
Robert Stone of Independence, MO. was a wagon maker who supplied vehicles for local sales and the Santa Fe traders, circa 1840–1860.

Stone
S.B. Stone, carriage makers of Doylestown, PA, and Fox Chase, 23rd ward, Philadelphia, PA, circa 1880–1910.

Stone (see Crandal, Stone & Co.)

Stoops
Joseph Stoops, wagon maker, 5th, between K and L; Sacramento, CA, circa 1853–1865.

Stopple
A.G. Stopple, blacksmiths, horseshoers, and wagon maker, 166 Camp, and 135 Ross Ave.; Dallas, Texas, circa 1905–1910.

Storch
Henry Storch, wagon maker, 174 South; Utica, NY, circa 1899.

Stoughton Wagon Company
Established in 1865, this company built bob sleighs, and they also built and sold thousands of wagons through their own efforts, and those of Moline Plow Company, acting as general agents for the Stoughton Wagon Co. Moline Plow Company eventually bought out this firm; Stoughton, WI, circa 1865–1910.

St. Paul Plow Works
Manufactured horse-drawn farm equipment, including their St. Paul Sulky Plow; St. Paul, Minnesota, circa 1890–1910.

Stratman
F.W. Stratman & Co., wagon makers; Dodgeville, Wisconsin, circa 1879–1903.

Stratton
The C.H. Stratton Carriage Co.; Muncie, Indiana, circa 1890–1910.

Stratton
Ezra M. Stratton served his apprenticeship under Charles Townsend of the Platt and Townsend firm in Connecticut (1824 to 1829). He established his own carriage making shop in New York City by 1836.

About this same time Ezra M. Stratton began publishing a trade journal entitled The New York Coachmakers Magazine. The magazine was absorbed by The Hub in 1871. Both publications were informative trade journals of the day, offering articles and illustrations of current styles of vehicles, technical drawings, details of construction, finish and trim; New York, NY., circa 1824–1871.

Straut
W.E. Straut, carriage and wagon materials, and carriage and wagon wheels, nw corner of Drumm and Sacramento; San Francisco, California, circa 1882–1894.

Strehly
Omar Strehly, blacksmith, wheelwright and horseshoer, se corner of 364 Bryan and Good; Dallas, Texas, circa 1900–1908.

Streich
A. Streich & Bro. was established in 1860. This Oshkosh, Wisconsin firm, circa 1860–1919, specialized in cutters and sleighs. They had produced over 100,000 by the 1890's, building 30,000 between 1889–1890 alone.

Streich
Gabriel Streich, wagon maker, Oshkosh, WI, circa 1885–1919.

Stringfellow J S & Co.
J.S. Stringfellow, wagons, 98 Polk; Amarillo, Texas, circa 1916.

Strode (see Weston & Strode)

Stromberg
Andrew Stromberg, wagon maker; Stockholm, Wisconsin, circa 1885–1919.

Strong (see Wilder-Strong Implement Co.)

Stroud
Z. Stroud, blacksmith and wagon maker; Fairburn, Idaho, circa 1905–1910.

Studebaker Bros. Mfgr. Co.
The Studebaker family came to America in 1736 from Germany. The great-frandfather, Clement Studebaker, built his first wagon here in 1750 in Ashland, Ohio.

Years later, grandsons, Clement and Henry Studebaker opened a wagon building and blacksmith shop in February of 1852 under the name of H & C Studebaker, shoeing horses and doing repair work, in South Bend, Indiana. It was said their original investment was $68.00 and two sets of blacksmith tools.

In 1858 John Studebaker, a brother, joined the firm and bought out Henry, who wanted to take up farming. Later that year two other brothers, Peter and Jacob, joined the firm.

In 1868 they became known as Studebaker Brothers Manufacturing Company. During this first year, business was very slow—and only two wagons were built.

Struggling for recognition, a contract for wagons from the U.S. government gave them a much needed boost. By 1876 they were producing 30,000 wagons annually. By 1893, their plant covered 95 acres in South Bend, Indiana. The Studebaker Brothers Manufacturing Company was considered the largest manufacturer of horse drawn vehicles in the world.

One of the many qualities of a Studebaker wagon was their wheels. It has been said a sign at the factory read "We didn't invent the wheel—We perfected it". A strong feature was their slope shoulder spokes. The spoke was sloped where it entered the hub. This distributed the stress over a wide surface and prevented the spoke from breaking off at the shoulder.

Each wheel was immersed in boiled linseed oil to seal the pores of the wood and joints from moisture. This also served as a foundation for painting later.

In 1902 they introduced their first automobile. It was electric. In 1904 they joined the Garford Company to make autos while still making wagons and carriages.

From 1913 to 1920 they made horse-drawn vehicles in South Bend and automobiles in Detroit. They built wagons through 1920 basically to support the military during the first world war.

After the war they converted their plant in South Bend to make automobiles and that was the end of their wagon business. They made autos until 1980 when McGraw Edison bought them out.

Studer
R. Studer, blacksmith and wheelwright; also carriage and wagon manufacturer, 328 E. Commerce; San Antonio, Texas, circa 1887–1900.

Stuhr (see Nicolaisen & Stuhr)

Stumpf
Joseph Stumpf, blacksmith and wheelwright; carriage, wagon, buggy and phaeton manufacturing and repairing; also carriage painters and trimmers, 510–12 Colorado; Austin, Texas, circa 1900–1918.

Stumpf (see Brower & Stumpf)

Sturtevant-Larrabee Co.
Manufacturer of carriages, wagons, sleighs, bobsleds, delivery wagons, and also pony size vehicles; Binghamton, NY, circa 1890–1920.

Sturtevant (see Isham & Sturtevant)

Suber & Cutts
Wagon makers; Marysville, CA, circa 1854–1880. (See listing for A.W. Cutts)

Suemann
N. Suemann & Co., carriage and wagon dealer; Adell, Wisconsin, circa 1890–1910.

Suhl
C.F. Suhl, blacksmith and wagon maker, 114 Drumm Street; San Francisco, California, circa 1882–1885.

Sullivan
P.H. Sullivan, manufactured farm wagons, 16 Cottage; Lockport, NY, circa 1899.

Sullivan Bros.
This firm manufactured sleighs and carriages, and were well known for their large exhibits at the dealers' conventions; Rochester, NY, circa 1880–1910.

Sullivan and Eagle
Builders of circus wagons for steam calliopes and other horse-drawn vehicles; Peru, Indiana, circa early 1900's.

Summers Buggy Co.
C.O. Summers, Barmesville, Georgia, circa 1890–1910.

Superior Drill Co.
This very early farm implement manufacturer can be traced back to 1840. They built a variety of farm equipment and later became part of the 1903 merger with American Seeding Machine Co.

The Superior name was used on equipment long after the merger; Springfield, Ohio, circa 1840–1920's.

Superior Hay Stacker Co.
Manufactured an automatic corn harvester and other implements; Linneus, Missouri, circa 1900–1920.

Suter
David Suter, wheelwright and wagon maker; Chrisman, Virginia, circa 1850–1900.

Sutton
A.S. Sutton, carriage and wagon maker; Casa Grande, Arizona, circa 1884–1890.

Suydam
W.D. Suydam & Co., carriage and wagon dealers, Denver, Colorado, circa 1884–1890.

Suydam & Co.
W.D. Suydam & Co., carriages and wagons, 15th and Wewatta and 387 Stout; Denver, Colorado, circa 1881–1890.

Suydam & Huffman
Carriage and wagon maker, 15th and Wazee; also 15th and Wewatta; Denver, CO, circa 1880–1890's.

Svendsen & Blessing
Blacksmiths and wagon makers; Casper, Wyoming, circa 1900–1905.

Swab Wagon Company, Inc.
Jonas Swab, blacksmith and civil war veteran, founded Swab's Wagon Works, December of 1868, in Elizabethville, Pennsylvania.

Known today as the Swab Wagon Company, Inc., they claim to be the oldest continuously operating transportation company in the the world.

Said to be the inventor of the Chilled Box Steel Axles, the company advertised "Wagons That Wear", and claimed there has never been a report of a Swab axle wearing out. Early manufacture included a variety of hub wheel wagons, two and four horse wagons, drag and timber wagons, covered platform spring wagons, delivery dump wagons, farm carts and wheelbarrows; also sleighs and one third size "Jr." wagons for hand or use by children.

Today, Swab Wagon Company, operated by the family of Jonas Swab, manufacture the finest quality solid fiberglass truck bodies for animal collection designed with the humane treatment of animals in mind. They continue to carry on the tradition of quality and integrity established by their founder in 1868.

Swales
A.E. Swales, blacksmith and wheelwright, 329 Fredericksburg road; San Antonio, Texas, circa 1901–1902.

Swalm & Doak
Blacksmiths and wagon makers; Lander, Wyoming, circa 1905–1910.

Swalm (see Lewis & Swalm)

Swan
Benjamin A. Swan, blacksmith and wheelwright, Montgomery road; Houston, Texas, circa 1900–1910.

Swanke
August Swanke, wagon maker; Princeton, WI, circa 1879–1903.

Sweet
B.F. & H.L. Sweet produced over 10,000 sleighs and cutters by the 1890's. The Sweet firm also offered carriages and buggies; Fond du Lac, Wisconsin, circa 1879–1919.

Sweetser (see Bliss & Sweetser)

Swenson
F. Howard Swenson, carriage painters and trimmers, 1615 Sabine; Austin, Texas, circa 1910–1917.

Swentzel
George Swentzel, buggy maker; Mifflinburg, PA, circa 1845–1851.

Swift
Charles Swift was a wagon maker, 44 Mercer Street; New York, NY, circa 1850's–1870's.

Swift-Caffall Carriage Co.
Carriage manufacturers and repairers, 814–818 Pearl; Beaumont, Texas, circa 1906–1912.

Swift (see Zeller, Phelps & Swift)

Swineford
Henry Swineford, buggy maker; Mifflinburg, PA, circa 1881.

Sylvestor
Adam F. Sylvestor, wagon maker; Philadelphia, PA., circa 1840's–1860.

Symons
D.A. Symons, carriage maker; Utica, NY, circa 1850's.

Syracuse Agricultural Works
Manufactured farm equipment and implements, circa 1870's–1912, many under the patents of Moses G. Hubbard, including their Reversible Sulky Plow.

The company became part of Deere & Co. in 1912; Syracuse, NY.

Syracuse Chilled Plow Co.
Farm implement and equipment manufacturer; Syracuse, NY, circa 1890–1920.

Taber Buggy Co.
A.B. Taber, carriages, wagons and buggies, 341–343 Elm; Dallas, Texas, circa 1898–1910.

Tait
F.B. Tait Manufacturing Co. built farm implements; Decatur, Illinois, circa 1900.

Talbert Buggy Co.
Isaah Talbert moved to West Elkton, Ohio from Miamisburg, where he learned the buggy trade under a Mr. Dan Augebright. Together with Tommy Stubbs (a sawmill operator) and a Mr. VanTrump (an undertaker), they started the VanTrump and Talbert buggy factory.

Talbert eventually bought out the interest of VanTrump and Stubbs; continued the business as Isaah Talbert and Sons, until a fire destroyed their factory in 1914.

Ta-Pat-Co
A 20-year old named Edward McClain started a business that became Ta-Pat-Co. He grew up in his father's saddlery shop in Greenfield. Through the years he watched as customers put make-shift collar pads around their horses' necks. He designed a pad that was open at the bottom so that it could be fitted to the neck of the horse easier. He also put special hooks on the pad to secure it to the collar and hold it in place; Greenfield, Ohio, circa 1890–1910.

Tarbora Buggy Co.
Tarbora, North Carolina, circa 1890–1910.

Tate & Buford
Rock Island, IL, (see Rock Island Plow Co.)

Tatum (see Gill & Tatum)

Tayler & Flint
Carriage and wagon materials, 31 Beale; San Francisco, California, circa 1888–1894.

Tayler (See Aultman & Tayler Machinery Co.)

Taylor
A.B. Taylor, Son & Co. of New York, NY. The Taylor company constructed three steam fire-engines. One of these saw extensive use at the Undine Engine Company No. 52 of New York City, circa 1865–1870.

Taylor
A.P. Taylor, carriage and wagon maker, Holladay and 27th St., also 27th and Larimer; Denver, Colorado, circa 1880–1890.

Taylor
C.V. Taylor & Co. manufactured carriages and sleighs; Pontiac, Michigan, circa 1880's–1900.

Taylor
H. Allison Taylor, buggy maker, 358 Walnut street; Mifflinburg, PA, circa 1872–1897.

Taylor
John T. Taylor, wagon maker; Monument, CO, circa 1882–1887.

Taylor
J.W. Taylor, carriage maker; Newfane, NY, circa 1899.

Taylor
Shapley P.R. Taylor, blacksmith and wheelwright, 215 E. Shepherd, and 521 W. Murray; Denison, Texas, circa 1887–1894.

Taylor
T. Brainard Taylor, buggy maker, 267–271 Market street; Mifflinburg, PA, circa 1869–1916.

Taylor
William Taylor, blacksmith and wagon maker; Rock Creek, Wyoming, circa 1901–1902.

Taylor & Ayala
Blacksmiths and wheelwrights, 224 S. Flores; San Antonio, Texas, circa 1890–1910.

Taylor & Hadley
Carriages and wagons, 29th and Stout; Denver, CO, circa 1881–1890.

Taylor (see Belcher & Taylor Agricultural Tool Co.)
Taylor (see Fowler & Taylor)
Taylor (see Nordling & Taylor)

Taylor (see Roberts, Willis, Taylor Co.)

Taylor (see Webb, Taylor & Perry)

Tebbett's (see Mansur & Tebbett's Implement Co.)

Tegetmeier & Riepe
Manufactured wagons and trucks, 771 First Avenue; New York, NY, circa 1899.

Telegraph Blacksmith Shop
Gibson & Sager, proprietors, blacksmithing and general jobbing, horseshoeing and plow work, 1228—J Street; Sacramento, California, circa 1882–1885.

Telles (see Garay & Telles)

Ten Brocke (see Coan & Ten Brocke)

Terbush
F. Terbush, wagon maker; Racine, Wisconsin, circa 1865.

Terry
Andrew Terry & Co. manufactured a variety of malleable iron castings used for carriage and harness trimmings; Terryville, CT, circa 1850–1890.

Teschner
C. Teschner, carriage and wagon dealer and representative; Amherst, Wisconsin, circa 1890–1910.

Tetreault (see King & Tetreault)

Tew
John W. Tew, blacksmith and wagon maker, Thomes and 18th; Cheyenne, WY, circa 1895–1905.

Texas Buggy Co.
Carriage, buggy and wagon dealer, N.F. Hood, manager, 1006 Houston; Ft.Worth, Texas, circa 1890–1900.

Texas Implement & Machine Co.
Carriages, wagons and buggies, ne corner of Patterson Ave. and Griffin; Dallas, Texas, circa 1897–1903.

Texas Implement & Transfer Co.
Carriage, buggy, wagon and phaetons, Alexander Rabyor, proprietor, 209–215 W. 1st; Ft.Worth, Texas, 1904–05, and later at the sw corner of Throckmorton and W. Belknap; Ft.Worth, Texas, circa 1900–1915.

Texas Moline Plow Co.
Carriages, wagons and buggies, W.N. Stroud manager, 101 N. Broadway corner of Main, and 275 Elm, also sw corner N. Austin and Pacific Ave., also ne corner N. Market and Pacific Ave.; Dallas, Texas, circa 1897–1910.

Thatcher
T.R. Thatcher, carriage painter; Silver Cliff, Colorado, circa 1882.

Thayer
L.P. Thayer, wagon maker, K street between 7th and 8th; Sacramento, CA, circa 1855–1875.

Thayer
W.D. Thayer, blacksmith and wagon maker; Boise, Idaho, circa 1905–1910.

Theobold
J.J. Theobold, blacksmith and wheelwright; carriage, buggy and wagon manufacturer, 303–25th, and 2501–2503 Mechanic; Galveston, Texas, circa 1893–1902.

The Rubber Tire Wheel Co.
Springfield, Ohio, established in June of 1894.

Theurer
John Theurer manufactured wagons and trucks, 804 Eleventh Avenue; New York, NY, circa 1899.

Thiede
William F. Thiede, wagon maker; Columbus, WI, circa 1879–1919.

Thofern
David Thofern, blacksmith, wheelwright, wagon maker, carriage painter and trimmer, 575 Ross Ave., also 158 N. Akard, Phone 1277; Dallas, Texas, circa 1891–1910.

Thofern & Monschke
Blacksmiths and wheelwrights, 152 N. Ervay, also 158 North Akard; Dallas, Texas, circa 1897–1906.

Thomas
Chauncey Thomas; Boston, MA, circa 1870–1890.

Thomas built and patented his unique style of Sedan Cab featuring a rear entrance door which, when opening, raised the divided seat—and then lowered the seat as the door was closed, thus placing the passengers in a forward-facing position.

The driver was able to balance the load, according to weight, or for ascending or decending hills, by adjusting a crank on the side of the vehicle.

Thomas
D.S. Thomas and Son operated a complete carriage factory consisting of: blacksmithing and ironing shop, office and showrooms, trimming shop, painting and finishing shop, woodworking department and handles. They made all kinds of carriages, served as a dealer for the "Emerson-Brantingham" buggy, manufactured in Rockford, Illinois; and kept on hand a variety of harnesses, lap robes, whips and other accessories; Bridgewater, Virginia, circa 1891–1930's.

Thomas
S.H. Thomas, blacksmith and wheelwright, 190 Leonard; Dallas, Texas, circa 1900.

Thomas
Thomas Thomas, carriage and wagon maker; Colorado Springs, Colorado, circa 1884–1890.

Thomas
William Thomas was born around 1802, in either New York or New Jersey. He also lived for a brief time in Iowa and Arkansas.

Thomas, an inventor, worked in a number of jobs, including the construction of a water powered gristmill. In his early years, he may even have been a sailor. However, he was best known for his dream to build a windwagon, having made two attempts. The first around 1846–1847, and the next when William Thomas received a patent—March 13, 1859 for his Sail Wagon.

Although he had some personal success with his Prairie Ship, the idea overall never caught on; Westport, Missouri, circa 1846–1860.

Thomas
W.L. (Bill) Thomas, blacksmith and wagon maker, 201 N Polk; Amarillo, Texas, circa 1920, also at 302 Tyler; Amarillo, Texas, circa 1919.

Thomas Manufacturing Co.
Built farm implements, including the Thomas Royal Hay Rake; Springfield, Ohio, circa 1870's–1900.

Thomas Caster Co.
Built circus wagons and other vehicles; Philadelphia, PA, circa 1890–1910.

Thomas (see Burgess, Baker & Thomas)

Thomas (see Morrow-Thomas Hardware Co.)

Thomas & Lewis
Carriage, wagon and buggy maker, Cascade Ave.; Colorado Springs, Colorado, circa 1877–1890.

Thomason
Thomas C. Thomason, blacksmith, wheelwright and horseshoer, 207 E. 5th; Austin, Texas, circa 1897–1910.

Thompson
Blacksmith and wagon maker; Cedron, Idaho, circa 1905–1910.

Thompson
Charles Thompson, wagon maker, 9th, between J and K; Sacramento, CA, circa 1853–1865.

Thompson
C.R. Thompson, carraige maker; Red Cliff, Colorado, circa 1882–1895.

Thompson
I.E. Thompson, blacksmith and wagon maker; Chesterfield, Idaho, circa 1905–1910.

Thompson
James Thompson, carriage and wagon maker; Black Hawk, Colorado, circa 1884–1890.

Thompson
John Thompson, wagon maker; Beloit, Wisconsin, circa 1865.

Thompson
J. Thompson & Sons manufacturer of farm implements, including the Ole Olson tongueless sulky plow; Beloit, Wisconsin, circa 1880–1940.

Thompson
Philip Thompson, blacksmith and wheelwright, 19 Liberty road; Houston, Texas, circa 1887–1895.

Thompson
Robert Thompson, blacksmith and wheelwright, S. Congress Ave., near St. Edward's college; Austin, Texas, circa 1898–1906.

Thompson
William A. Thompson, carriage painters and trimmers, 304 W. Weatherford; Ft. Worth, Texas, circa 1904–1912.

Thompson
Zenas Thompson & Bro.; manufacturer of light vehicles, also built several styles of sleighs and cutters; Portland, Maine, circa 1876–1910.

Thompson & Co.
Manufactured farm equipment and implements, including harvesters and mowers; Rockford, Illinois, circa 1850's–1880.

Thomson
Peter Thomson, blacksmith and wheelwright; carriage, wagon, buggy and phaeton manufacturer and carriage repairer; 106 Congress Ave. and 410 Colorado; Austin, Texas, circa 1887–1918.

Thornburgh Manufacturing Co.
Built farm implements; Bowling Green, Ohio, circa 1900–1940.

Thornhill Wagon Co.
Benjamin Thornhill, Lynchburg, Virginia, circa 1898–1948.

Thorpe (see Klom & Thorpe)

Thorp (see Roberts, Thorp & Co.)

Thrasher
W.H. Thrasher, blacksmith and wheelwright, 401 W. Bonham; Paris, Texas, circa 1891–1900.

Threadgold
J.F. Threadgold, carriage and wagon dealer and representative; Argyle, Wiscosnin, circa 1890–1910.

Threefoot Brothers
Harness; Meridian, Mississippi, circa 1890–1910.

Thuerer (see Moeller & Thuerer)

Thun
Charles Thun, carriage and wagon makers; Alpine, Colorado, circa 1884–1890.

Thurr
C.J. Thurr, carriage and wagonmakers; Alpine, Colorado, circa 1884–1890.

Tibbets
A.B. Tibbets, carriage maker; Niagara, NY, circa 1850's.

Tiede
A.C. Tiede, blacksmith and wagon maker; Corral, Idaho, circa 1905–1910.

Tiedmann
J. Tiedmann, carriage trimmers; Denver, Colorado, circa 1884–1890.

Tierney
John Tierney manufactured light carriages; Niagara Falls, NY, circa 1899.

Tiffin Wagon Co.
Manufacturer of farm wagon—garbage, stone and asphalt wagons.
They also built heavy self-dumping wagons and a little know line of corn shellers; Tiffin, Ohio, circa 1890–1910.

Tifft
R.C. Tifft & Co., carriage and wagon maker; LaCrosse, Wisconsin, circa 1865.

Tiger Wagon & Carriage Co.
In Illinois, circa 1870's–1900.

Tignor & Mosse
Blacksmiths and wheelwrights;and carriage, buggy and wagonmanufacturers, 424–426 WestMain; Denison, Texas, circa 1887–1910.

Tilley
S. Tilley, carriage and wagon dealer and representative; Albany, Wisconsin, circa 1890–1910.

Tilton (see Stivers & Tilton)

Timken Roller Bearing Axle
Canton, Ohio, circa 1890–1910.

Tinls
Baac Tinls made wagons and sleighs; Clay, NY, circa 1850's.

Tips
Walter Tips, carriage and wagon woodwork, 708–712 Congress Ave.; Austin, Texas, circa 1887–1911.

Tobey
E.H. Tobey, carriage and wagon maker, 285 15th, Denver, Colorado, 1880–1881, also 384 Hall; Denver, Colorado, circa 1879.

Tolbot
S.B. Tolbot, blacksmith and wheelwright; Sherman, Texas, circa 1893–1900.

Toledo Bending Co.
Carriage maker; Toledo, OH, circa 1890–1910.

Toledo Carriage Woodwork Co.
Manufactured hubs, spokes, rims, shafts, poles and trimmings; Toledo, OH, circa 1880's–1910.

Tolman
C. Tolman, blacksmith and wagon maker; Irwin, Idaho, circa 1905–1910.

Tolman
Joseph H. Tolman, blacksmith and wagon maker; Auburn, Wyoming, circa 1900–1910.

Tomlinson
John Tomlinson, blacksmith and wagon maker; Black Hawk, Colorado, circa 1879–1880's.

Tomlinson (see Austin & Tomlinson)

Topfer
John Topfer & Son, carriage maker; Brooklyn, NY, circa 1880–1900.

Topliff
I.N. Topliff Mfg. Co. was a manufacturer of carriage parts and bow sockets. They were located in Cleveland, Ohio and St. Catharines, Ontario, Canada, circa 1870–1910.

Topperwein & Schulz
Wagon makers, 552 East 144th Street; New York, NY, circa 1899.

Torat
John H. Torat & Co., wagon makers; Ironton, WI, circa 1865.

Torry (see Martin & Torry)

Tower
I.S. Tower & Bro., carriage and sleigh builders; Chicago, Illinois, circa 1880–1900.

Tower
J.D. Tower & Sons Co. built farm implements; Mendota, Illinois. circa 1900–1920.

Townsend & Radle
Manufacturer of carriages, wagons, carts and wheel barrows. (see Manchester Wagon Factory).
This firm was one of the first to use a steam engine power source to operate hammers, forges, blowers,

and woodworking machinery; Manchester, PA, circa 1835–1860.

Townsen (see Laurence & Townsen)

Townsend (see Platt and Townsend)

Townsend (see Tucker & Townsend)

Tracy
L. Tracy & Co., wagon maker; Fond du Lac, Wisconsin, circa 1865.

Tracy (see Galt & Tracy)

Travers
R.C. Travers, carriage painters and trimmers, 140 Fisher Lane; Dallas, Texas, 1897–1903.

Traxell Bros.
Wagon makers; Boonville, NY, circa 1899.

Treloar
E.P. Treloar, blacksmith and wagon maker; Forney, Idaho, circa 1905–1910.

Treat & Lenfesty
Carraige makers; Trinidad, Colorado, circa 1882–1890.

Tri-City Carriage Works
Davenport, Iowa, circa 1899.

Tricts
Isaac Tricts, carriage and wagon maker; Clay, NY, circa 1850's.

Trousch (see Sior & Trousch)

Trout
William Trout, blacksmith and wheelwright, 2006 N. New Braunfels Ave.; San Antonio, Texas, circa 1897–1910.

Troy Bending Company
Offered all sizes, grades and shapes of shafts and poles to the carriage trade; Troy, Ohio, circa 1870–1900.

Troy Buggy Works Co.
This firm manufactured a full line of carriages, buggies, fancy surries and carts. They also built farm equipment and a variety of wagons; Troy, Ohio, circa 1880–1920.

Troy Buggy & Carriage Works
Manufacturer of carriages and buggies. They also produced several styles of cutters and sleighs; Troy, NY, circa 1880–1910.

Troy Wagon Works
Manufactured farm wagons and related vehicles. The firm became Troy Trailer & Wagon Company by the 1930's; Troy, Ohio, circa 1880's–1930's.

Truax
George E. Truax, blacksmith and wagon maker; Glenrock, Wyoming, circa 1900–1905

Truax
George Truax. blacksmith and wagon maker; Pinedale, Wyoming, circa 1902–1910.

Truckey
Alex Truckey, blacksmith and wagon maker, 18th and Bent; Cheyenne, Wyoming, circa 1900–1905.

Trullinger
R.R. Trullinger, blacksmith and wagon maker; Ketchum, Idaho, circa 1905–1910.

Truman, Hooker & Co.
Carriages, wagons, surries and buggies. 421–427 Market Street; San Francisco, California, circa 1884–1894.

Tucker
Dan Tucker, blacksmith and wagon maker; Arapahoe Agency, Wyoming circa 1902–1908.

Tucker
John Tucker, blacksmith and wagon Maker, 219 S. Oregon; El Paso, Texas, circa 1904–1911.

Tucker
S.H. Tucker, blacksmith and wagon maker; Saguache, Colorado, circa 1880–1885.

Tucker & Loungen
Blacksmith and wagon makers; Saguache, CO, circa 1879–1880's.

Tucker & Townsend
Blacksmith and wagon makers; Saguache, Colorado, circa 1880.

Tucker (see Ashbrook, Tucker & Co.)

Tucker (see Farrington & Tucker)

Tudhope Carriage Co.
Carriage manufacturer; Orillia, Ontario, Canada, circa 1890–1910.

Tuller Buggy Co.
Buggy maker; Columbus, OH, circa 1890–1910.

Tulloch
A.E. Tulloch, blacksmith and wagon maker, 109 South Spruce; Leadville, Colorado, circa 1880–1890.

Tulloss (see Lyles, Tulloss Hardware Co.)

Turner
D.B. Turner, blacksmith and wagon maker; Gold Hill, Colorado, circa 1878, and also Golden, Colorado, circa 1879.

Turner
G.A. Turner, blacksmith and wheelwright, sw corner of Main; Dallas, Texas, circa 1897–1903.

Turner
Joseph T. Turner, blacksmith and horseshoer, 136 S. Jefferson, Dallas, Texas, circa 1905.

Turner
Sam Turner, blacksmith and wagon maker; Barber, Wyoming, circa 1902–1910.

Turner
S.Turner, blacksmith, carriage and wagon maker; Canon City, Colorado, and Caribou, Colorado, circa 1877–1880's.

Turner
Vance Turner, carriage and wagon maker; Coal Creek, Colorado, circa 1884–1890.

Turner (see Wood & Turner)

Turton & Hawks
Wagon makers; Beaver Dam, Wisconsin, circa 1865.

Tuthill
E. Tuthill & Co. of Port Jefferson was the largest manufacturer of carriages in Suffolk County. They built every type of vehicle. They also did painting, trimming and repair work; Long Island, NY, circa 1855–1890.

Tuttle (see Duncan & Tuttle)

Twentieth Century Storm Buggy Co.
Buggy manufacturers; St. Henry, OH, circa 1890–1910.

Tyke
George Tyke, carriage and wagon maker; Skaneateles, NY, circa 1850's.

Tyler
A.H. Tyler, wagon maker; Richland Center, Wisconsin, circa 1865.

Tyler
H.E. Tyler established his company in 1871. They built carriages and sleighs; Morrisville, NY, circa 1871–1900.

Tyson & Jones Buggy Co.
Buggy and carriage makers; Carthage, NC, circa 1850–1926.

Uglow
C.E. Uglow, blacksmith and wagon maker, 118 McKinney Ave.; Dallas, Texas, circa 1910.

Uhle
Frederick Uhle, wagon maker, 87 Manhattan; New York, NY, circa 1899.

Uhler
Matthew Uhler, carriage and wagon maker; LaCrosse, Wisconsin, circa 1865–1898.

Ullrich
L.F. Ullrich, carriage painter and trimmer, 326 Elm; San Antonio, Texas, circa 1887–1890's.

Underwood (see Coleman & Underwood)

Union Carriage Co.
Carriage manufacturer; Cadiz, OH, circa 1890–1910.

Union Carriage & Gear Co.
Established in 1888, manufacturing vehicles and equipment for wagons, carriages and sleighs; Watertown, NY, circa 1888–1910.

Union City Carriage Mfg. Co.
Buggy manufacturers; Union City, Indiana, circa 1890–1910.

Union Foundry & Machine Co.
Built farm equipment—including their Perfection Straw Spreader in 1915; Ottawa, KS, circa 1910–1920.

Union Hardware
Supplied a variety of metal parts needed to build buggies; Mifflinburg, PA, circa 1870–1880.

Union Mercantile Co.
Carriage and wagon makers; Cheyenne, WY, circa 1884–1890's.

United States Carriage Co.
Carriage manufacturer; Columbus, OH, circa 1890–1910.

Universal Plow Co.
Built plows and farm implements. They moved to Canton, Ohio in the 1880's, circa 1870–1900.

Unlandherm
C. Unlandherm manufactured wagons and trucks, 339 East 48th; New York, NY, circa 1899.

Unlandherm
F. Unlandherm & Sons manufactured wagons and trucks, 403 East 117th; New York, NY, circa 1899.

Urieta
Euleterio Urieta, blacksmith, 3710 Texas Pacific; El Paso, Texas, circa 1906–1918.

U.S. Buggy & Cart Co.
Manufactured buggies and carts. They also built a line of commercial vehicles and carriages, including their #2841 auto top buggy, #2931 turn-under delivery wagon and #2810 rubber tired runabout—selling for $47.50 in 1906; Cincinnati, Ohio, circa 1880–1920.

Usinger Co.
Buggy manufacturer; Cincinnati, Ohio, circa 1880–1910.

Vail (see A.E. Hallock)

Valdez
Juan M. Valdez, blacksmith, wheelwright and wagon maker, 610 Colorado; Austin, Texas, circa 1889–1900.

Valdez
Paul Valdez, blacksmith and wheelwright, 412 E. 7th; 1212 S. Congress Ave.; 1300 E 12th; and 1205 Angelina; Austin, Texas, circa 1893–1907.

Valdosta Buggy Co.
Valdosta, GA, circa 1890–1910.

Valencia
Miguel Valencia, blacksmith and wagon maker, Bassett Ave.; El Paso, Texas, 1906, and later at S. Piedras and l S. Alameda; El Paso, Texas, circa 1911–1918.

Valentine
L.W. Valentine, carriage and wagon maker; Hempstead, Long Island, NY, circa 1880–1910.

Valentine
Lawson Valentine Company of New York, NY manufactured coach and carriage varnishes and paints.

Their factory was located at Hunters Point and the main office in the Times building in New York, circa 1860–1900.

Valentine & Company
Henry C. Valentine was president of one of the foremost suppliers and manufacturers of carriage makers supplies, paints and varnishes.

With offices in New York, Chicago, Boston and Paris, France, Valentine distributed his products to agents and importers throughout the world; 245 Broadway; New York, NY, circa 1850–1910.

Valentine (see Stimson, Valentine & Co.)

Valley Implement & Vehicle Co.
Carriages, wagons and buggies, 504–508 San Francisco; El Paso, Texas, circa 1910–1920.

VanAlstyne (see Dennis and Van-Alstyne)

Van Brunt Manufacturing Co.
D.C. Van Brunt of Horicon, WI, circa 1860–1912, started building farm equipment, including seeding machines, as early as 1860.

The company also operated under the name Van Brunt & Wilkins Manufacturing Co.

The firm built a reputation for quality and was bought out by John Deere in 1912.

Vance
David Vance, wagon maker; Jackson County, Missouri, circa 1850–1860.

Van Court
John Van Court, carriage and wagon materials, 25 Washington; San Francisco, California, circa 1888–1894.

Vanderbelt (see Robinson & Vanderbelt)

Vandiver Corn Planter Co.
Manufactured corn planters and other farm implements. Many of their planters were designed by J.C. Barlow. Barlow went on to form the J.C. Barlow Corn Planter Co. around 1890. Vandiver continued in business for several more years; Quincy, Illinois, circa 1863–1900.

Vandyke
J.S. Vandyke, blacksmith and wagon maker, 9th, between J and K; Sacramento, CA, circa 1853–1865.

Van Hess
William Van Hess, blacksmith and wagon maker; Garland, Wyoming, circa 1902–1908.

Van Ness Co.
Builders of light carriages, wagons, carts and sulkies; New York, NY, circa 1890–1910.

Van Pelt
John Van Pelt, carriage maker; Pineville, PA, circa 1880–1910.

Van Pelt & Bright
Carriage makers; Pineville, PA, circa 1880–1910.

Van Sickel (see Ling & Levoy)

Van Tassel & Kearney
Agents in the carriage and wagon business and built vehicles, including a line of dog carts; New York, NY, circa 1890–1910.

Van Ulzen (see Harb & Van Ulzen)

Varian & Dillon
Carriage makers, 18th Ward; New York, NY, circa 1850's.

Varner
W. Varner, blacksmith and wagon maker; Greer, Idaho, circa 1905–1910.

Varney
Thomas B. Varney, carriage and wagon materials, 22 Fremont; San Francisco, CA, circa 1888–1894.

Vaudervort
G.W. Vaudervort, wagon maker; Fond du Lac, Wisconsin, circa 1865.

Vaughn
Daniel Vaughn, wagon yards, corner E. 8th and Calhoun; Ft. Worth, Texas, circa 1896–1904.

Vehrkamp Carriage Co.
Buggy manufacturer; Cincinnati, Ohio, circa 1880–1910.

Velasquez
Luis Velasquez, blacksmith, 107 E. 6th; El Paso, Texas, circa 1910–1920.

Velie Carriage Co.
This company was established in 1902 by W.H. Velie, a grandson of John Deere.

Velie manufactured carriages and light wagons, including some commercial vehicles—and offered others in their catalog.

They eventually went into the automobile business; Moline, Illinois, circa 1902–1920's.

Ventress (see Evans & Ventress)

Verhu
J. Verhu, wagon and carriage maker; Milwaukee, WI, circa 1865.

Vickery
Wesley Vickery, blacksmith and wagon maker; Halfway, Idaho, circa 1905–1910.

Viele (see Babcock & Viele Carriage Co.)

Vigorelli
Charles Vigorelli manufactured carriages and push carts, 11 Baxter; New York, NY, circa 1899.

Vipond
George Vipond, carriage and wagon dealer and representative; Ashland, WI, circa 1890–1910.

Virden
James Virden, wagon maker; St. Louis, Missouri, circa 1850–1870.

Virginia Buggy Co.
L.R. Jones; Franklin, Virginia, circa 1890–1910.

Voekle
Andrew Voekle, wagon maker, 525 East 19th; New York, NY, circa 1899.

Vogel
A.J. Vogel, blacksmith and wagon maker; Jackson, Wyoming, circa 1902–1910.

Vogt
F. Vogt, wagon maker, 474 Water; New York, NY, circa 1899.

Voigt & Ritter
Carriage and wagon makers; LaCrosse, Wisconsin, circa 1879–1903.

Vollmer
Bennett Vollmer, carriage and wagon maker, also for an unknown period of time, leased a shop from J;.L. Darling; Cazenovia, NY, circa 1870–1890's.

Vollrath
F.H. Vollrath, blacksmith and wheelwright; carriage and wagon manufacturer; and carriage painter and trimmer, 317 S. Flores; San Antonio, Texas, circa 1887–1905.

Vollrath
L. Vollrath, carriage painters and trimmers, 217 S. Flores; Houston, Texas, circa 1897–1912.

Von Emden
I. Von Emden, blacksmith and wagon maker, corner of Clara and 5th; San Francisco, California.

Von Gerichten
Theodore Von Gerichten, wagon maker, 610 Bergen Avenue; New York, NY, circa 1899.

Von Hees
William Van Hees, blacksmith; Burlington, WY, circa 1905–1910.

Vorwick Road Cart Co.
Manufactured road carts and other light vehicles; Monmouth, Illinois, circa 1880's–1900.

Vossbeck & Arnett
Wagon makers; Trinidad, Colorado, circa 1881–1887.

Vossbeck (see Baldwin & Vossbeck)

Vulcan Plow Co.
This firm offered plows and tillage equipment, before merging with others to form Farm Tools, Inc; Evansville, IN, circa 1880–1920's.

Wade
C.W. Wade, blacksmith and wheelwright, 700–725 Elm; Dallas, Texas, circa 1897–1904.

Wade
W. and J. Wade, wagon makers; Beaver Dam, Wisconsin, circa 1865.

Wade & Leverich
Carriage and coach maker; New York, NY, circa 1820–1840.

Credited with building one of the first American carriages for public service in cities, around 1827. It provided regular service on Broadway—between Bleecker and Wall street.

Waechter
Alfred Waechter, blacksmith, wheelwright and wagon maker, 801 W. 6th; 1609 Guadalupe; 306 W. 25th, and 106 E. 30th; Austin,Texas, circa 1887–1918.

Waechter (see Day & Waechter)

Wagaman
John Wagaman, wagon maker, K, between 7th and 8th; Sacramento, CA, circa 1853–1865.

Wagner
G.W. Wagner built carriages and sleighs, and offered several sytles of cutters, like their Wagners's Swell Body Cutter; Philadelphia, PA, circa 1870–1900.

Wagner
M. Wagner, blacksmith and wagon maker, 9th, between J and K; Sacramento, CA, circa 1853–1865.

Wagon Co.
Henderson, Kentucky, circa 1890–1910.

Wagons
Boone, Iowa, circa 1890–1910.

Waite (see Birdsall, Waite & Perry Mfg. Co.)

Wakeham & Florance
Blacksmiths and wheelwrights, 209 Lancaster Ave.; Dallas, Texas circa 1900.

Wakeman
F.W. Wakeman, blacksmith and wagon maker; Durango, Colorado, circa 1881–1888.

Walborn & Riker
Freeman Riker and Will Walborn considered themselves manufacturers of pony vehicles, as opposed to pony carts or pony wagons. The term of pony wagon was, however, the most common used slang among the rank-and-file of the carriage building trade.

Walborn & Riker started their business in 1881 in St. Paris, Ohio, a city just 70 miles north of Cincinnatti, the hub of the national wagon industry.

They were meticulous in every detail, from proper sizing and proportions to the finishing touches.

There business grew rapidly and they soon became outstanding in a field of only a handful of pony-wagon builders. They were not only the biggest, but probably also the best.

Mr. Walborn, the imaginative artist, had a fine sense of color and design. Mr. Riker, the pragmatic perfectionist, took care or production and business details. Together they produced pony wagons that in their time were as close to works of art as such vehicles could get, and today are valued collector's items.

By the early 1900's they printed their twentieth catalog. They even printed one in Spanish. They had a thriving mail-order business and a lucrative international one, too. They had agents in New York, Paris, London and the British Colonies.

So, once upon a different age, a Walborn & Riker pony cart was the ultimate status symbol, a beautifully made, terribly expensive full-sized toy. They were all custom made, and only the well-to-do could afford the luxury of ownership.

Walbrandt
William Walbrandt, wagon maker; Troy, WI, circa 1879–1903.

Walker
Addison Walker, carriage painter and trimmer, 171 Elm; Dallas, Texas, circa 1898–1907.

Walker
Alfred J. Walker, was a builder of light and heavy carriages, carts and other light vehicles; New York, NY, circa 1890–1910

Walker
A.P. Walker, manufacturer of carriages, buggies and wagons, 207 Houston; Ft. Worth, Texas, circa 1896–1903.

Walker
Frederick William Walker lived in Cincinnati, Ohio. The work of this famous artist can be found on the wagons built at the Bode Wagon Company of Cincinnati.

He painted a variety of subjects—from biblical scenes to portraits of circus owners on tableau and portrait wagons. Walker's work is also found on other commercial vehicles and carriages, circa 1900–1930.

Walker
G.W. Walker, carriage manufacturer; Gainesville, Georgia, circa 1890–1910.

Walker
John C. Walker, blacksmith and wheelwright, 1301 Houston; Ft. Worth, Texas, 1904–1905, also 1420 S. Main; Ft.Worth, Texas, circa 1905–1915.

Walker
J.T. Walker, maker of carriages, wagons and carts; New York, NY, circa 1890–1910.

Walker
William Walker, blacksmith and wheelwright, Avenue L, between 38th, 39th; Galveston, Texas, circa 1888–1895.

Walker (see Fulton & Walker)

Walker (see Fulton & Walker Wagon Co.)

Walker Brothers
Blacksmiths and wagon makers, 110 Pine; Leadville, Colorado, circa 1881–1890.

Wall
David K. Wall, blacksmith and manufacturer and dealer in carriages, wagons, fine buggies and harness. As early as 1874, Wall made special arrangements with Studebaker Brothers to sell their buggies and wagons in the Colorado territory; 188 and 190—15th Street; Denver, Colorado, circa 1870–1890.

Wall
J.T. Wall, blacksmith and wheelwright, 1104 S. Flores; San Antonio, Texas, circa 1900–1910.

Wall & Pursel
Carriages and wagons, 351–357 Wazee; Denver, Colorado, circa 1884–1895.

Wall, Witter & Co.
Wagons and carriages, 188–204 15th; Denver, Colorado, 1877–1883, and at West 2nd & 206 Chestnut; Leadville, Colorado, circa 1880–1890.

Wallenburg
O.F. Wallenburg, carriage and wagon manufacturer and dealer; Wallace, Idaho, circa 1908.

Waller
G.W. Waller, blacksmith and wheelwright, nw corner of Cedar Spring and Gillespie Ave.; Dallas, Texas, circa 1897–1903.

Walmer & Fox
Carriage works; Hummelstown, PA, circa 1890–1900.

Walsh
Charles Walsh, blacksmith and wheelwright, 2 blocks east of city limits on 5th; Austin, Texas, circa 1896–1906.

Walsh
Martin Walsh, carriage painter, 1615–1621 Market; San Francisco, California, circa 1888–1894.

Walsh
U.L. Walsh, wagon maker, Longmont; CO, circa 1882–1890.

Walters
A. Walters, blacksmith and wheelwright, 203 W Crawford; Denison, Texas, circa 1887–1890's.

Walters
S.C. Walters, carriage and wagon dealer and representative; Albany, Wisconsin, circa 1890–1910.

Walton
Peter Walton, carriage maker; Las Animas, CO, circa 1882–1890.

Walton
See Electric Wheel Co.

Walton Carriage Co.
Lynbrook, New York, circa 1890–1910.

Wanamaker
H.C. Wanamaker, carriage maker; Stockton, NJ, circa 1880–1910.

Wanamaker
John Wanamaker, carriage maker, New York, NY, circa 1890's.

Wanamaker & Arenburg
Blacksmiths and wagon makers; Maysville, Colorado, circa 1881–1890.

Wapakonetta Wheel Co.
Manufacturer of buggy wheels; Wapakonetta, Ohio, circa 1890–1910.

Ward
Charles W. Ward, blacksmith and wheelwright, 2502 Dallas Ave.; Houston, Texas, circa 1900–1910.

Ward
W.H.L. Ward, blacksmith and wheelwright, 10th between Lancaster and Ewing Avenues and Oak Cliff; Dallas, Texas, circa 1891–1900.

Ward Plow Co.
Manufactured farm implements and their Universal Bean Harvester; Batavia, NY, circa 1890–1920.

Ward & Rowland
Blacksmiths and wagon makers; Caldwell, Idaho, circa 1905–1910.

Warden
George J. Warden & Co. of Cleveland, Ohio manufactured carriages, wagons and sleighs, circa 1880–1900.

Warden & Illo
Blacksmiths and wagon makers, se corner Wood and S Houston; Dallas, Texas, circa 1910.

Warder, Bushnell & Glessner Co.
This Springfield, Ohio implement manufacturing company is listed as Warder, Brokaw & Child in the 1850's—building the Champion mower. In the 1860's they are under the name of Warder, Mitchell & Company—building the Marsh harvester. By the 1870's they were building Whiteley's Champion reaper, a design by William N. Whiteley.

Eventually, the firm became known as Warder, Bushnell & Glessner—before their 1902 merger with The International Harvester Co., circa 1850–1902.

International Harvester sold the Champion line of equipment to B.F. Avery Company about 1918.

Ware
Samuel Ware, wagon maker; Philadelphia, PA, circa 1840's–1860.

Ware & Watson
Blacksmiths, 1400 Myrtle Ave.; El Paso, Texas, circa 1910.

Warner Pole & Top Co.
Buggy maker; Cincinnati, Ohio, circa 1880–1910.

Warner
W.M. Warner, carriage and wagon maker; Coyoto, Utah, circa 1884–1890.

Warner & Co.
Established in 1877, this firm manufactured fine carriage lamps. They also offered repair work and nickel and silver plating, 409 Cherry Street; Philadelphia, PA, circa 1877–1910.

Warner (see Riling, Warner & Co.)

Warren
Alex Warren, blacksmith and wagon maker; Alamosa, Colorado, circa 1884–1890.

Warren
The Joseph W. Warren Co., manufacturer of carriages and sleighs; Worcester, MA, circa 1890–1910.

Warren
W.H. Warren, blacksmith and wagon maker; Mackay, Idaho, circa 1905–1910.

Warren (see Paige & Warren)

Warrior Mower Co.
Built horse-drawn farm equipment like the Warrior mower; Little Falls, NY, circa 1870–1880.

Warth
August C. Warth, carriage painters and trimmers, 3107 M; Galveston, Texas, circa 1900–1910.

Wassmuth
A.J. Wassmuth, blacksmith and wagon maker; Greencreek, Idaho, circa 1905–1910.

Waterhouse
C. Waterhouse, wagon maker, 199 J; Sacramento, CA, circa 1853–1865.

Waterhouse & Lester
Manufacturers, agents and dealers in carriages, carts, wagons, hardware, trimmings, tops, umbrellas, wagon and carriage bodies and wheels, 16–22 Beale; San Francisco and Sacramento, CA, circa 1870–1905.

Waterloo Mfg. Co.
Manufactured carriage, buggy and cart bodies for the trade. They also produced a line of road wagon bodies; Waterloo, IN, circa 1880–1900.

Waterloo Threshing Machine Co.
Offered a line of implements and equipment; Waterloo, Iowa, circa 1890–1910.

Waterloo Wagon Co.
Manufactured carriages, sleighs and wagons; Waterloo, New York, circa 1880–1900.

Waterous Engine Works Co.
This St. Paul, MN firm specialized in the construction of smaller and lighter weight steam fire-engines, for sale to the volunteer fire companies in smaller towns and villages, circa 1888–1900.

Their No. 1 engines were known as the "Villiage Steam Fire Engine". They weighed about 1,500 lbs. and sold for about $2,000 in the late 1800's. One of their first machines, built in 1888, met with great praise from Fire Chief Knell of the Perry, Iowa Volunteer Fire Department, where it served for many years.

Watkins & Slaughter
Manufacturer of saddles, harness and saddlery hardware; Terre Haute, Indiana, circa 1858.

Watland (see Ratliff & Watland)

Watson
Oliver Watson, carriage maker; Hatboro, PA, circa 1880–1910.

Watson
P. Watson, wagon maker; Poynette, Wisconsin, circa 1865.

Watson
W.L. Watson, blacksmith and horseshoer, 222 Cedar Springs, Dallas, Texas, circa 1905.

Watson & Cunningham
Blacksmiths and wagon makers; Encampment, Wyoming, circa 1905–1910.

Watson & Williams
Carriage and wagon makers; Austin, Nevada, circa 1884–1890.

Watson (see Ware & Watson)

Wayne Works
Carts and light spring wagons; Richmond, IN, circa 1890–1910.

Weakley
J. Weakley, blacksmith and wheelwright, 280 Live Oak; Dallas, Texas, circa 1891–1900.

Weatherford & Coolidge
Blacksmiths and wheelwrights; manufacturers of carriages, buggies, and phaetons, 102 N. Rusk; Ft. Worth, Texas, circa 1904–1916.

Weaver & Mayer
Carriage and wagon makers; Deming, New Mexico, circa 1884–1890.

Webb
J.A. Webb & Brothers, carriage, wagon, buggy and phaeton dealers; carriage and wagon woodwork, 212–216 E. 6th; Austin, Texas, circa 1887–1901.

Webb Brothers
Blacksmiths, horseshoers, and wagon makers, 162 Lancaster Ave.; Dallas, Texas, circa 1908–1910.

Webb, Taylor & Perry
Carriage, wagon and buggy dealers; carriage and wagon woodwork, 212 214 E. 6th; Austin, Texas, circa 1906–1916.

Weber
F.S. Weber, wagon maker and repair work; Kansas City, Missouri, circa 1860–1880.

Weber
J. Weber, wagon maker; Schenectady, NY, circa 1870–1890.

Weber
Peter Weber, wagon maker; Waukau, Wisconsin, circa 1865.

Weber
Peter Weber, wagon maker; South Osborn, WI, circa 1885.

Weber Wagon Co.
Henry Weber was born in Hockwiller, Germany in 1830, and is said to have traveled to the United States as an indentured servant, for his passage. He worked about three years as an apprentice in a New York wagon factory before moving on to Chicago, where he established one of the nation's largest wagon factories.

They manufactured thousands of vehicles in their 59 years of wagon building. The company advertised that they were makers of the "King of all Farm Wagons".

The firm was established in 1845 and sold out to International Harvester in 1904. I.H.C. continued to build and sell Weber wagons for several more years; Chicago, Illinois, circa 1845–1904.

Weber & Damme Wagon Co.
Wagon makers, 1613 and 1615 N. Broadway; St. Louis, Missouri, circa 1880–1920.

Weber (see Ackerman & Weber)
Weber (see Menick & Weber)
Weber (see Rhody & Weber)
Webster
Charles Webster, blacksmith and wagon maker; Loveland, Colorado, circa 1879–1880.

Webster Wagon Co.
Manufacturer of farm, freight, lumber and plantation wagons; Moundsville, West Virginia, circa 1880–1910.

Webster (see Stokey & Webster)

Weddle
H. Weddle, blacksmith and wheelwright; Sherman, Texas, circa 1893–1900.

Weekes
S.C. Weekes, blacksmith and wagon maker; Irwin, Idaho, circa 1905–1910.

Weick
P. Weick's Sons, wagon makers, 405 West 36th; New York, NY, circa 1899.

Weidel
Joseph Weidel, wagon maker; Terre Haute, Indiana, circa 1858.

Weidensaul
H.A. Weidensaul, carriage and wagon maker; Lewisburg, PA, circa 1840–1860.

Weidner & Co.
Blacksmith and wagon maker; Alamosa, Colorado, circa 1880's.

Weir
James Weir, early coach and carriage maker; Staten Island, NY, circa 1800–1840.

Weir
John Weir, wagon maker; Kenosha, Wisconsin, circa 1865.

Weir Plow Co.
This early Monmouth, Illinois manufacturer of farm implements, circa 1860–1920, offered a number of styles, including the Iron Beam Spring Cultivator and their well-known Wild Irishman Sulky plow, in the 1890's.

Weir operated into the early 1900's, with spare parts still available in the 1920's from Martin & Kennedy of Kansas City, MO.

Weirick
Charles & Robert Weirick, buggy makers, 531 Green street (rear) circa 1870–1889 and 433 Green street (rear); Mifflinburg, PA, circa 1889–.

Robert Weirick was also a coach trimmer and top maker.

Weirick
John Weirick started out as a harness maker, before turning to the carriage and buggy building trade; Mifflinburg, PA, circa 1880's.

Weirick
Uriah Weirick built wagons and carriages until he lost his shop to fire, in 1867; Laurelton, PA, circa 1850's–1867.

Welbasky
W. Welbasky, carriage trimmer, 194 K street; Sacramento, CA, circa 1855–1875.

Welbers & Newman
Blacksmiths and wheelwrights, 108 Congress Ave.; Austin, Texas, circa 1895–1905.

Welch
A.S. Welch, dealer in piano box top buggies, platform and spring wagons; Mt. Union, PA, circa 1890–1910.

Welch
H.C. Welch, blacksmith and wagon maker; Colorado Springs, Colorado, circa 1879–1886.

Wells
Joseph Wells, blacksmith and wagon maker; Monitor, Idaho, circa 1905–1910.

Wells (see Shaw-Wells Co.)
Welniack
Michael Welniack & Son, carriage and wagon makers; Algoma, Wisconsin, circa 1890–1910.

Wendell
Robert A. Wendell, buggy maker, 620 Chestnut street (rear) circa 1868–1880 and north fifth and Mill streets (body shop); Mifflinburg, PA, circa 1880–1894.

Wenke
Franz Wenke, government blacksmith, wagon maker and repairer; Fort Wingate, New Mexico. Military reservation in McKinley County, NM, circa 1900–1910.

Werlein
Jacob Werlein, wagon maker, 514 West 15th; New York, NY, circa 1899.

Werner Wagon Works
Don Werner, wheelwright, wainwright and wagon maker; Horton, Kansas. Don is one of a few craftsmen today who still make covered wagons. He is a great example of the authentic work being done in response to the growing interest in the history of horse drawn vehicles.

Don also spends a lot of time repairing and restoring old wagons for other people. Whether it's a buggy, buckboard, box wagon or chuck wagon, his countless hours of research into various types of 1800's vehicles make certain everything he builds or repairs is historically correct. (If it's a Werner, its right). Don likes to hitch up his mules and test drive every wagon before it leaves his shop.

He, and wife Connie, have traveled in their wagons across the country giving demonstrations for schools and museums, including a trip on the Oregon trail—celebrating the 150th anniversary. While Don puts on a wheelwright demonstration, Connie will display an authentic covered wagon with all the supplies and equipment needed in those early days. (See more on contemporary craftsmen in forthcoming Vol. II).

Wessel
C.L. Wessel, blacksmith and wagon maker; Ashton, Idaho, circa 1905–1910.

West
W.N. West, wagon maker; De Soto, Wisconsin, circa 1865.

Westcott Carriage Co.
Anderson, Indiana, circa 1890–1910.

West End Wagon Co.
Wagon makers, 50 West 67th; New York, NY, circa 1899.

Western Land Roller Co.
Built farm implements, including their popular three-gang roller; Hasting, Nebraska, circa 1900–1940.

Westinghouse Co.
Before moving his company to Schenectady, NY in 1856, George Westinghouse, circa 1835–1925, had been building threshing machines for nearly 20 years.

The company offered their implements into the 1920's.

Westlund (see Karling & Westlund)

Weston
Robert Weston, wagon maker and blacksmith, doing business as Weston & Strode by 1860; Independence, Missouri, circa 1840–1860. (see Jacob Leader).

Weston & Sparks
Blacksmiths and wagon makers, 2109 Polk; San Francisco, California, circa 1882–1890.

Weston & Strode
Wagon makers who also did repair work; Independence, Missouri, circa 1860–1880.

West Tire Setter Co.
Rochester, New York, NY, circa 1890–1910.

Wheeler
L. Wheeler, wagon maker in Everett, Colorado, a small quartz mill town settled in 1879 on Lake Creek in Lake County, circa 1882–1889.

Wheeling Axle Co.
Wheeling, W. Virginia, circa 1890–1910.

Whiffen (see Seaton & Whiffen)

Whitaker
G.H. Whitaker, blacksmith and wheelwright, 211 Lancaster Ave. between 9th and 10th; Dallas, Texas, circa 1897–1905.

Whitaker
William Whitaker of Hurley & Whitaker, blacksmith and wagon maker, corner K and 8th; Sacramento, CA, circa 1853–1864.

Whitaker (see Hurley & Whitaker)

Whitcomb
J.B. Whitcomb, wagon maker; Beloit, Wisconsin, circa 1865.

White
Charles White, blacksmith; Sacramento, CA, circa 1853–1865.

White
Edward F. White of Smith & White, coach, sign and ornamental painters and coach trimmers, 115 K street, between 4th and 5th; Sacramento, CA, circa 1853–1865.

White
E.F. White, of White & Mallard, carriage painter, 4th street between I and J; Sacramento, CA, circa 1855–1875.

White
George White & Sons Co. Ltd. manufactured horse-drawn farm equipment, implements and steam traction engines; London, Ontario, Canada, circa 1870–1930.

White
Hiram White made wagons and sleighs; Pompey, NY, circa 1850's.

White
J.V. White, dealers in carriages, buggies and phaetons, 217 Tremont; Galveston, Texas, circa 1886–1896.

White
Peter White manufactured wagons and horse-drawn trucks, 514 West 37th; New York, NY, circa 1899.

White
Samual J. White was a builder of sleighs and buggies; Wilmington, Delaware, circa 1880–1900.

White
Thomas J. White of New York, NY. This wood carver worked in the shops of Sameul Robb and worked on many circus wagons, circa 1860–1890.

White Bros.
Carriage and wagon materials, 13–15 Main; San Francisco, California, circa 1882–1894.

White Manufacturing Co.
The White firm built lamps of every description, for all styles of vehicles; Bridgeport, CT, circa 1880–1910.

White Star Buggy Co.
Buggy maker; Atlanta, Georgia. (see Atlanta Buggy Co.), circa 1890–1914.

White & Beaghen
Blacksmiths and horseshoers, 101 Collin; Dallas, Texas, circa 1905.

White & Mallard
Carriage painters, 4th street between I and J; Sacramento, CA, circa 1855–1875.

White (see Easton & White)

White (see Joubert & White)

White (see Smith & White)

White (see Wise & White)

Whitesides & McInturff
Blacksmiths and wheelwrights, 1309 N. Main; N. Ft. Worth, Texas, circa 1904–1905.

Whitlow
Dabney A. Whitlow, blacksmith and wheelwright, 311 W. Belknap; Ft.Worth, Texas, circa 1904–1912.

Whitman Agricultural Co.
Built a variety of farm implements, including a special seeder mounted onto the wagon floor box; St. Louis, MO, circa 1880's–1920's.

Whitmire
J.D. Whitmire, blacksmith and wagon maker; Clearmont, Wyoming, circa 1902–1910.

Whitney Carriage Works
Manufactured wagons and light carriages, Basin Court; Syracuse, NY, circa 1899.

Whittet & Boyd
Blacksmiths and wheelwrights, 151 S. Lamar; Dallas, Texas, circa 1900–1910.

Whittet & Hatley
Blacksmiths and wagon makers, 239 Young; Dallas, Texas, circa 1910.

Whittier (see Campbell & Whittier)

Wiard Plow Co.
This Batavia, NY firm was founded by George Wiard, the son of a plow maker, circa 1870's–1940's.

Wiard's company offered a wide variety of tillage implements and farm equipment. One of the popular designs by George Wiard was their Reversible Sulky Plow. George died in 1913.

George's nephew, Harry Wiard was also in the plow business, as part owner of the Syracuse Chilled Plow Company.

Parts for their equipment were still available through 1940.

Wiborg (see Ault & Wiborg Co.)

Wicker & Janney
Wagon makers; Muscoda, Wisconsin, circa 1865.

Wickersham
T. Wickersham, wagon makers; Mars, Wisconsin, circa 1885.

Wigmore
John Wigmore & Son, carriage and wagon materials, 129–147 Spear; San Francisco, California, circa 1888–1894.

Wilber, Stevens & Co.
Under the patents of J.D. Wilber, this company manufactured implements like their Eureka mower; Poughkeepsie, NY, circa 1860–1880.

Wilburn
William Wilburn, wagon yards, ne corner East 8th and Calhoun; Ft. Worth, Texas, circa 1896–1902.

Wilcock
John Wilcock, blacksmith and wagon maker, 410 west 17th; Cheyenne, Wyoming, circa 1902–1908.

Wilcox & Son
Blacksmiths and wagon makers, 410 west 17th; Cheyenne, Wyoming, circa 1903–1910.

Wilcox Mfg. Co.
Manufactured fifth wheels and accessories, including its Prong King Bolt Fifth Wheels and the King Bolt Yokes and Braces; Mechanicsburg, PA, and Howard, PA, circa 1880–1910.

Wilcox & Harwood
Blacksmiths and horseshoers, 534–536 N Haskell Ave.; Dallas, Texas, circa 1908–1912.

Wilder & Palm
Manufactured a variety of farm implements and wagons. Much of the machinery used to build the vehicles in this factory was propelled by a windmill; Lawrence, Kansas, circa 1860–1880.

Wilder-Strong Implement Co.
Built farm equipment; Monroe, Wisconsin, circa 1900–1910.

Wiley
William U. Wiley, carriage maker, also advertised a variety of vehicles for sale, including "Ambulances for the plains"; Kansas City, Missouri, circa 1850–1880.

Wilheinus
George Wilheinus, carriage maker; Westmoreland, NY, circa 1850's.

Wilkinson & McCain
Blacksmiths and wheelwrights, Rosen Heights; Ft.Worth, Texas, circa 1904–1910.

Will
Lewis Will, wagon and buggy maker was born in 1817. Opened his own shop near Forestville in 1838 and later in the vicinity of Timberville, Virginia. He died in 1895 at the age of 78.

Willett
W.S. Willett, carriage and wagon maker; Baxter Springs, Nevada, circa 1884–1890.

Willey Co.
Paint; New York, NY, circa 1890–1910.

Williams
B.M. Williams, wagon maker; Boulder, Colorado, circa 1877–1884.

Williams
Charles Williams, blacksmith and wagon maker; Hyattville, Wyoming, circa 1902–1908.

Williams
D.D. Williams manufactured light carriages, 116 John; Rome, NY, circa 1899.

Williams
D.T. Williams, carriage and wagon makers; Milwaukee, Wisconsin, circa 1865.

Williams
Hillary A. Williams, carriages, wagons, buggies and phaetons, 213–315 W. 2nd; Ft.Worth, Texas, circa 1904–1908.

Williams
Julius Williams, blacksmith and wheelwright, 410 Grand Ave.; Paris, Texas, circa 1891–1900.

Williams
W.H. Williams, wagon maker; Brodhead, Wisconsin, circa 1865.

Williams & Son
Carriage painters and trimmers, 108 Commerce; Dallas, Texas, circa 1897–1903.

Williams & Harlis
Blacksmiths and wagon makers; Rock Springs, WY, circa 1901–1902.

Williams & Smith
Carriages, buggies and wagons, 116 S. Rusk Ave.; Denison, Texas, circa 1899–1910.

Williams (see Edwards & Williams)

Williams (see Healey, Williams & Co.)

Williams (see Morgan & Williams)

Williams (see Watson & Williams)

Williamson
Samuel Williamson, blacksmith and carriage maker, carriage painter and trimmer, 619 E. Overland; El Paso, Texas, circa 1911–1914

Willie & Hein
Carriage and wagon makers; Staten Island, NY, circa 1870–1900.

Willingham
J.P. Willingham, blacksmith and wheelwright, 520–524 Main, also 541 Main; Dallas, Texas, circa 1891–1908.

Willing (see Kennedy, Willing & Co.)

Willis
A.J. Willis, blacksmith and wagon maker, Lancaster Ave. and 1 S. Zang's Blvd.; Dallas, Texas, circa 1910.

Willis
Henry M. Willis was born in 1848 near Hempstead, New York. He started out in the livery business, and later sold agricultural implements.

In 1890, Willis applied for, and was later granted, a patent for his invention of the East Williston Cart. This popular vehicle advertised as a cart for the people" was in use for many years for both pleasure and competitive driving, circa 1890–1910.

Willis
J.F. Willis, blacksmith and wheelwright; Sherman, Texas, circa 1893–1900.

Willis (see Roberts, Willis, Taylor Co.)

Willoughby
Owen Willoughby Co. manufactured light carriages, 86 Genesee; Utica, NY, circa 1899.

Willoughby
Mr. Willoughby designed and built carriages, coaches and sleighs; Rome NY, circa 1880's–1910.

Wills
Leven P. Wills, wagon maker; Jackson County, Missouri, circa 1850–1860.

Wilmans
F.A. Wilmans, blacksmith and wheelwright, 166 S. Harwood, Dallas, Texas, circa 1891–1900.

Wilson
A. Wilson, wagon maker; Janesville, WI, circa 1865–1879.

Wilson
Bert Wilson, carriage lines, 109 W. 4th; Amarillo, Texas, circa 1906–1912.

Wilson
E.S. Wilson, blacksmith and wagon maker; Dubois, Wyoming, circa 1900–1905.

Wilson
James F. Wilson, carriage trimmers and painters, 503 Preston; Houston, Texas, circa 1900–1910.

Wilson
James M. Wilson, carriage and wagon maker, 485 Larimer; Denver, Colorado, circa 1884–1890.

Wilson
James Wilson, carriage and wagon dealers, Denver, Colorado, circa 1884–1890.

Wilson
J. Wilson, carriage maker; Whitestown, NY, circa 1850's.

Wilson
Samuel Wilson, buggy maker, southwest corner of Market and third street (rear); Mifflinburg, PA, circa 1876–1886.

Wilson Brothers
Wilson, SC, circa 1890–1910.

Wilson Buggy Co.
Wilson, SC, circa 1890–1910.

Wilson Carriage Co.
C.R. and J.C. Wilson produced a full line of carriages, including a few commercial vehicles and a number of sleighs and cutters; Detroit, Michigan, circa 1880's–1910.

Wilson, Childs & Co.
David G. Wilson, a wheelwright and J. Childs, a blacksmith, formed a partnership in 1829, at 305 N. 3rd Street in Philadelphia, PA. They built the famed Wilson Wagon used by the Army in the west. This 6-mule wagon was designed by Major George H. Grosman, of the U.S. Army Quartermaster Dept., and was manufactured with an unmatched uniformity in all its parts.

By the 1860's, August Staacke of San Antonio, Texas offered the Chihuahua Wagon. This large, four thousand pound wagon, with iron axles, was built in the Wilson, Childs & Co. factory; for use on the rocky and mountainous roads of west Texas and Mexico.

The Childs factory was known for an impresseve feat accomplished in 1857, in conjunction with the Simons, Coleman & Co., also of Philadelphia. They produced 550 wagons in about five weeks for the U.S. Army's Utah Expedition.

The firm also sold wagons through its sales agents in other states—like Messrs. Barnwell & Fitler of Mobile, Alabama and their agents at 24 Perdido Street, New Orleans, LA, circa 1829–1880's.

Wilson & Mummer
Carriages and wagons; Denver, Colorado, circa 1882–1890.

Wilson & Shacker
Blacksmiths, 615 W San Antonio; El Paso, Texas, circa 1918.

Wilson (see Cann & Wilson)

Wilson (see Keyes & Wilson)

Winans, Pratt & Co.
Manufacturers of buggies, surries and road wagons. They also built a line of road, speeding and pleasure carts; 49 to 59 Pitcher St., Kalamazoo, MI, circa 1870–1910.

Winchell
William Winchell made sleighs and wagons; Lysander, NY, circa 1850's.

Winchester & Mulligan
Blacksmiths and wagon makers; Caldwell, Idaho, circa 1905–1910.

Windsor
Francis E. Windsor, blacksmith; wagon and carriage maker; Marion, Iowa, circa 1855–1871.

Francis was born in Devonshire, England in 1832. When he was just two years old, his family arrived in Canada.

Windsor
H.C. Windsor, blacksmith and livery; Marion, Iowa, circa 1861–1876.

Windsor purchased the old Hoppough livery stable building in 1866. It was fitted up for a blacksmith andmachine shop.

Wingett & Fisher
Carriage makers; South Pueblo, Colorado, circa 1882–1890.

Winkler Bros.
Manufactured carriages, wagons and commercial delivery wagons; South Bend, IN, circa 1890–1910.

Winkler Bros.
Blacksmiths and wagon makers; Council, Idaho, circa 1905–1910.

Winner
E.B. Winner, wagon maker with Hall & Fox, corner 8th and K; Sacramento, CA, circa 1853–1865.

Winner Wagon Co.
Buggy manufacturer; Cincinnati, Ohio, circa 1880–1910.

Winters (see Burroughs, Winters & Co.)

Wisconsin Carriage Top Co.
Successors to Lawrence Carriage Top Company, they manufactured a variety of tops for all styles of carriages and buggies; and a full line of carriages for wholesale or retail including their open panel-seat Stanhope; Janesville, Wisconsin, circa 1880's–1915.

Wisconsin Wagon Company
This firm specialized in the manufacture of carriages and wagons for use in the hotel and livery trade. Makers of the Madison six-passenger cut-under vis-à-vis and other fine commercial vehicles; Madison, WI, circa 1880's–1915.

Wise
Jacob Wise, coach and wagon maker; Pittsburgh and Allegheny, PA, circa 1840–1870.

Wise
Philip S. Wise Wagon Factory, manufacturers of farm and express wagons, carts and wheelbarrows, Water and Cross Streets; New Market, Virginia, circa 1880–1900.

Wise
W.D. Wise & Co., carriages, wagons and buggies, sw corner of Chihuahua and 2nd; El Paso, Texas, circa 1910–1920.

Wise & White
Carriages, wagons and buggies, sw corner of 2nd and Chihuahua; El Paso, Texas, circa 1905.

Wiser
John B. Wiser, carriage and wagon maker; Madison, Wisconsin, circa 1865–1879.

Wistrand
Wistrand Manufacturing Co., built farm implements and the Blue Star corn planter; Galva, Illinois, circa 1905–1910.

Witt
J.C. Witt, blacksmith and wheelwright, 220 N. Flores; San Antonio, Texas, circa 1897–1903.

Witt (see McGoldrick & Witt)

Witter & Ball
Amos Witter learned wagon making in Connecticut, while Francis Ball learned his trade in Springfield, MA. They established their carriage and wagon making shop on Main street in Milton, PA around 1822. Here they manufactured wagons, carriages, gigs, barouches, sulkeys and dearborns.

They were also advertised as Agents of Blair and Company, selling their patented Elastic Spring Cushions, Seats and Footboards, circa 1822–1840.

Witter (see Wall, Witter & Co.)

Witwer
J.S. Witwer, carriages, buggies and wagons, 275 Elm; Dallas, Texas, circa 1891–1899.

Woderdalek
Joseph Woderdalek, carriage and wagon dealer; Algoma, Wisconsin, circa 1890–1910.

Woeber Brothers Carriages
Manufacturer of carriages andwagons, 230 and 242 11th St.;Denver, Colorado, circa 1877–1890—also 3rd

Wheels Across America 157

and Harrison St.; Davenport, Iowa, circa 1880.

Wolcken
C.M. Wolcken, blacksmith and nwheelwright; also carriage and wagon manufacturer, 318 South Flores; San Antonio, Texas, circa 1887–1890's.

Wolf
Christian Wolf, blacksmith, wheelwright, horseshoer; wagon maker, and carriage and wagon repairing, 604 East Ave, and 504 Trinity; Austin, Texas, circa 1895–1901.

Wolf
G. Wolf, wagon maker; Middleton, Wisconsin circa 1879–1903.

Wolf
Henry Gast Wolf was a wholesale dealer in carriages, buggies and wagon parts; Philadelphia, PA, circa 1850–1880's.

Wolf
Hugo G. Wolf, carriage painters and trimmers, 1711 Lavaca; Austin, Texas, circa 1910–1915.

Wolf
John H. Wolf, wagon maker; St. Cloud, Wisconsin, circa 1879–1903.

Wolf (see Kruger & Wolf)

Wolff & Sons
Buggy manufacturer; Cincinnati, Ohio, circa 1880–1910.

Wolfington
Alex Wolfington, carriage maker, 12–14 N. 10th street; Philadelphia, PA, circa 1880–1910.

Wolfram
August E. Wolfram, carriage and wagon dealer and representative; Appleton, WI, circa 1890–1910.

Wolfram
F.A. Wolfram, carriage and wagon maker, 125 Live Oak; Dallas, Texas, circa 1908–1912.

Wolfram (see Chandler & Wolfram)

Wollman & Co.
A.G. Wollman, carriage painters and trimmers, 362 Commerce; Dallas, Texas, circa 1898–1902.

Wollman & McMellon
Carriage painters and trimmers, 362 Commerce; Dallas, Texas, circa 1897–1906.

Wolter
B.C. Wolter, carriage and wagon dealer and representative; Appleton, Wisconsin, circa 1890–1910.

Womack & Miller
Blacksmiths and wagon makers; Emmett, Idaho, circa 1905–1910.

Wood
D.P. Wood, wagon maker; Warrenton, VA, circa 1880–1910.

Wood
George L. Wood & Son, was established in 1853. This firm specialized in the manufacture of coach and car varnishes, supplying carriage painters throughout the region.

An 1891 advertisement reads "Our varnishes are reliable, uniform, brilliant and durable in every instance"; Long Island, NY, circa 1853–1910.

Wood
Walter A. Wood Mowing & Reaping Machine Co. started building farm implements as early as 1850, growing to offer a variety of equipment, including the New Century Grain Binder.

Mr. Wood died in 1892, but the company continued on for many years and in the 1920's parts were still available through Hoosick Falls Implement Co.; Hoosick Falls, N.Y, circa 1850–1920's.

Wood
William Anson Wood built the Eagle mower and other implements; Albany, NY, circa 1875–1890.

Wood
William Wood manufactured wagons and other horse drawn vehicles that they sold throughout the U.S. and a number of foreign countries: Philadelphia, PA, circa 1840's–1860.

Wood Bros.
Manufactured carriages, 74 Cortland Alley; New York, NY, circa 1850's–1870's.

Wood Bros. Co.
Carriage and wagon manufacturing company, 740 Broadway, New York, NY, circa 1870–1890.

Wood Bros. Threshing Co.
F.J. and R.L. Wood started building implements as early as the 1890's. They moved to Des Moines around 1899 and soon after, the company incorporated as Wood Bros. Steel Self Feeder Co.; Des Moines, Iowa, circa 1890–1930.

Wood & Turner
Blacksmiths and wheelwrights, 713 Rusk; Ft.Worth, Texas, circa 1905–1910.

Wood & Wood
Carriages, wagons, buggies and phaetons dealers, 401–403 Houston; Ft. Worth, Texas, circa 1904–1906.

Wood (see Frost & Wood)

Woodburn & Scott
Manufactured wheels, hubs, spokes and rims, including the Sarven Patent Wheel; St. Louis, Missouri, circa 1840–1900.

Woodcock (see Blankenship & Woodcock)

Woodhall
Carriage and wagon maker; Dayton, Ohio, circa 1880's–1910.

Woodhull Carriage Co.
L. & Morris Woodhull built carriages, buggies and sleighs; Dayton, Ohio, circa 1878–1922.

Woodhull's son, James started working in his father's carriage company at the age of 14. He later operated the business under his name.

Woodside (see Osman & Woodside)

Woodson
A.W. Woodson, blacksmith and wheelwright, 700 N. Jefferson; Paris, Texas, circa 1891–1900.

Woodward
D.J. Woodward, carriages and wagons, 117–121 Main Ave.; San Antonio, Texas, circa 1897–1902.

Woodward & Co.
Carriage and wagon maker, 221 W. Commerce; Houston, Texas, circa 1900–1905.

Woodworth
A. Woodworth of Leavenwoth, Kansas was an agent and wagon dealer who owned and operated the Great Western Wagon Depot, offering numerous styles and types of wagons—complete with harness for horse or mule.

The company was known for supplying equipment for use on freight lines headed west.

Most of the Woodworth inventory was that of the so called "Jackson Wagons"—meaning they were manufactured in Jackson, Michigan. (see Austin & Tomlinson), circa 1860's–1890's.

Wooley
E.L. Wooley, wagon maker; Boonville, NY, circa 1899.

Woolsey
C.A. Woolsey's Paint & Color Co. manufactured fine coach and carriage colors and offered a variety of varnishes, stripping and artist tools of the trade; Jersey City, NJ, circa 1880–1910.

Worden & Smith
Blacksmiths, horseshoers and wheelwrights, corner of Houston and Elm, also 113 N. Houston; Dallas, Texas, circa 1886–1892.

Work
A.J. Work & Co., wagon makers; Berlin, Wisconsin, circa 1865–1879.

Works
Edwin A. Works manufactured wagons, carriages and sleighs; Manlins, NY, circa 1850's.

Worlaumont (see Brennan & Worlaumont)

Worshel
Peter Worshel, carriage and wagon maker; Salina, NY, circa 1850's.

Worthen & Co.
H.A. Worthen & Co. manufactured sleighs and carriages; Dover, New Hampshire, circa 1880–1900.

Woy & Scott
Agents for the "Old Reliable" Schuttler wagon, and dealers in agricultural implements; Clinton, Illinois, circa 1870–1910.

Wren Buggy Co.
Norfolk, VA, circa 1890–1910.

Wright
Frank Wright, carriage and wagon dealer and representative; Appleton, WI, circa 1890–1910.

Wright
O.P. Wright & Co. offered a variety of vehicles, including coaches, carriages and a line of commercial styles. The Wright company was also known as one of the leading sleigh manufactures, producing nearly 100,000 before 1900; Nyack, NY, circa 1880's–1910.

Wright, Campbell & Co.
Carriage and wagon maker; Greeley, CO, circa 1879–1880's.

Wright (see Hills Bros. & Wright)

Wroe
W.T. Wroe & Sons, carriage, buggy and wagon dealers, 421–423 Congress and 117 E. 5th; Austin, Texas, circa 1909–1911.

Wuest
F & C Wuest carriage and buggy manufacturer; Cincinnati, Ohio, circa 1880–1910.

Wuest (see Hoepfner & Wuest)

Wurster (see Kolinsky & Wurster)

Wyatt
J.B. Wyatt, blacksmith and wagon maker, 760–762 S Ervay; Dallas, Texas, circa 1910.

Wyland (see Corrigall & Wyland)

Wyman
M.E. Wyman, blacksmith and wagon maker; Georgetown, Colorado, circa 1880.

Wyman (see Andrews & Wyman)

Wyoming Hardware Co.
Dealer in carriages and other vehicles, 310 west 17th; Cheyenne, Wyoming, circa 1900–1905.

Yarber & Son
Blacksmiths, horseshoers and wheelwrights, ne corner Main and Ervay; Dallas, Texas, circa 1886–1890.

Yates
Frank B. Yates, blacksmith and wheelwright, 475 Fannin; Beaumont, Texas, circa 1906–1911, and 225 East Buford; Beaumont, Texas, circa 1910–1915.

Yeaman (see Leuty & Yeaman)

Yegen Brothers
This Billings, MT firm advertised in the 1890's as Montana's largest department store.

The Yegen brothers offered everything needed to outfit the farmer, rancher, or cowboy. This included a full line of wagons, buggies and agricultural implements from manufacturers around the country, circa 1870–1920.

York Carriage Company
Carriage maker; York, PA, circa 1890–1910.

York Wagon Gear Company
York, PA, circa 1890–1910.

Young
G.H. Young, blacksmith and wagon maker; Fairplay, Colorado, circa 1878–1880's.

Young
Hiram Young established a wagon building shop, in 1851, where he also manufactured ox yokes. Young was a former slave. He purchased his freedom in 1847 and first settled

in Liberty—later moving on to Independence, Missouri in 1850. Here he worked as a carpenter for a brief time before opening his wagon and ox yoke business.

Young took on another former slave, Dan Smith, as a partner—operating as Young & Smith, circa 1854–1855. Within two years this company dissolved.

Hiram Young continued building a very successful business, supplying freighters, government contracts, and others.

By 1860, Young employed 25 men, producing six thousand yokes and three hundred wagons per year.

In December of 1861, Young relocated to Leavenworth, Kansas. He built wagons for the nearby military post, before retiring to Independence, Missouri in 1868. Most of his business was in the manufacture of ox yokes, circa 1851–1870's.

Young
James Young made wagons and sleighs; Manlius, NY, circa 1859.

Young
John Young, wagon maker, L, between 8th and 9th; Sacramento, CA, circa 1853–1865.

Young
W.F. Young, blacksmith, horseshoer and wagon maker, 556 Main; Dallas, Texas, circa 1908–1910.

Young Wagon Works
Carriage and wagon makers; Del Norte, CO, circa 1877–1882.

Young (see McCabe, Young & Co.)

Youngstown Carriage & Wagon Co.
Youngstown, Ohio, circa 1890–1910.

Zane & Richardson
Dealers in agricultural implements; Basin, WY, circa 1900–1910.

Zanesville Gear Wood Co.
Carriage manufacturers; Zanesville, OH, circa 1890–1910.

Zartman
William Zartmen & Co., manufacturer of road machines and all kinds of vehicles, including a large stock of buggies, phaetons, etc. at prices to suit; Petaluma, California, circa 1888–1894.

Zeckendorf & Co.
Louis Zeckendorf, 33 & 34 Thomas St., New York, and Albert Steinfeld, Tucson, Arizona; dealers in general merchandise. They were sole agents for Anheuser beer, and Fish Brothers' wagons; miners supplies and mining goods a specialty; Tucson, Arizona, circa 1882–1885.

Zeibig
August Zeibig, blacksmith and wagon maker; Oriental City, Colorado, (mining camp in Saguache County 20 miles ne of Saguache) circa 1881–1887.

Zeller
John M. Zeller, carriage and wagon dealer and representative; Arcadia, WI, circa 1890–1910.

Zeller, Phelps & Swift
Little known company that built farm implements in the late 1800's; Rock Falls, Illinois, circa 1885–1900.

Zellers
Charles S. Zellers, buggy maker; Mifflinburg, PA, circa 1880–1890.

Zellers
I.L. and C.S. Zellers, buggy maker, 267 Market street; Mifflinburg, PA, circa 1868–1870.

Zellers
Isaac Zellers, buggy maker, 216 Market street (rear); Mifflinburg, PA, circa 1869–1881.

Zimm
F. Zimm, carriage and wagon maker; Milwaukee, WI, circa 1865.

Zimmerman
Calvin G. Zimmerman of Seven Points, Rockerfeller Township, PA was a builder of buggies, wagons, sleds and sleighs, circa 1880's–1910.

Zimmerman
F.F. Zimmerman (and Sons—1903), wagon makers; Waupun, Wisconsin, circa 1879–1911.

Zimmerman
Fred Zimmerman, wagon maker; Ripon, Wisconsin, circa 1879–1903.

Zimmerman
Jacob Zimmerman, buggy seat maker, 200 block, north third street; Mifflinburg, PA, circa 1910.

Zimmerman
Samuel Zimmerman, buggy maker; Mifflinburg, PA, circa 1876.

Zirhut
M.C. Zirhut, carriage and wagon makers; a complete line of wagons, carriages and buggies of all kinds in stock. They also did carriage painting and trimming; Albuquerque, New Mexico, circa 1884–1890's.

Zork (see Krakauer, Zork & Moye)

Zufelt
Jerome Zufelt, wagon maker; Sheboygan Falls, WI, circa 1865.

Zumhof & Collins
Blacksmiths and wagon makers; Moscow, Idaho, circa 1905–1910.

Zwick, Greenwald & Co., Ltd.
Established in 1859, manufactured fine wheels, including wood hub, banded hub, Curtis' patent, Warner, Sarven and Shell band; Dayton, Ohio, circa 1859–1910

Vintage Ad's, Catalogs and Images

The Aaron Kratz "Improved Hay Wagon" Circa 1900. From A Small One Room Blacksmith Shop In The Early 1850's To A Three Story, Fifty Foot Long Factory By 1857, Aaron Kratz Business Soon Reached The $100,000 Annual Income Mark, Making Him One Of The largest Employers In The Plumsteadville, Pennsylvania Area. (Courtesy Bucks County Historical Society)

Advertisement Circa 1880's (Courtesy John Hardy Family)

Business Card Circa 1900 (Courtesy John Hardy Family)

Probably Photographed In The 1890's, This Image Shows The Hardy Factory, Located At Main And Market Streets In Staunton, Virginia. Established In 1848 By John M. Hardy, The Business Would Remain At This Location For 81 Years, Until Consumed By Fire December 23, 1929. Hardy's Son Edward Had Worked In The Shop With His Father Since He was 12 Years Old. By 1884 The Senior Hardy Had Made His 17 Year Old Son A Partner, Then Owner After John M. Hardy Died In 1894. *(Courtesy John Hardy Family)*

Posed In This 1905 Photograph Are Seven Of The Many Workers That Contributed To The William Gray & Sons, Sixty One Years Of Success In The Manufacturing Of Carriages And Sleighs, (1855–1916). The Company Switched Their Main Operation To The Production Of Automobiles In 1916. *(Courtesy James Gray, Gray-Dort Motors, William Gray & Sons)*

William Gray & Sons Company Letterhead, Circa 1910. By The Early 1900's They Had Expanded Their Market Beyond The Construction Of Carriages And Sleighs To Include The Production Of Fanning Mills, Kitchen Cabinets, Farm Scales And Automobile Bodies. *(Courtesy James Gray, Gray-Dort Motors, William Gray & Sons)*

Founder, William Gray Sr., Son Robert Gray And Grandson William Gray. *(Courtesy James Gray, Gray-Dort Motors, William Gray & Sons)*

Two Sided Promotional Token From The William Gray & Sons Carriage Company Of Chatham, Ontario, Canada. Circa 1890. *(Courtesy James Gray, Gray-Dort Motors, William Gray & Sons)*

Robert Gray, Posed With The last Buggy Built By His Fathers Company In 1916. 283,456 Carriages, Sleighs And Cutters Were Built Before The Firm Switched Over To The Production Of Automobiles.
(Courtesy James Gray, Gray-Dort Motors, William Gray & Sons)

(Below) The Gray-Dort Offices And Factories in Chatham, Ontario, Canada.

Wheels Across America 165

Sometimes Refereed To As a Storm Buggy, This Winter Vehicle (Circa 1900 Heinzelman Bros. Catalog) Could Be Easily Converted Into A Summer Vehicle By Removing The Doors, Front And Attaching Leather Dash. Their Patented Buggy Design Was So popular With Country Doctors That It was Awarded First Prize At The 1904 St. Louis Worlds Fair. Heinzelman Brothers Carriage Company Belleville, Illinois. *(Image Courtesy Andy Miller Collection)*

Circa 1890's Cut From Minneapolis Harvester Works, Minneapolis, Minnesota. Featuring Their Steel Binder. *(Image Courtesy Andy Miller Collection)*

1897 Annual Booklet From Parlin And Orendorff Company Of Canton, Illinois. Founded By William Parlin In 1842, The Company Quickly Grew Into One Of The Leaders In The Farm Implement Design And Construction Business. International Harvester Acquired Parlin And Orendorff In 1919, But Continued To Sell Their "Canton Clipper Plow" And Other Popular Lines. *(Image Courtesy Andy Miller Collection)*

John Heinzelman, President Of The Heinzelman Brothers Carriage Company In Belleville, Illinois. Circa 1900 *(Image Courtesy Andy Miller Collection)*

Circa 1892 Catalog Cover From The Sullivan Brothers Carriage Company In Rochester, New York. This Firm Was Well Know For Their Large Exhibits At The Dealers' Convention. *(Image Courtesy Andy Miller Collection)*

Circa 1890's Advertisement For The Two Horse Binder By Adriance, Platt & Company Of Poughkeepsie, New York. A Variety Of Farm Implements Was Manufactured By This Firm, Before They Were Bought Out By Moline Plow Company In 1912. *(Image Courtesy Andy Miller Collection)*

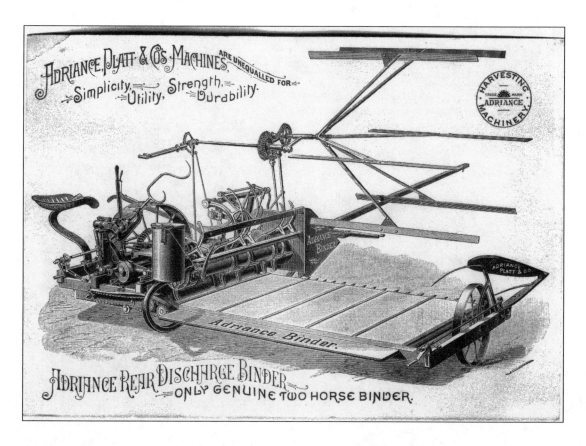

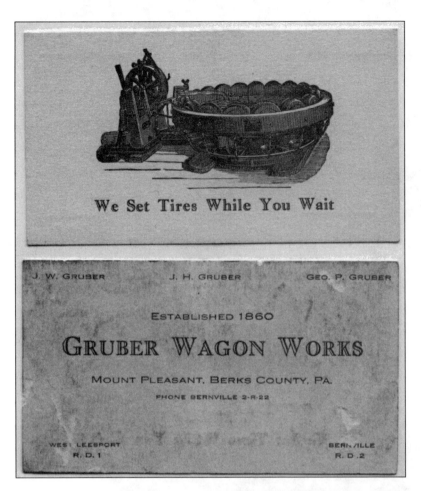

Business Card Featuring The Tire Machine Purchased In 1908 By The Gruber Wagon Works Of Mount Pleasant, Berks County, Pennsylvania. The Card Also Lists Three Of Founder Frank H. Gruber's Five Sons. John W. Gruber–Woodworker And Plant Manager After His Fathers Death In 1898, Jacob H. Gruber–Wheelwright, George P. Gruber–Blacksmith, Not Listed On This Business Card Was Adam Gruber, (Adam Was Killed In A Runaway Horse Accident In 1903) He Operated The Paint Department. *(Image Courtesy Of: Berks County Heritage Center)*

Gruber Employees Posed In This 1890's Photograph Outside Of The Old Wagon Works. This Image Shows What The Factory Looked Like Before The Addition Of The Elevator In 1905. *(Photo Courtesy Of: Berks County Heritage Center)*

Wheels Across America

Pictured Here, The Gruber Wagon Works After It Was Moved To Its New Home At The Berks County Heritage Center Around 1975 or 1976. The Elevator Was Added Circa 1905. *(Image: Courtesy Berks County Heritage Center)*

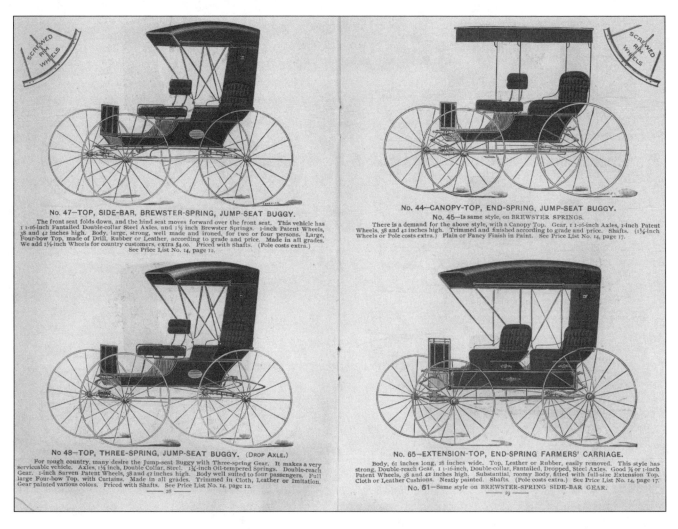

From Their 1899 #14 Catalog, A Sample Of Four Vehicles Available At Wholesale Only Through The American Carriage Company In Cincinnati, Ohio. *(Image Courtesy: Carriage Museum Of America, Bird-In-Hand, PA)*

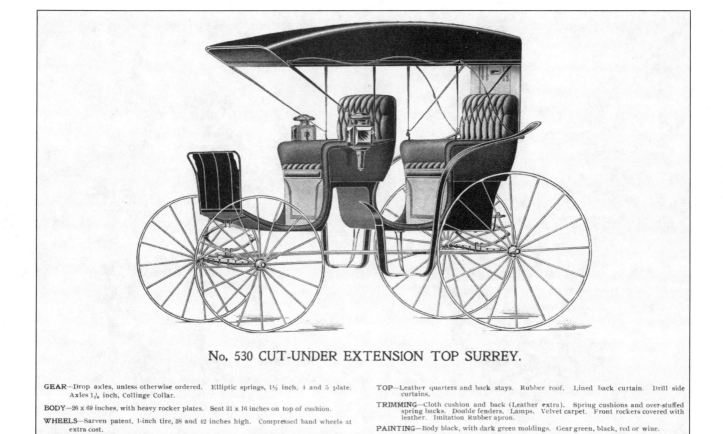

Cincinnati, Ohio Based Acorn Buggy Company, Offered This #530 Cut-Under Extension Top Surrey In Their 1907 Catalog #20. *(Image Courtesy: Carriage Museum Of America, Bird-In-Hand, PA)*

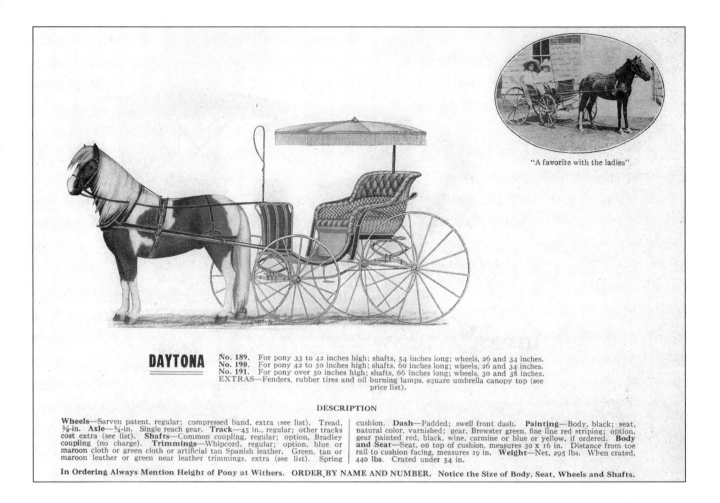

The "Daytona", By Eagle Carriage Company Of Cincinnati, Ohio Circa 1900. Eagle Specialized In Pony Vehicles And Harness. *(Image Courtesy: Carriage Museum Of America, Bird-In-Hand, PA)*

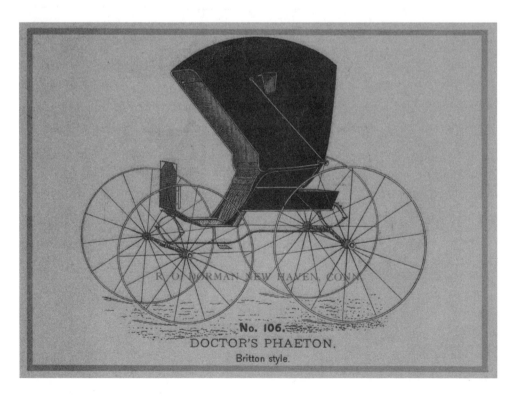

"Britton Style", #106 Doctor's Phaeton, Displayed In The 1877 Catalog Of R.O. Dorman From New Haven, Connecticut. *(Image Courtesy: Carriage Museum Of America, Bird-In-Hand, PA)*

| DURANT-DORT CARRIAGE CO. | No. 158. FANCY TOP BUGGY | FAMOUS BLUE RIBBON LINE |

GEAR — Axles, self oiling, dust proof, with Collinge collar 15-16 inch; beds, hand fitted, cemented and full clipped. Fifth wheel, double perch, full bottom circle, rear kingbolt. Springs, 1¼ x 36 inches, 3-plate front, 4-plate rear; Bailey hangers.

WHEELS — Sarven patent, compressed band or Warner, whalebone AA grade with screwed rims, ¾, ⅞ or 1 inch, 36-40, 39-43 or 41-45.

BODY — Piano, 20, 22 or 24 x 54 inches; concave risers; oval panel irons; 22 inch polished panel spring back.

TRIMMING — All wool brown carriage cloth; diamond center with roll; spring cushion; padded seat ends; red welts and bindings; brass buttons and tacks; fancy velvet carpet, toe and side panel carpets; leather dash; solid board rubber covered boot; apron; antique dash and lazyback rails, hub-bands and prop-nuts.

TOP — Rubber, 3- or 4-bow, lined throughout with all wool brown cloth; stitched back stays; fancy welts; curved joints.

PAINTING — Body fancy rosewood, floral decoration in natural colors. Gear Aztec red with black stripe.

EXTRAS — See price list.

From Catalog #15 Circa 1895, This #158 Fancy Top Buggy, Was Part Of The Famous "Blue Ribbon" Line Of Vehicles Manufactured By Durant-Dort In Their Flint, Michigan Factory. They Had A Capacity Of 35,000 Vehicles In Their Peak Production Years. *(Image Courtesy: Carriage Museum Of America, Bird-In-Hand, PA)*

Front Cover Of The J.J. Deal & Son Catalog #50, Circa 1900. Featuring Their "Quick Deal Wagons" Manufactured At Deal's, Jonesville, Michigan Factory. *(Image Courtesy: Carriage Museum Of America, Bird-In-Hand, PA)*

No. 77 Business Wagon

Body—6 feet 4 inches long, 30 inches wide. Bolted pattern. Wood dash. Drop end gate.
Gear—1⅛ inch, double collar axles. The original *"Quick Deal Wagon,"* built by us for over 20 years.
Wheels—Sarven, 40 and 44 inches. Tire, 1 x ⅞ inch.
Paintings—Body, black. Gear, red and neatly striped.
Trimmings—Imitation leather. Spring cushions and backs. Weight, 400 pounds. Crated, 450 pounds.

#77 Business Wagon Illustrated In The J.J. Deal & Son Catalog #50, Circa 1900. The Deal Business Was Established In Jonesville, Michigan Around 1857. They Advertised As Builders Of The "Quick Deal Wagons." *(Image Courtesy: Carriage Museum Of America, Bird-In-Hand, PA)*

Circa 1889 Catalog Cover From The Elkhart Carriage And Harness Manufacturing Company Of Elkhart, Indiana. They advertised, "We Have No Agents But Sell Direct To You". *(Image Courtesy: Carriage Museum Of America, Bird-In-Hand, PA)*

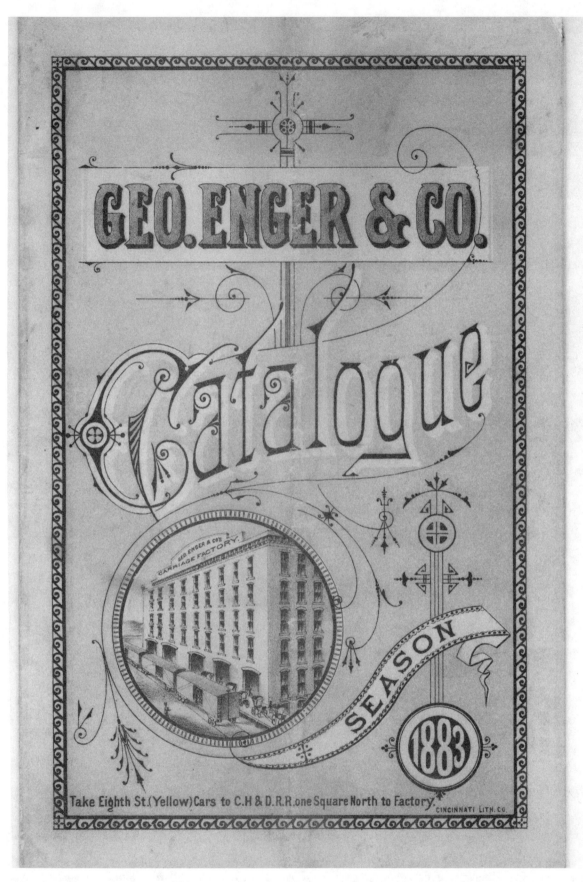

1883 George Enger & Company Catalog, Cincinnati, Ohio. *(Image Courtesy: Carriage Museum Of America, Bird-In-Hand, PA)*

GEO. ENGER & CO.'S CATALOGUE.

No. 60—BASKET PHÆTON.

MADE IN TWO GRADES— A AND AA. TWO OR THREE SPRINGS.

Grade **A**, duck top, heavy fine fringe, leather or cloth trimmed, $\frac{7}{8}$ or 1 inch wheel, inch axle, 1¼ inch springs, lamps, back cross straps, and leather fenders, painted fancy or plain.

Grade **AA**, the best wheels and axles, steel tire, painted and finished in elegant style.

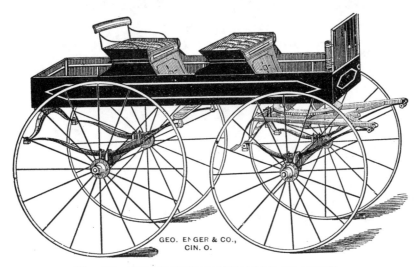

No. 70—PLATFORM SPRING WAGON.

MADE IN TWO GRADES—A AND AA, WITH TWO SEATS. SEATS MOVABLE.

Grade **A**, rubber trimmed, 1⅛ inch axles, 1⅛ inch wheels, painted fancy or plain.
Grade **AA**, leather trimmed, the best wheels and axles, steel tire, painted and finished in fine style.

None but Skilled Mechanics Employed.

This Cut From An 1883 George Enger & Company Catalog, Shows The Wide Range Of Vehicles Built At Their Cincinnati, Ohio Plant. *(Image Courtesy: Carriage Museum Of America, Bird-In-Hand, PA)*

SEIDEL BUGGY COMPANY — RICHMOND, INDIANA.

No. 530. Straight-Sill Surrey, Auto Seats.
HIGH GRADE.

GEAR—1 x 1 1/16-inch axles, long distance; genuine Brewster slotted fifth wheel; reaches second growth hickory, bent and mortised through the head block; springs 36 inches; hickory axle caps, cemented to the axles; rear spring bar select second growth hickory, front bar drop forged steel; track 4 feet 8 inches, 5 feet, 5 feet 1 inch, or 5 feet 2 inches.

BODY—Poplar panels; heavy ash sills; ash frame work; oak step-board; round edge bottom boards.

SEAT—Poplar panels; ash frame work.

WHEELS—7/8 or 1-inch, 40-44 only; select second growth hickory spokes and rims; 6 1/2-inch hub; either Sarven or shell band.

TOP—Either leather quarter, full leather or full rubber; heavy all-wool head lining.

TRIMMINGS—16 oz. all-wool cloth or imitation leather; oil burning lamps; fenders; velvet carpet full length; spring cushion and back. (Leather trimmings extra.)

SHAFTS—Select second growth hickory, high bend; bolted off with bullet-head bolts.

PAINTING—See schedule on page 37.

Circa 1905 Sample Of The Vehicles Available From This Richmond, Indiana Maker. The Heading On This Catalog Page From Seidel Buggy Company Reads, "Quality Our Watchword." *(Image Courtesy: Carriage Museum Of America, Bird-In-Hand, PA)*

DESCRIPTION.

This is one of the finest and most elegant carriages made in the U. S. Handsomely trimmed inside with either green morocco or green cloth; morocco and silver toilet set, and ivory pull to handles. Best crystal plate or beveled-edge glass in windows. The very finest quality of lamps; silver-plated toe board, dickey seat and door handles. Hub bands partly or fully silver-plated, whichever may be desired. The finest quality of English collinge axles; wood hub wheels, made from the best selected second growth stock and all made by hand, under our own care and supervision; oil tempered Swede's steel springs and steel tire.

Size of Springs, 1¾ x 5 plate. Size of Tire, 1⅜ x ½ inches. Size of Axles, 1⅜ inches.

Cut #263, (Circa 1890) Displays One Of Many Elegant, First Class Carriages Constructed In The Ravina, Ohio Shops Of Merts & Riddle. This Firm Established Itself Early On As One Of The Foremost Carriage, Coach & Hearse Builders In The World, Employing Only The Finest Wood Carvers And Craftsmen Of The Day. *(Courtesy: Image Carriage Museum Of America, Bird-In-Hand, PA)*

No. 40—Four Passenger.

A stylish and comfortable vehicle. AXLES, 1⅛ inch, Double Collar, Steel. SPRINGS, 1½ x 36, Five-Leaf Front; two 1¼ x 36, Four-Leaf, back, Berlin Head, Elliptic. WHEELS, 38 x 46 x 1 inches. PERCH, Double. TRIMMING, Cloth or Leather. PAINTING, Black, extra finished.

FOR PRICES WRITE TO THE STANDARD WAGON CO., CINCINNATI, O.

Simply Listed As Their #40-Four Passenger In An 1890's Catalog From The Standard Wagon Company Of Cincinnati, Ohio. Under The Direction Of Company President, Mr. Burrows, The Firm Also Operated Branch Offices In Atlanta, Albany, Chicago And Dallas, Texas. *(Image Courtesy: Carriage Museum Of America, Bird-In-Hand, PA)*

No. 321 Heavy Concord, With Top

AXLES—1 1/16 inch, three-perch Concord gear, made extra strong, all reaches ironed, equalizers front and rear.

SPRINGS—1⅜ inch, five plate, 52½ inches long, double sweep.

WHEELS—1 inch tread, Sarven, riveted rims, 40 and 44 inches high, steel tire.

SHAFTS—Selected hickory. Fernald quick-shift couplers, 36 inch point trimmings, selected shaft straps.

BODY—28 inches wide, 58 inches long, panels extra thick, iron corners, panels ironed on top edge in front. Seat, extra wide. Back 22 inches high, cushion 33 inches long.

PAINTING—Gear, black or red, appropriately striped. Body and seat, black, neatly striped.

TRIMMINGS—Genuine leather. Spring back and spring cushion. Padded seat ends. Full length bottom mat. Solid panel rubber covered boot. Curved dash with line rail made solid in frame, dash braces. Storm apron.

TOP—Four bow, 30 ounce rubber, lined throughout, except side curtains, welted on bows, padded back stays, colored back rubber side curtains. Regular track, 4 feet 8 inches.

Illustrated Here With Top In An 1890 Catalog, The #321 Heavy Concord Was One Of The Most Popular Lines Sold By Noyes Carriage Company From Elkhart, Indiana. Known For Their Sturdy Construction Practices, The Noyes Firm Would Eventually Go Into The Manufacture Of House Trailers. *(Image Courtesy: Carriage Museum Of America, Bird-In-Hand, PA)*

#13 Surrey Body Hung On A Set Of light Bobs, Complete With Either #6 Single Harness Or #66 Double Harness. Displayed In This Circa 1900 Hitchcock Manufacturing Company Catalog From Cortland, New York. *(Image Courtesy: Carriage Museum Of America, Bird-In-Hand, PA)*

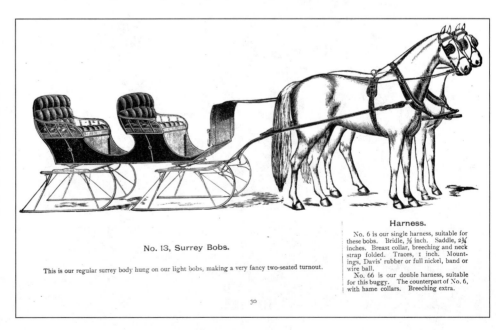

No. 13, Surrey Bobs.

This is our regular surrey body hung on our light bobs, making a very fancy two-seated turnout.

Harness.

No. 6 is our single harness, suitable for these bobs. Bridle, ½ inch. Saddle, 2¾ inches. Breast collar, breeching and neck strap folded. Traces, 1 inch. Mountings, Davis' rubber or full nickel, band or wire ball.

No. 66 is our double harness, suitable for this buggy. The counterpart of No. 6, with hame collars. Breeching extra.

No. 090

Seats—Phaeton style.
Gear—Axles, $1\frac{1}{16}$ inch, double collar; four and five plate springs; Bailey loops.
Wheels—Sarven's patent, 1 inch rims; height 39-43 inches; steel tires.
Top—Leather quarters and stays; rubber roof; heavy back and side curtains; wool faced head lining.
Painting—Body, black, neatly striped. Gear, Brewster green.
Trimmings—Imitation leather; spring backs and cushions; padded seat ends; carpet; storm apron; leather dash; anti-rattlers.
Shafts—Double braced and neatly trimmed.
For further detail and options, see page No. 60.

Buggy #090 From Hercules Buggy Company Of Evansville, Indiana Circa 1890's. They Also Built Vehicles For Sears, Roebuck & Company. The Chicago Based Company Of Sears & Roebuck Also Had Their Buggy Factory In Evansville. *(Image Courtesy: Carriage Museum Of America, Bird-In-Hand, PA)*

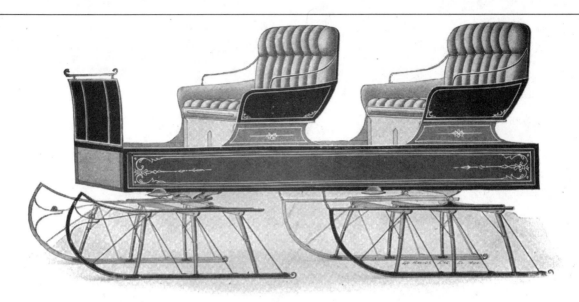

No. 19 Pleasure or Business Sleigh

PAINTING: Body black, neatly ornamented; gear, Brewster green or carmine.
TRIMMINGS: Cloth or whipcord. Panel spring backs and spring cushions.
DASH: Metal, with nickle dash rail.
BODY: 7 feet by 34 inches; drop end gate; 7½ feet by 3 feet, and 8½ feet by 3 feet at added cost.
SHAFTS: Extra strong and well ironed. Shifting bar furnished. Pole to order. Heavy channel steel shoes.
NOTE: Seats wide and roomy.

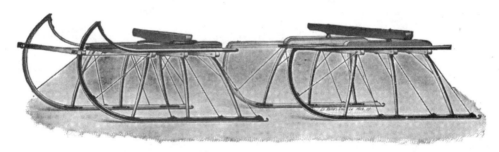

No. 32 Three-Kneed Business or Pleasure Bobs
Capacity, 1,800 Pounds

With bolster and full circle in front and oscillating bolster in the rear. Made of the best of selected hickory throughout, and very strongly ironed and braced. Capacity, 1,800 pounds. Painted red or Brewster green, nicely striped.

Heavy channel shoes. Shafts or pole extra.

Offered Here In A Circa 1905 Catalog From The American Carriage Company Of Kalamazoo, Michigan Are Two Versatile Styles Suitable For Business Or Pleasure. The #19 Sleigh And The #32 Bobs. *(Image Courtesy: Carriage Museum Of America, Bird-In-Hand, PA)*

Employees And Officers Of The Joseph S. Kemp Manufacturing Company In Waterloo, Iowa Circa 1906. Makers Of The 20th Century Spreaders. *(Author's Collection)*

Circa 1906 Catalog Cut Showing The Kemp 20th. Century Spreader From Joseph S. Kemp Manufacturing Company In Waterloo, Iowa. *(Author's Collection)*

Full Side View And Rear Elevation Of The Swab Wagon Company Standard Butcher Wagon, From Their Circa 1897 Catalog. Elizabethville, Pennsylvania. *(Author's Collection)*

Circa 1885 Catalog Cover From Columbus Buggy Company of Columbus, Ohio. *(Courtesy The Long Island Museum Of American Art, History & Carriages)*

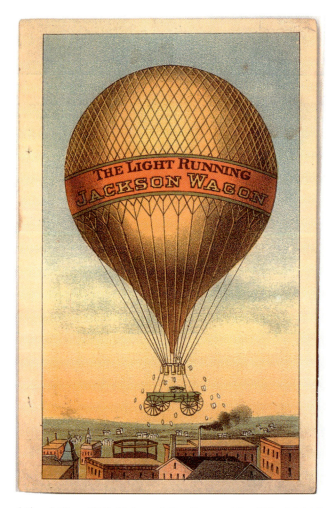

Circa 1880's Business Card From Woy & Scott Of Clinton, Illinois, Another One Of The Countless Agents Selling The Schuttler "Old Reliable" Wagons. *(Courtesy Mark Gardner Collection)*

(Above) Circa 1880, Unique Advertisement For "The Light Running" Jackson Wagon. Jackson, Michigan. *(Courtesy Mark Gardner Collection)*

(Below) Circa 1870's Christoph Hotz Business Card Featuring A Peter Schuttler Wagon. Schuttler Was One Of The First To Utilize Agents, Dealers And Retail Outlets To Ensure The Wide Spread Popularity Of His "Old Reliable" Wagons. *(Courtesy Mark Gardner Collection)*

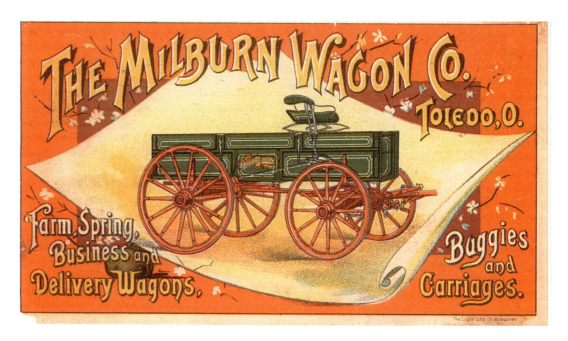

Circa 1880's Business Card From The Milburn Wagon Company Of Toledo, Ohio. They Offered A Full Line Of Carriages And Wagons From A Number Of Branch Office Locations In Several Mid-Western States, Including Their Popular "Milburn Hollow-Axle Farm Wagon."
(Courtesy Mark Gardner Collection)

1879 Catalog Cover Featuring The Birdsell "Steel Skein" Wagon, From The John C. Birdsell Wagon Company Of South Bend, Indiana. Birdsell Moved To South Bend Indiana From West Henrietta, New York 1863. *(Courtesy Mark Gardner Collection)*

Circa 1890's Business Card From The South Bend Wagon Company Of South Bend, Indiana. A Similar South Bend Advertisement Stated, "We Confine Our Entire Factory To The Exclusive Manufacture Of Wagons" *(Courtesy Mark Gardner Collection)*

Circa 1880's Mitchell & Lewis Wagon Company Advertisement. This Well Known Wisconsin Firm Was Originally Established In Racine Around 1832 As Mitchell Wagon Company, They Manufactured Tens Of Thousands Of Wagons Over The Years, Including A Number Of Covered Wagons. They Frequently Advertised Their Vehicles As "Monarch Of The Road." By 1918 Mitchell Wagons Were Being Built By John Deere Company. *(Author's Collection)*

Circa 1897 Catalog Cover From The Swab Wagon Company Of Elizabethville, Pennsylvania. Founded In 1868 By Jonas Swab, Inventor Of The Chilled Box Steel Axle, They Advertised "Wagons That Wear". The Company Is Still In Business Today Constructing Fiberglass Truck Bodies. *(Author's Collection)*

(Above)
Catalog Cover #263 Circa 1905.
From Studebaker Brothers Manufacturing Company Of South Bend, Indiana.
(Author's Collection)

(Right)
Circa 1892 Catalog Cover From Binghamton Wagon Company Of Binghamton, New York. *(Courtesy The Long Island Museum Of American Art, History & Carriages)*

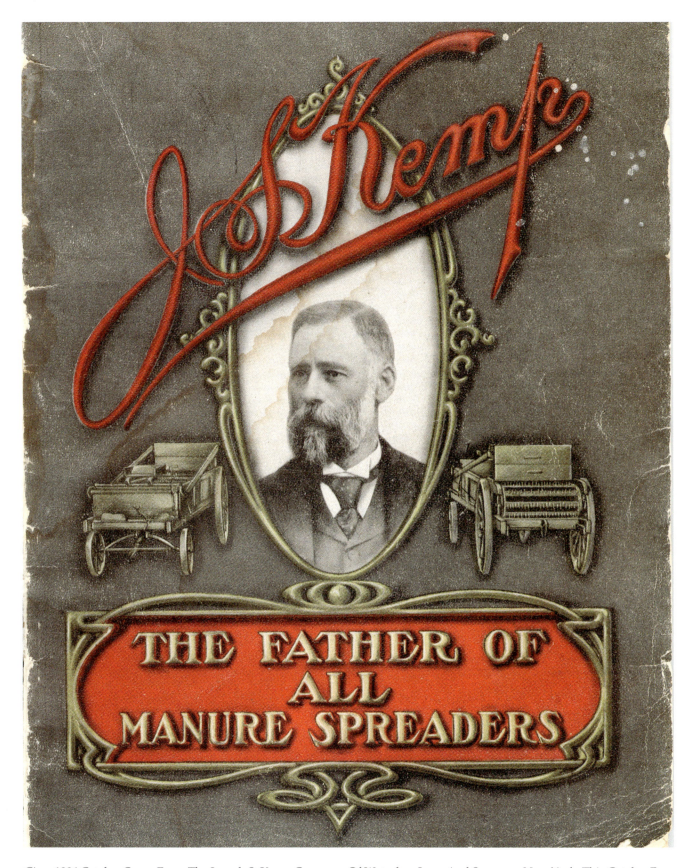

Circa 1906 Catalog Cover From The Joseph S. Kemp Company Of Waterloo, Iowa And Syracuse, New York. This Catalog Features The Kemp 20th. Century Spreader And Other Farm Implements, Kemp Is Credited With What May Have Been The First Practical Spreader Ever Built, In 1875. They Eventually Grew Into The Largest And Strongest Manure Spreader Organizations In The World. *(Author's Collection)*

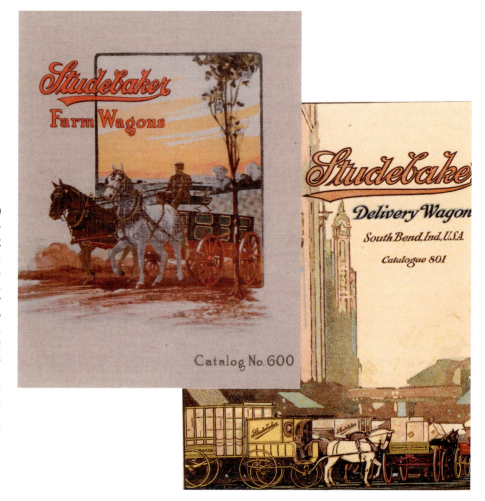

Catalog Covers #600 Circa 1910 And # 801 Circa 1903 From Studebaker Brothers Manufacturing Company Of South Bend, Indiana. These Two Fine Catalogs Contain A Wide Range Of Farm And Delivery Wagons. The Studebaker Family Came To America In 1736 From Germany, And It Is Said That Clement Studebaker Built His First Wagon In 1750. Years Later His Grandsons Would Build A Wagon Empire. By 1876 They Were Producing 30,000 Wagons A Year, By 1893 Their Plant Covered 95 Acres. A Sign In Their Factory Read "We Didn't Invent The Wheel—We Perfected It." *(Author's Collection)*

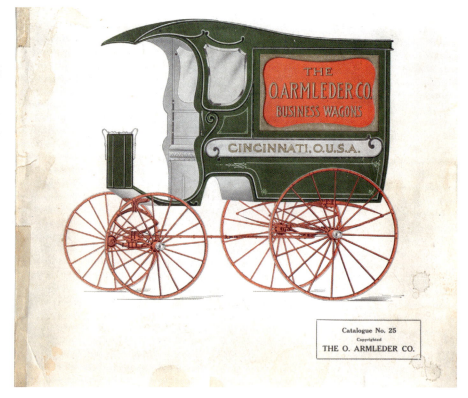

Catalog #25 Cover, Circa 1895 From The Otto Armleder Company Of Cincinnati, Ohio. This Issue Offered A Line Of Their Commercial Vehicles. *(Courtesy The Long Island Museum Of American Art, History & Carriages)*

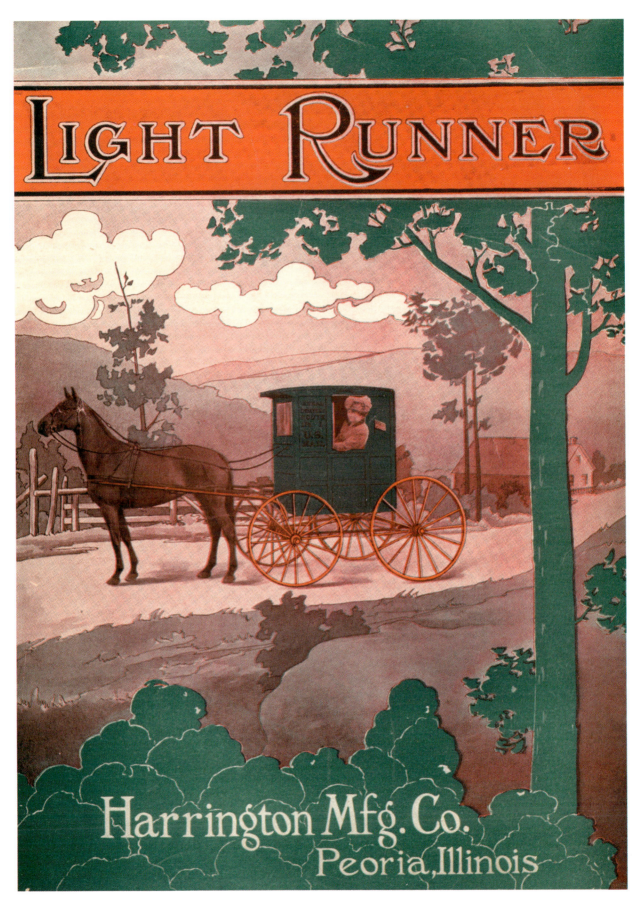

Circa 1900 Catalog Cover From The Harrington Manufacturing Company Of Peoria, Illinois, Featuring Their "Light Runner" Line Of Vehicles. *(Courtesy The Long Island Museum Of American Art, History & Carriages)* (See more on this maker and many others in volume 2 of Wheels Across America)

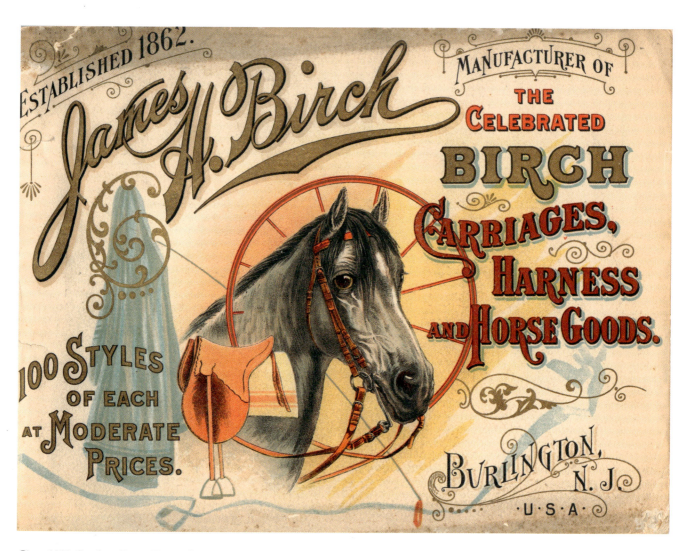

Circa 1892 Catalog Cover From The James H. Birch Company Of Burlington, New Jersey. They Also Operated A Plant In Philadelphia, Pennsylvania Offering A Full Line Of Vehicles, Harness And Horse Goods. *(Courtesy The Long Island Museum Of American Art, History & Carriages)*

Circa 1895 Sechler And Company Catalog Cover From Their Cincinnati, Ohio Factory.

Founder D. M. Sechler Apprenticed In The Carriage Building Trade As Early As 1835 In Milton, Pennsylvania Before Moving To Cincinnati Around 1877. The Sechler Name Was Well Known In The Carriage, Wagon And Farm Implement Business With Outlets In Numerous Locations. The Company Name Changed To Trailmobile Company In The 1900's And Was Later Acquired By The Pullman Company In 1950. *(Courtesy The Long Island Museum Of American Art, History & Carriages)*

Circa 1890 Catalog Cover From The Enterprise Carriage Manufacturing Company Of Miamisburg, Ohio. They Also Offered A Line Of Farm And Hay Wagons. *(Courtesy The Long Island Museum Of American Art, History & Carriages)*

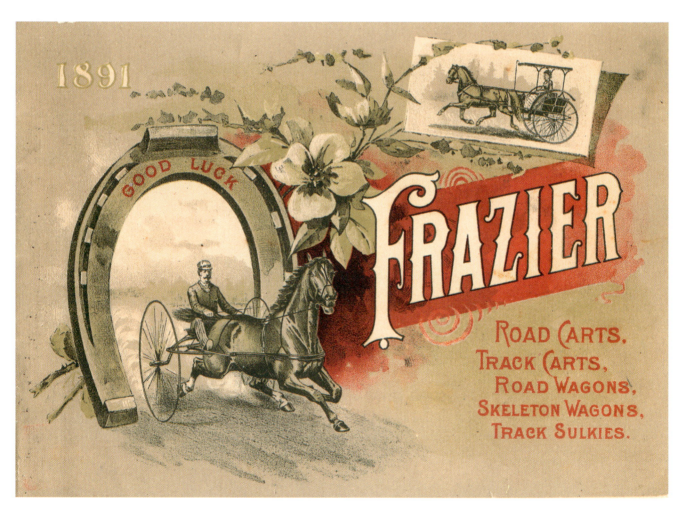

1891 Catalog Cover From The W. S. Frazier & Company Of Aurora, Illinois. *(Courtesy The Long Island Museum Of American Art, History & Carriages)*

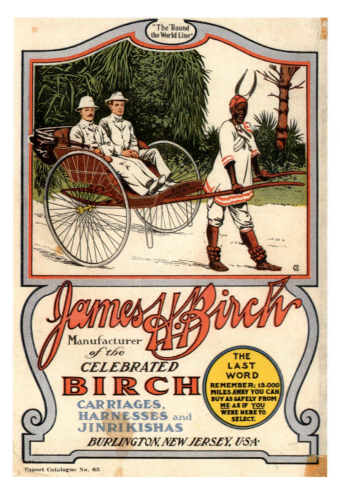

(Left) Back Cover Of #65 Special Export Catalog Circa 1900 From The James H. Birch Company Of Burlington, New Jersey And Philadelphia, Pennsylvania. Birch Established A Large Foreign Market For Their Vehicles Through An Aggressive Marketing Campaign Including The Employment Of Foreign Sales Representatives. *(Courtesy The Carriage Museum of America, Bird-In-Hand, PA)*

(Right) Front Cover Of The Birch #65 Special Export Catalog Circa 1900 Portraying Themselves As The Leader In The World Wide Export Of Wheeled Vehicles And Harness. *(Courtesy The Carriage Museum of America, Bird-In-Hand, PA)*

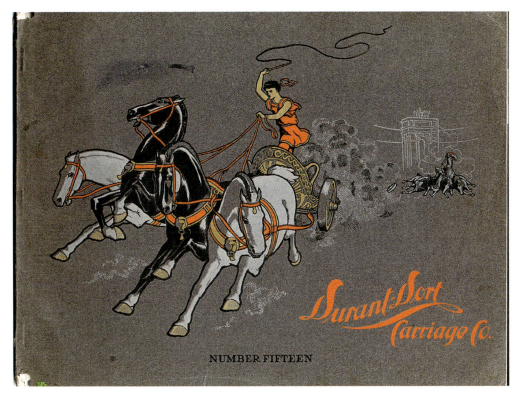

Catalog #15 Cover, Circa 1895 From The Durant-Dort Carriage Company Of Flint, Michigan. This Catalog Features Their Famous Blue Ribbon Line Of Vehicles. (The Firm Was Formerly Known As The Flint Road Cart Company Before 1886). *(Courtesy The Carriage Museum of America, Bird-In-Hand, PA)*

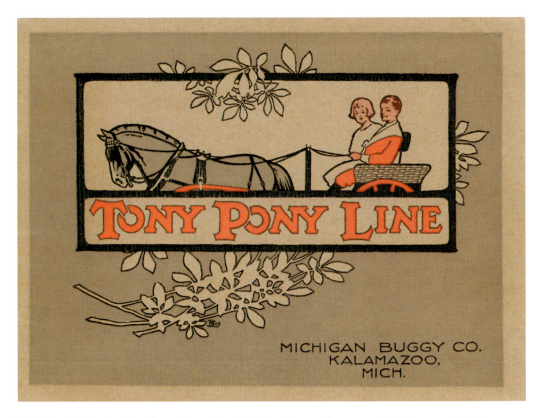

Circa Late 1890's Catalog Cover From The Michigan Buggy Company Of Kalamazoo, Michigan Featuring Their Tony Pony Line. This Firm Also Produced Over 20,000 Sleighs Before 1900. *(Courtesy The Carriage Museum of America, Bird-In-Hand, PA)*

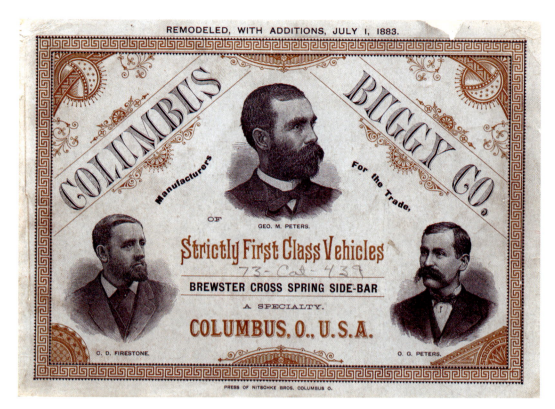

(Above) 1883 Catalog Cover From The Columbus Buggy Company Of Columbus, Ohio Showing Co-Founders C. D. Fire Stone, Geo. M. Peters And O. G. Peters. The Company Also Operated Under The Name Columbus Vehicle Company With Branches In Cincinnati, Chicago, Kansas City, Detroit And San Francisco. *(Courtesy The Long Island Museum Of American Art, History & Carriages)*

(Below) Circa 1900 Catalog Cover From The Hitchcock Manufacturing Company Of Cortland, New York.
(Courtesy The Long Island Museum Of American Art, History & Carriages)
(See more on this maker and many others in Volume 2 of *Wheels Across America*)

(Above) Circa 1900 Catalog Cover From The Eagle Carriage Company Of Cincinnati, Ohio Featuring Their Pony Carts, Carriages And Harness. *(Courtesy The Carriage Museum of America, Bird-In-Hand, PA)*

(Below) Circa 1900 Cover The Hitchcock Manufacturing Company Of Cortland, New York. This Issue Displays Several Styles Of Sleighs And Bobs. *(Courtesy The Carriage Museum of America, Bird-In-Hand, PA)* (See more on this maker and many others in Volume 2 of *Wheels Across America*)

(Top left) Circa 1900 Catalog Cover From Noyes Carriage Company Of Elkhart, Indiana. Noyes Offered A Competitive Line Of Vehicles Well Into The 1900's Before Business Slowed Due To The Coming Of The Automobile, At That Time The Company Went Into The Construction Of House Trailers. *(Courtesy The Carriage Museum of America, Bird-In-Hand, PA)*

(Top right) # 20 Catalog Cover From The Acorn Buggy Company Of Cincinnati, Ohio in 1907. *(Courtesy The Carriage Museum of America, Bird-In-Hand, PA)*

(Middle right) Circa 1890 Catalog Cover From Merts & Riddle Of Ravenna, Ohio. Originally Known As Clark Carriage Company, Established In 1831. The Name Changed To Merts & Riddle Coach And Hearse Company In 1861 And They Soon Became Known As A Leader In The Construction Of These Vehicles. Merts & Riddle Employed Some Of The Foremost Wood carvers And Craftsmen Of The day. Over The Years, Many Famous People Were Carried To There Graves In A Riddle Hearse Including Two Presidents, McKinley And Harding, And A Cowboy Named Roy Rogers, Who was Buried From A Restored Riddle Hearse In 1998. *(Courtesy The Carriage Museum of America, Bird-In-Hand, PA)*

(Bottom right) Circa 1905 Catalog Cover From The American Carriage Company Of Kalamazoo, Michigan, The Catalog Illustrates A Number Of Sleighs & Bobs For Pleasure And Business Use. *(Courtesy The Carriage Museum of America, Bird-In-Hand, PA)*

(Bottom left) 1886 Catalog Cover From W. S. Frazier & Company Of Aurora, Illinois Featuring Their Extensive Line Of Road Carts And Related Vehicles. *(Courtesy The Carriage Museum of America, Bird-In-Hand, PA)*

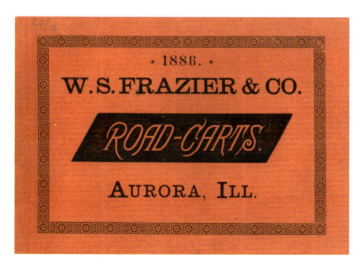

(Below) 1899 Catalog #14 Cover From The American Carriage Company Of Cincinnati, Ohio. A Large Wholesale Business Was Established While Under The Direction Of Company President Perrin P. Hunter. *(Courtesy The Carriage Museum of America, Bird-In-Hand, PA)*

(Above) 1916 Cover Of Catalog #34 From The Perfect Banner Buggy Company In St. Louis, Missouri. *(Courtesy The Carriage Museum of America, Bird-In-Hand, PA)*

(Below) Circa 1910 Catalog Cover From The Empire Manufacturing Company Of Quincy, Illinois Showing Their Wheels And Wagons. They Also Built Farm Implements At Their Rock Falls, Illinois Location. *(Courtesy The Carriage Museum of America, Bird-In-Hand, PA)*

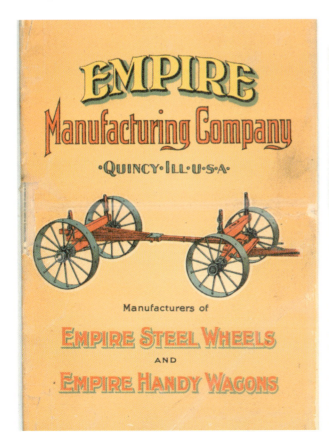

(Above) Circa 1890's Catalog Cover From The D. M. Sechler Carriage Company In Moline, Illinois. Sechler Established His Carriage Business In Cincinnati, Ohio Around 1877 And Manufactured That Type Of Vehicle There. In Moline He Mostly Manufactured Wagons And Farm Implements Including His Popular Black Hawk Corn Planter. Sechler Products Were Available Through Out The Country By The Way Of His Extensive Use Of Agents, Jobbers, Dealers, And Retail-Wholesale Outlets. *(Courtesy The Carriage Museum of America, Bird-In-Hand, PA)*

(Above left) 1896 Hand-Drawn Chemical Fire Wagon By Fire Extinguishers Manufacturing Company Of Chicago, Illinois. On Display At The Jung Carriage Museum, It Was Purchased New For $900.00 By The Plymouth, Wisconsin Fire Department. When In Use The Large Tank Was Filled With Soda And Water, Then Activated With Sulfuric Acid That Is Stored In The Wooden Box Up Front. The Chemical Reaction Process Produced Pressure In The Same Way As An Ordinary Soda-Acid Fire Extinguisher. *(Courtesy Jung Carriage Museum Collection—Image Courtesy The Author)*

(Above right) Wesley W. Jung, Grandson Of Jacob, Jung Restored This 1888 Silsby Steam Powered Fire Engine. The Engine Was Originally Owned And Used By The Berlin, Wisconsin Fire Department. Silsby Manufacturing Company Of Seneca Falls, New York Was One Of The Foremost Names In The Construction Of Steam Fire Pumps. Horace C. Silsby Produced Various Pumps And Equipment From 1845 Until 1891 When He Joined Several Other Manufacturers To Form The American Fire Engine Company. *(Courtesy Jung Carriage Museum Collection—Image Courtesy The Author)*

(Left) Circa 1910 Open Delivery Wagon Built By Jung Carriage Company In Sheboygan, Wisconsin. This Light Little Utility Vehicle Was Used By The Jung Department Store In Sheboygan. It Was Equipped With A Fifth Wheel To Enable Quick And Easy Turning With Improved Stability As Well As Leaf Springs Allowing The Wagon To Carry Heavy Loads. *(Courtesy Jung Carriage Museum Collection—Image Courtesy The Author)*

(Right) Restored, Circa 1900 Street Sprinkler By Studebaker Bros. Of South Bend, Indiana. Now Part Of The Jung Carriage Museum Collection, This Vehicle was Used Before The Extensive Paving Of Roads And Streets. Originally Built As A Water Sprinkler It Was Later Converted To A Road Oiler, Note The Tight Cooperage And Heavy Suspension Needed To Support Its Great Weight When Fully Loaded. *(Courtesy Jung Carriage Museum Collection— Image Courtesy The Author)*

(Above and Right) Side And Back View Of This Rare Old Tobacco Wagon Which Still Exhibits Its Original Paint And Decoration. This Adorable Little Wagon Was Built By The Jung Carriage Company Of Sheboygan, Wisconsin Circa 1900 For Use On The Streets Of That Same City By Herman Schuelke A Local Business Man. *(Courtesy Jung Carriage Museum Collection—Image Courtesy The Author)*

(Left) Meat Wagon, Built In 1906 By Jung Carriage Company For The George W.F. Herzog Company. The Heavy Leaf Spring Suspension Identifies This As A Heavy Wagon Or Sometimes Called A Dray, Capable Of Hauling Whole Carcasses. It Was The Restoration Of This Vehicle That Inspired Wesley Jung (Grandson Of Jacob Jung) To Begin Collecting And Restoring The Carriages, Wagons And Sleighs That Would Eventually Become Part The Jung Carriage Museum On Display In Greenbush, Wisconsin Today. *(Courtesy Jung Carriage Museum Collection—Image Courtesy The Author)*

(Right) Circa 1900 Wholesale Meat Dealers' Delivery Sled, Designed And Manufactured By The Jung Carriage Company To Haul Whole Carcasses From The Herzog Slaughterhouse Two Miles North Of Sheboygan, Wisconsin To Retail Meat Markets In Town. The Sled Is Suspended On Two Bob Runners, Allowing It Turn Easily And Smooth The Ride Over Rough Or Uneven Terrain. *(Courtesy Jung Carriage Museum Collection—Image Courtesy The Author)*

Bostock & Wombwell's Menagerie Band Carriage. Built: Circa 1883, Unidentified Builder, Burton-On-Trent, Great Britain.

Original Owner: Bostock & Wombwell's. Presentation Appearance: Circa 1883.

This Exemplary Band Carriage Is The Finest Example Of The Style Still In Existence Today. It Led The Street Parades Of One Of The Bostock Family's Several Menageries From Its Construction In The Early 1880's Until The Last Enterprise Was Closed By E.H. Bostock In 1932. Imported To The United States By Animal Importer John T. Benson, It Was A Feature Of His New Hampshire Farm Until Acquired At Auction By Circus World Museum In 1987. The Six-foot Diameter Rear Wheels Are The Largest On Any Parade Wagon In Existence Today. At One Time It Was Drawn By A Thirteen-In-Line Hitch Of Horses, The Longest Such Team In Outdoor Show History. *(Courtesy Circus World Museum: Identification Courtesy Circus World Museum, Image Courtesy The Author)*

Christy Bros. "Beauty". Tableau #76. Built: 1883; Wagon By Fielding Brothers, New York, New York; Carvings, Likely Samuel Robb Shop. Original Owner: Barnum & London Greatest Show On Earth. Altered: Circa 1911–1915; Christy Bros. Circus Presentation Appearance: 1926. This Wagon Was Originally Fabricated As One Of Ten To Twelve Tableau Cages For The Barnum & London Circus. The Outside Of These Dual Service Vehicles Was Decorated To Serve As A Tableau In The Daily Street Parade. Once Parked In The Menagerie, Or Traveling Zoo Tent, The Removable Sideboards Were Taken Off Of One Side, Exposing The Animals Housed Therein To Educate The Public. In The 1920's The Wagon Was Rebuilt Into Strictly Tableau Service And Then Substantially Re-Decorated In The Late 1920's. The Name "Beauty" Was Bestowed On It, In Honor Of The Six Carved Maidens That Adorn The Body.

Walt Disney Studios Donated The Wagon To Circus World Museum In 1962. *(Courtesy Circus World Museum: Identification Courtesy Circus World Museum, Image Courtesy The Author)*

Cole Bros. "America" Steam Calliope #76. Built: 1903; Wagon By Sebastian Wagon Company, New York, NY; Carvings By Samuel Robb Shop, New York, NY. Original Owner: Barnum & Baily Greatest Show On Earth. Altered: 1917, Ringling Bros. Circus; 1940, Cole Bros. Circus Presentation Appearance: 1940. The "America" Was One Of Four Continental-Themed Floats Constructed For The 1903 Return Of The Barnum & Bailey Greatest Show On Earth From A Five-Year Tour Of Europe, Part Of A Mammoth Thirteen Wagon Order. In Its Original Form It Carried A Carved Wooden Statuary Group On Top, An Allegorical Representation Of America, Which Telescoped Upward From The Lower Body. It Existed In That Format Untill The Season Of 1917, When The Ringling Brothers, Who Had Bought The Show In 1907, Removed The Statuary And Increased The Box Body To Its Current Height. It Was Utilized By The Ringlings As A Baggage-Carring Tableau Wagon From 1917 Through 1920, Then Later By Christy Bros. Circus 1928-1930 And Cole Bros. Circus 1935–1937. In 1940 It Was Altered To House And Carry A 32-Whistle Steam Calliope Instrument And Apparatus, Serving In That Manner Through 1950. Acquired Thereafter By Cleaver-Brooks Company Of Milwaukee, WI, The Firm Donated It To Circus World Musem In 1959. *(Courtesy Circus World Museum: Identification Courtesy Circus World Museum, Image Courtesy The Author)*

Ringling Bros. Bell Wagon. Built: 1892; wagon And Assembly By Henry Moeller & Sons, Baraboo, WI; Bells By G. Campbell & Sons Centennial Bell Foundry, Milwaukee, WI; Carvings By Milwaukee Ornamental Carving Company, Milwaukee, WI. Original Owner: Ringling Bros.' World's Greatest Shows. Altered: Circa 1903–1905, Ringling Bros. Circus / H. Moeller & Sons. Presentation Appearance: 1905. The Most Emposing Bell Wagon Ever Costructed Was This Vehicle, Which May Have Been The First Entirely New parade Wagon Fabricated For The Ringling Bros.' World's Greatest Shows. The Nine Heavy Bells Are Played By Means Of A Mechanical Keyboard Located At The Rear Of The Vehicle. It Was A Feature From 1892 Until About 1909, When It Was Stored For Future Use. The Wagon Came Back Into Service In 1934 On Ringling-owned Hagenbeck-Wallace Circus And Was Subsequently Utilized On Ringling Bros. And Barnum & Bailey Combined Shows In The 1940's And As Late As 1952. It Has Been On Loan To The Wisconsin Historical Society's Circus World Museum, Baraboo, Wisconsin By Kenneth Feld And Ringling Bros. And Barnum & Bailey Since 1984. *Wagon Identifications: Copyright Circus World Museum & Tempo International Publishing Company. (Courtesy Circus World Museum: Identification Courtesy Circus World Museum, Image Courtesy The Author)*

(Above) Looking In On A Cowboy Camp. This Chuck Was Built By Contemporary Craftsman Doug Hansen At His Hansen Wheel And Wagon Shop In Letcher, South Dakota. The Wagon Is Set Up To Pull A Trail Pup And Was Constructed On An Original Peter Schuttler Gear, It Is Part Of Their Dakota Series. *(Courtesy Doug Hansen)*

(Right) A First Class Team OF Show Horses Will Be Extremely Proud To Pull This Top Of The Line Hitch Wagon By Hansen Wheel And Wagon Shop Into Any Competition. This One Was Custom Built For The Express Ranch's Of Yukon, Oklahoma. *(Courtesy Doug Hansen)*

(Left) A Truly Diverse Range Of Vehicles Pass Through The The Letcher, South Dakota Shops Of Hansen Wheel And Wagon. Evidence This Original Old Gypsy Wagon, First Restored In England Before It Was Acquired By Hansen. It Was Then Finished, Complete with Stove, Bed, Table Benches, Etc. *(Courtesy Doug Hansen)*

Circa 1890's Standard Oil Wagon, Maker Unknown. A Fine Example Of The Restoration Work Being Done Today In The Shops Of Master Craftsman Doug Hansen. *(Courtesy Doug Hansen)*

Reminiscent Of The Late 1800's, This Totally New Army Scout Wagon Shows The Commitment To Detail And Love Of History That Goes Into Each Vehicle Built Or Restored Under The Supervision Of Master Craftsman Doug Hansen, Who Also Built The Authentic Reproduction 1897 Abbot-Downing Stage Coach On The Front Cover Of This Book. *(Courtesy Doug Hansen)*

This Original 1910 John Deere Surrey Was Fitted With A New Top And Gear Paint, The Original Body Paint Is Preserved With Varnish, All Courtesy Of Hansen Wheel And Wagon Shop. *(Courtesy Doug Hansen)*

(Above) Old Style Meets New Idea In This Interesting Combination By Doug Hansen. Featured Here Is An Entirely New Modified Conestoga Wagon, Fitted With A Full Fifth Wheel Gear.

(Below) Doug Hansen Is Truly One Of The Foremost Craftsmen In The Horse Drawn Vehicle Business Today, So It Is No Wonder That The South Dakota Historical Society Selected Him To Restore This Beautiful Five Glass Landau Made By E.M. Miller Circa 1895. In The Early Days This Vehicle Saw Extensive Use On The Streets Of Pierre, South Dakota As A Livery Service. *(Both Images Courtesy Doug Hansen)*

(Top) Jens Ole (J.O) Aplan Pictured In The Doorway Of His Blacksmith And Wagon Shop In Gettysburg, South Dakota Circa 1890.

(Bottom) South Dakota Blacksmith And Wagon Maker Jens (J.O.) Aplan Pictured In Doorway Of His Shop Circa 1890.

Jens (J.O.) Pictured At The Anvil In His Blacksmith And Wagon Shop In Gettysburg, South Dakota Circa 1890.

The Above Image And The Two Images on Page 187 Are Courtesy Of Peg And James Aplan, Grandson Of J.O. Aplan (See More On Jens (J.O.) Aplan In Volume Two Of Wheels Across America.*)*

Rare 1902 Raffle Ticket Or Coupon, Good For One Chance To Win This #50 Pneumatic Runabout By The E.R. Jeffrey Company In Arizona. *(Author's Collection)*

Circa 1900 Catalog Cover From The Harrington Manufacturing Of Peoria, Illinois. Makers Of The "Light Runner" Vehicles. *(Courtesy Dan Bussy Collection)*

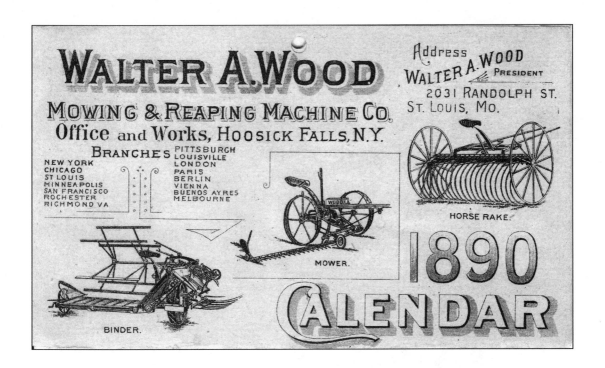

(Above) 1890 Walter A. Wood Calendar, Offered As Advertisement For Their St. Louis Branch. The Extensive Line Of Wood Implements Were Available Coast To Coast And Several Foreign Countries By The 1880's, Fifteen Branch Locations Are Listed In This Ad Alone. The Main Factory Was In Hoosick Falls, New York. *(Author's Collection)*

(Right) Circa 1905 Advertisement For The #6 McCormick Mower. McCormick Harvesting Company Of Chicago, Illinois Was A Leader In The Reaper Business Circa 1860–1902. *(Author's Collection)* This Advertisement Was After They Were Acquired By International Harvester Company. *(See More On The Latter In Volume Two Of* Wheels Across America*)*

Unknown Street Vendor With Lunch Wagon Circa 1905. *(Author's Collection)*

Jonas Swab, Inventor Of The Chilled Box Steel Axle, Blacksmith And Civil War Veteran, Founded Swab's Wagon Works December Of 1868 In Elizabethville, Pennsylvania. The Company Is Still In Business Today, Operated By The Family Of Jonas Swab Building Solid Fiberglass Truck Bodies, Making Them One Of The Oldest Continuously Operating Transportation Companies In The World. *(Author's Collection)*

Circa 1900 Advertisement From The Pattee Plow Company Of Monmouth, Illinois, Listing A Number Of Their Popular Brands And Claiming To Be The only Exclusive Cultivator Factory In America. *(Author's Collection)*

Wheels Across America

Advertisement In The 1880 Carriage Monthly For Miles Brothers New Standard Varnish Brush. (*Author's Collection*)

Colorado Style, Cooper Wagon From The 1915 Parlin & Orendorff Company Catalog. (*Author's Collection*)

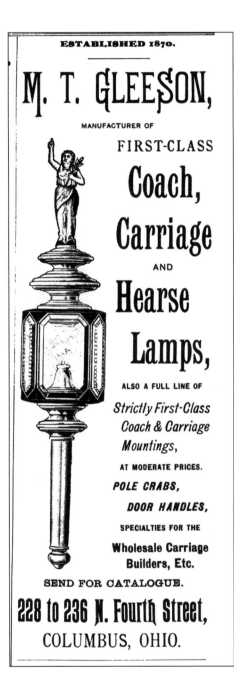

Circa 1880's Advertisement From The M.T. Gleeson Manufacturing Company Of Columbus, Ohio. In addition To First Class Coach lights They Also Offered For Sale, Mountings And Trimmings To The Wholesale Carriage trade.

Circa 1899 Acme Road Machine Company Catalog, Showing Horse Drawn Graders And Other Road Construction Equipment. *(Author's Collection)*

#1150 Victor Auto Seat Surrey, Offered In The 1915 Parlin & Orendorff Company Catalog. This Firm Was Established By William Parlin, In Canton Illinois Around 1842.
(Author's Collection)

The #650 Anchor Livery Buggy Sold For $142.00 Complete With Either Pole Or Shafts, In The 1915 Parlin & Orendorff Company Catalog.
(Author's Collection)

1915 Anchor Buggy Advertisement From The Parlin & Orendorff Company Catalog. (*Author's Collection*)

May 1888 Front Cover Of "The Hub", A Major Carriage Trade Publication Of The Day. *(Author's Collection)*

(Top) Illustration Of An Early Clapp & Jones Steam Pump Fire Engine. This Well Know Hudson, New York Firm Constructed Over 600 Machines Between 1862 And 1891 When They Joined With Others To Form The American Fire Engine Company.

(Bottom) Illustration Of A Manchester Locomotive Works Steam Pump Fire Engine Circa 1880. Prior To 1877 The Company Name Was Amoskeag Manufacturing Company Of Manchester, New Hampshire. The Latter Constructed Over 700 Engines Before The Company Name Changed To Manchester Locomotive Works.

This #1304 Lion Brand Three-Seated Spring Wagon Cut, Was Shown In An Unidentified Manufacturers Catalog, Circa 1910. *(Author's Collection)*

Circa 1855 Illustration Of The Woodburn Wheel Factory In St. Louis, Missouri. The Company Manufactured Wheels, Hubs, Spokes And Rims, Including The "Sarven Patent Wheel".

#242 Depot Wagonette, Or Paul-Bearer Wagon By Kelk Carriage Works Of Sedalia, Missouri Circa 1902. Established In 1868 By Thomas Kelk, The Firm Grew To Employ A Number Of Craftsmen Including His Future Partner, Harvey F. Keens. Mr. Keens Would Eventually Become Sole Owner After The Death Of Thomas Kelk. 1916 Was The Factories Peak Production Year, With Over 750 Vehicles Constructed.

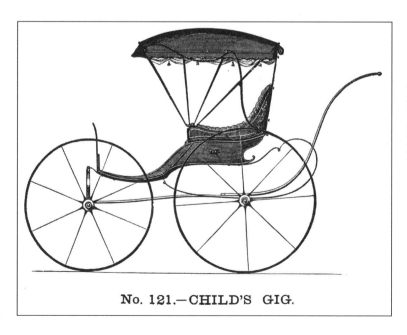

No. 121.—CHILD'S GIG.

A Fine Selection Of Children's Carriages Were Offered In This Circa 1860 Catalog Including The #121 Child's Gig Featured Here By Lawrence, Bradley And Pardee Of New Haven, Connecticut.

Lawrence, Bradley & Pardee,

No. 184.—Albany Cutter.

No. 185.—Light Two Seat Sleigh.

No. 186.—Fine Pony Sleigh.

New Haven, Conn.

Sleighs And Cutters Represented a Significant Portion Of The Lawrence, Bradley & Pardee Business In New Haven, Connecticut, Circa 1862 Catalog.

$38.50 AMERICAN BEAUTY.
No. 11S105
Don't buy a cheaper buggy, for while our lower priced top buggies are covered by our binding guarantee, and are much better in quality and much lower in price than you can buy elsewhere, and will give satisfaction in every case, you get more for your money when you order our American Beauty at $38.50.
See full description on opposite page

Sears, Roebuck & Company Of Chicago, Illinois Played A Major Roll In The Production And Distribution Of Horse Drawn Vehicles Across America. This "American Beauty" Buggy, Selling At The Price Of $38.50 Could Be Purchased By Almost Anyone In 1905. It Was One Of 53,464 Vehicles Manufactured That Year Alone, In The Sears, Roebuck & Company's Vehicle Factory In Evansville, Indiana.

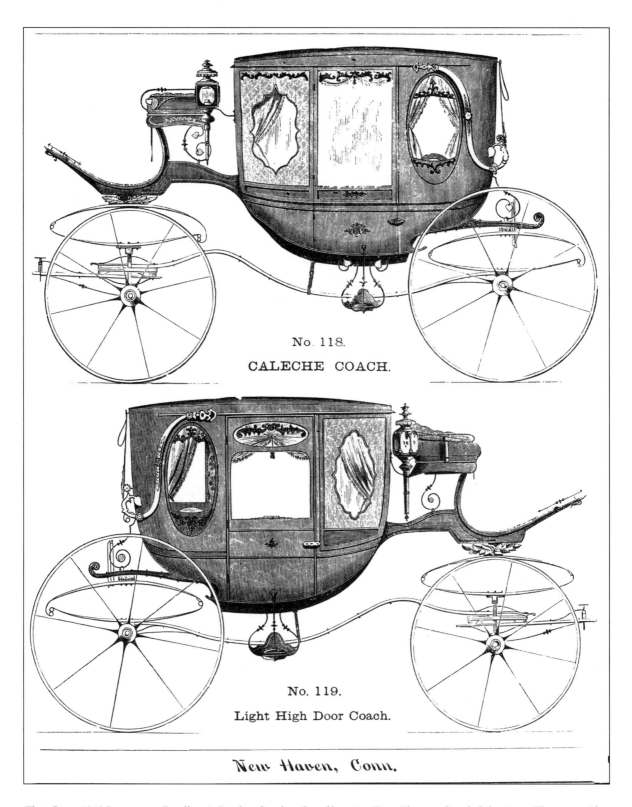

This Circa 1862 Lawrence, Bradley & Pardee Catalog Cut, Showing Two Elegant Coach Selections, Illustrates The Famed James Brewster Style And Influence Seen In The Vehicles Produced By This Group Of Three Carriage, Sleigh And Buggy Builders In New Haven, Connecticut.

Description.—Body 5-17 or 54 or 56 in. Concave Risers, Rear Concord Post Convex, Seat latest style, 22x17½ in. on bottom, Rubber covered steps, Bradley Toe Rail, Solid Foot Grain Front Dash.
Gear, Ball Bearing Axles, Bailey 5th wheel, or Brewster. Weight 140 pounds, Front Axle clearing 23 inches from floor, Body 30 inches from bottom to floor, Solid Shaft Connections, Rear Axle Solid Center, Center Springs Timpkin, Brewster or Storm other forgings best Norway Iron, Side Bars Select Hickory, Shafts High Bend Best Hickory, Wheels Best Wire Spokes, Tire 1¾ inch, Best Pneumatic Sulkey, Workmanship first-class. Track to suit. Wheels 30 in. and 32 in. high. Height of Gear is made to order to suit customer. Price, A Grade, $160 00.
Trimming above job, Best Whip Cord or Best Leather, Velvet Rug Toe Mat, Storm Apron, Leather Covered Whip Socket, 36 inch Shaft Leathers, $19 00.

The Vehicle And Gear Displayed In This 1901 Cut, Was Available At Retail Or Wholesale Prices From The Schubert Brothers Gear Company Of Oneida, New York. They Also Manufactured Carriages, Wagons, Carts, Automobile Bodies, Tops And Trimmings.

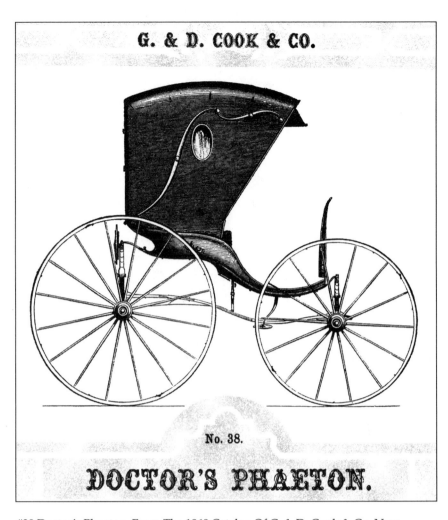

#38 Doctor's Phaeton, From The 1860 Catalog Of G. & D. Cook & Co. New Haven, Connecticut.

Sleek And Stylish, The #129 Calash By G. & D. Cook & Company Of New Haven, Connecticut Circa 1858.

D.W. Johnson & Company Of Hartford, Connecticut Manufactured Horse And Pony Drawn Vehicles, As Well As A Line Of Hand Push Carriages Like The Fine Example Show Here In The 1860 G. & D. Cook & Company Catalog.

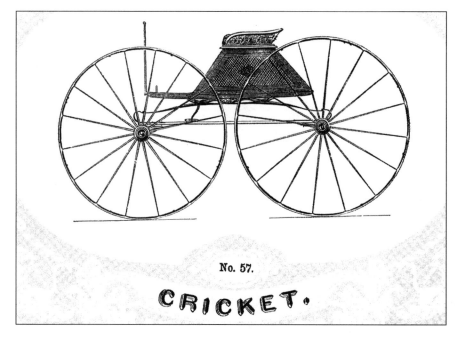

This Unusual Looking #57 Cricket Is One More Example Of The Diverse Array Of Vehicles Offered In The 1860 Catalog By G. & D. Cook & Company Of New Haven, Connecticut.

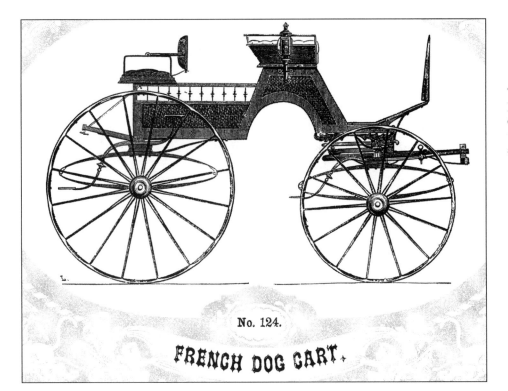

The Seemingly Endless Inventory Of Vehicles In G. & D. Cook & Company's 1860 Catalog Included This #124 French Dog Cart.

G. F. Kimball Of New Haven, Connecticut Operated A Retail, Wholesale Wheel Manufacturing Business Throughout Most Of The 1800's And Into The Early 1900's. They Maintained A Massive Inventory, Able To Supply Wheels And Related Items For Vehicles Of Every Description.

Wheels Across America 205

(Above) Available From The New Haven, Connecticut Shop Of H. Galbraith Every Thing Needed To Iron And Trim Your Carriage, Displayed Here In An 1860 Advertisement In The G. & D. Cook & Company's Catalog.

(Right) 1863 Advertisement For "Wood's Mower", Just One Of Dozens Designed And Patented By The Farm Implement Manufacturing Giant, Walter A. Wood Mowing & Reaping Machine Company Of Hoosick Falls, New York. *(Author's Collection)*

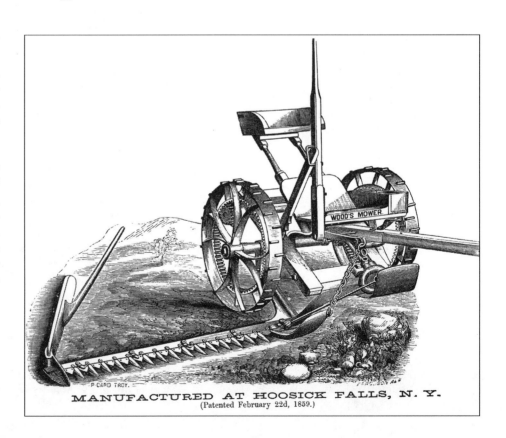

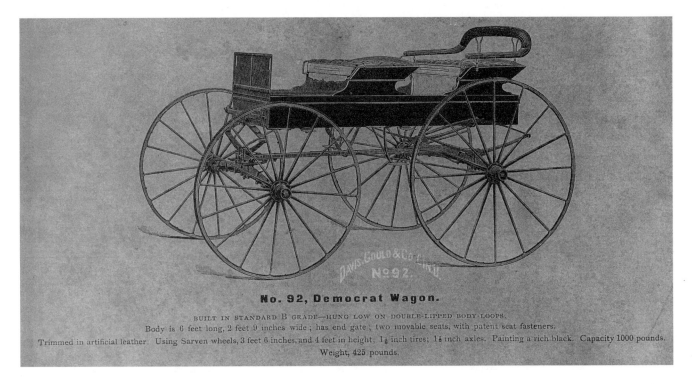

(Above) #92 Democrat Wagon In The Circa 1870's Catalog By Davis, Gould & Company Of Cincinnati, Ohio. *(Courtesy Mark Gardner Collection)*

(Below) #45 White Chapel Body—Top Buggy In The Circa 1870's Catalog By Davis, Gould & Company Of Cincinnati, Ohio. *(Courtesy Mark Gardner Collection)*

The smallest member of the "BIRDSELL" Wagon Family

On the opposite side we illustrate our Miniature Farm Wagon. We will ship subject to your approval and if not as described you may hold subject to our order. It is not a toy but is constructed on the same lines as a heavy farm wagon.

The wheels are 14 and 20-inches high with heavy welded tires, clipped felloes and staggered spokes. The gear is heavily ironed throughout, has bent front hound and adjustable reach.

The body is handsomely painted and measures 16 x 36 inches. The sides and ends can be removed leaving the bottom with stakes. Furnished regular with seat, hand tongue and a pair of shafts. Pole with neckyoke and whiffletrees furnished when wanted at extra charge.

Weight, 65 lbs. crated.

BIRDSELL MANUFACTURING COMPANY

Manufacturers of Cast and Steel Skein Farm Wagons

SOUTH BEND, INDIANA

Freight on two no more than on one.

According To This Advertisement From Birdsell Manufacturing Company Of South Bend, Indiana. This Cute Little Wagon Is Not A Toy, But A Smaller Scale Version Of Their Popular Farm Wagon. In Other Birdsell Ad's (Circa 1880's) They Claimed To Be The largest "Steel Skein" Wagon Works In The World. *(Courtesy Mark Gardner Collection)*

To the Wagon Users of the World:

PETER SCHUTTLER III
President

CARL SCHUTTLER
Vice-President

WALTER SCHUTTLER
Sec'y-Treas.

ADOLPH B. SCHUTTLER
Ass't to Pres.

COPYRIGHT 1920 BY PETER SCHUTTLER CO.

IF YOU are looking for a farm wagon that will stand up to its work for many, many years—a farm wagon that will need mighty few trips to your blacksmith shop during its lifetime—a wagon that is made by the slow, painstaking, old-fashioned method of quality, not quantity—if you are willing to pay just a trifle more to get a substantial wagon—you're the very man I want to talk to about

The Old Reliable
Peter Schuttler Farm Wagons

I'm a wagon man through and through—so are my three brothers in this great business. There isn't a thing in wagon making from the selection of lumber to the paint finishing that we four brothers have not learned in thorough Schuttler fashion in the thorough Schuttler shops. We were all brought up in the business and devote our whole time to it.

My brothers and I are the grand-children of Peter Schuttler who started building good, honest farm wagons in 1843—over 78 years ago, when Chicago was little more than a country town. The thoroughness of his work spread through the west like a prairie fire in those early days.

He didn't leave a big business to our father but he left him something far greater—*a reputation for downright conscientious workmanship*. Farmers were proud then and are prouder still today to be the owner of a Schuttler farm wagon. My father in turn stuck to the same last, making two blades of grass grow where one grew before.

Now the business is ours—a business that has grown from a tiny acorn to a grand, big, solid oak and kept in the same Schuttler family for three generations. Anything that grows like this business has grown must surely have something solid about it.

You want to get the biggest wagon value for your money—read this short catalogue carefully—your wagon's right here.

Yours very truly,
PETER SCHUTTLER COMPANY,
PETER SCHUTTLER III,
President.

This Letter From The Four Grandsons Of Founder Peter Schuttler, Appeared In Their 1920 Company Catalog. Established In 1843, The Company Grew Into One Of The Largest Wagon Producing Factories In The World. By The Mid-1850's Schuttler's Factory Already Employed 100 Workers, Building Over 120 Of His "Old Reliable" Wagons Per Month.
(Courtesy Mark Gardner Collection)

(Above) Davis, Gould & Company Factory In Cincinnati, Ohio, Shown Here On The Outside Back Cover Of Their Circa 1870's Catalog. *(Courtesy Mark Gardner Collection)*

(Below) Circa 1870's Front Cover Image Of The Cincinnati, Ohio Based Davis, Gould & Company Catalog. They Offered At Wholesale Prices, A Complete Line Of Private & Commercial Vehicles. *(Courtesy Mark Gardner Collection)*

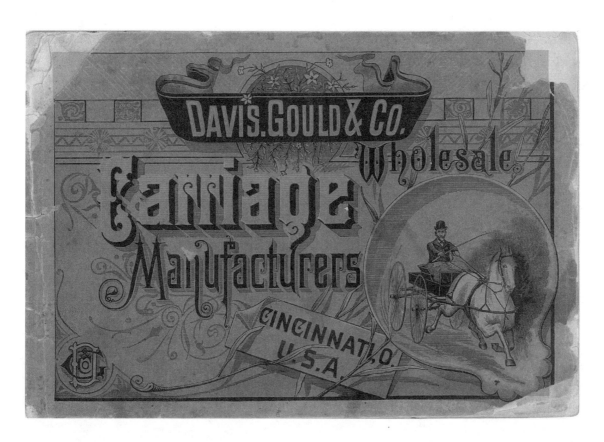

Posed Around 1880, This Gent Seems To Be The Proud New Owner Of An Americus Company, "Eureka" Wagon. This Americus, Missouri Wagon Manufacturer Was Just One Of Many Who Used The Eureka Name On Their product. *(Courtesy Mark Gardner Collection)*

(Left) 1891 Calendar Featuring The One Horse Wagon From The Harrison Wagon Works Of Grand Rapids, Michigan. Founded In 1850 By William Harrison, The Company Also Maintained A Branch Office In Kansas City, Missouri. *(Courtesy Mark Gardner Collection)*

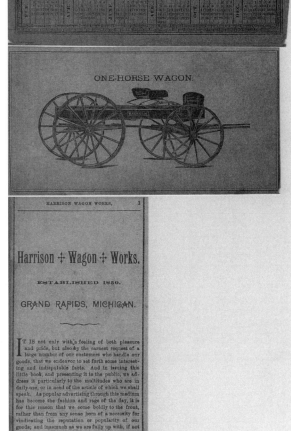

#89 Coal Box—Top Buggy In The Circa 1870's Catalog By Davis, Gould & Company Of Cincinnati, Ohio. *(Courtesy Mark Gardner Collection)*

Wheels Across America   211

(Above) Circa 1890's Letterhead From The Kentucky Wagon Manufacturing Company Of Louisville, Kentucky. This Firm Built Wagons Well Into The 1950's Including Their Famous "Old Hickory" Farm Wagon And A Popular Line Of Miniature Wagons.
(Courtesy Mark Gardner Collection)

(Right) Circa 1900 Business Card From The John E. Harvey Carriage And Wagon Shop In South Bend, Indiana. The Card States That He Operated His Business From The Rear Portion Of Crofoot And Doane's Grocery Store.
(Courtesy Mark Gardner Collection)

(Left) Luedinghaus Wagon And Letterhead As It Appeared In An Advertisement By Suttle & Jones Trading Company, One Of Thousands Of Agents, Dealers And Retail Stores Selling The Wagons And Carriages Manufactured By Luedinghaus And Many Other Factories.
(Courtesy Mark Gardner Collection)

We take pleasure in presenting you a cut of our **Business Wagon**, which we make **a specialty of manufacturing.** We make full platform, half platform, and three springs, and of **any size axle required.** A **better** advertisement of your business you could not have, as they are the **FINEST** finished wagons ever turned out.

For price apply to our agents.

Respectfully,
MILBURN WAGON CO.,
TOLEDO, OHIO.

Letterhead From The Memphis, Tennessee Branch Office And A Cut Of The Milburn Wagon Company's Business Wagon. They Also Built The "Milburn Hollow-Axle Wagon" At Their Main Factory In Toledo, Ohio.
(Courtesy Mark Gardner Collection)

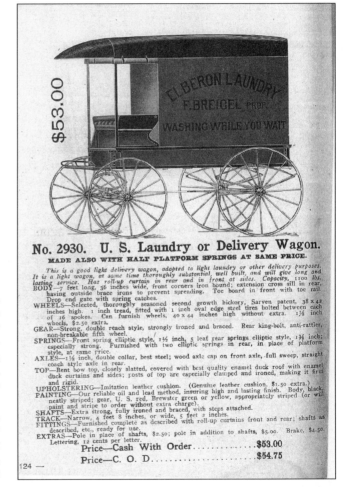

(Above) Mitchell, Lewis & Company's 1884 Annual Booklet. Established In 1832, This Racine, Wisconsin Wagon Manufacturing Firm Enjoyed A Long And Successful Run. They Advertised Their Wagons As "Monarch Of The Road", Selling Thousands Of Them Before Being Acquired By John Deere Wagon Company Of Moline, Illinois Circa 1918.
(Courtesy Mark Gardner Collection)

(Right) Another Circa 1890 Catalog Cut From The U. S. Buggy & Cart Company Of Cincinnati, Ohio. Your Company Name Or Message Could Be Added On To Any Of Their Vehicles At The Extra Charge Of Twelve Cents Per-Letter.
(Courtesy Mark Gardner Collection)

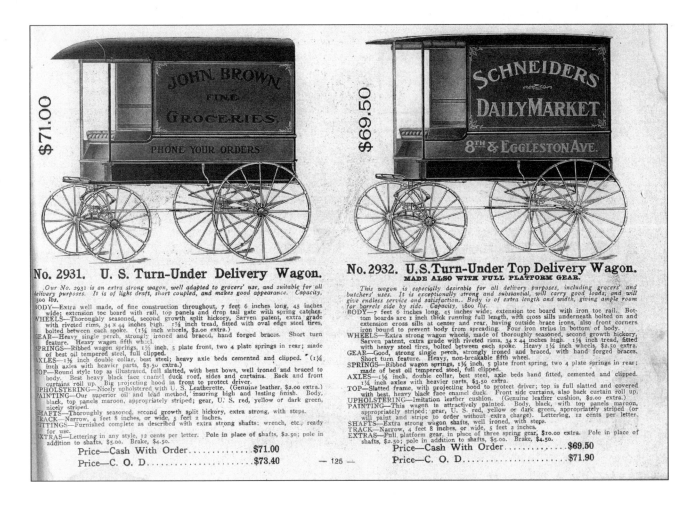

(Above) Two Examples Of The Special Line Of Commercial Vehicles Offered By The U. S. Buggy & Cart Company From Cincinnati, Ohio Circa 1890. *(Courtesy Mark Gardner Collection)*

(Below) Posed In Dodge City, Kansas Around 1900, This Group Of Proud Factory Workers Take A Break Outside Of Their Wagon & Wheel Works. *(Courtesy Mark Gardner Collection)*

Wheels Across America

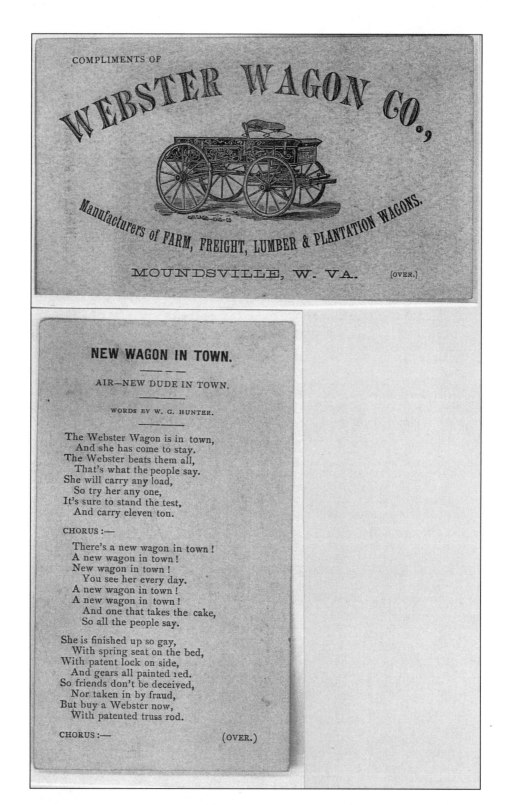

Front And Back View Of An 1880's Promotional Business Card From The Webster Wagon Company Of Moundsville, West Virginia. *(Courtesy Mark Gardner Collection)*

Carriage House:
Presenting the Foremost Businesses in the Carriage Industry Today

COLORADO DRAFT HORSE & EQUIPMENT AUCTION

Adams County Fairgrounds • Brighton, Colorado
(18 miles North of Denver) 1.5 miles West of HWY 85 on 124th Ave.

The largest Draft Horse Auction in the West

AUCTION DATES:

April 2 & 3, 2004	April 1 & 2, 2005	March 31 & April 1, 2006
Oct 1 & 2, 2004	Sept. 30 & Oct. 1, 2005	Oct. 6 & 7, 2006
July 9 & 10, 2004	July 15 & 16, 2005	July 14 & 15, 2006

Also Colorado Light Driving Horse, Mule & Carriage Auction held each July.

Troyer Harness & Equipment Company
Pioneer Equipment Dealer

For further information contact: **Harley D. Troyer Auctioneers, Inc.**
Fort Lupton, Colorado • 970-785-6282
e-mail: troyerauctioneers@msn.com • www.troyerauctions.com

WHEEL REPAIRS- All sizes of wheels repaired, up to 84"

NEW WHEELS
Can build new wheels on your old hubs.
RESTORATION
Will restore completely on most all horse drawn vehicles.
Presently working on vehicles for Collectors, Museums and Historical Societies

Greenman Carriage CO.
500 Monroe St. / P.O. Box 250
Floyd, IA 50435
Charles Greenman & Dwight Mitchell
641-398-2299   Cell 641-420-4620
wheelwright@mchsi.com

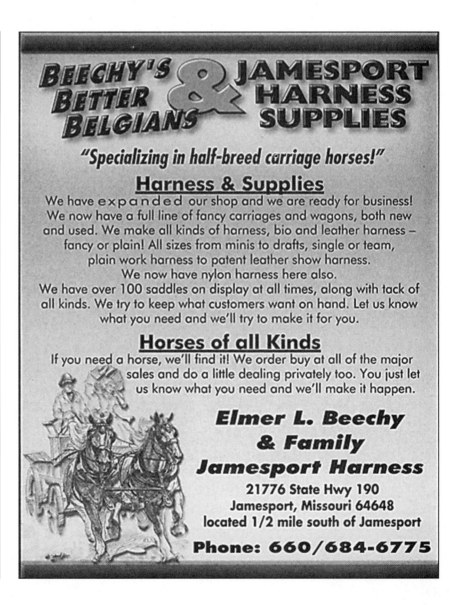

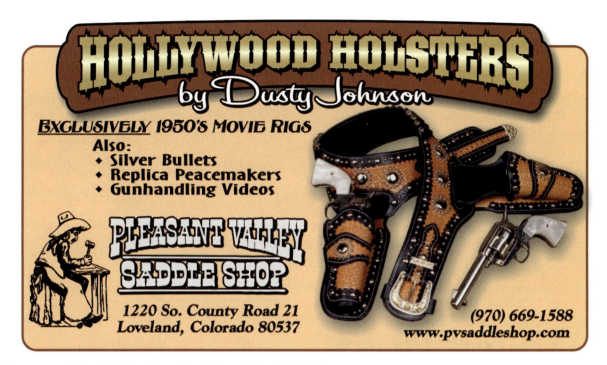

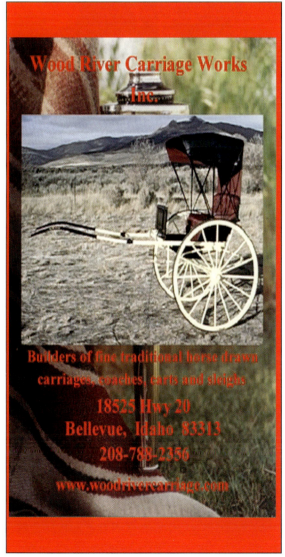

Mp Mischka Press
PUBLISHING & BOOKSELLERS

For over 25 years Mischka Press has provided the draft horse and driving horse enthusiast with calendars, books, videos and other unique items. Our wall calendars have become a tradition in literally thousands of homes throughout North America. Our full color catalog is available for the asking and many of our products can be viewed on our website.

PO Box 2067 | Cedar Rapids IA 52406-2067
www.mischka.com | 1-877-647-2452 (toll free)

Draft Horse Calendars *Driving Horse Calendars*

CARRIAGE DRIVING World Magazine
Serving the carriage driving community since 1986

SUBSCRIBE TODAY!

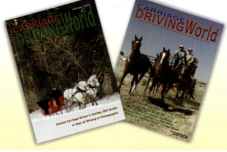

Dedicated entirely to the recreation and sport of carriage driving. The only publication written by carriage drivers for carriage drivers.

Carriage Driving World Magazine
P.O. Box 36 • Springtown, TX 76082-0036 U.S.A.
Tel 817-220-4CDW (817-220-4239)
On the Web at www.carriagedrivingworld.com

New Englands Finest!

- 19th Century Craftsmanship &
- 21st Century works of art

Horsedrawn Antiques
Hebron, Conn
860-649-4601
e-mail: restoresleigh@aol

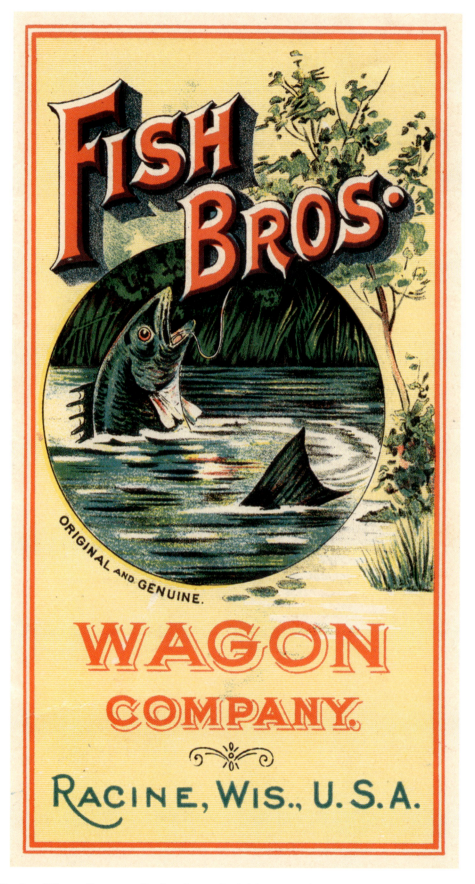

Circa 1895 Fish Brothers Wagon Company Catalog Cover. In Addition To There Main Plant In Racine, Wisconsin They Also Had Outlets In Angelica, Wisconsin And Others. *(Courtesy The Long Island Museum Of American Art, History & Carriages)*

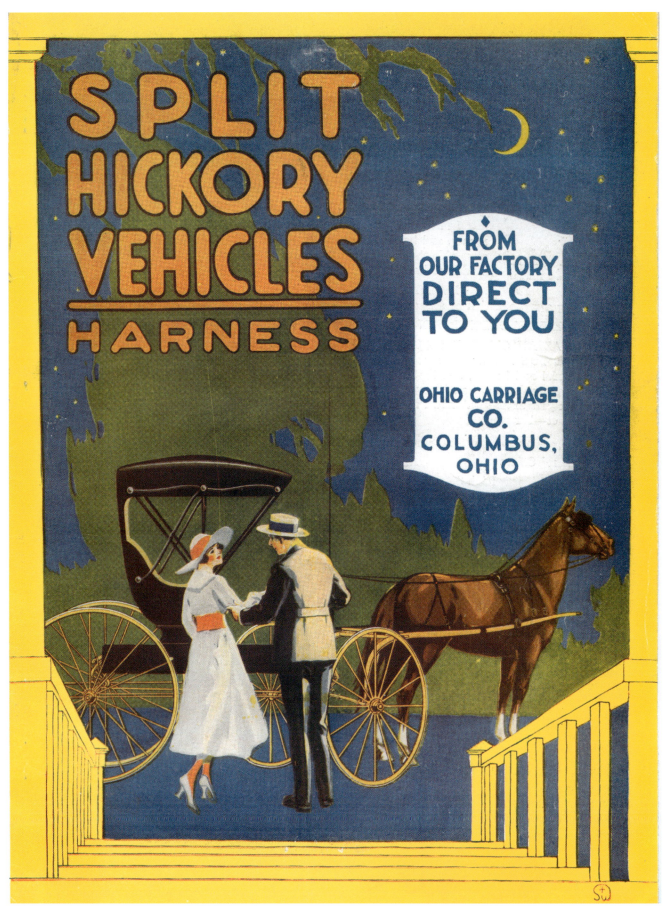

Circa 1900 Catalog Cover From The Ohio Carriage Company Of Columbus and Cincinnati, Ohio Featuring Their Split Hickory Vehicles. Under The Direction Of Company President H. C. Phelps This Firm Built One Of The Most Extensive Direct Mail Order Businesses In Their Field. *(Courtesy The Long Island Museum Of American Art, History & Carriages)*

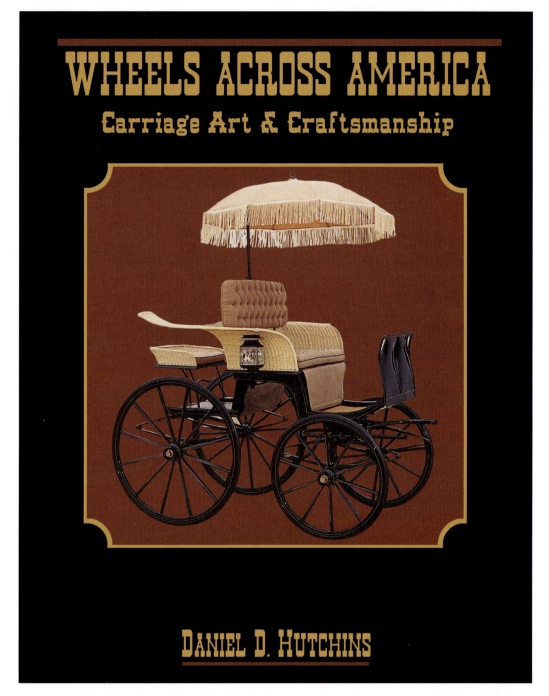

Forthcoming: WHEELS ACROSS AMERICA, Volume 2
ISBN: 0-9745106-1-0
"All New"

Over 5,000 New Listings, From Early And Rare Makers To Major Names In Horse-Drawn Vehicle Construction; Expanded Contemporary Section Of Today's Craftsmen; Important New Additions To Makers Previously Listed In Volume I; Excellent Variety Of Photos & Images; Fun And Entertaining Old Advertisements, Promotions, Trade Cards And Catalog Samples; New Carriage House Section Featuring The Foremost Dealers Of Today, Including Carriage & Wagon Makers, Shows, Sales & Auctions, Books, Magazines, Wheelwrights, Collar Shops, Saddle & Tack Shops, Antiques Dealers, Museums, Galleries And Much More!
This Is Your Largest Reference To The Makers Of All Horse-Drawn Vehicles!!
Don't Miss A Single Book In This Multi-Volume Sequential Set Of Books!
For More Information On This And Other Forthcoming Books, Call Or Write The Author, Daniel D. Hutchins,
At Tempo International Publishing Company, P.O. Box 28845, Santa Fe, NM 87592 / (505) 426–8633
www.tempopublishing.com; e-mail tempopub@msn.com

H&B Sales Fall Sale
Annually on Thanksgiving Weekend - Rock Springs, WY
The largest sale of its kind in the western United States - 3 days of selling

- Draft, Saddle, & Driving
- Horses, Mules & Ponies
- Wagons, Buggies & Sleighs
- Farming Implements
- Wagon Wheels & Sleigh Bells

- Western & Cowboy Collectibles
- Military Items
- Saddles & Bridles
- Chaps
- Spurs & Bits

- Harness & Collars
- Pack Equipment
- Furniture
- Blacksmith Tools
- 100's of small antiques

Tom Harrower - Auctioneer
8603 Powderhouse
Cheyenne, WY 82009
(307) 432-0404

HandBSales.com

Chuck Bonomo - Auctioneer
280 Hoskins Lane
Rock Springs, WY 82901
(307) 362-2071

The Luminary Shoppe
Division of Patrick Enterprises, Inc.

Specializing in Fine Carriage Lamp Restorations

www.luminaryshoppe.com

RR.1, Box 336A • Joliet, MT 59041
Rick & Pat Bischoff
Ph. 406-962-3677
lampltr@montana.com

HORSE DRAWN VEHICLES
Bought & Sold

Dave Shea
(203) 879-3169

48 Center St. - Rt. 322
Wolcott, CT 06716

---

brakes, steel, rubber, bolts,

axles, springs, singletrees

WITMER COACH SHOP
1070 West Main Street
New Holland Pa 17557
717-656-3411

Buggy Parts & Wheels
Wooden Wheel Repair

We ship to all 50 states and numerous forign countries.

CATALOG - $3.00 MAILING CHARGE

lights-LED & conventional, shafts, paints, steps

top parts, whips, fringe

Wheels Across America

Waverly Midwest Horse Sale

Largest Draft Horse and Equipment Auction of its kind in the United States and Canada
Selling hundreds of Draft and Draft cross horses to people all over America and Canada
Also selling several thousands of items of equipment and tack.
All of us here at Waverly Midwest Horse Sale say **Thank You** to Buyers and Sellers for all their years of support.
We feel like all of you are like family at our sales and welcome you to come and see our sales and stop to say hello.

Located at **2212 5th Ave. NW, Waverly, IA 50677   319-352-2804**
Bill Dean   319-352-1682
Ron Dean   319-352-6670
David Beyer 319-352-5615
Mailing Address: PO Box 355, Waverly, IA 50677   www.waverlysales.com

Waverly Midwest Horse Sale Dates

2004 Spring Dates ~ March 23–27	2006 Spring Dates ~ March 28–31, April 1
2004 Fall Dates ~ October 5–9	2006 Fall Dates ~ October 3–7
2005 Spring Dates ~ March 29–31, April 1–2	2007 Spring Dates ~ March 27–31
2005 Fall Dates ~ October 4–8	2007 Fall Dates ~ October 2–6
2005 Spring Sale Date is later because of Easter	2008 Spring Dates ~ March 25–29
	2008 Fall Dates ~ October 7–11

Hunts Harness Inc.
The Finest Workmanship
for all unique projects requiring Quality
Harness, Carriage appointments, Museum reproductions and repair, for discerning customers!
Please call 920-387-5057
greghunt@huntsharness.com

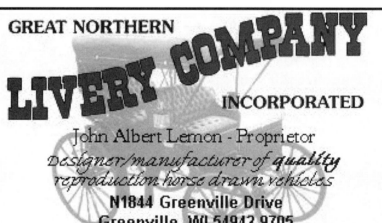

GREAT NORTHERN LIVERY COMPANY INCORPORATED
John Albert Lemon - Proprietor
Designer/manufacturer of quality reproduction horse drawn vehicles
N1844 Greenville Drive
Greenville, WI 54942-9705
920/757-5529
http://www.liveryone.net
67 different vehicle body styles to date

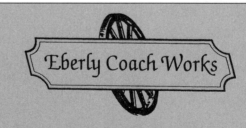

—Manufacturing of standard and custom vehicles
—Restoration of buggies and wagons
—Complete wheel wright services
—Replacement buggy parts
(715) 229-2222
N15133 Frenchtown Ave. Withee, WI 54498

Dixie Draft Horse, Mule & Carriage Auction

2 day sale— November & March

**Iredell County Fairgrounds
Troutman, NC**

Friday, 9:00 am **Tack Auction:**
New Tack
Horse-Drawn Equipment, Farm Equipment
5:00 pm **Harness Auction:**
200+ New and Used Harnesses & Saddles
7:00 pm **Carriage Auction:**
150+ Wagons, Buggies & Sleighs

Call for Flyer

Auctioneer & Info
Dean Beachy NC #5771
PO Box 367, Berlin
OH 44610
Fax (330) 893-3545
Phone (330) 893-3541

Saturday, 9:00 am **Horse Auction:**
450+ Draft Horses
Mules
Driving Horses
Ponies
Amish broke Teams
Haflingers

Over 24 Years

Largest Tack and Equipment Auction in the Southeast!

Wade House Historic Site and Wesley Jung Carriage Museum

Featuring Wisconsin's Largest Collection of Horse and Hand Drawn Vehicles

Wade House is open Mid-May through Mid-October from 9:00am to 5:00pm

Please contact the site for more information:

Wade House
P.O. Box 34
Greenbush, WI 53026
Phone: (920)526-3271
Fax: (920)526-3626

www.wisconsinhistory.org

 Wade House is owned and operated by the Wisconsin Historical Society

---

- Hitchwagons
- Carriages
- Vis-Vis
- Sleighs

Send $3.50 for catalog

Woodlyn Coach, LLC

Ivan Burkholder, Owner

4410 TR 628 • Millersburg, OH 44654
(330) 674-9124 Fax (330) 674-3589

Restoring Antique Carriages • Parts and Supplies

Henning Art Gallery AND SLEIGH MUSEUM

"A Wee Place Of Distictive Art"
E. 21001 Henning Road
Augusta, WI 54722
715-286-2464

*Original Paintings
Signed and Numbered Prints
Cards and Gifts

Specializing in Draft and Light
Horse & Winter Sleigh Scenes

Call or Write for color brochures
of prints*

#1 SOURCE OF TECHNICAL BOOKS FOR HORSE-DRAWN VEHICLES

Carriage Museum of America
Post Office Box 417
Bird-In-Hand, Pennsylvania 17505
phone: 717-656-7019
web site:
www.carriagemuseumlibrary.org

Wheels Across America

Anvil Wagon Works

522 E. Park St.
PO Box 1382
Livingston, MT
59047
(406) 222-7390
Fax (406) 222-5926

Custom built and rebuilt sheepwagons, chuck wagons, buggies, specialized wagons, canvas covers, wheelwrighting, rubber tiring, blacksmithing and more.

www.whitebuffalolodges.com
e-mail: tipisandwagons@aol.com

Nolt's Wheel Shop

New Wheels • Wheels Repaired

We Manufacture Wheels For Carriages And Spring Wagons

Surries, push carts,
ornamental wheels
wheel sizes 20"–54"
Also can make under 20"
with wood hubs
We buy & sell new and used
horse drawn vehicles
New road carts in stock!
—Rear enter and front enter—
—Pony size to draft size—
We also make wagon wheel
chandeliers

717–355–9182

Aaron M. Nolt
214 N. Shirk Rd. • New Holland,
PA 17557

THE ART OF THE WHEELWRIGHT
FIRST TIME ON VIDEO

FROM THE WORK SHOP OF MASTER WHEELWRIGHT, DAVE ENGEL COMES THE VIDEO DEBUTS OF

"BUILDING LIGHT TRADITIONAL WHEELS".
THIS 90 MINUTE INSTRUCTIONAL VIDEO IS AN EXCELLENT LEARNING TOOL FOR THOSE WHO WANT TO BUILD BUGGY WHEELS & THOSE WHO WANT TO UNDERSTAND HOW THEIR WHEELS ARE MADE.

"EVALUATING WHEELS"
THIS 20 MINUTE COMPANION VIDEO COULD SAVE THE FIRST TIME BUYER TROUBLE IN THE LONG RUN BY DISCUSSING CONDITION OF WHEELS ... FROM FIT & STYLE TO ISSUES OF AUTHENTICITY.

FILLED WITH CLEAR EXAMPLES, METHODS AND EXPLANATIONS!

BOTH TAPES ONLY $89.95 PLUS $8.50 FOR S & H (U.S. FUNDS)

Engel's Coach Shop
105 S. Main • P.O. Box 247
Joliet, MT 59041
(406) 962-3573
www.engelscoachshop.com

WERNER WAGON WORKS

DON & CONNIE WERNER
1705 YATES ROAD
HORTON, KANSAS 66439
TEL- 785-486-3758   FAX- 785-486-6690
wagons@rainbowtel.net
www.rainbowtel.net/~wagons
877-460-4978

family owned and operated since 1988

Stage Coaches
Prairie Schooner   Box Wagons
Conestoga   Spring Wagons
Buckboards   Chuck Wagons
"Real McCoy" Hub Inserts

WERNER WAGON WORKS
Wheelwright & Wainwright

Don & Connie Werner   1705 Yates Rd.
Home 785-486-3758   Horton, KS 66439
Fax   785-486-6690   e-mail: wagons@rainbowtel.net

www.rainbowtel.net/~wagons

MORGAN CARRIAGE WORKS INC.
OAK VIEW, CALIFORNIA

Restoration ★ Sales ★ Repairs
Fine Carriages ★ Carts
Competition Vehicles
Antiques ★ Reproductions
Rubber Tire Settings
Approved Distributor for
Smucker's® Harness

We have a large inventory of harness, carriage parts, wheels and driving accessories in stock.

We invite you to visit our shop.
(Between Ventura and Ojai)

250 Riverside Road, Oak View, CA 93022
805/649-1723 or 649-3155 (Eve.)
Fax: 805/649-5538
www.morgancarriage.com

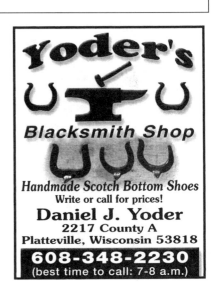

Yoder's Blacksmith Shop

Handmade Scotch Bottom Shoes
Write or call for prices!

Daniel J. Yoder
2217 County A
Platteville, Wisconsin 53818

608-348-2230
(best time to call: 7-8 a.m.)

Wild Horse Books & Art

*The World's largest supplier for Books & Plans on building full size and model Horse Drawn Vehicles, also books on driving horses, & more.
Equine Art by over 15 Artists*

Kayo Fraser
Proprietor

406-846-3686

Email: info@wildhorsebooks.com

Web site:
www.wildhorsebooks.com

Antiques & Art
James Aplan

21424 Clover Place
Piedmont, SD 57769
605-347-5016
AntiquesandArt.com

Cowboy & Western
Indian Crafts & Relics
Western Art
Old Photographs
Old Documents
Dakota & Black Hills Items
Antique Guns
Rare Books

Annual Catalog Subscription $5.00

HOMESTEAD HARNESS SHOP

Makers of Quality Leather Harness
at affordable prices. We make what
we use and use what we make

Custom-fit leather harness
miniature to draft
single driving & team

All types of accessories in stock
collars, hames, pads
halters (leather and nylon)
lead ropes
also tongues, wagon bows, shaves,
eveners & neckyokes (wood & steel)
Good Broke Teams and Single Driving Mules & Horses
for Sale Most of the Time

Dealers in Pioneer Equipment
Forecarts & accessories in stock for prompt shipment.
Horse-Drawn Machinery for sale
Give us a call for all your Harness and Accessory needs.

Homestead Harness Shop
J.R. & Jim Johnston
11085 Monroe Road 881
Paris, Missouri 65275
Phone: 660-327-4875
Fax: 660-327-1074
e-mail: homestead@mcmsys.com

SHIRK'S BUGGY SHOP
MOSES SHIRK

Buggy Repair & Parts

Wheelwright & Horseshoes

2002 KY 910
Liberty, KY 42539

PHONE
606-787-0337

COLORADO CARRIAGE CONNECTION

INDEPENDENT DISTRIBUTOR FOR

LES VOITURES
Robert

New
Used
Repairs
Parts

THE WOOLLY BEAR TRADING CO.
NATHROP, CO 81236
www.thewoollybear.com
(719) 395-8228
woolly@amigo.net

Charles & Barbara Abel

BuggyTowne™
Early Pioneer Transportation
Historic Horse-drawn transportation

Tremonton, Utah
Over 200 restored buggies and other pioneer memorabilia
For more information, visit www.tremontoncity,com

A leatherworking bi-monthly with how-to, step-by-step instructional articles using full-size patterns for leathercraft, leather art, custom saddle, boot and harness making, etc. A large resource for leather, tools, machinery, related goods & services plus leather industry news.

SUBSCRIBE TODAY!

1 YEAR SUBSCRIPTION RATES

US 6 BIG issues	$29 U.S.
Canada	$33 USD
Foreign Surface	$37 USD
Foreign Air	$71 USD

2 YEAR SUBSCRIPTION RATES

US 12 BIG issues	$58 U.S.
Canada	$66 USD
Foreign Surface	$74 USD
Foreign Air	$142 USD

Order Toll Free
1-888-289-6409

The Leather Crafters
& Saddlers Journal
331 Annette Court, Dept WAA,
Rhinelander WI 54501
Tel: 715-362-5393
Fax: 715-365-2493
E-mail: journal@newnorth.net

WORK HORSE HANDBOOK *second edition* & TRAINING WORKHORSES/TRAINING TEAMSTERS

Two important books by Lynn R. Miller

The *Work Horse Handbook second edition* is a brand new 368 page volume, completely revised and expanded. It is a sensitive and intelligent examination of, and introduction to, the craft of the teamster. 850+ photographs and illustrations support current information covering every aspect; from care and feeding through hitching and driving. The companion text to *"The Work Horse Handbook", "Training Workhorses/Training Teamsters"* includes 482 photographs and hundreds of drawings on 352 pages. This text covers the subjects of: training horses to work in harness, correcting behavior problems with work horses - and training people to drive and work horses.

Send check or money order: $32.95 each for
The Work Horse Handbook and/or
Training Workhorses/Training Teamsters

$4 shipping for 1st book, $6 other countries, $1.50 each for addl. books
Small Farmer's Journal, PO Box 1627
Sisters, Oregon 97759-1627
Phone for credit card orders 800-876-2893

MILLER BUGGY SHOP

RESTORATIONS AND NEW CARRIAGES

OWNERS
ANDY MILLER   MENNO MILLER

19743 212th St.

BLOOMFIELD, IOWA 52537

ALASKA HORSE JOURNAL

- **Monthly** - we publish 11 issues and an annual Guide to the Alaska Horse Community
- **Calendar of Events** - keeping you current on what is happening now!
- **Statewide Coverage** - we distribute 4,000+ copies every month
- **Advertising Opportunities** - reach some very hard to reach people

(907) 376-4470   sandy@alaskahorsejournal.com
310 N. Harriette St., Wasilla, AK 99654-7627

www.alaskahorsejournal.com

Ox Bow Trade Company
Collector, Dealer & Restoration of Horse Drawn Vehicles
Buggies – Wagons – Surreys – Vis-A-Vis – Victorias – Sleighs
Harness – Collars – New Wheels – Wheel Repair
(Standard, 3/4 Size or Miniature)

Jim Jensen, Owner
Shop (541) 575-2911
FAX (541) 575-2675

P. O. Box 658
Higyway 395 South
Canyon City, Oregon 97820

Sugar Valley Collar Shop

—since 1980
Quality & Service!
Most collars are in stock for same day shiping.

Manufacturing...
- Pulling Collar ◆ Work Collars ◆ Adjustable Top Collars ◆
- Tick Faced Collars ◆ Pony Collars ◆ Llama Collars ◆
- All Purpose Collars ◆ Driving Collars ◆ Collar Clocks ◆
- Collar Mirrors ◆ Closed Top Show Collars ◆ Vinyl Healing Pads ◆

Special sizes and styles available

- Farm and pulling hames in stock ◆
- A complete line of farm and pulling pads in stock for prompt shipment ◆
- Free Catalog - retail or wholesale ◆

No. 150 Heavy Pulling Collar

18 Wagon Wheel Lane ◆ Loganton ◆ PA 17747

Dick's Wicker & Buggy Shop

Specializing In:
- Quality Handcrafted Buggies
- All Types of Wicker Work
- Wicker Repair & Restoration
- Sleigh Repair & Restoration

Phone: 740-599-7282

Richard Craven
207 State Street • Brinkhaven Ohio 43006
www.DicksWickerandBuggy.com
E-Mail: DicksBuggy@yahoo.com

SAMSON HARNESS SHOP, INC.

Custom Harness Manufacturer

Quality Harness Since 1975

Light Driving Harness • Draft Horse Harness
Show, Work & Pleasure

6543 Akonerva Road • Gilbert, Minnesota 55741 • 218-865-4602

Johnson & Son Coach Shop

Carriage Restoration
Wheels Repaired • Parts
• Tires Replaced
Trim Work • Appraisals

Jeffrey P. Johnson
8191 N. Armstrong
Clovis, CA 93611
Phone (559) 299–1647

Does your Cinderella need a carriage?
We can build it for you!

Thanks to Stan Wilhelm and family on the purchase of this carriage.

Give us a call for Custom-Made Carriages,
Chuckwagons, Farm Wagons, Hitch Wagons and Show Carts.
We also do restoration work and wheel rebuilding.

McGilvray Farms

P.O. Box 169 · Woodrow, Colorado 80757 · **(970) 386-2276**

http://www.sandhillclydes.com · mcgilvrm@flci.net

Custom Spring Wagons & Running Gears
Wheel Work & Wagon Parts

NOLT WAGON WORKS

927 Newswanger Rd.
Ephrata, PA   17522-9352

Elam H. Nolt
Phone (717) 354–2732

Wanted For Volume Two

Names of craftsmen, makers and manufacturers of carriages & wagons from yesterday and today, including: photos, old ad's, business cards, catalogs and promotional information with history, location and dates of operation. Also interested in additional information on companies and individuals listed in this edition.

Please contact the author, Daniel D. Hutchins, through the publisher at:

Tempo International Publishing Company
P.O. Box 28845
Santa Fe, NM 87592
505-426-8633 www.
tempopublishing.com

Leola Coach Shop

We specialize in painting, finishing, trimming and upholstery

---

THE 2004 REACH
LOOKING FOR A ONE SOURCE GUIDE . . . .
. . . to locate a wide variety of driving horse equipment suppliers?
. . . to find horse services (transportation, auctions, supplies, clinics, etc.)?
. . . to locate horse sales, shows, pulls or events?
. . . to find contacts in breed associations?
. . . to locate a "Helping Hand" when you travel with your horse?

The price of THE 2004 REACH is: $7.00 - U.S.; $9.00 - Canada; $10.00 - Overseas *(You may discount $3.00 each on purchases of 5 to 9 books; $4.00 each on purchases of 10 or more books.)* All payments are to be in U.S. Funds.

Please send _____ copy(s) of THE 2004 REACH @ $_____ = $_____
Please check method of payment: __ Check; __ Money Order   (Total Enclosed)
SEND TO: REMIT TO:
Name _____
Address _____   **THE REACH**
         _____   DEPT. WA
                                             P.O. BOX 932
City _____   KENDALLVILLE, IN 46755
State/Zip_____   Phone: (260) 347-8223
                                             Email kcp@mchsi.com

"America's Harness Horse Newspaper"

Published Monthly & Distributed Free At Driving Horse Events Nation Wide

Subscription Rates: $24.00 (12 Issues) 1 Year • $46.00 (24 Issues) 2 Years

www.HorseDrawnNews.com • 1-888-864-2299

Reserve your space now for Wheels Across America, Voume Two

5th WHEEL CHASSIS

SHILOH

SINCE 1985

5th WHEEL WAGONS

PRECISION BUILT AND HITCH READY 5th WHEEL WAGON CHASSIS6

Chassis built with a Roller Bearing 5th wheel. Comes complete with rear brakes, springs and pole. Will tow behind vehicle at highway speeds. Also ski-kits available.

Show and Hitch Wagons, Covered Wagons or passenger multipurpose wagons. All sizes.

We manufacture the entire chassis.

Purchase the chassis and build your own wagon box **OR** . . .
we can build complete wagons—12 models to choose from. Call or write for free brochure.

SHILOH WAGON WORKS

15980 County Hwy 59, Vining, Minnesota 56588
Phone: (218) 769-4444

Monday–Friday
8:00 a.m. – 5:00 p.m.
Closed Weekends

At times we are away from the the phone—if no there is no immediate answer, please call back!

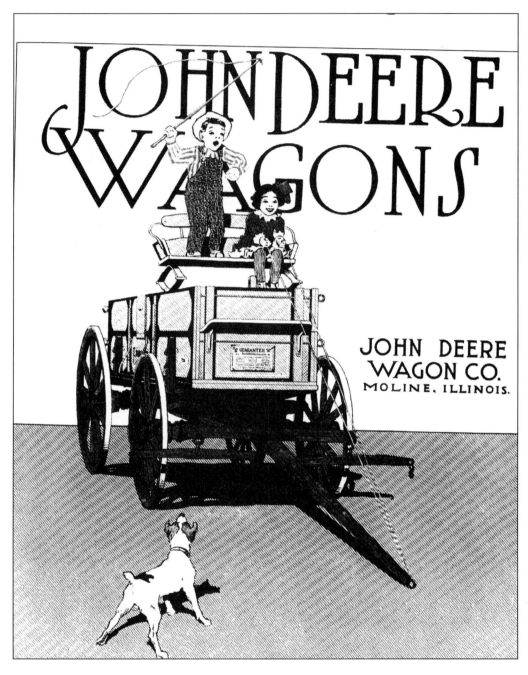

Circa 1911 Front Cover Of A John Deere Wagon Company Circular, This Little Catalog Was Produced Shortly After Deere Acquired The Moline Wagon Company In 1910. Featuring Their Light, Medium, Standard & Heavy Farm Wagons, With Load Capacities Ranging From 1,500 Pounds To 6,000 Pounds. *(Author's Collection)*